Keyboarding & Word Processing

16e

Lessons 1-60
Microsoft® Word 2003

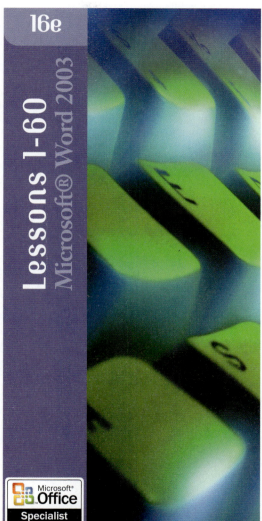

Microsoft® Office
Specialist
Approved Courseware

Susie H. VanHuss, Ph.D.
University of South Carolina

Connie M. Forde, Ph.D.
Mississippi State University

Donna L. Woo, Ph.D.
Cypress College, California

Linda Hefferin, Ed.D.
Elgin Community College

THOMSON
SOUTH-WESTERN

Australia · Canada · Mexico · Singapore · Spain · United Kingdom · United States

THOMSON

*

SOUTH-WESTERN

College Keyboarding: Keyboarding and Word Processing, Microsoft Word® 2003, Lessons 1-60
Susie H. VanHuss, Connie M. Forde, Donna L. Woo, and Linda Hefferin

VP/Editorial Director:
Jack W. Calhoun

VP/Editor-in-Chief:
Karen Schmohe

Acquisitions Editor:
Jane Phelan

Project Manager:
Dave Lafferty

Consulting Editor:
Mary Todd, Todd Publishing Services

Production Manager:
Patricia Matthews Boies

Production Editor:
Colleen A. Farmer

Vice President/Director of Marketing:
Carol Volz

Marketing Manager:
Lori Pegg

Marketing Coordinator:
Georgi Wright

Manufacturing Coordinator:
Charlene Taylor

Art Director:
Stacy Jenkins Shirley

Compositor:
GEX Publishing Services

Internal Designer:
Ann Small, a small design studio

Cover Designer:
Ann Small, a small design studio

Cover Photo Source:
© CORBIS

Printer:
Quebecor

ASIA (including India)
Thomson Learning
5 Shenton Way
#01-01 UIC Building
Singapore 068808

AUSTRALIA/NEW ZEALAND
Thomson Learning Australia
102 Dodds Street
Southbank, Victoria 3006
Australia

LATIN AMERICA
Thomson Learning
Seneca, 53
Colonia Polanco
11560 Mexico
D.F.Mexico

CANADA
Thomson Nelson
1120 Birchmount Road
Toronto, Ontario
Canada M1K 5G4

[CONTENTS]

What does this logo mean?

It means this courseware has been approved by the Microsoft® Office Specialist Program to be among the finest available for learning *Microsoft Word 2003*. It also means that upon completion of this courseware, you may be prepared to become a Microsoft Word 2003 Specialist.

What is a Microsoft Office Specialist?

A Microsoft Office Specialist is an individual who has certified his or her skills in one or more of the Microsoft Office desktop applications of Microsoft Word, Microsoft Excel, Microsoft PowerPoint®, Microsoft Outlook®, or Microsoft Access. The Microsoft Office Specialist Program typically offers certification exams at the "Specialist" and "Expert" skill levels.* The Microsoft Office User Specialist Program is the only Microsoft approved program in the world for certifying proficiency in Microsoft Office desktop applications. This certification can be a valuable asset in any job search or career advancement.

More information:

To learn more about becoming a Microsoft Office Specialist, visit www.microsoft.com/learning/mcp/officespecialist

To learn about other Microsoft Office Specialist approved courseware from Thomson/South-Western, visit www.swlearning.com/keyboarding/mosp/mosp-page1.html.

* The availability of Microsoft Office Specialist certification exams varies by application, application version, and language. Visit www.microsoft.com/officespecialist for exam availability.

Microsoft, the Microsoft Office Specialist Logo, PowerPoint and Outlook are either registered trademarks or trademarks of Microsoft Corporation in the United States and/or other countries.

THE LATEST WORD IN KEYBOARDING

Building a skill takes practice, and that's what you'll get with the *College Keyboarding* series. More timed writings, five supplemental keyboarding lessons using the keyboarding software, and technique drills throughout.

Keyboarding Pro—Now with Web Reporting, especially designed for distance education

Keyboarding Pro 4
Now with Web reporting and Spanish instruction!

Keyboarding Pro 4 software uses graphics, games, progress graphs, videos, 3-D models for viewing proper posture and hand positions, sound effects, and a full-featured word processor to keep learning fun and meaningful. Students also have the option of e-mail or the Web for transferring their assignments to the instructor. Instruction available in Spanish.

Extra skillbuilding lessons using *Keyboarding Pro*

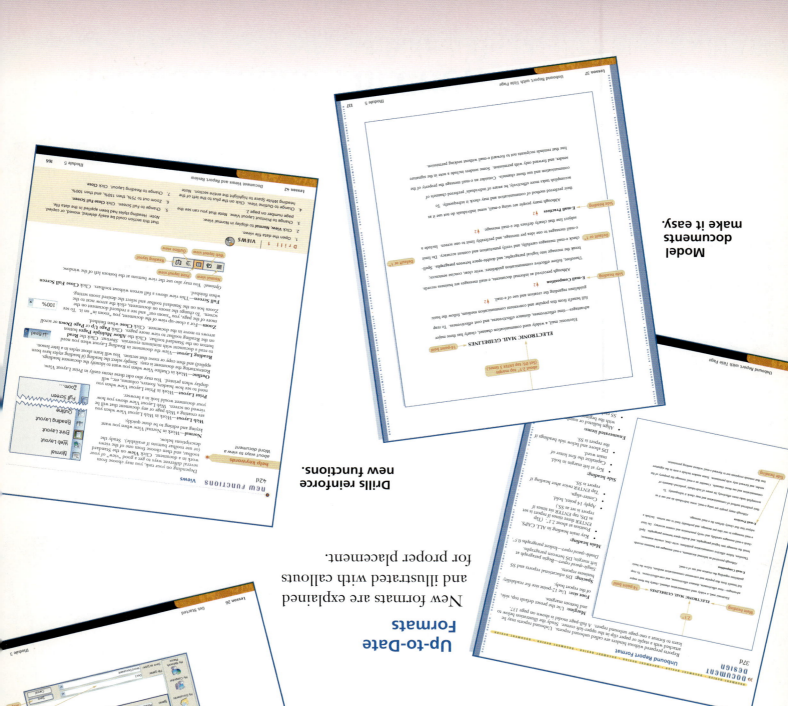

Model documents make it easy.

Drills reinforce new functions.

Up-to-Date Formats

New formats are explained and illustrated with callouts for proper placement.

The Latest Word!
Microsoft® Office Specialist Certified for Microsoft® Word 2003

College Keyboarding teaches document formatting using the functions of Microsoft Word 2003. This is the *only* keyboarding text on the market that integrates the Microsoft Office Specialist competencies into each lesson. Only South-Western delivers the most fundamental keyboarding skills and current word processing software in one convenient package.

CLEARLY FOCUSED ON YOUR NEEDS

Document Processing

That's the focus of Lessons 61-120. Users will apply advanced word-processing functions to business correspondence, tables, reports, and administrative and employment documents.

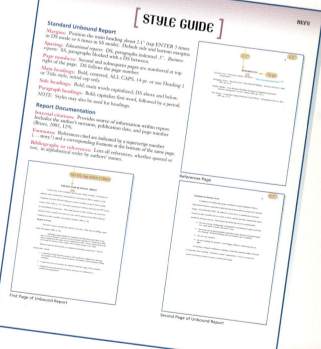

CheckPro 2003
Now with Web reporting for distance education!

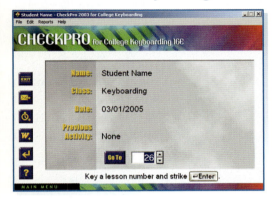

Transferring student data between students and instructors just gets easier. *CheckPro 2003* is your answer to handling distance education with ease.

Reference Manual
provides easy access to model documents.

Communication Skills

Proofreading, capitalization, composition, and other language arts skills are reinforced. Supplemental Communication Skill Builder pages provide extra practice.

THE LATEST WORD IN KEYBOARDING

Product Family

Advanced Word Processing, Lessons 61–120
0-538-72823-X
Intensive document processing text that includes many document types: budgets, financial statements, a wide variety of forms, minutes, reports, agendas, itineraries, and merged documents. A Software Training Manual reviews functions learned in L1–60.

College Keyboarding Complete Course, Lessons 1–120
0-538-72824-8

Instructor's Manual & Key, Lessons 1–60 (0-538-72829-9) and *Instructor's Resource CD, Lessons 1–60* (0-538-72832-9)
Solutions, data files, teaching tips, and tests—all in an easy-to-use format.

Technology Solutions

Keyboarding Pro 4
0-538-72802-7, Individual License.
With Web reporting and Spanish.

CheckPro for College Keyboarding
0-538-72836-1, Individual License.
Now with Web reporting for your distance education needs.

MicroPace Pro, 2.0
0-538-72912-2, Individual License.
Program software that correlates to *Keyboarding Essentials* and provides additional skillbuilding practice to increase technique and accuracy. Comprehensive error diagnostics.

KeyChamp, 2E
0-538-43390-6
Textbook and program software that builds speed by analyzing student's two-stroke key combinations and provides drills for building speed.

Instructor Approved

Angela Butler
Mississippi Gulf Coast Community College
Gautier, Mississippi

Dorie Forkenbrach
Kirkwood Community College, Iowa City Campus
Iowa City, Iowa

Robyn Hart
Fresno City College
Fresno, California

Ruth Levy
SUNY/Westchester Community College
Valhalla, New York

Juanita Marquez
Dallas Community College, El Centro
Dallas, Texas

Sonia Wilson Pusey
Eastfield College
Mesquite, Texas

Hilda Roberts
Santa Ana College
Orange, California

Sheryl Shields
Sullivan University
Louisville, Kentucky

Beverly Stowers
Ivy Technical State College
Valparaiso, Indiana

Vicky York
Surry Community College
Dobson, North Carolina

A Word from the Authors

Thank you for your support of our keyboarding texts over the past many years. We have designed this text especially for those who need a traditional keyboarding and document formatting approach. We hope our new series meets your needs.

Susie VanHuss
Connie Forde
Donna Woo
Linda Hefferin

[WELCOME TO WINDOWS®]

Microsoft® Windows® is an operating system, a program that manages all other software applications on your computer and its peripherals such as the mouse and printer. Software applications that run under *Windows* have many common features. Depending on the version of your operating system, some features may look, work, or be named slightly differently on your computer.

The Desktop

When your computer is turned on and ready to be used, a Welcome screen showing the names of every computer user on the computer will display. Click your user icon, key your password in the textbox, and then click the **Next** button to access the desktop. The illustration below shows a *Windows XP* **desktop**, which is the main working area. Your desktop will have many of the same features. Your desktop may look different depending on the programs installed on your computer and the way the desktop has been arranged.

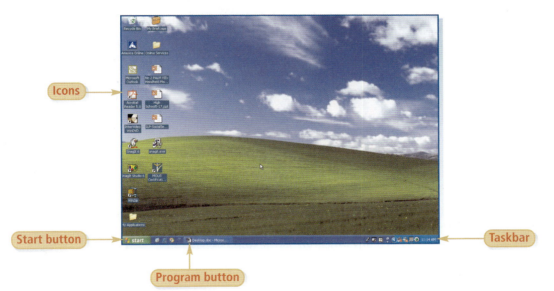

Icons

Start button

Program button

Taskbar

The desktop displays icons and a taskbar. Icons provide an easy way to access programs and documents that you frequently use. Desktop icons will vary. Two common icons are:

 My Computer displays the disk drives, CD-ROM drives, and printers that are attached to your computer.

 Recycle Bin stores files and folders that have been deleted from the hard drive. Documents in the Recycle Bin may be restored and returned to their folders. However, once you empty the Recycle Bin, the documents are deleted and cannot be restored.

The bar at the bottom of the desktop is the taskbar. The **taskbar** displays the Start button on the left, a button for each program or document that is open, and the system clock on the right (your taskbar may have additional icons). The taskbar enables you to open programs and navigate on your computer.

The Mouse

Windows requires the use of a mouse or other pointing device such as a touch pad built into your keyboard. The *Windows* software utilizes the left and right mouse buttons. The left button is used to select text or commands, to open files or menus, or to drag objects. The right button is used to display shortcut menus.

The pointer (arrow) ➤ indicates your location on the screen. To move the pointer, you must first move the mouse. If you have a touch pad on your keyboard, move the pointer by moving your finger on the touch pad. The mouse or touch pad is used to perform four basic actions.

Point: Move the mouse so that the pointer touches something displayed on the screen.

Click: Point to an item, quickly press the left mouse button once, and release it. You will always use the left mouse button unless directions tell you to right-click, which means click the right mouse button.

Double-click: Point to an item; quickly press the left mouse button twice, and release it.

Drag: Point to an item, then hold down the left mouse button while you move the mouse to reposition the item.

The mouse pointer changes in appearance depending on its location on the desktop and the task being performed.

| | The *vertical blinking bar* indicates the current position of the cursor.

I | The *I-beam* indicates the location of the mouse pointer. To reposition the cursor at this point, you must click the mouse button.

➤ | The *arrow* indicates that you can select items. It displays when the mouse is located outside the text area. You can point to a toolbar icon to display the function of that icon.

⧗ | The *hourglass* indicates that *Windows* is processing a command.

↔ | A *double-headed arrow* appears when the pointer is in the border of a window; it is used to change the size.

The Start Button

The **Start** button opens the Start menu, which lists a variety of items from which to choose such as programs and documents.

The Start menu is divided into three sections and displays some of the programs and folders on your computer. The top of the menu displays the user icon and name. The middle section contains two columns of commands. The bottom section contains the Log Off and Turn Off Computer commands.

Let's take a closer look at the middle section of the Start menu. Separator lines divide sections of the Start menu. The section in the upper left is called the pinned items list, which contains an icon for your Web browser and your e-mail program. The next section below contains icons for your six most frequently used programs. The top right section contains commands to access various folders and My Computer. If your computer is connected to a network, the My Network Places command displays below My Computer. The next section contains commands to customize the computer and peripherals. The bottom section contains commands for Help, searching, and launching programs (Run).

If you do not see the program you need displayed, point to the All Programs arrow to display a full list of programs available on your computer. To open an item listed on the Start menu, point to the item and click the left mouse button. A right arrow beside a menu item indicates that a submenu with more options is available for that item. (*Note* If an icon is displayed on the desktop, you can double-click the icon to open the program, document, or folder that it represents.)

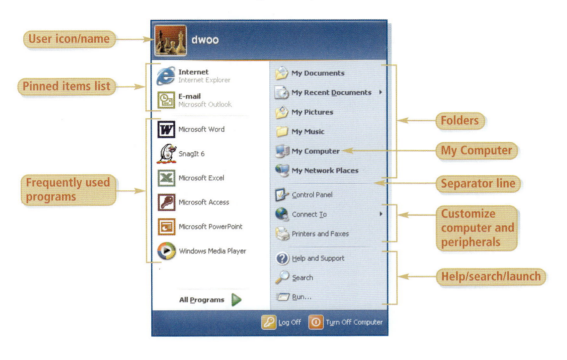

Windows features

Windows displays folders, applications, and individual documents in windows. A **window** is a work area on the desktop that can be resized or moved. To resize a window, point to the border. When the pointer changes to a double-headed arrow, drag the window to the desired size. To move a window, point to the title bar, drag it to the new position, and release the mouse button.

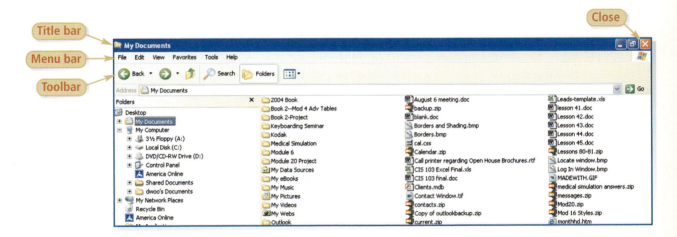

The basic features of all windows are the same. Each window contains the following:

Menu bar: Displays commands available in the software.

Toolbars: Display icons that offer a convenient way to access frequently used commands. Applications programs have different toolbars for different tasks.

Scroll bars: Enable you to see material that does not fit on one screen. You can click the arrows on the scroll bars or drag the scroll box to move through a document.

Title bar: Displays the name of the application that is currently open and the path (folder name). The Title bar also includes several buttons at the right.

Minimize button: Reduces the window to a button on the taskbar. To restore the window, click the button on the taskbar.

Maximize button: Enlarges a window to full-screen size.

Restore button: When you maximize a window, the Maximize button is replaced with a Restore button that, when clicked, returns the window to its original size.

Close button: Closes the application.

Minimize   Maximize   Close   Restore

Help

Help is available for *Windows.* Help is also available with each software application that you use. Generally you will use the Help feature provided with the application. To access *Windows* Help, click the **Start** button, and then click **Help and Support.** You can choose from the list of Help topics displayed, or key your topic in the Search box and click the green arrow.

Index button   Search box

You can also click the **Index** button on the toolbar to display a list of specific items in alphabetical order. As you key the characters of the topic in the entry box, the program automatically moves to items beginning with the keyed letters. When the correct topic displays, highlight it and choose **Display.** If you prefer, you can scroll through the list of topics until you find what you are looking for.

Drill 1

1. Click the **Start** button. Choose **Help** and **Support.**
2. Click **What's new in Windows XP** from the Help topics.
3. Click **Taking a tour or tutorial** in the left pane.
4. Choose **Take the Windows XP tour** in the right pane. Follow the directions on the screen to complete the *Windows XP Tour.* When finished, close the Help and Support Center.

[FILE MANAGEMENT]

File Management includes the processes of creating and managing the electronic files on your computer. You will learn to format a floppy disk, understand basic file structure, manage files and folders, and log off from the computer.

format a Diskette

Data that needs to be used again in the future must be saved on a storage device such as floppy diskettes, CD/DVD, zip disk, or the hard drive. Floppy diskettes are often used in school settings. A floppy diskette must be formatted before it can be used for storing data. Some diskettes are shipped from the manufacturer preformatted; they will not require additional formatting. If you purchase unformatted disks, they will need to be formatted before use. Formatting the disk means that the operating system will erase the disk, check for bad sectors, and place tracks and sectors on the disk so that files can be saved on the disk.

To format a disk:

The following steps will instruct you to format a high-density diskette in the A: drive. Ask your instructor what drive you are to use to format a diskette.

1. Insert the disk to be formatted in the disk drive (A:).

2. Double-click the **My Computer** icon to open the My Computer window.

3. Select the drive containing the disk to be formatted (A:).

4. Click the File menu and select **Format**; the Format dialog box displays.

The maximum capacity for the disk displays in the Capacity drop list.

The *File system* and *Allocation unit size* boxes display the defaults for the disk to be formatted.

The *Volume label* box allows you to enter an electronic label that is recorded during the formatting process.

The *Format options* box allows you to select a format option other than the standard. *Quick Format* should only be used on previously formatted disks that you know are in good condition; it does not check for bad sectors on the disk.

5. Click the **Start** button to begin the formatting. A warning box displays so you do not format a disk that might contain data you need to keep.

6. Click **OK** when the warning box displays.

7. Click **OK** when the message box displays telling you the formatting is complete.

8. Click **Close** to close the Formatting dialog box.

9. Close the My Computer window.

D r i l l   2

1. Format a 3½" floppy disk.   Use your name for the volume label on the disk.

2. Double-click **My Computer** to display the My Computer dialog box.

3. Right-click **3½" Floppy (A:)** and select **Properties** from the menu.

4. Click the **General** tab in the Properties dialog box. Your name should display in the text box at the top. Notice the amount of free space on your disk. Click **OK** to close the Properties dialog box.

5. Close the My Computer window.

Understand the File System

As with paper files, it is important to establish a logical and easy-to-use computer file management system to organize your files efficiently so that you can find them quickly and easily. You can manage files from the desktop or from My Computer or Windows Explorer.

Computer files are stored on **disks** specified by their location. The storage drives can be identified in My Computer.

The computer in this example has a hard disk drive (C), a floppy disk drive (A), and a DVD/CD drive (D).

View Contents of a Drive

1. To view the contents of a drive through My Computer, double-click the **My Computer** icon on the desktop. If the icon is not available, choose **My Computer** from the Start menu.

2. Double-click the desired disk drive to display the contents.

View Contents of a Folder

Folders are listed in numerical and alphabetic order. Folders with numerical names will be listed before those with alphabetic names, as shown in the figure above. To see the contents of a folder, double-click the folder. Folders may contain files, programs, and folders.

headings

Name ▲	Size	Type	Date Modified
Assignments		File Folder	3/17/2005 11:17 AM
Term Papers		File Folder	3/22/2005 11:18 AM
Work in Progress		File Folder	9/21/2005 11:18 AM

View Data and Arrange Files

Files and folders can be viewed in different ways: as Thumbnails, Tiles, Icons, List, and Details. The figure above shows the items in List View.

To change the view, click **View** on the menu; then choose a view. You may want to experiment with each of the views to decide which one you prefer.

As previously mentioned, folders are listed in alphabetical order. You can also arrange them in descending order by date, size, or type of file. To rearrange the order of files or folders, select **Details** from the View menu, and then click the heading displayed above the files or folders such as **Size**, **Type**, or **Date Modified**.

D r i l l   3

1. Insert your data CD in its drive. Use My Computer to display the contents of that CD.

2. Use the View menu to change to Thumbnails View.

3. Change the view to List View.

4. Change to Details View. Click the **Name** heading. Notice the files are displayed in ascending order.

5. Click the **Date Modified** heading to place the documents back in ascending order by date.

6. Double-click on a file folder to display the files in the folder.

7. Click the Up button on the toolbar to return to the previous level displaying the folders.

8. Click the **Back** button on the toolbar to return to the My Computer screen.

Work with Folders and Files

Folders are extremely important in organizing files. You will want to create and manage folders and the files within them so that you can easily locate them. Managing files and folders also involves renaming and deleting items.

Create Folder

Folders can be created in My Computer or in Windows Explorer.

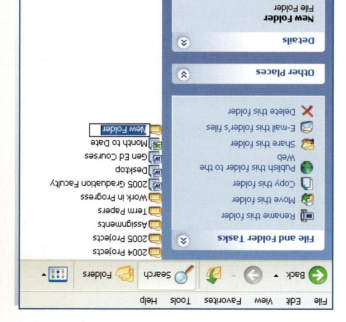

1. To create a folder in My Computer, display the drive that is to contain the new folder.

2. Click **Make a new folder** in the left pane.

3. A new folder displays at the end of the list of files labeled **New Folder**. Delete the words *New Folder* and replace them with a new name.

4. Tap ENTER.

To create a folder in Windows Explorer, point to **All Programs** on the Start menu. Choose **Accessories**, and then choose **Windows Explorer**. Click the drive or folder that will contain the new folder. Select **New** from the File menu and choose **Folder**. Select and replace **New Folder** with the new name.

Name Files and Folders

Good file organization begins with giving your folders and files names that are logical and easy to understand. In the previous figure, a folder was created for Assignments, Term Papers, and Work in Progress. You may want to create a folder named *Module 3* to hold all work that you key in Module 3. You will save the files by the exercise name such as *26b-d1* or *26b-d2*. A system like this makes finding files simple.

Rename Files and Folders

Occasionally, you may want to rename a file or folder. To do so, click the file or folder, choose **Rename this file** or **Rename this folder**, key the new name, and press ENTER. You can also rename files using the Windows Explorer menu; select the file or folder, and then choose **Rename** on the File menu.

Move and Copy Files and Folders

1. To move or copy files using My Computer, click the file/folder to be copied or moved.
2. Click **Copy this file** or **Move this file** in the left pane. The Copy Items window displays.
3. Click the drive or the folder in which the copy is to be placed.

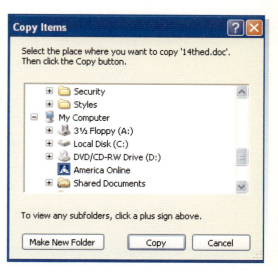

To copy or move files using Windows Explorer:

1. In the Windows Explorer screen, click the drive that contains the file or folder you want to move, then locate the item.
2. Be sure the place you want to move the file or folder to is visible. Press and hold down the left mouse button and drag the pointer to the new location.

To copy a file or folder, press and hold down CTRL while you drag.

Note: If you drag a file or folder to a location on the same disk, it will be moved. If you drag an item to a different disk, it will be copied. To move the item, press and hold down SHIFT while dragging.

If you wish to copy or move several items at once, click the first item; then hold down the CTRL key as you select each additional item. This allows you to copy or move all the files at one time. If the items you wish to copy or move are consecutive, click the first item, hold down SHIFT, and click the last item—now you can copy or move the entire list at once.

Delete Files and Folders

Files and folders can be deleted in My Computer or Windows Explorer. You can select and delete several files and folders at once, just as you can select several items to move or copy. If you delete a folder, you automatically delete any files and folders inside it.

To delete a file or folder and send it to the Recycle Bin, right-click the item and choose **Delete**. Answer Yes to the question about sending the item to the Recycle Bin.

Restore Deleted Files and Folders

When you delete a file or folder, the item goes to the Recycle Bin. If you have not emptied the Recycle Bin, you can restore files and folders stored there. Items deleted from the A drive will be deleted permanently and do not go to the Recycle Bin.

To restore a file in the Recycle Bin:

1. Double-click the **Recycle Bin** icon on the desktop to open the Recycle Bin window.
2. Select the file you want to restore, right-click to display the shortcut menu, and choose **Restore**. You can also choose Restore from the File menu.
3. Close the Recycle Bin window. Click the folder where the file was originally located, and it should now be restored.

Log Off and Shut Down

Log Off

When you are finished using the computer, you should close your user account by logging off the computer. Logging off performs three functions: (1) any applications software left often will be closed; (2) you will be prompted to save any unsaved documents; and (3) you will end your *Windows* session and allow another person to use your computer. This procedure should always be followed if your computer has more than one user account listed in the Welcome screen. It is a good idea to log off, even if you are the sole user of the computer.

To log off, click the **Start** button and click the **Log Off** button on the Start menu. Confirm the log off in the dialog box that displays. The Welcome screen displays.

Shut Down

To shut down the computer after logging off, click the **Turn off computer** button on the Welcome screen, then click the **Turn Off** button in the Turn off computer dialog box.

Drill 4

1. Using My Computer, create a new folder on Drive A called *XP Intro*.
2. Rename the folder *Win XP*.
3. Make a copy of this folder on Drive C. (If you cannot do this, ask your instructor for the location to which you can copy.)
4. Delete the folder you created on Drive A and the copy you made on Drive C.

Drill 5

You will need to copy files from the data CD to your floppy diskette when you perform the exercises in this book. This exercise will walk you through the steps of copying a file folder and its contents from the CD to the diskette in Drive A. You will use Windows Explorer.

1. Insert your data CD in the CD Drive and a floppy diskette in Drive A.
2. Display the Windows Explorer window.
3. Click the + symbol to the left of My Computer to display the drives on the computer.
4. Double-click the CD drive to display the contents of the CD in the right pane.
5. Click the **View** menu and select **Details**.
6. Click a file folder, hold down the left mouse button, and drag the folder to Drive A. The folder and its contents will be copied to Drive A. Next, check to see that the folder and its contents were copied to Drive A, then delete the folder.
7. Double-click **3½" Floppy (A:)** in the left pane under My Computer to display the contents of Drive A.
8. Double-click the file folder to view the files in the folder.
9. Click the **Up** button in the toolbar to display the higher level (file folders).
10. Select the file folder, click the **File** menu, and select **Delete**.
11. Click **Yes** to confirm the deletion of the folder.
12. Go back to your desktop. Ask your instructor if you should log off or shut down the computer.

[KNOW YOUR COMPUTER]

The numbered parts are found on most computers. The location of some parts will vary.

1. **CPU (Central Processing Unit)**: Internal operating unit or "brain" of computer.

2. **Disk drive**: Reads data from and writes data to a disk.

Keyboard Arrangement

3. **Monitor**: Displays text and graphics on a screen.

4. **Mouse**: Used to input commands.

5. **Keyboard**: An arrangement of letter, figure, symbol, control, function, and editing keys and a numeric keypad.

6. **CD-ROM drive**: Reads data from and writes data to a CD.

1. **Alphanumeric keys**: Letters, numbers, and symbols.

2. **Numeric keypad**: Keys at the right side of the keyboard used to enter numeric copy and perform calculations.

3. **Function (F) keys**: Used to execute commands, sometimes with other keys. Commands vary with software.

4. **Arrow keys**: Move insertion point up, down, left, or right.

5. **ESC (Escape)**: Closes a software menu or dialog box.

6. **TAB**: Moves the insertion point to a preset position.

7. **CAPS LOCK**: Used to make all capital letters.

8. **SHIFT**: Makes capital letters and symbols shown at tops of number keys.

9. **CTRL (Control)**: With other key(s), executes commands. Commands may vary with software.

10. **ALT (Alternate)**: With other key(s), executes commands. Commands may vary with software.

11. **Space Bar**: Inserts a space in text.

12. **ENTER**: Moves insertion point to margin and down to next line. Also used to execute commands.

13. **DELETE**: Removes text to the right of insertion point.

14. **NUM LOCK**: Activates/deactivates numeric keypad.

15. **INSERT**: Activates insert or typeover.

16. **BACKSPACE**: Deletes text to the left of insertion point.

[WELCOME TO KEYBOARDING PRO]

Keyboarding Pro 4 combines the latest technology for distance education with South-Western's superior method for teaching keyboarding.

Installing the Software

If you are using the Individual User version of *Keyboarding Pro 4* on your home computer, you must first install the software on your computer. Refer to the Individual User's Guide that accompanies *Keyboarding Pro 4*.

Getting Started with Keyboarding Pro

Click the **Start** button and then select **Programs.** Select the South-Western Keyboarding program group and click **Keyboarding Pro 4.** After a few seconds you will see the Log In dialog box.

The first time you use *Keyboarding Pro*, you must enter your user information and create a student record. You will create a student record *only once* so that the results of all lessons are stored in one file.

From the Log In dialog box, click the **New User** button to create a student record. A wizard will guide you through several screens.

Step 1: On the first screen, enter your first and last name and a password. Write the password in a safe place; you will need to enter it each time you log into the software. Then click the **Next** button.

Notice that your default student record is C:\ Program Files\ Keyboarding Pro 4\Students.

If you will be saving on drive A or if you have a subdirectory on the network, click the **Folder** icon and browse to identify the path.

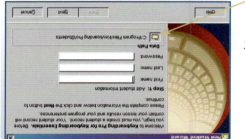

Note: The graphic in the illustration above may be slightly different in your software.

Step 2: *If you are not a distance learning student,* do not enter anything on this screen, simply click the **Next** button.

If you are a distance education student, you must enter the data on this screen in order to send your files to the Keyboarding Pro Web server or to e-mail your files to your instructor. Enter your instructor's e-mail address and/or the course code your instructor has given you. Click the **Next** button.

Step 2: (Optional) Add distance learning information
If you do not know this information, request it from your instructor and enter it at a later time by choosing **Preferences** from the **Edit** menu.

Step 3: Select your class from the list shown. If your class is not available, select **No Class Assigned.**

Step 4: From the final screen in the wizard, click the **Finish** button.

Each time you enter *Keyboarding Pro* after the first time, the Log In dialog box displays (as in Step 3). Select your name and enter your password. If you do not see your name, click the **Folder** button to locate the drive where your student record is located (Drive A or your folder on the network).

Main Menu

The Main Menu provides access to the four main modules of the software, beginning with Alphabetic (Lessons 1–13). To access any module, click its name from the Main menu.

Alphabetic: Begin with this module to learn the alphabetic keys. Each lesson includes a variety of exercises. You will key from the software screen and from your textbook. In *Textbook Keying* and *Timed Writing*, the software directs you to key the exercise from the textbook.

Numeric and Skill: Activities focus on building skill and learning the top-row and symbol keys.

Skill Builder: After you know the alphabetic keys, use these 20 lessons to boost your keyboarding skill. Each lesson can be completed in both speed and accuracy mode.

Numeric Keypad: You will learn the numeric keypad operation by completing four lessons in this module.

Additional Features

Keyboarding Pro 4 includes several important features. Three of these features are described below.

 Open Screen: The Open Screen is a word processor; it has a timer option. You will be directed to key various exercises and timings in the Open Screen. These files may be saved and sent to your instructor.

 Diagnostic Writings: Numerous timed writings in the textbook can be keyed as Diagnostic Writings. This feature is available from either the Numeric and Skill Lesson menu or the Skill Builder Lesson menu. You will key each timing twice. Results are saved in your Summary Report (see Reports below).

Student Reports: *Keyboarding Pro 4* creates several reports. The two reports that you will use most frequently are the Lesson Report and the Summary Report. The Lesson Report shows your performance data for a specific lesson. The Summary Report provides an overview of your progress on each of the modules and your Diagnostic Writings (Timed Writings). To access all reports, select **Reports** from the Menu bar, and then choose the desired report. Reports can be printed.

Sending Files to Your Instructor

If you are a distance learning student, you can send files to your instructor through the Keyboarding Pro Web server or by e-mail. Your instructor will advise you as to which method you should use. (**Note:** You must have entered your Course Code or instructor's e-mail address. See Step 2 on the previous page.)

You can send three types of files; each file type has a different file extension:

- .swk   Your student record that includes the results of all lessons completed and diagnostic writings.

- .kdwq   Diagnostic writings that were saved.

- .kos   Documents or timings created and saved in the Open Screen.

Send Files to Keyboarding Pro Web Server:

1. Log in as a student with a valid course code.

2. Click the Send File button on the Main menu or the Lesson Report menu.

3. Your student data file is automatically selected. To attach additional files, click the **Attach Files** button and click the file you want to attach.

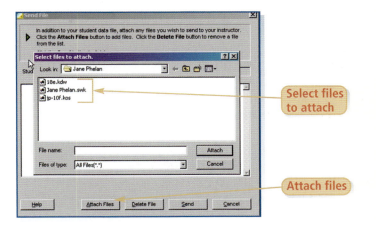

Send Files Using E-mail:

1. Log in as a student.

2. Click the Send File button on the Main menu or the Lesson Report menu.

3. The student data file is automatically attached. To attach additional files, click the **Attach Files** button and locate the files you wish to add.

Note: To use Send File, a MAPI-compliant e-mail program must be installed and properly configured on your computer. (MAPI stands for *Messaging Application Program Interface,* which is a Microsoft Windows program interface that enables the user to send e-mail from within a Windows application and attach documents.) Microsoft Outlook is an example of a MAPI-compliant program.

If you are using an e-mail program such as Hotmail or Yahoo that is not MAPI compliant, you will not be able to use the automatic Send File feature. However, you can still send your student files to your instructor using your e-mail program by attaching the data files manually.

Create an e-mail to your instructor in the usual manner. Use the attach function of your e-mail program. Use the Browse or Attach function to navigate to the **C:\Program\ Keyboarding Pro\Students** folder on your hard drive. When you have located your Student Record (username.swk) in the Students folder, highlight it and click Open or Select.

[WELCOME TO CHECKPRO]

CheckPro verifies the accuracy of the keystrokes in drills, timed writings, and selected documents that you key beginning in Module 3. The drill practice and timed writings features are built into the *CheckPro* program. For the document exercises, *CheckPro* works in conjunction with Microsoft *Word*. You will key documents using *Word* and then *CheckPro* error-checks your work.

Getting Started With CheckPro

To launch the program, click the **Start** button and then select **Programs.** Select the South-Western Keyboarding program group and then click **CheckPro 2003.** Once the splash screen is removed, the New Student Wizard dialog box displays. **Note:** The graphics illustrated below will be slightly different than your software.

The first time you use *CheckPro 2003*, you must key your user information and create a student record. You will create a student record *only once* so that the results of all lessons are stored in one file.

From the Log In dialog box, click the **New** button to create a student record. A Wizard will guide you through several screens.

Step 1: Key your name and password.

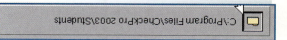

New Student Wizard

Welcome to CheckPro 2003 for College Keyboarding. Before you begin, you must create a student record. Your student record will contain your lesson results and your program preferences.

Please complete the information below and click the Next button to continue.

Step 1: Add student information

First name: John
Middle initial: D
Last name: Doe
Password: ********

Your files will automatically save to the *Students* folder within the program (**C:\Program Files\CheckPro 2003\Students**) unless you change the location. To save to another drive or a zip drive, click the folder icon and browse to the desired drive. Select **Next** when you are ready to proceed.

C:\Program Files\CheckPro 2003\Students

Step 2: *If you are not a distance learning student,* do not key anything on this second screen; simply click the **Next** button.

Step 3: Select your class from the list shown. If your class is not available, select **No Class Assigned.**

New Student Wizard

Step 3: Select a class

Select a class from the list below. If you are not using CheckPro as part of a class, or your class is not available, select **No Class Assigned.**

Class List:
No Class Assigned
Keyboarding
DT-101

Help   Back   Next   Cancel

Step 4: From the final screen in the Wizard, click the **Finish** button.

New Student Wizard

Step 2: (Optional) Add distance learning information

CheckPro allows you to send your student data files to your instructor via e-mail or the CheckPro Web server. If you do not know your course code, you should request it from your instructor.

IMPORTANT: Enter the information below only if you plan to use the distance learning features.

Instructor e-mail address:

Course code:

If you do not know your instructor's e-mail address or the CheckPro course code, you may enter it later by accessing the **Preferences** option from the Edit menu.

Help   Back   Next   Cancel

If you are a distance learning student, key either your instructor's e-mail address or a course code. Click the **Next** button if your instructor has not provided you with this information. You can key it at a later time by choosing the **Edit** menu and then **Preferences.**

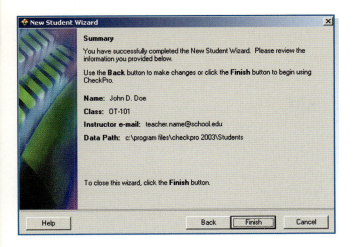

Each time you enter *CheckPro 2003* after the first time, the Log In dialog box displays. Select your name and key your password. If you do not see your name, click the **Folder** button to locate the drive where your student record is located (Drive A, zip drive, or your folder on the network).

Main Screen

After you start the program and log in, the program displays the *CheckPro 2003* main screen. The main screen is the central navigation point for the entire program. From here you can select a lesson, e-mail a data file, or access the supplemental/timings documents or send your documents to your instructor. **Note:** Your software will look *different* but *similar* to the example below.

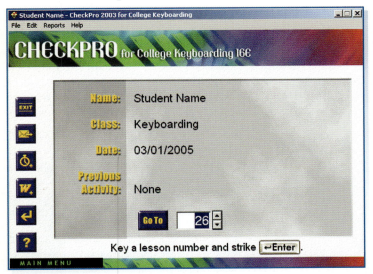

Lesson Screen

Choose a lesson by keying the lesson number or clicking the arrows to the right of the Go To field. Then click on the **Go To** button or tap ENTER. The exercises to be keyed from the lesson are listed on the Lesson menu as shown at the right.

The Lesson menu corresponds directly with the activities that are to be keyed in *CheckPro 2003*. Click on the button next to an activity title to complete the activity. In Lesson 26, only two documents are keyed within *CheckPro*. When you click on either activity, the software will launch *Microsoft Word* for you to complete the activity.

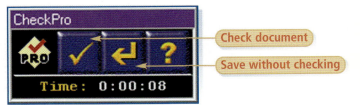

Lessons may include drills, timed writings, documents, and production tests. Each of these is described below:

Drill Practice: For a drill practice activity, key each drill line as it appears on the screen. You can choose to repeat the activity when you finish the drill practice. A check mark appears next to the menu option on the lesson screen when you complete it.

Timed Writings: Click a **Timed Writing** button to take a timed writing. Then select the timing length and source. Key the timed writing from your textbook. The program shows the *gwam*, error rate, and actual errors when you finish the writing. You can print the timed writing report or save it to disk.

Documents and Production Tests: Select a document or assessment activity and choose **Begin new document**. You'll get a dialog box with important information, and then your word processor will be launched. *CheckPro* creates a document for you with the correct filename. The *CheckPro* toolbar will appear on top of the *Word* document window.

When you are finished proofreading the document, click the check mark on the *CheckPro* toolbar. *CheckPro* will then save your document and open a checked version for you to review your results.

To save a document without checking it, click the **Back** button on the *CheckPro* Toolbar.

To finish an exercise or revise a checked document at a later time, select the exercise and choose **Open existing document**. You may also check or print a completed document from this dialog box.

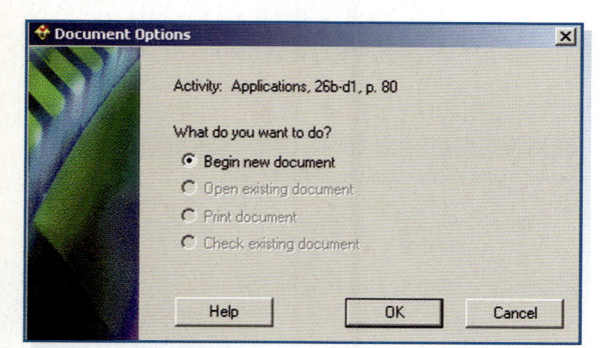

Reports

There are a number of reports available in *CheckPro*. Click the **Reports** menu to see the selection. The Lesson Report provides a snapshot of your results for a specific lesson. The Activity Checklist is an overview of the activities completed. This report indicates the date each activity was completed. The Summary Report displays progress on all Drills, Timed Writings, Documents, and Production Tests. All of the information for creating these reports is saved in your student record.

Special Features

CheckPro 2003 includes several important features. Three of these features are described below:

Timed Writings: Click this button to access timings that are located in a Skill Builder or someplace other than a numbered lesson.

Word document: Click this button to access tests and supplementary documents not within a numbered lesson.

Send File: Click this button to send your student record and lesson documents to the website or via a MAPI-compliant e-mail such as Yahoo.

Send Files to Your Instructor

If you are a distance learning student, you can send files to your instructor through the Web server or by e-mail. Your instructor will advise you as to which method you should use.

Send Files to CheckPro Web Server:

1. Log in as a student with a valid course code. (Your instructor will give you the course code. See step 2, page xxii.)

2. Click the **Send File** button on the Main menu. Your student record (*user name.ckc*) is automatically selected. To attach additional files, click the **Attach Files** button and select the files you want to attach. You can send three types of files. Each file type has a different extension:

- *User name.ckc* Your student record. All reports can be created from this file.
- *.ctw* Timed writing created and saved with a filename.
- *.rtf* The checked version of the exercise, such as *61e-d1.rtf*.

Send Files Using E-mail:

1. Log in as a student.

2. Click the **Send File** button on the Main menu.

3. The student data file is automatically attached. To attach additional files, click the **Attach Files** button and locate the files you wish to add.

Note: To use Send File, a MAPI-compliant e-mail program must be installed and properly configured on your computer. (MAPI stands for *Messaging Application Program Interface*, which is a Microsoft Windows program interface that enables the user to send e-mail from within a Windows application and attach documents.) Microsoft Outlook is an example of a MAPI-compliant program.

If you are using an e-mail program such as Hotmail or Yahoo that is not MAPI compliant, you will not be able to use the automatic Send File feature. However, you can still send your student files to your instructor using your e-mail program by attaching the data files manually.

Create an e-mail to your instructor in the usual manner. Use the attach function of your e-mail program. Use the Browse or Attach function to navigate to the **C:\ Program\ CheckPro2003\Students** folder on your hard drive. When you have located your student record (*username.cwk*) in the *Students* folder, highlight it and click **Open** or **Select**.

1

Developing Keyboarding Skill

Keyboarding

- To key the alphabetic and number keys by touch with good technique.
- To key approximately 25 *wam* with good accuracy.

Communication Skills

- To apply proofreaders' marks and revise text.
- To create simple documents in a basic word processor.

Document 10, continued

4. Format all first-level headings using Heading 1 style, and all second-level headings using Heading 3 style.

5. Reapply Numbering to the two items in *Desired Objectives*, and reapply bullets using the same bullet format to the last three sections of the report.

6. Turn on Show/Hide. Select the first paragraph under Desired Objectives and the numbered items. Format using the paragraphs, using 6-point Spacing after. Repeat the same action for the first paragraph and bulleted items in the last three sections of the report.

7. Check the report carefully. Ensure that no headings are left alone at the bottom of the page and that the main heading is positioned at approximately 2.1". Adjust spacing, if necessary.

TIP

Do not select the last paragraph marker when applying numbering and bullets to these items.

Document 11
Announcement

Format the following Announcement for Miguel Enterprises, Inc.:

- Copy the photo from *picture-kayla anez* in the data files. Position it at the left and increase its size.

- Use landscape orientation, 1" margins on all sides, and a large font.

- Format the following announcement on one page:

Please Welcome

Kayla Anez

Manager

Miguel Emporium

Kayla has six years of very successful managerial experience with Miguel Enterprises. She comes to Columbia from San Juan, Puerto Rico, where she managed our top-producing retail store.

Elena T. Miguel

- After you print and save as *mod9-d11*, save as a Single File Web page named *mod9-d11-web*. Use your browser to preview the document.

PLEASE WELCOME

KAYLA ANEZ

MANAGER

MIGUEL EMPORIUM

KAYLA HAS SIX YEARS OF VERY SUCCESSFUL MANAGERIAL EXPERIENCE WITH MIGUEL ENTERPRISES. SHE COMES TO COLUMBIA FROM SAN JUAN, PUERTO RICO, WHERE SHE MANAGED OUR TOP-PRODUCING RETAIL STORE.

ELENA T. MIGUEL

Document 12
Newsletter

Prepare a newsletter:

- Open *news and views* from the data files.

- Use WordArt (Style in Column 1, Row 1) to add the banner head: **TruAcc News and Views**. Format with blue color.

- Select the text and format in two equal, balanced columns.

TruAcc News and Views

TruAcc, Inc. has had a banner month! In addition, to all the accounts that we manage on retainer, TruAcc has managed two major projects—one for a former client and one for a new client.

Miguel Enterprises, Inc.
Elena Miguel, a client we worked with several years ago, asked us to manage all of the activities related to the grand opening and the marketing of Miguel Emporium. Both the Pre-Grand Opening Celebration for major customers and the Grand Opening Celebration for the public were huge successes. They also liked the opening marketing plan we implemented.

Kayla Anez, the new manager of Miguel Emporium, is working with us on the ongoing marketing plan. Kayla was so pleased with the publicity on the opening and the resulting sales that she has more than doubled the marketing budget. She also indicated she would like us to work on two new out-of-state projects.

Midlands Business Partnership
Mackenzie J. Sakakibara, President of the Midlands Business Partnership, retained us to analyze their previous annual report and recommend ways to improve this year's annual report. The process included focus groups with their leadership and top-level representatives from the business community.

Our analysis and recommendations were well received, and Midlands Business Partnership gave us the opportunity to produce this year's annual report. The report has been completed and distributed to their stakeholders and to the general public. Their distribution list included top leaders in business, the professions, government, and education.

Midlands included an acknowledgement that the report was designed and produced by TruAcc, Inc. As a result of that acknowledgement, we have been asked to submit proposals to several top corporate executives.

www.collegekeyboarding.com

Keyboarding Assessment/Placement

WARMUP

1. Open *Keyboarding Pro*. Create a student record. (See page xx.)
2. Go to the Open Screen.
3. Key the drill twice.
4. Close the Open Screen ☒. Do not save or print the drill lines.

alphabetic

1 Zack quipped that Marny will get five or six jobs.
2 Quin Gaf's wax mock-up had just dazzled everybody.

Tap ENTER twice

figures

3 Room 2938 holds 50 people, and Room 1940 holds 67.
4 Call 803-555-0164 and then ask for extension 1928.

easy

5 Ken may go downtown now and then go to their lake.
6 Did he bid on the bicycle, or did he bid on a map?

Straight-Copy Assessment

1. Go to Skill Builder. From the Lesson menu, click the **Diagnostic Writing** button.
2. Choose 3'. Select **pretest** from the Writings list. Tap TAB to begin. Key from the text.
3. Take a second 3' timing. Click the Timer to begin.
4. Print your results.

| | gwam | 1' | 3' |

I have a story or two or three that will carry you away	11 4
to foreign places, to meet people you have never known, to	23 8
see things you have never seen, to feast on foods available	35 12
only to a few. I will help you to learn new skills you want	47 16
and need; I will inspire you, excite you, instruct you, and	59 20
interest you. I am able, you understand, to make time fly.	71 24
I answer difficult questions for you. I work with you	11 27
to realize a talent, to express a thought, and to determine	23 31
just who and what you are and want to be. I help you to	35 35
know words, to write, and to read. I help you to comprehend	47 40
the mysteries of the past and the secrets of the future. I	59 44
am your local library. We ought to get together often.	70 47

1' | 1 | 2 | 3 | 4 | 5 | 6 | 7 | 8 | 9 | 10 | 11 | 12 |
3' | | 1 | | 2 | | 3 | | 4 | |

Statistical Assessment

1. Follow the steps for the straight-copy assessment.
2. Take two 3' writings using the Diagnostic Writing feature. Choose the writing **placement2**.

| | gwam | 1' | 3' |

Attention Wall Street! The Zanes & Cash report for the end	4 38
of the year (Report #98) says that its last-quarter income was up	8 42
26% from the record earnings of last year. The report also says	12 46
that it was caused by a rise in gross sales of just over 4 1/3%.	16 50
The increase is the 7th in a row for last-quarter earnings; and	20 54
the chief executive of this old firm—Paul Cash—has told at	24 58
least one group that he is sure to ask the board (it will meet on	28 62
the last day of the month) for an "increase of up to $1.50 a share	33 66
as its dividend for the year."	34 68

1' | 1 | 2 | 3 | 4 | 5 | 6 | 7 | 8 | 9 | 10 | 11 | 12 |
3' | | 1 | | 2 | | 3 | | 4 | |

Document 6
Title Page

Prepare a title page for the report you revised in Document 5.

- Format the title page attractively; center the page vertically.
- Use the report title and current date. Prepared for **Ms. Mackenzie J. Sakakibara, President; Midlands Business Partnership**. Prepared by President Hartman's full name and title on one line, company name on the next.
- Add a blue page border to match the TruAcc letterhead color.

Document 7
Letter

Prepare the following transmittal letter for the report to **Ms. Sakakibara**. The Midlands Business Partnership address is: **2678 Elmwood Avenue, Columbia, SC 29204-1259**.

The attached report contains our analysis of the Midlands Business Partnership's last annual report and our recommendations for preparing the report for this year. We noted the many strengths of the last report and ways to build on those strengths in this year's report.

A complete summary of the data we collected and our detailed analysis of that data are stored electronically, and we will e-mail the files to you. We think you will be especially pleased to see the comments made in the focus groups. If you have any questions after you review the report and the backup data, please let us know.

Ms. Sakakibara, we thoroughly enjoyed working on this project with you. We would be very happy to prepare a proposal to assist you in preparing next year's annual report if you would like us to do so.

Document 8
Labels

Prepare a label for Ms. Sakakibara, since the report will be sent in a large envelope so that it will not be folded. Also prepare a label for **Mr. Esteban Pinango, Chair of the Board**. Use the Midlands Business Partnership address.

Document 9
E-mail

Compose a short e-mail to your instructor with three or four sentences about the report you prepared in Document 5. Point out that the report illustrates good communication tips that could be applied to other documents as well. Also comment on the formatting of the document and something you may have learned from preparing the report. Attach Documents 5, 6, and 7.

Document 10
Reformat Report

Reformat Document 5; complete the steps in the following order:

1. Select all text and clear the formatting.
2. Use single spacing and remove indent to the block paragraphs.
3. Format the title using Heading 1 style centered; convert the all caps heading to Title Case.

Continued on next page

MODULE 1

OBJECTIVES

- Key the alphabetic keys by touch.
- Key using proper techniques.
- Key at a rate of 14 *gwam* or more.

Alphabetic Keys

LESSON 1

Home Row, Space Bar, Enter, I

1a Home-Row Position and Space Bar

Practice the steps at the right until you can place your hands in home-row position without watching. Key the drill lines several times.

Home-Row Position

1. Drop your hands to your side. Allow your fingers to curve naturally. Maintain this curve as you key.
2. Lightly place your left fingers over the **a s d f** and the right fingers over the **j k l ;**. You will feel a raised element on the *f* and *j* keys, which will help you keep your fingers on the home position. You are now in **home-row position**.

Space Bar and Enter

Tap the Space Bar, located at the bottom of the keyboard, with a down-and-in motion of the right thumb to space between words.

Enter   Reach with the fourth (little) finger of the right hand to ENTER. Tap it to return the insertion point to the left margin. This action creates a **hard return**. Use a hard return at the end of all drill lines. Quickly return to home position (over ;).

Key these lines:

```
a  s  d  f  SPACE  j  k  l  ;  ENTER
a  s  d  f  SPACE  j  k  l  ;  ENTER
```

Data
~~Information~~ Collected for Report Analysis

Several methods of data collection were used. Leaders _of the organization_ were interviewed to determine the objectives they sought to achieve. Public relations and communication professionals _employed by TruAcc, Inc._ analyzed the last annual report in depth. Consultants conducted ~~three~~ _two_ focus groups: one with stakeholders and one with business community representatives to get their impressions of the last report and ideas of what they would like to see in future reports.

Desired Objectives

The ~~clear~~ consensus of the leaders _of the Midlands Business Partnership_ about the objectives was that the report was designed for ~~three~~ _two_ purposes:

1. To provide stakeholders with information about the accomplishments as well as accurate financial data.

2. To serve as a PR [_write out_] tool with stakeholders, the business community, and the public in general.

Add the following paragraph at the end of the report:

Implementing these recommendations would retain the strengths of the previous report and would improve the areas that were not as effective as they could be. These changes would enhance the public relations aspect of the report significantly.

nɛw kɛɣs

1b Procedures for Learning New Keys

Apply these steps each time you learn a new key.

1. Find the new key on the illustrated keyboard. Then find it on your keyboard.

2. Watch your finger make the reach to the new key a few times. Keep other fingers curved in home position. For an upward reach, straighten the finger slightly; for a downward reach, curve the finger a bit more.

3. Repeat the drill until you can key it fluently.

1c Home Row

1. Go to the Open Screen of *Keyboarding Pro*.

2. Key each line once. Tap Enter at the end of each line. Tap Enter twice to double-space (DS) between 2-line groups.

3. Close the Open Screen without saving your text.

Tap Space Bar once.

```
1 fff    jjj    fjf    fff    jjj    fjf    fjf    jfj    jfj    fjf
2 ddd    kkk    dkd    ddd    kkk    dkd    dkd    kdk    kdk    dkd
```
Tap ENTER twice to DS
```
3 sss    lll    sls    sss    lll    sls    sls    lsl    lsl    sls
4 aaa    ;;;    a;a    aaa    ;;;    a;s    a;a    ;a;    ;a;    a;a

5 ff  jj  ff  jj  fj  fj  fj  dd  kk  dd  kk  dk  dk  dk
6 ss  ll  ss  ll  sl  sl  sl  aa  ;;  aa  ;;  a;  a;  a;

7 f  j  d  k  s  l  a  ;
```
DS
```
8 ff  jj  dd  kk  ss  ll  aa  ;;

9 fff  jjj  ddd  kkk  sss  lll  aaa  jjj  ;;;
```

1d i

1. Apply the standard plan for learning the letter *i*.

2. Keep fingers curved; key the drill once.

i Reach *up* with *right second* finger.

```
10 i  ik  ik  ik  is  is  id  id  if  if  ill  i  ail  did  kid  lid
11 i  ik  aid  ail  did  kid  lid  lids  kids  ill  aid  did  ilk
12 id  aid  aids  laid  said  ids  lid  skids  kiss  disk  dial
```

Miguel Enterprises, Inc.
Cordially invites you and your guest to attend a special
Pre-Grand Opening Celebration
of the Miguel Emporium
3483 Devine Street
7:30 p.m. (one month from today)
RSVP, 555-0167

Document 4
Table

Use a table to prepare the following budget for the Pre-Grand Opening Celebration:

- Key the heading **Pre-Grand Opening Celebration Budget** at approximately 2.1". Use 14 point, all caps, bold.
- Key the following table a DS below the heading. Center-align the text vertically in each cell. Specify row height as 0.3". Shade row 1 15% gray.
- Convert the all caps column heads to Title Case. Adjust widths of columns so that only one line is needed for the column heads. Set decimal tabs, where necessary.
- Calculate the total price for each item. Sum the last column (cell D7).

DESCRIPTION	QUANTITY/ NUMBER	UNIT COST	ESTIMATED COST
Food and beverages	120	$24.50	
Floral arrangements	4	65.75	
Decorations	1	250.00	
Party favors	125	4.25	
Invitations/mailing	1	65.75	
Total Cost			

Document 5
Report

Revise the sections of the report shown on the next page:

- Open *annual report analysis* from the data files.
- Add **Midlands Business Partnership** as AutoText.
- Turn Track Changes on and make the revisions listed here and in the sections shown on the next page.
- Change the bullet format to a symbol similar to that used in TruAcc letterhead (◈).
- Find all occurrences of text formatted in *Italic* and replace it with regular text.
- Revise the footer by replacing **Annual Report Analysis** with **TruAcc, Inc.**
- Review the changes made and accept all changes.
- Review the document summary and make sure your name is listed as author. Add Mr. Hartman's name as manager and TruAcc, Inc. as the company. Also review the statistics.

1e Lesson 1 from Software

Read the information at the right. Then do Lesson 1 from *Keyboarding Pro.*

STANDARD PLAN [for Using Keyboarding Pro]

1. Select a lesson from Alphabetic by clicking the lesson number (Figure 1-1).

2. The first activity is displayed automatically. In Figure 1-2, *Learn Home Row* is in yellow because this activity is active. Follow the directions on screen. Key from the screen.

Figure 1-1 Alphabetic Keyboarding Lesson Menu

Figure 1-2 Alphabetic Keyboarding (Lesson 1: Learn Home Row and i)

3. Key the Textbook Keying activity from your textbook (lines 13–18 below). Tap ESC or the **Stop** button to continue.

4. Figure 1-3 shows the Lesson Report. A check mark opposite an exercise indicates that the exercise has been completed.

5. At the bottom, click the **Print** button to print your Lesson Report. Click the **Send File** button to send your student record to your instructor. Click the **Graph** button to view the Performance Graph.

6. Click the **Back** button twice to return to the Main menu. Then click the **Exit** button to quit the program. Remove your storage disk if necessary. Clean up the work area.

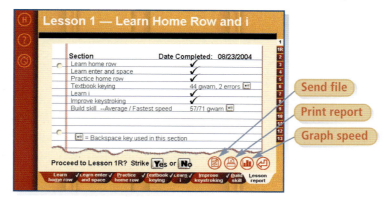

Figure 1-3 Lesson Report Screen

Textbook Keying

1. Key the lines at the right in Textbook Keying. Key each line once. Tap ENTER at the end of each line. Keep your eyes on the book. Do not look back at the screen until you complete the entire line.

2. When you complete the lesson, print your Lesson Report (step 5 above) and exit the software.

```
13 a  a;  al  ak  aj  s  s;  sl  sk  sj  d  d;  dl  dk  dj

14 j  ja  js  jd  jf  k  ka  ks  kd  kf  l  la  ls  ld  lf

15 a;  sl  a;sl  dkfj  a;sl  dkfj  a;sldkfj  asdf  jk

16 a;  sl  a;sl  dk  fj  dkfj  a;sl  dkfj  fkds;a;  fj

17 f  ff  j  jj  d  dd  k  kk  s  ss  l  ll  a  aa  ;  ;;  fj

18 afj;  a  s  d  f  j  k  l  ;  asdf  jkl;  fdsa  jkl;
```

Lesson 1   Home Row, Space Bar, Enter, I   Module 1   5

Document 1
Letter

Prepare the following letter:

Ms. Elena T. Miguel, President | Miguel Enterprises, Inc. | 3476 Devine Street | Columbia, SC 29205-1902 | Dear Ms. Miguel

Thank you for accepting our proposal to manage the grand opening and marketing of your new gift shop, Miguel Emporium. We are very pleased to have the opportunity to work with you again.

The senior staff of TruAcc, Inc. would be happy to meet with you on (insert day and date—one week from today) at 10:30 a.m. in our offices as you requested. Prior to that meeting, we will prepare a proposed plan for the Grand Opening event. As we discussed, we will build on the same model that we used on your previous store openings.

Please sign the enclosed agreement and return one copy to us. We look forward to an exciting event.

Sincerely | Enclosure

Document 2
Memo

Prepare the following memo:
- Use the data file memo template and key the memo.
- Use Find and Replace to locate all instances of *contract* and replace with *agreement*.

To: Senior Staff | Subject: Miguel Contract

Miguel Enterprises accepted the TruAcc, Inc. proposal to manage the grand opening and marketing of the new Miguel Emporium. Elena Miguel called me today to indicate that she had signed the contract, and she was having it hand delivered to us today.

Ms. Miguel also requested that our senior staff meet with her on (insert day and date—one week from today) at 10:30 a.m. in our offices. Please plan to attend this important session. Marlene Delhomme, who is no longer with us, was the manager responsible for the last two Miguel events. Karl Metze has been assigned as the senior account manager for the Miguel account. Please work with Karl on the proposed plan that we will present at the meeting.

Document 3
Draft Invitation

Prepare the invitation on the next page:
- Center-align each line except the *rsvp*, which should be left-aligned. Select 3.0 spacing from the Line Spacing button on the Formatting toolbar. Center the page vertically.
- Use a decorative font such as script or Harlow Solid Italic; apply 16 point, dark red color.
- Compose a short e-mail to your instructor. Attach the draft invitation and ask her or him to review the draft you prepared and make suggestions for improving it.

WARMUP

1Ra Review Home Row

1. Open *Keyboarding Pro* software.
2. Click the ↓ next to *Class* and select your section. Click your name.
3. Key your password and click **OK**.
4. Go to Lesson R1.
5. Key each exercise as directed. Repeat if desired.

Note: All drill lines on this page may be keyed in the Open Screen. See 2d on page 8 for instructions.

Fingers curved and upright

```
1  f j fjf jj fj fj jf dd kk dd kk dk dk dk
2  s ; s;s ;; s; s; s; aa ;; aa ;; a; a; a;

3  fj dk sl a; fjdksla; jfkdls;a ;a ;s kd j
4  f j fjf d k dkd s l sls a ; fj dk sl a;a

5  a; al ak aj s s; sl sk sj d d; dl dk djd
6  ja js jd jf k ka ks kd kf l la ls ld lfl

7  f fa fad s sa sad f fa fall fall l la lad s sa sad
8  a as ask a ad add j ja jak f fa fall; ask; add jak
```

SKILLBUILDING

1Rb Keyboard Review

Key each line once; repeat as time permits.

```
9   ik ki ki ik is if id il ij ia ij ik is if ji id ia
10  is il ill sill dill fill sid lid ail lid slid jail

11  if is il kid kids ill kid if kids; if a kid is ill
12  is id if ai aid jaks lid sid sis did ail; if lids;

13  a lass; ask dad; lads ask dad; a fall; fall salads
14  as a fad; ask a lad; a lass; all add; a kid; skids

15  as asks did disk ail fail sail ails jail sill silk
16  ask dad; dads said; is disk; kiss a lad; salad lid

17  aid a lad; if a kid is; a salad lid; kiss sad dads
18  as ad all ask jak lad fad kids ill kill fall disks
```

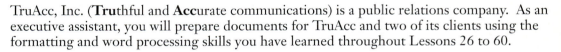

TruAcc, Inc.

OBJECTIVES

- Apply keying, formatting, and word processing skills.
- Work independently with few specific instructions.

TruAcc, Inc. (**Tru**thful and **Acc**urate communications) is a public relations company. As an executive assistant, you will prepare documents for TruAcc and two of its clients using the formatting and word processing skills you have learned throughout Lessons 26 to 60.

Use these instructions for all documents:

- Set up a folder named *TruAcc Reference Manual*.

- TruAcc uses block letter format and unbound report style.

- Unless instructed otherwise, all documents are from Mark C. Hartman, President.

- Use the date function to add the current date; add your reference initials.

- Before you begin, add **TruAcc, Inc.** as AutoText to avoid keying it repeatedly.

- Use the TruAcc letterhead and memo templates provided as data files for all letters and memos. Use appropriate salutations, closing lines, and subject lines.

- Proofread, spell-check, preview, and print each document.

- Save each document as *mod9-d*+document number (*mod9-d1*, *mod9-d2*, etc.).

- Rename the folder as *TruAcc Style Guide*.

E and N

WARMUP

2a

1. Open *Keyboarding Pro*.
2. Locate your student record.
3. Select **Lesson 2**.

```
1 ff dd ss aa ff dd ss aa jj kk ll ;; fj dk sl a; a;
2 fj dk sl a; fjdksla; a;sldkfj fj dk sl a; fjdksla;

3 aa ss dd ff jj kk ll ;; aa ss dd ff jj kk ll ;; a;
4 if a; as is; kids did; ask a sad lad; if a lass is
```

NEW KEYS

2b E and N

Key each line once; DS between groups.

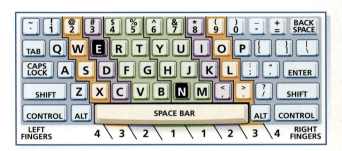

e Reach *up* with *left second* finger.

n Reach *down* with *right first* finger.

e
```
5 e ed ed led led lea lea ale ale elf elf eke eke ed
6 e el el eel els elk elk lea leak ale kale led jell
7 e ale kale lea leak fee feel lea lead elf self eke
```

n
```
8 n nj nj an an and and fan fan and kin din fin land
9 n an fan in fin and land sand din fans sank an sin
10 n in ink sink inn kin skin an and land in din dink
```

all reaches learned
```
11 den end fen ken dean dens ales fend fens keen knee
12 if in need; feel ill; as an end; a lad and a lass;
13 and sand; a keen idea; as a sail sank; is in jail;
14 an idea; an end; a lake; a nail; a jade; a dean is
```

2c Textbook Keying
Key each line once; DS between groups.

```
15 if a lad;
16 is a sad fall

17 if a lass did ask
18 ask a lass; ask a lad

19 a;sldkfj a;sldkfj a;sldkfj
20 a; sl dk fj fj dk sl a; a;sldkfj

21 i ik ik if if is is kid skid did lid aid laid said
22 ik kid ail die fie did lie ill ilk silk skill skid
```

> Reach with little finger; tap Enter key quickly; return finger to home key.

Objective Assessment
Answer the questions below to see if you have mastered the content of this module.

1. A dynamic, graphic form of print that provides for adding color and shading and that is ideal for formatting banner headings in newsletters is created using the _____ feature.

2. A chart that is used effectively to show percentages of a whole is a(n) _____.

3. Text columns that flow down one column to the top of the next column are known as _____ columns.

4. To change the format of a document and have a different format on the same page, insert a(n) _____ section break.

5. Section breaks are shown as a dotted line with the type of break indicated in _____ view.

6. To move clip art, you must first click the Text Wrapping button on the _____ toolbar.

7. To insert shapes such as an octagon or triangle, click _____ on the Drawing toolbar.

8. A(n) _____ arrow is needed to size clip art.

9. A(n) _____ arrow is needed to move clip art.

10. To balance columns so that all columns end at the same point, insert a(n) _____ at the end of the text.

Performance Assessment

Document 1

Newsletter

1. Open *safety net* from the data files.
2. Change the side margins for the entire document to .75".
3. Use WordArt for the banner.
4. Format the document in two equal-sized columns.
5. Create a Line chart to replace the Workplace Accidents Table. Change the line color to red.
6. Use a 1.5-point line across the column to separate components of the newsletter except when it would be positioned at the top of a column.
7. Insert a picture of a handheld cell phone positioned at the left side of the column after the cell phone is mentioned in the text.
8. Insert a picture of an individual at a computer workstation within the paragraph after the ergonomics seminar has been introduced.
9. Adjust the newsletter so that it will fit on one page with balanced columns.
10. Save the document as *checkpoint8d-1* and print.

Document 2

Revise Newsletter

1. Open *checkpoint 8d-1*.
2. Delete the lines across the columns and change the format to three columns.
3. Move the picture of the individual at a computer workstation to the end of the third column.
4. Slightly decrease the size of the line chart. Delete any blank space to fit the newsletter on one page. Balance the columns.
5. Save as *checkpoint8d-2* and print.

2d **Open Screen**

The Open Screen is a word processor. Exercises to be keyed in the Open Screen are identified with an Open Screen icon. For these exercises, follow the instructions in the textbook and key from your textbook. Keep your eyes on the textbook copy as you key— not on your fingers or the screen.

Open Screen - Untitled.kos
File Edit View Insert Format Table Help

Times New Roman ▼ 11 ▼   B I U

Student·Name¶
¶

1. Click the **Open Screen** button at the left edge of the Main menu of *Keyboarding Pro*.
2. Key your name and tap ENTER twice.
3. Follow the directions in the textbook for the drill.
4. Print what you key in the Open Screen.
5. Click the **Close** button in the upper-right corner to exit the Open Screen. ⊠

> **TIP**
>
> Click the **View** menu; then click **Show Codes**. The dot between words indicates that you tapped the Space Bar. The ¶ indicates that you tapped the ENTER key. Check these codes to verify that you inserted correct spacing between words and lines.

SKILLBUILDING

2e **Reinforcement**

1. In the Open Screen, key each line twice. DS between 2-line groups.
2. Print but do not save the exercise.
3. Close the Open Screen and you will return to Lesson 2 in the software.

> **TECHNIQUE TIP**
>
> Keep your eyes on the textbook copy.

i

23 ik ik ik if is il ik id is if kid did lid aid ails

24 did lid aid; add a line; aid kids; ill kids; id is

n

25 nj nj nj an an and and end den ken in ink sin skin

26 jn din sand land nail sank and dank skin sans sink

e

27 el els elf elk lea lead fee feel sea seal ell jell

28 el eke ale jak lake elf els jaks kale eke els lake

all reaches

29 dine in an inn; fake jade; lend fans; as sand sank

30 in nine inns; if an end; need an idea; seek a fee;

2f
End the lesson.

1. Print the Lesson Report.
2. Exit the software; remove the storage disk if appropriate.

Asset Allocation

The Investment Committee agreed on an aggressive asset allocation of 75% equity and 25% fixed income securities. The Foundation endows its assets in perpetuity and spends only 5% of the income earned on these assets each year. Therefore, the extremely long time horizon of the investment portfolio justifies the aggressive investment in equities.

Asset Classes

The Committee considered eight classes of assets: large cap core, large cap value, large cap growth, small cap value, small cap growth, international equities, fixed income, and alternative assets. The Committee included all classes of assets except alternative investments in its recommendation. Alternative investments are so named because these assets have not traditionally been included in the portfolios of foundations. Alternative investments include assets such as hedge funds, venture capital funds, real estate funds, and direct investment in startup ventures. The Committee recommends that investments in alternative investments be deferred for at least a year.

Asset Weightings

Obviously, some of the equity classes deserve higher weightings than other classes. Small cap stocks and international stocks play a less predominate role in traditional foundation portfolios than large cap stocks. The portfolio structure diagram shown below contains the Investment Committee's recommendations for weighting the various asset classes.

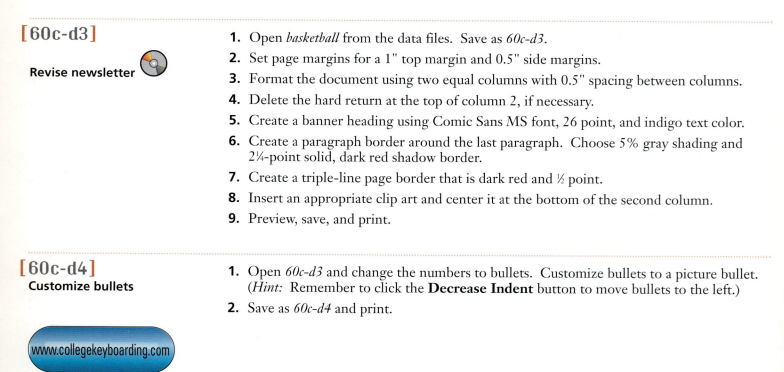

[60c-d3]

Revise newsletter

1. Open *basketball* from the data files. Save as *60c-d3*.
2. Set page margins for a 1" top margin and 0.5" side margins.
3. Format the document using two equal columns with 0.5" spacing between columns.
4. Delete the hard return at the top of column 2, if necessary.
5. Create a banner heading using Comic Sans MS font, 26 point, and indigo text color.
6. Create a paragraph border around the last paragraph. Choose 5% gray shading and 2¼-point solid, dark red shadow border.
7. Create a triple-line page border that is dark red and ½ point.
8. Insert an appropriate clip art and center it at the bottom of the second column.
9. Preview, save, and print.

[60c-d4]
Customize bullets

1. Open *60c-d3* and change the numbers to bullets. Customize bullets to a picture bullet. (*Hint:* Remember to click the **Decrease Indent** button to move bullets to the left.)
2. Save as *60c-d4* and print.

www.collegekeyboarding.com

Review

WARMUP

3a

Key each line at a steady pace; tap and release each key quickly. Key each line again at a faster pace.

home	1	ad ads lad fad dad as ask fa la lass jak jaks alas
n	2	an fan and land fan flan sans sand sank flank dank
i	3	is id ill dill if aid ail fail did kid ski lid ilk
all	4	ade alas nine else fife ken; jell ink jak inns if;

SKILLBUILDING

3b Rhythm Builder

Key each line twice.

Lines 5–8: Think and key words. Make the space part of the word.

Lines 9–12: Think and key phrases. Do not key the vertical rules separating the phrases.

easy words

5 if is as an ad el and did die eel fin fan elf lens
6 as ask and id kid and ade aid eel feel ilk skis an

7 ail fail aid did ken ale led an flan inn inns alas
8 eel eke nee kneel did kids kale sees lake elf fled

easy phrases

9 el el|id id|is is|eke eke|lee lee|ale ale|jill jill
10 is if|is a|is a|a disk|a disk|did ski|did ski|is a

11 sell a|sell a|sell a sled|fall fad|fall fad|did die
12 sees a lake|sees a lake|as a deal|sell a sled|all

3c Technique Practice

Key each 2-line group twice; SS.

home row: fingers curved and upright

13 jak lad as lass dad sad lads fad fall la ask ad as
14 asks add jaks dads a lass ads flak adds sad as lad

upward reaches: straighten fingers slightly; return quickly to home position

15 fed die led ail kea lei did ale fife silk leak lie
16 sea lid deal sine desk lie ale like life idea jail

double letters: don't hurry when stroking double letters

17 fee jell less add inn seek fall alee lass keel all
18 dill dell see fell eel less all add kiss seen sell

[60c-dl]
Radial Diagram

1. Create the radial diagram shown below. Click **Insert Shape** four times to have seven circles.
2. Key the text in bold. Tap ENTER once above the text to center it in the circle.
3. Save as *60c-d1*.

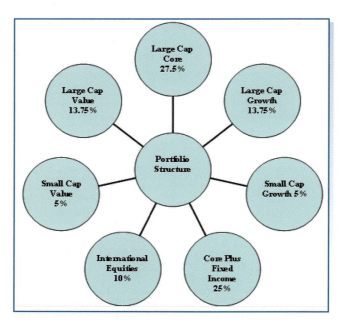

[60c-d2]
Newsletter

1. Key a newsletter using the information that follows.
2. Set page margins for a 1" top margin and 0.5" side and bottom margins.
3. Use a banner heading with the design in column 1, row 3 of the WordArt Gallery, and change the color to dark red. Extend the heading from margin to margin.
4. Use 11-point Times New Roman for body text and Heading 1 for all headings.
5. Format the document using two equal columns with 0.5" spacing between columns.
6. Key the text and balance columns.
7. Copy the radial diagram from *60c-d1* and paste it at the bottom of the newsletter at the approximate horizontal center.
8. If necessary, adjust the newsletter so that it fits on one page.
9. Save the newsletter as *60c-d2* and print a copy.

Central Foundation Update

Central University Foundation committees met this past week, and this newsletter is designed to update all Board Members of the actions taken by one of the Investment Committee. At its last meeting, the Foundation Board charged the Investment Committee to work with its consultants to diversify the Foundation's investment portfolio and present the proposed portfolio structure to the full Board for its approval at its next meeting.

3d Textbook Keying

Key each line once; DS between 2-line groups.

reach review

19 ea sea lea seas deal leaf leak lead leas fleas keas

20 as ask lass ease as asks ask ask sass as alas seas

DS

21 sa sad sane sake sail sale sans safe sad said sand

22 le sled lead flee fled ale flea lei dale kale leaf

DS

23 jn jn nj nj in fan fin an; din ink sin and inn an;

24 de den end fen an an and and ken knee nee dean dee

phrases (think and key phrases)

25 and and land land el el elf elf self self ail nail

26 as as ask ask ad ad lad lad id id lid lid kid kids

27 if if|is is|jak jak|all all|did did|nan nan|elf elf

28 as a lad| ask dad| fed a jak| as all ask| sales fad

29 sell a lead|seal a deal|feel a leaf|if a jade sale

30 is a|is as if|a disk|aid all kids|did ski|is a silk

3e Reinforcement

1. In the Open Screen, key your name and tap ENTER twice.
2. Key each line once. DS between 2-line groups.
3. Print the exercise.
4. Click the **X** box in the upper-right corner to close the Open Screen.
5. Print your Lesson Report and exit.

d/e
31 den end fen ken dean dens ales fend fens keen knee

32 a deed; a desk; a jade; an eel; a jade eel; a dean

n/a
33 an an in in and and en end end sane sane sand sand

34 a land; a dean; a fan; a fin; a sane end; end land

nj
35 el eel eld elf sell self el dell fell elk els jell

36 in fin inn inks dine sink fine fins kind line lain

all reaches
37 an and fan dean elan flan land lane lean sand sane

38 sell a lead; sell a jade; seal a deal; feel a leaf

Assessment

alphabet	1	Jayne Cox puzzled over workbooks that were required for geometry.
figures	2	Edit pages 308 and 415 in Book A; pages 17, 29, and 60 in Book B.
one hand	3	Plum trees on a hilly acre, in my opinion, create no vast estate.
easy	4	If they sign an entitlement, the town land is to go to the girls.

| 1 | 2 | 3 | 4 | 5 | 6 | 7 | 8 | 9 | 10 | 11 | 12 | 13 |

60b Timed Writings

Take one 3' and one 5' writing at your control level.

 all letters

	gwam	3'	5'

What is a college education worth today? If you asked that question to a random sample of people, you would get a wide range of responses. Many would respond that you cannot quantify the worth of a bachelor's degree. They quickly stress that many factors other than wages enhance the quality of life. They tend to focus on the benefits of sciences and liberal arts and the appreciation they develop for things that they would never have been exposed to if they had not attended college.

3'	5'
4	2
9	5
13	8
18	11
22	13
26	16
31	18
33	20

Data show, though, that you can place a value on a college education—at least in respect to wages earned. Less than twenty years ago, a high school graduate earned only about fifty percent of what a college graduate earned. Today, that number is quite different. The gap between the wages of a college graduate and the wages of a high school graduate has more than doubled in the last twenty years.

37	22
41	25
45	27
50	30
54	32
58	35
59	36

The key factor in economic success is education. The new jobs that pay high wages require more skills and a college degree. Fortunately, many high school students do recognize the value of getting a degree. Far more high school graduates are going to college than ever before. They know that the best jobs are jobs for knowledge workers and those jobs require a high level of skill.

63	38
68	41
72	43
76	46
81	48
85	51

| 3' | 1 | 2 | 3 | 4 |
| 5' | 1 | 2 | 3 | |

[APPLICATIONS]

[60c]

Assessment

→ Continue

✓ Check

With *CheckPro*: When you complete a document, proofread it, check the spelling, and preview for placement. When you are completely satisfied with the document, click the **Continue** button to move to the next document. You will not be able to return and edit a document once you continue to the next document. Click the **Check** button when you are ready to error-check the test. Review and/or print the document analysis results.

Without *CheckPro*: On the signal to begin, key the documents in sequence. When time has been called, proofread all documents again and identify errors.

Left Shift, H, T, Period

WARMUP

4a
Key each line twice SS.
Keep eyes on copy.

home row 1	al as ads lad dad fad jak fall lass asks fads all;
e/i/n 2	ed ik jn in knee end nine line sine lien dies leis
all reaches 3	see a ski; add ink; fed a jak; is an inn; as a lad
easy 4	an dial id is an la lake did el ale fake is land a

NEW KEYS

4b Left Shift and h
Key each line once.

> Follow the "Standard Plan for Learning New Keyreaches" on page 4 for all remaining reaches.

left shift Reach *down* with *left fourth* (little) finger; shift, tap, release.

h Reach to *left* with *right first* finger.

left shift

5 J Ja Ja Jan Jan Jane Jana Ken Kass Lee Len Nan Ned
6 and Ken and Lena and Jake and Lida and Nan and Ida
7 Inn is; Jill Ina is; Nels is; Jen is; Ken Lin is a

h

8 h hj hj he he she she hen aha ash had has hid shed
9 h hj ha hie his half hand hike dash head sash shad
10 aha hi hash heal hill hind lash hash hake dish ash

all reaches learned

11 Nels Kane and Jake Jenn; she asked Hi and Ina Linn
12 Lend Lana and Jed a dish; I fed Lane and Jess Kane
13 I see Jake Kish and Lash Hess; Isla and Helen hike

4c Textbook Keying
Key the drill once. Strive for good control.

14 he she held a lead; she sells jade; she has a sale
15 Ha Ja Ka La Ha Hal Ja Jake Ka Kahn La Ladd Ha Hall
16 Hal leads; Jeff led all fall; Hal has a safe lead
17 Hal Hall heads all sales; Jake Hess asks less fee;

TIPS ON CULTURE AND CUSTOMS

North American business executives need knowledge of customs and practices of their international business partners. The following suggestions provide an important starting point for understanding other cultures.

1. *Know the requirement of hand shaking.* Taking the extra moment to shake hands at every meeting and again on departure will reap benefits.

2. *Establish friendship first if important for that culture.* Being a friend may be important first; conducting business is secondary. Establish a friendship; show interest in the individual and the family. Learn people's names and pronounce them correctly in conversation.

3. *Understand the meaning of time.* Some cultures place more importance on family, personal, and church-related activities than on business activities. Accordingly, they have longer lunches and more holidays. Therefore, they place less importance on adherence to schedules and appointment times.

4. *Understand rank.* Protocol with regard to who takes precedence is important; i.e., seating at meetings, speaking, and walking through doorways. Do not interrupt anyone.

5. *Know the attitudes of space.* Some cultures consider 18 inches a comfortable distance between people; however, others prefer much less. Adjust to their space preferences. Do not move away, back up, or put up a barrier, such as standing behind a desk.

6. *Understand the attitude of hospitality.* Some cultures are generous with hospitality and expect the same in return. For example, when hosting a party, prepare a generous menu; finger foods would be considered "ungenerous."

7. *Share their language appropriately.* Although the business meeting may be conducted in English, speak the other language in social parts of the conversation. This courteous effort will be noted.

[59d-d3]
Customize Bullets

1. Open *59d-d2* and save as *59d-d3a*.

✳ 2. Select the numbered items and change to bullets by clicking Bullets and Numbering button. Customize the bullets as a picture of your choice (**Format**, **Bullets and Numbering**, **Customize**, and **Picture**). Save.

✳ 3. Select the bullets again and customize as a character of your choice. Choose a character from any of the Wingdings fonts.

4. Save as *59d-d3b*.

✳ DISCOVER

To customize a bullet, click the **Format** menu and choose **Bullets and Numbering**. On the **Bulleted** tab, click **Customize**. Click **Picture** or **Character** and select the desired bullet.

4d t and . (period)

Key each line once.

Period: Space once after a period that follows an initial or an abbreviation. To increase readability, space twice after a period that ends a sentence.

t Reach *up* with *left first* finger.

. (period) Reach *down* with *right third* finger.

t

18 t tf tf aft aft left fit fat fete tiff tie the tin

19 tf at at aft lit hit tide tilt tint sits skit this

20 hat kit let lit ate sit flat tilt thin tale tan at

. (period)

21 .l .l l.l fl. fl. L. L. Neal and J. N. List hiked.

22 Hand J. H. Kass a fan. Jess did. I need an idea.

23 Jane said she has a tan dish; Jae and Lee need it.

all reaches learned

24 I did tell J. K. that Lt. Li had left. He is ill.

25 tie tan kit sit fit hit hat; the jet left at nine.

26 I see Lila and Ilene at tea. Jan Kane ate at ten.

SKILLBUILDING

4e Reinforcement

Follow the standard directions for the Open Screen (page 8).

Lines 27–34: Key each line twice; DS between groups. Try to increase your speed the second time.

Lines 35–38: Key the lines once.

reach review

27 tf .l hj ft ki de jh tf ik ed hj de ft ki l. tf ik

28 elf eel left is sis fit till dens ink has delt ink

h/e

29 he he heed heed she she shelf shelf shed shed she

30 he has; he had; he led; he sleds; she fell; he is

i/t

31 it is if id did lit tide tide tile tile list list

32 it is; he hit it; he is ill; she is still; she is

shift

33 Hal and Nel; Jade dishes; Kale has half; Jed hides

34 Hi Ken; Helen and Jen hike; Jan has a jade; Ken is

enter

35 Nan had a sale.

36 He did see Hal.

37 Lee has a desk.

38 Ina hid a dish.

4f End the lesson

Print the lines keyed in the Open Screen and print your Lesson Report. Exit the software.

TECHNIQUE TIP

Tap Enter without pausing or looking up from the copy.

provide maximum schedule flexibility. The three core modules are required for all employees. At least three modules must be selected from the six modules that are designated as electives. Descriptive information and schedules are available from the Training Department and will be posted on the Crown Lake Online Bulletin Board.

Students Function as Professional Consultants

In late spring, President John Marcus notified us that a team of international MBA students from the Business School at State University would be working with us to develop an export strategy for Crown Lake and asked us to cooperate fully with the team. Most of us felt that we were being asked to take on a project that was essentially a "public service" contribution to the University. Were we ever wrong!!! It only took us one day to realize that these five graduate students were truly professionals in every respect and that they were going to function as a highly effective, results-oriented professional consulting team. A faculty member advised the team, and they had access to a wide range of expertise at the University. This past week the team presented the final results of their field-consulting project to the division management team. The bottom line is that we now have an export strategy for three of our product lines and a viable implementation plan to begin exporting to Canada and Mexico early next year. The team also performed extensive country analyses of 12 European and South American countries and laid the groundwork for future expansion to those markets. Partnering with the University was truly a win-win situation!

—Roberta C. West
Vice President of Marketing

✉ **Mail from Employees**

—Student's Name
Production Associate

R, Right Shift, C, O

WARMUP

5a
Key each line twice.

home keys	1	a; ad add al all lad fad jak ask lass fall jak lad
t/h/i/n	2	the hit tin nit then this kith dint tine hint thin
left shift/.	3	I need ink. Li has an idea. Hit it. I see Kate.
all reaches	4	Jeff ate at ten; he left a salad dish in the sink.

NEW KEYS

5b r and Right Shift
Key each line once.

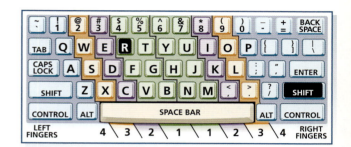

r Reach *up* with *left first* finger.

right shift Reach *down* with *right fourth* finger; shift, tap, release.

r

5 r rf rf riff riff fir fir rid ire jar air sir lair
6 rf rid ark ran rat are hare art rant tire dirt jar
7 rare dirk ajar lark rain kirk share hart rail tart

right shift

8 D D Dan Dan Dale Ti Sal Ted Ann Ed Alf Ada Sid Fan
9 and Sid and Dina and Allen and Eli and Dean and Ed
10 Ed Dana; Dee Falk; Tina Finn; Sal Alan; Anna Deeds

all reaches learned

11 Jane and Ann hiked in the sand; Asa set the tents.
12 a rake; a jar; a tree; a red fire; a fare; a rain;
13 Fred Derr and Rai Tira dined at the Tree Art Fair.

5c Textbook Keying
Key each line once; DS between 2-line groups.

14 ir ir ire fir first air fair fire tire rid sir
15 fir jar tar fir flit rill till list stir dirt fire
DS
16 Feral is ill. Dan reads. Dee and Ed Finn see Dere.
17 All is still as Sarah and I fish here in the rain.
DS
18 I still see a red ash tree that fell in the field.
19 Lana said she did sail her skiff in the dark lake.

Crown Lake News and Views

Current date

Newsletter Staff

Eric Burge
    Editor

Nancy Suggs
Christopher Hess
Anne Reynolds
    Associate Editors

Wayne Martin
    Editorial Assistant

The *Crown Lake News and Views* is a weekly newsletter compiled by the staff of the Human Resources Department, and it is sent to all employees. Employees are invited to share ideas with others by writing a letter to the editor to be included in the Mail from Employees column.

New Development Project

Crown Lake won the bid to develop and construct the new multimillion-dollar Business Center adjacent to Metro Airport. Connie McClure, one of the three senior project managers, has been named as the Business Center project manager. The project is expected to take more than two years to complete. Approximately fifty new permanent employees will be hired to work on this project. All jobs will be posted within the next two weeks. The recruiting referral program is in effect for all jobs. You can earn a $100 bonus for each individual you recommend who is hired and remains with Crown Lake for at least six months. You may pick up your recruiting referral forms in the Personnel Office.

Blood Drive Reminder

The Crown Lake quarterly blood drive is set for Friday, April 4, in the Wellness Center. The Community Blood Bank needs all types of blood to replace the supplies sent to the islands during the recent disaster caused by Hurricane Lana. Employees in all divisions are being asked to participate this quarter because of the current supply crisis. All three donation sites will be used. Several volunteers will be needed to staff the two additional sites. The regular division rotation will resume next quarter.

Lee Daye Honored

The Community Foundation honored Lee Daye of the Marketing

Department with the Eagle Award for outstanding service this year. The Eagle Award is presented each year to three citizens who have made a significant impact on the lives of others. The Community Foundation recognized Lee for his work with underprivileged children, the Community Relations Task Force, the Abolish Domestic Violence Center, and the Community Transitional Housing Project. Congratulations, Lee, you made a difference in the lives of many citizens in our community. Your award was richly deserved.

New Training Program

The pilot test of the new Team Effectiveness training program was completed last month, and the results were excellent. Thanks to all of you who participated in the development and testing of the program. Your input is vital to the program's success. The program is designed as a series of nine modules ranging from two to four hours long to

5d c and o

Key each line once.

c Reach *down* with *left second* finger.

o Reach *up* with *right third* finger.

c

20 c c cd cd cad cad can can tic ice sac cake cat sic
21 clad chic cite cheek clef sick lick kick dice rice
22 call acid hack jack lack lick cask crack clan cane

o

23 o ol ol old old of off odd ode or ore oar soar one
24 ol sol sold told dole do doe lo doll sol solo odor
25 onto door toil lotto soak fort hods foal roan load

all reaches learned

26 Carlo Rand can call Rocco; Cole can call Doc Cost.
27 Trina can ask Dina if Nick Corl has left; Joe did.
28 Case sent Carole a nice skirt; it fits Lorna Rich.

SKILLBUILDING

5e Keyboard Reinforcement

Key each line once SS; key at a steady pace. Repeat, striving for control.

o/r

29 or or for for nor nor ore ore oar oar roe roe sore
30 a rose|her or|he or|he rode|or for|a door|her doll

i/t

31 is is tis tis it it fit fit tie tie this this lits
32 it is|it is|it is this|it is this|it sits|tie fits

e/n

33 en en end end ne ne need need ken ken kneel kneels
34 lend the|lend the|at the end|at the end|need their

c/o

35 ch ch check check ck ck hack lack jack co co cones
36 the cot|the cot|a dock|a dock|a jack|a jack|a cone

TECHNIQUE TIP

Reach up without moving hands away from your body. Use quick keystrokes.

all reaches

37 Jack and Rona did frost nine of the cakes at last.
38 Jo can ice her drink if Tess can find her a flask.
39 Ask Jean to call Fisk at noon; he needs her notes.

[59d-dl]

Two-page Newsletter with Unequal Columns

✳ **1.** Frequently used text can be added as an AutoText entry so that you don't have to key the entire text each time it occurs. Before keying the newsletter, add **Crown Lake** as an AutoText entry. Then key the newsletter on the next two pages as straight text (no columns). When *Word* suggests the complete Crown Lake entry, press ENTER to accept it.

2. Set left and right margins of 0.75".

3. Use WordArt for the banner heading, and adjust the size so the banner spans all columns. Leave two or three blank lines; then insert a continuous break.

4. Use 14-point Times New Roman for headings within the document and 12-point Times New Roman for body text.

5. Format the document after the banner as a three-column document with lines between the columns. Use the following settings:

First Column: 1.5"

Space between all columns: 0.025"

Second and third columns: 2.5"

6. Use the first column for editorial information as shown, then insert a column break.

7. Insert an eagle from clip art similar to what is shown. Center it in the column after the Eagle Award is mentioned.

8. When text wraps to the second page, insert a column break in the first column to shift the text to the second column so that you will reserve the first narrow column for editorial information.

9. In the first column of the second page, key the name of the newsletter in 14-point bold and the current date and **Page 2** in 12-point bold.

10. Insert a mailbox symbol from Wingdings for the Mail from Employees column.

11. Compose an article to fill the space left in the last column of the second page. You may choose your own topic or use one of the following:

- The value of participating in community service activities (write from the perspective of both the employee and the company).

- Invite employees to participate in an activity such as an investment club, an exercise group, a club sport, or some other area of interest. Share benefits of being involved and provide information about the activity.

- Tips for keeping physically fit and why it is important to do so.

- Tips for traveling on a tight budget.

- Tips for managing time effectively.

12. Use an appropriate title for your article, and add your name and title **Production Associate** at the end of your article.

13. Save the document as *59d-d1* and print a copy.

[59d-d2]

Report with Columns

1. Key the text on page 264; SS between numbered items.

2. Create two columns of equal width; balance the columns so that both end at about the same point.

3. At the right of two of the numbered items, insert an appropriate graphic. Wrap text around the graphics using square wrapping and right alignment; size the graphic appropriately.

4. Save as *59d-d2*.

W, Comma, B, P

WARMUP
6a
Key each line twice; avoid pauses.

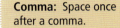

home row 1 ask a lad; a fall fad; had a salad; ask a sad jak;

o/t 2 to do it; to toil; as a tot; do a lot; he told her

c/r 3 cots are; has rocks; roll cot; is rich; has an arc

all reaches 4 Holt can see Dane at ten; Jill sees Frank at nine.

NEW KEYS
6b w and , (comma)
Key each line once.

> **Comma:** Space once after a comma.

w Reach *up* with *left third* finger.

, (comma) Reach *down* with *right second* finger.

w

5 w ws ws was was wan wit low win jaw wilt wink wolf

6 sw sw ws ow ow now now row row own own wow wow owe

7 to sew; to own; was rich; was in; is how; will now

, (comma)

8 k, k, k, irk, ilk, ask, oak, ark, lark, jak, rock,

9 skis, a dock, a fork, a lock, a fee, a tie, a fan,

10 Jo, Ed, Ted, and Dan saw Nan in a car lift; a kit

all reaches learned

11 Win, Lew, Drew, and Walt will walk to West Willow.

12 Ask Ho, Al, and Jared to read the code; it is new.

13 The window, we think, was closed; we felt no wind.

6c Textbook Keying
Key each line once.

14 walk wide sown wild town went jowl wait white down

15 a dock, a kit, a wick, a lock, a row, a cow, a fee

16 Joe lost to Ron; Fiji lost to Cara; Don lost to Al

17 Kane will win; Nan will win; Rio will win; Di wins

18 Walter is in Reno; Tia is in Tahoe; then to Hawaii

To enter a section break:

1. Select **Break** from the Insert menu.
2. Click the type of Section break desired, and then click **OK**.

   Next page: Begins a new page at the point the section break is entered.

   Continuous: Begins a new section on the same page.

   Even page: Begins a new section on the next even-numbered page.

   Odd page: Begins a new section on the next odd-numbered page

In Normal View, section breaks appear as a dotted line with the type of break indicated. *Word* displays the current section number on the status bar. To copy the format of one section to a different section, select the section break and copy it to the new location.

```
Section 1, page 1
......................................................Section Break (Continuous)...........
Section 2, page 1
......................................................Section Break (Next Page)...........
Section 3, page 2
......................................................Section Break (Even Page)...........
Section 4, page 4
......................................................Section Break (Odd Page)...........
Section 5, page 5
```

D r i l l   1   NEXT PAGE BREAKS

1. Open *time* from the data files.
2. Format the title using WordArt of your choice; leave two or three blank lines after the WordArt.
3. At the beginning of the text, insert a Continuous section break. Format the text as two equal columns.
4. At the end of the text, insert a Next Page section break.
5. Drag the pie chart to the approximate center of the page if it is not centered.
6. Save the document as *59c-drill1* and print a copy.

D r i l l   2   CONTINUOUS SECTIONS

1. Open *59c-drill1* and change the Next Page section break to a Continuous section break.
2. Drag the pie chart to the approximate center of the page if it is not centered.
3. Save the document as *59c-drill2* and print a copy.

6d b and p

Key each line once.

b Reach *down* with *left first* finger.

p Reach *up* with *right fourth* (little) finger.

b

19 bf bf bf biff fib fib bib bib boa boa fib fibs rob

20 bf bf bf ban ban bon bon bow bow be be rib rib sob

21 a dob, a cob, a crib, a lab, a slab, a bid, a bath

p

22 p; p; pa pa; pal pal pan pan pad par pen pep paper

23 pa pa; lap lap; nap nap; hep ape spa asp leap clap

24 a park, a pan, a pal, a pad, apt to pop, a pair of

all reaches learned

25 Barb and Bob wrapped a pepper in paper and ribbon.

26 Rip, Joann, and Dick were all closer to the flash.

27 Bo will be pleased to see Japan; he works in Oslo.

SKILLBUILDING

6e Keyboard Reinforcement

Key each line once; key at a steady pace.

reach review

28 ki kid did aid lie hj has has had sw saw wits will

29 de dell led sled jn an en end ant hand k, end, kin

s/w

30 ws ws lows now we shown win cow wow wire jowl when

31 Wes saw an owl in the willow tree in the old lane.

b/p

32 bf bf fib rob bid ;p p; pal pen pot nap hop cap bp

33 Rob has both pans in a bin at the back of the pen.

6f Speed Builder

1. Follow the standard Open Screen directions on page 8.
2. Key each line twice. Work for fluency.

all reaches

34 Dick owns a dock at this lake; he paid Ken for it.

35 Jane also kept a pair of owls, a hen, and a snake.

36 Blair soaks a bit of the corn, as he did in Japan.

37 I blend the cocoa in the bowl when I work for Leo.

38 to do|can do|to bow|ask her|to nap|to work|is born

39 for this|if she|is now|did all|to see|or not|or if

Sections and Newsletters

59a

Key each line twice SS.

alphabet	1	Loquacious, breezy Hank forgot to jump over the waxed hall floor.
figures	2	Invoices 675 and 348, dated June 29 and August 10, were not paid.
one hand	3	Polk traded Case #789—24 sets of rare carved beads—as rare art.
easy	4	They may dismantle the eight authentic antique autos in the town.

| 1 | 2 | 3 | 4 | 5 | 6 | 7 | 8 | 9 | 10 | 11 | 12 | 13 |

COMMUNICATION

59b

1. Key each enumerated item that follows, correcting the redundancies as you key. (*Hint:* A redundancy is a phrase that repeats an idea in an accompanying word, e.g., *true facts* or *full and complete*.)

2. Save the document as *59b*.

1. The witness was instructed to tell the honest truth.
2. Attendance is a necessary requirement for a keyboarding course.
3. The two twins were greeted by their brother and sister.
4. Past history should assist us in blocking an appropriate number of rooms for each night of the convention.
5. Please refer back to page 25 for exact wording of the research questions.
6. Would you like my personal opinion?
7. Children left unattended are in serious danger.
8. Let me know whether or not you will attend the meeting at 2 p.m. in the afternoon.
9. Each and every contestant will receive a prize for being on the show.
10. Waiting for my plane to leave, I watched the sun set in the west.

NEW FUNCTIONS

59c

Sections

Often long documents such as reports and newsletters are formatted in sections so that different formats may be applied on the same page or on different pages using section breaks. *Word* provides several different types of breaks. Page breaks, column breaks, and text wrapping breaks can all occur in the same section of a document.

Page break: To move to the next page of a document.

Column break: To move to the next column of text.

Text wrapping break: To move text to the next line.

help keywords

sections

Section breaks differ from the breaks just described in that they divide a document into sections. Each section can have its own format and page numbering scheme.

Review

WARMUP

7a

Key each line twice; begin new lines promptly.

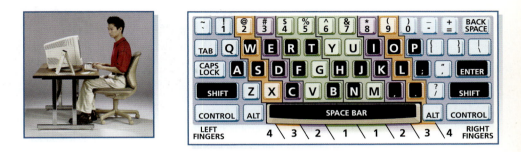

all 1	We often can take the older jet to Paris and back.
home 2	a; sl dk fj a;sl dkfj ad as all ask fads adds asks
1st row 3	Ann Bascan and Cabal Naban nabbed a cab in Canada.
3d row 4	Rip went to a water show with either Pippa or Pia.

SKILLBUILDING

7b Reach Mastery

Key each line once; DS between 3-line groups.

5 ws ws was was wan wan wit wit pew paw nap pop bawl

6 bf bf fb fb fob fob rib rib be be job job bat back

7 p; p; asp asp pan pan ap ap ca cap pa nap pop prow

DS

8 Barb and Bret took an old black robe and the boot.

9 Walt saw a wisp of white water renew ripe peppers.

10 Pat picked a black pepper for the picnic at Parks.

7c Rhythm Builder

Key each line once; DS between 3-line groups.

words	11	a an pan so sot la lap ah own do doe el elf to tot
phrases	12	if it|to do|it is|do so|for the|he works|if he bid
sentences	13	Jess ate all of the peas in the salad in the bowl.

DS

words	14	bow bowl pin pint for fork forks hen hens jak jaks
phrases	15	is for|did it|is the|we did a|and so|to see|or not
sentences	16	I hid the ace in a jar as a joke; I do not see it.

DS

words	17	chap chaps flak flake flakes prow prowl work works
phrases	18	as for the|as for the|and to the|to see it|and did
sentences	19	As far as I know, he did not read all of the book.

TECHNIQUE TIP

words: key as a single unit rather than letter by letter;
phrases: say and key fluently;
sentences: work for fluency.

Arena Update

Get Your Shovels Ready!

The architects have put the final touches on the arena plans and the groundbreaking has been scheduled for March 18. Put the date on your calendar and plan to be a part of this exciting time. The Groundbreaking Ceremony will begin at 5:00 at the new arena site. After the ceremony, you will join the architects in the practice facility for refreshments and an exciting visual presentation of the new arena. The party ends when we all join the Western Cougars as they take on the Central Lions for the final conference game.

Cornerstone Club Named

Robbie Holiday of the Cougars Club submitted the winning name for the new premium seating and club area of the new arena. Thanks to all of you who submitted suggestions for naming the new club. For his suggestion, which was selected from over 300 names submitted, Robbie has won season tickets for next year and the opportunity to make his seat selection first. The Cornerstone Club name was selected because members of our premium clubs play a crucial role in making our new arena a reality. Without the financial support of this group, we could not lay the first cornerstone of the arena.

Cornerstone Club members have first priority in selecting their seats for both basketball and hockey in a specially designated section of the new arena. This section provides outstanding seats for both basketball games and hockey matches. Club members also have access to the Cornerstone Club before the game, during halftime, and after the game. They also receive a parking pass for the lot immediately adjacent to the arena. If you would like more information about the Cornerstone Club and how you can become a charter member of the club, call the Cougars Club office during regular business hours.

What View Would You Like?

Most of us would like to sit in our seats and try them out before we select them rather than look at a diagram of the seating in the new arena. Former Cougar players make it easy for you to select the perfect angle to watch the ball go in the basket. Mark McKay and Jeff Dunlap, using their patented Real View visualization software, make it possible

for you to experience the exact view you will have from the seats you select. In fact, they encourage you to try several different views. Most of the early testers of the new seat selection software reported that they came in with their minds completely made up about the best seats in the house. However, after experiencing several different views with the Real View software, they changed their original seat location request.

7d Technique Practice

Key each set of lines once SS; DS between 3-line groups.

▼ Space once after a period following an abbreviation.

spacing: space *immediately* after each word

20 ad la as in if it lo no of oh he or so ok pi be we

21 an ace ads ale aha a fit oil a jak nor a bit a pew

22 ice ades born is fake to jail than it and the cows

spacing/shifting   ▼   ▼

23 Ask Jed. Dr. Han left at ten; Dr. Crowe, at nine.

24 I asked Jin if she had ice in a bowl; it can help.

25 Freda, not Jack, went to Spain. Joan likes Spain.

7e Timed Writings in the Open Screen

PROCEDURE [for Using the Open Screen Timer] 🕐

You can check your speed in the Open Screen using the Timer.

1. In the Open Screen, click the **Timer** button on the toolbar. In the Timer dialog box, check **Count-Down Timer** and time; click **OK**.

2. The Timer begins once you start to key and stops automatically. Do not tap ENTER at the end of a line. Wordwrap will cause the text to flow to the next line automatically.

3. To save the timing, click the **File** menu and **Save as**. Use your initals (*xx*), the exercise number, and number of the timing as the filename. Example: *xx-7f-t1* (your initials, exercise 7f, timing1).

4. Click the **Timer** button again to start a new timing.

5. Each new timing must be saved with its own name.

7f Speed Check ◉

1. Take two 1' writings on the paragraph in the Open Screen.

2. Follow the directions in **7e**. Do not tap ENTER at the ends of the lines.

Goal: 12 *gwam*

Note: The dot above the text represents two words.

```
              •            4              •            8              •
It is hard to fake a confident spirit.  We will do
            12             •            16             •
better work if we approach and finish a job and
20             •            24             •            28             •
know that we will do the best work we can and then
            32
not fret.
| 1 | 2 | 3 | 4 | 5 | 6 | 7 | 8 | 9 | 10 |
```

7g Guided Writing ◉

1. In the Open Screen, key each line once for fluency. Do not save your work.

2. Set the Timer in the Open Screen for 30". Take two 30" writings on each line. Do not save the timings.

Goal: to reach the end of the line before time is up

gwam

26 Dan took her to the show.   12

27 Jan lent the bowl to the pros.   25

28 Hold the wrists low for this drill.   37

29 Jessie fit the black panel to the shelf.   49

30 Jake held a bit of cocoa and an apricot for Diane.   61

31 Dick and I fish for cod on the docks at Fish Lake.   73

32 Kent still held the dish and the cork in his hand.   84

| 1 | 2 | 3 | 4 | 5 | 6 | 7 | 8 | 9 | 10 |

D r i l l   3 | REVISE COLUMN STRUCTURE

1. Open *58b-drill2* and save it as *58b-drill3*.
2. Change the format to three equal columns with .3" space between columns and a line between them.
3. Resize the graphic to fit within a column. Position it attractively in column 3.
4. Balance the columns so that they will end at approximately the same point on the page.
5. Save, preview, and print.

APPLICATIONS

[58c-d1]
Newsletter

1. Key the newsletter shown on the next page. Use 0.5" left and right margins, and apply what you have learned.
2. Use the WordArt shown or select another style for the banner.
3. Insert clip art files, as shown in the newsletter. You may substitute any appropriate clip art you find if you cannot find the same images. Wrap the text around the graphics.
4. Use 18-point Albertus Medium type for the internal headings in the newsletter.
5. Balance columns so that all columns end at about the same place.
6. Create a double-line page border that is dark red and 1½ point. (*Hint:* Choose **Options** and then **Measure from Text**.)
7. Save the document as *58c-d1*.

[58c-d2]
Revise Newsletter

1. Reformat document *58c-d1* as a three-column newsletter. Change the spacing between columns to 0.3".
2. Delete the second graphic in the third column. Resize the first graphic in that column so that it is the same width as the column. Balance the columns if the last column is shorter than other columns.
3. Save the document as *58c-d2* and print.

[58c-d3]
Compose Newsletter

1. Design a family newsletter that would be interesting to your immediate family and your extended family.
2. Key the newsletter and apply what you have learned. Be creative in choosing graphics—clip art, scanned pictures, or your digital pictures. See your instructor for directions for scanning and for using a digital camera if available.
3. Save as *58c-d3*. E-mail the newsletter to your teacher and to your family members.

G, Question Mark, X, U

WARMUP
8a
Key each line twice. Keep eyes on copy.

all 1 Dick will see Job at nine if Rach sees Pat at one.
w/b 2 As the wind blew, Bob Webber saw the window break.
p/, 3 Pat, Pippa, or Cap has prepared the proper papers.
all 4 Bo, Jose, and Will fed Lin; Jack had not paid her.

NEW KEYS
8b g and ?
Key each line once; repeat.

> **Question mark:** The question mark is usually followed by two spaces.

g Reach to *right* with *left first* finger.

? Left shift; reach *down* with *right fourth* finger.

g

5 g g gf gaff gag grog fog frog drag cog dig fig gig
6 gf go gall flag gels slag gala gale glad glee gals
7 golf flog gorge glen high logs gore ogle page grow

?

8 ? ?; ?; ? ? Who? When? Where? Who is? Who was?
9 Who is here? Was it he? Was it she? Did she go?
10 Did Geena? Did he? What is that? Was Jose here?

all reaches learned

11 Has Ginger lost her job? Was her April bill here?
12 Phil did not want the boats to get here this soon.
13 Loris Shin has been ill; Frank, a doctor, saw her.

8c Textbook Keying
Key each line once; DS between groups.

reach review
14 ws ws hj hj tf tf ol ol rf rf ed ed cd cd bf bf p;
15 wed bid has old hold rid heed heed car bed pot pot

g
16 gf gf gin gin rig ring go gone no nog sign got dog
17 to go|to go|go on|go in|go in|to go in|in the sign

?
18 ?; ?;? who? when? where? how? what? who? It is I?
19 Is she? Is he? Did I lose Jo? Is Gal all right?

TECHNIQUE TIP

Concentrate on correct reaches.

To force the starting of a new column:

1. Position the insertion point where the new column is to start.
2. From the Insert menu, choose **Break**.
3. Click **Column break**.

Drill 1 SIMPLE COLUMNS

1. Open *training* from the data files. Save it as *58b-drill1*.

2. Click **Columns** and format the document in three even columns. Preview to see how it looks.

3. Format the same document in two columns and balance the columns. Preview to check the appearance.

4. Select the heading **Productivity Enhancement Program**; click **Columns** and select one column. Double space below the heading. Apply 24 point, bold. Center-align the heading. Save again and close.

Wrap Text Around Graphics

When graphic elements are included in documents such as newsletters, text usually wraps around the graphic.

To wrap text around graphics:

1. Insert the graphic; then place the insertion point over the graphic and right-click.
2. Select **Format picture** to display the Format Picture dialog box.
3. Click the **Layout** tab and select the desired wrapping style (**Square**).
4. Click the desired alignment (**Right**) and then click **OK**.

Drill 2 WRAP TEXT AROUND GRAPHIC

1. Open *productivity* from the data files. Save as *58b-drill2*.

2. Go to the end of the document and select the graphic. Change handles to moving handles (click the **Text Wrapping** icon on the Picture toolbar; click **Square**).

3. Move the graphic and position it before the paragraph that begins with *Integration*. Work patiently.

4. Wrap the text around the graphic using square wrapping and center alignment.

5. If the graphic moves to the left column, drag it back so it is positioned above the *Integration* paragraph. Be sure it is center-aligned.

6. Preview and print when you are satisfied.

To revise the column structure:

1. Click **Format, Columns**. Click the number of desired columns.
2. In the Width and spacing section, key the desired spacing between columns. (**Note:** If different spacing is desired between each column, deselect the **Equal column width** option box.) Select the **Line between** option to add a line between columns.

8d x and u

Key each line once; repeat.

x Reach *down* with *left third* finger.

u Reach *up* with right first finger.

x

20 x x xs xs ox ox lox sox fox box ex hex lax hex fax

21 sx six sax sox ax fix cox wax hex box pox sex text

22 flax next flex axel pixel exit oxen taxi axis next

u

23 u uj uj jug jut just dust dud due sue use due duel

24 uj us cud but bun out sun nut gun hut hue put fuel

25 dual laud dusk suds fuss full tuna tutus duds full

all reaches learned

26 Paige Power liked the book; Josh can read it next.

27 Next we picked a bag for Jan; then she, Jan, left.

28 Is her June account due? Has Lou ruined her unit?

SKILLBUILDING

8e Reinforcement

Optional: In the Open Screen, key each line once; DS between groups. Repeat. Print.

29 nut cue hut sun rug us six cut dug axe rag fox run

30 out of the sun|cut the action|a fox den|fun at six

31 That car is not junk; it can run in the next race.

32 etc. tax nick cure lack flex walls uncle clad hurt

33 lack the cash|not just luck|next in line|just once

34 June Dunn can send that next tax case to Rex Knox.

8f Speed Check

In the Open Screen, take a 1' writing on each paragraph. Tap ENTER only after you have keyed the entire paragraph. Save the timings as *xx8f-t1* and *xx8f-t2*, substituting your initials for *xx*.
Goal: 14 *gwam*

```
                        .       4       .       8       .
How a finished job will look often depends on how
        12      .       16      .       20
we feel about our work as we do it.  Attitude has
        .       24      .       28      .
a definite effect on the end result of work we do.
```
Tap ENTER once
```
                        .       4       .       8       .
When we are eager to begin a job, we relax and do
        12      .       16      .       20
better work than if we start the job with an idea
        .       24      .       28      .
that there is just nothing we can do to escape it.
```

Columns and Newsletters

alphabet	1	Jimmy Favorita realized that we must quit playing by six o'clock.
figure	2	Joell, in her 2001 truck, put 19 boxes in an annex at 3460 Marks.
double letter	3	Merriann was puzzled by a letter that followed a free book offer.
easy	4	Ana's sorority works with vigor for the goals of the civic corps.

| 1 | 2 | 3 | 4 | 5 | 6 | 7 | 8 | 9 | 10 | 11 | 12 | 13 |

NEW FUNCTIONS
58b

Columns

help keywords

columns; newspaper columns

Text may be formatted in multiple columns on a page to make it easier to read. A newsletter, for example, is usually formatted in columns. Typically, newsletters are written in an informal, conversational style and are formatted with **banners** (text that spans multiple columns), newspaper columns, graphic elements, and other text enhancements. In newspaper columns, text flows down one column and then to the top of the next column. A simple, uncluttered design with a significant amount of white space is recommended to enhance the readability of newsletters.

Productivity Enhancement Program

The Executive Committee's new Productivity Enhancement Program resulted in standardizing all computer software applications for the company in all locations. The Training and Development Team, at the request of the Executive Committee, developed a training program designed to help all employees learn how to integrate applications available in the standardized suite and to use electronic mail and the Internet.

The Productivity Enhancement Program specifies that each employee must develop in-depth skill in at least two applications, basic skill in the other applications, and be able to produce a compound document—that is, a document that includes elements from multiple software applications in the suite. Employees must also be able to use electronic mail. The Productivity Enhancement Program specifies that most internal documents will be distributed electronically.

To meet the needs of all employees, the Training and Development Team structured the Integrating Computer Applications training program in three phases.

Assessment provides employees who already have developed skill in an application to demonstrate that competence without taking the training module. Two levels of assessments—basic skill and in-depth skill—are available for each application. Each computer-administered and scored assessment contains three versions.

An employee who does not successfully complete the assessment in three tries or who elects not to take the assessment option must take the training module for that application. Assessments are also used at the conclusion of training modules.

Development follows assessment. Two options are available for developing skill in the various applications. Employees may sign up for regular training classes or may elect to use the new computer-based training programs (CBT) to develop the skill. The advantage of using the CBT program is that it can be completed at your own workstation. A combination of both instructor-led training and the CBT program may be the best alternative for most employees. An assessment must be completed at the end of each training session to demonstrate the level of skill attained on each software application. Assessment applies to both CBT and instructor-led training.

Integration is the final phase of the program. The integration program accomplishes two objectives—teaching employees how to prepare documents that use objects from the various applications in the suite and standardizing the format for frequently used documents. Detailed information about the integration phase will be provided at least three weeks prior to the training so that participants can assemble the appropriate documents for the training session.

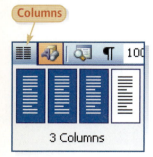

Columns

3 Columns

To create columns of equal width:

1. Click the **Columns** button on the Standard toolbar.
2. Drag to select the number of columns. Using this method to create columns will format the entire document with columns of equal widths.

Column format may be applied before or after keying text. If columns are set before text is keyed, use Print Layout View to check the appearance of the text. Generally, column formats are easier to apply after text has been keyed.

Occasionally, you may want certain text (such as a banner or headline) to span more than one column.

To format a banner:

1. Select the text to be included in the banner.
2. Click the **Columns** button, and drag the number of columns to one.

To balance columns:

To balance columns so that all columns end at the same point on the page, position the insertion point at the end of the text to be balanced and insert a **Continuous section break** (**Insert, Break, Continuous, OK**).

Q, M, V, Apostrophe

WARMUP
9a
Key each line twice.

all letters 1 Lex gripes about cold weather; Fred is not joking.

space bar 2 Is it Di, Jo, or Al? Ask Lt. Coe, Bill; he knows.

easy 3 I did rush a bushel of cut corn to the sick ducks.

easy 4 He is to go to the Tudor Isle of England on a bus.

NEW KEYS
9b q and m
Key each line once; repeat.

q Reach *up* with *left fourth* finger.

m Reach *down* with *right first* finger.

q

5 q qa qa quad quad quaff quant queen quo quit quick

6 qa qu qa quo quit quod quid quip quads quote quiet

7 quite quilts quart quill quakes quail quack quaint

m

8 m mj mj jam man malt mar max maw me mew men hem me

9 m mj ma am make male mane melt meat mist amen lame

10 malt meld hemp mimic tomb foam rams mama mire mind

all reaches learned

11 Quin had some quiet qualms about taming a macaque.

12 Jake Coxe had questions about a new floor program.

13 Max was quick to join the big reception for Lidia.

9c Textbook Keying
Key each line once for control. DS between 2-line groups.

m/x 14 me men ma am jam am lax, mix jam; the hem, six men

15 Emma Max expressed an aim to make a mammoth model.

q/u 16 qa qu aqua aqua quit quit quip quite pro quo squad

17 Did Quin make a quick request to take the Qu exam?

g/n 18 fg gn gun gun dig dig nag snag snag sign grab grab

19 Georgia hung a sign in front of the union for Gib.

[57d-d2]
Memo with Pie Chart

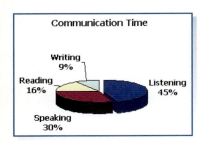

1. Use the Contemporary memo template and key the following memo to **Customer Service Representatives** from you. Use the current date.
2. Use **Report from Consultants** as the subject. Send a copy to **Roger Massaro**.
3. Create a 3-D pie chart using the following data:

   Headings for Pie Slices: **Listening**, **Speaking**, **Reading**, and **Writing**
   Data: Listening **54**, Speaking **36**, Reading **19**, and Writing **11**
   Chart Title: **Communication Time**
   Legend: None
   Data Labels: *Category name* and *Percentage*
4. Edit the pie chart as follows:
   a. Drag bottom right handle to 4" on the ruler line. Click center-align.
   b. Delete the plot area.
   c. Change the color of largest pie slice to dark blue and explode the pie slice.
   d. Format the chart title in 14-point Tahoma; format the data labels in 8-point Tahoma.
5. After creating the pie chart, continue keying the last paragraph of the memo. You should have one blank line before and after the chart.
6. Save the memo as *57d-d2*.

The consultants sent me the results of the initial phase of their study of our customer service operation. One of the interesting findings was the average distribution of communication time of our customer service representatives.

The approach the consultants used was to observe each representative for 120 minutes over a two-week period. Ten-minute observations were randomly scheduled during this period. The following chart shows how our customer representatives spend their communication time.

These findings clearly support the need for our new Listening Skills Training Program.

[57d-d3]

Copy and Paste Chart

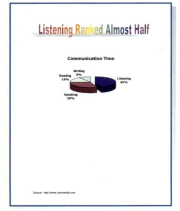

1. Open *57d-d2* and open the data file *listening*. Save the data file as *57d-d3*.
2. In *57d-d2*, click the pie chart and click the **Copy** button. Close the file.
3. In *57d-d3*, click **Edit**, **Paste Special**. Choose the **Microsoft Graph Chart Object** paste option. Resize the chart attractively.
4. Add a text box at the bottom left of the page that includes the following text: **Source: http://www.commskills.com**. Format it with no fill and no lines. Use a font of your choice.
5. Save. E-mail this file as an attachment to your teacher using the **Mail Recipient (as Attachment)** command. Compose an appropriate subject line and message.

9d v and ' (apostrophe)

Key each line once; repeat.

> **Apostrophe:** The apostrophe shows (1) omission (as Rob't for Robert or it's for it is) or (2) possession when used with nouns (as Joe's hat).

v Reach *down* with *left first* finger.

' Reach to ' with *right fourth* finger.

v

20 v vf vf vie vie via via vim vat vow vile vale vote
21 vf vf ave vet ova eve vie dive five live have lave
22 cove dove over aver vivas hive volt five java jive

' (apostrophe)

23 '; '; it's it's Rod's; it's Bo's hat; we'll do it.
24 We don't know if it's Lee's pen or Norma's pencil.
25 It's ten o'clock; I won't tell him that he's late.

all reaches learned

26 It's Viv's turn to drive Iva's van to Ava's house.
27 Qua, not Vi, took the jet; so did Cal. Didn't he?
28 Wasn't Fae Baxter a judge at the post garden show?

SKILLBUILDING

9e Reinforcement

1. Follow the standard Open Screen directions on page 8.
2. Key each line twice; DS between groups. Strive to increase speed.

v/?

29 Viola said she has moved six times in five months.
30 Does Dave live on Vine Street? Must he leave now?

q/?

31 Did Viv vote? Can Paque move it? Could Val dive?
32 Didn't Raquel quit Carl Quent after their quarrel?

direct reach

33 Fred told Brice that the junior class must depart.
34 June and Hunt decided to go to that great musical.

double letter

35 Harriette will cook dinner for the swimming teams.
36 Bill's committee meets in an accounting classroom.

9f Speed Check

In the Open Screen, take two 1' writings on the paragraph. Press ENTER only after keying the entire paragraph. Save the timings as *xx-9f-t1* and *xx-9f-t2*, substituting your initials for *xx*.

```
            .           4           .           8           .
We must be able to express our thoughts with ease
        12          .          16          .          20
if we desire to find success in the business world.
        .          24          .          28
It is there that sound ideas earn cash.
```

Drill 5 | PIE CHART

1. Create a pie chart to show the percentage of the total fourth quarter sales each region had.

2. On the Insert menu, click **Picture**, and then click **Chart**.

3. On the Chart menu, click **Chart Type**, and select **Pie** from the list.

4. In the Chart Sub-Type box, select the second chart, **Pie with a 3-D Visual Effect**.

5. Select the datasheet, and select and replace the labels and data with information shown below. The data for a pie chart is formatted in a row. Each heading represents a slice of the pie.

6. Click **Chart**; then **Chart Options**. Click the **Title** tab and key **Fourth Quarter Sales** in the chart title box.

E:\College Keyboarding 16t... - Datasheet						
		A	B	C	D	E
		East	West	North	South	
1	3-D Pie 1	250	325	245	205	
2						

7. Click the **Legend** tab and click the **Show legend** box to deselect it.

8. Click the **Data Labels** tab, and then click **Category name** and **Percentage**. Click **OK**.

9. Click the plot area and tap DELETE.

Plot area

10. Click once to select the pie slices; then click the West slice to select only it. Click it again and drag it away from the other pie slices to explode it.

11. Click outside the chart.

12. Save it as *57c-drill5* and print.

Fourth Quarter Sales

South 20%
East 24%
North 24%
West 32%

Drill 6 | CHANGE CHART TYPE

1. Open *57c-drill4* and save it as *57c-drill6*.

2. Double-click on the chart to open it.

3. Click **Chart**, then **Chart Type**, and select **Line** as the chart type.

4. In the Chart Sub-Type box, select the first option in row 2, Stacked line with markers displayed at each data value. Click **OK**.

5. Click **Chart**, and then click **Chart Options**.

6. Click the **Title** tab, and then click in the chart title box, and key **Sales Trends for 2006**.

7. Click outside the chart. Save again and print.

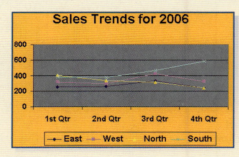

Sales Trends for 2006

800, 600, 400, 200, 0

1st Qtr, 2nd Qtr, 3rd Qtr, 4th Qtr

— East — West — North — South

APPLICATIONS

[57d-d1]
Radial Diagram

1. Prepare a radial diagram for a report you are writing.

2. Key **Critical Success Skills** in the center core element circle. (*Hint:* Tap ENTER to center the text vertically in the diagram.)

3. Add one additional circle to the three shown around the center.

4. Key **Reading**, **Writing**, **Listening**, and **Speaking** in the four circles.

5. Bold and center the text in each circle.

6. Save the document as *57d-d1* and print.

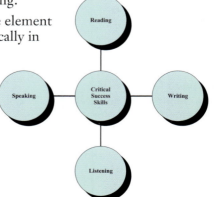

Reading

Speaking

Critical Success Skills

Writing

Listening

Z, Y, Quotation Mark, Tab

WARMUP
10a
Key each line twice.

all letters	1	Quill owed those back taxes after moving to Japan.
spacing	2	Didn't Vi, Sue, and Paul go? Someone did; I know.
q/v/m	3	Marv was quite quick to remove that mauve lacquer.
easy	4	Lana is a neighbor; she owns a lake and an island.

NEW KEYS
10b [z] and [y]
Key each line once; repeat.

z Reach *down* with *left fourth* finger.

y Reach *up* with *right first* finger.

z

5 za za zap zap zing zig zag zoo zed zip zap zig zed
6 doze zeal zero haze jazz zone zinc zing size ozone
7 ooze maze doze zoom zarf zebus daze gaze faze adze

y

8 y yj yj jay jay hay hay lay nay say days eyes ayes
9 yj ye yet yen yes cry dry you rye sty your fry wry
10 ye yen bye yea coy yew dye yaw lye yap yak yon any

all reaches learned

11 Did you say Liz saw any yaks or zebus at your zoo?
12 Relax; Jake wouldn't acquire any favorable rights.
13 Has Mazie departed? Tex, Lu, and I will go alone.

10c Textbook Keying
Key each line once. DS between groups.

14 Cecilia brings my jumbo umbrella to every concert.

direct reach	15	John and Kim recently brought us an old art piece.
	16	I built a gray brick border around my herb garden.

DS

17 sa ui hj gf mn vc ew uy re io as lk rt jk df op yu

adjacent reach	18	In Ms. Lopez' opinion, the opera was really great.
	19	Polly and I were joining Walker at the open house.

To modify a chart:

1. Double-click on the chart to display the datasheet or grid that is similar to an *Excel* spreadsheet. New information in the form of labels (words) and data (figures) can be either keyed in the data sheet or imported from a spreadsheet.

2. Select and edit the data as desired.

3. Right-click any part of the chart and select the **Format** option (**Format Chart Area**, **Format Chart Walls**, etc.). Make formatting selections from the dialog box that displays.

4. Click outside the chart area when you have finished.

E:\College Keyboarding 16t... - Datasheet

		A	B	C	D	E
		1st Qtr	2nd Qtr	3rd Qtr	4th Qtr	
1	East	257	265	340	250	
2	West	321	302	420	325	
3	North	402	340	320	245	
4	South	385	380	460	205	

D r i l l   3   COLUMN CHART

1. Create the column chart illustrated on the previous page using the data chart above.

2. On the Insert menu, click **Picture**, and then click **Chart** to display the default column chart along with the data sheet. The *Microsoft Graph* commands become available on the menu bar and toolbars.

3. Click in the datasheet cell below *North* and key **South**. Note that the software adds a unique color for the columns displaying the data for the South region.

4. Click in each cell in columns A–D, and key the data shown below for the four quarters.

5. On the menu, click **Chart** and then **Chart Options**.

6. Click the **Titles** tab and then click in the chart title box and key **Sales by Region**.

7. Click the **Legend** tab, and click the **Show legend** box if it is not already checked. Click the **Right** button, and then click **OK**.

8. Click outside the chart area.

9. Save the document as *57c-drill3* and print.

D r i l l   4   MODIFY COLUMN CHART

1. Open *57c-drill3*, save it as *57c-drill4*, and double-click the chart.

2. Refer to the illustration on page 251 for the parts of the chart. Right-click the chart area and click **Format Chart Area**. Select a color of your choice.

3. Change the value of the fourth quarter sales in the South to **580**.

4. Right-click the chart title, click **Format Chart Title**, and format it in 14 point.

5. Right-click the Category-Axis, click **Format Axis**, and format it in 10 point. Repeat for the Value-Axis.

6. Click the first column (data series). Right-click and choose **Format Data Series**. Select a color of your choice. Repeat for each series.

7. Right-click the legend and choose **Format Legend**. Click the **Placement** tab and select **Bottom**.

8. Right-click the chart walls and choose **Format Walls**. Select a color of your choice.

9. Size the chart by dragging the bottom right handle to 4.5" on the Horizontal Ruler. (*Hint:* Drag the datasheet out of the way.)

10. Save and print.

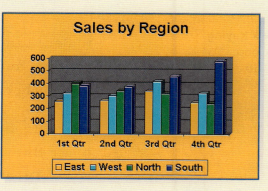

10d " (quotation mark) and TAB

Key each line once; repeat.

" Shift; then reach to " with *right fourth* finger.

TAB Reach up with *left fourth* finger.

SKILLBUILDING

10e Reinforcement

Follow the standard directions on page 8 for keying in the Open Screen. Key each line twice; DS between groups.

10f Speed Check

Take two 1' writings of paragraph 2 in the Open Screen, using wordwrap. Save as *xx-10f-t1* and *xx-10f-t2*.

Goal: 15 *gwam*

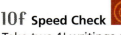

TECHNIQUE TIP

Wordwrap: Text within a paragraph moves automatically to the next line. Tap ENTER only to begin a new paragraph.

" (quotation mark)

20 "; "; " " "lingo" "bugs" "tennies" I like "malts."
21 "I am not," she said, "going." I just said, "Oh?"

tab key

22   The tab key is used for indenting paragraphs and aligning columns.
23   Tabs that are set by the software are called default tabs, which are usually a half inch.

all reaches learned

24   The expression "I give you my word," or put
25 another way, "Take my word for it," is just a way
26 I can say, "I prize my name; it clearly stands in
27 back of my words." I offer "honor" as collateral.

tab 28   Tap the tab key and begin the line without a pause to maintain fluency.
29   She said that this is the lot to be sent; I agreed with her.
30   Tap Tab before starting to key a timed writing so that the first line is indented.

gwam 1'

Tab ➝ All of us work for progress, but it is not   8
always easy to analyze "progress." We work hard   18
for it; but, in spite of some really good efforts, 28
we may fail to receive just exactly the response we 39
want.   40
Tab ➝ When this happens, as it does to all of us,   9
it is time to cease whatever we are doing, have   18
a quiet talk with ourselves, and face up to the   28
questions about our limited progress. How can we   38
do better?   40

| 1 | 2 | 3 | 4 | 5 | 6 | 7 | 8 | 9 | 10 |

---

1. Open *57c-drill1*, save it as *57c-drill2*, and change the page setup to **Landscape**.

2. Select the box with your name, and add **Mason McGee, Administrative Assistant** as an assistant (**Insert Shape, Assistant**).

3. Add **Marcus Clements, Division Head** as a subordinate to the Executive Vice President (select box; **Insert Shape**; **Left Hanging Layout**).

4. Add **Angela Westin, Division Head** as a subordinate to the Vice President for Finance (select box; **Insert Shape**; **Standard Layout**).

5. Add **Lynn Watson, Division Head** as a subordinate to the Vice President for Marketing (select box; **Insert Shape**; **Right Hanging Layout**).

6. Select and drag the Canvas to the approximate center of the page.

7. Save the document again and print one copy.

Optional: Insert several of the other diagrams from the Drawing toolbar, and discover how to add elements to each and to format them.

---

help keywords

chart, graph

◉ Microsoft Graph

Different types of charts can be created using *Microsoft Graph*. The most common are bar charts, column charts, line charts, and pie charts. Bar and column charts compare values across categories—the length of the bar or the height of the column is used to show the differences. Line charts show trends over time or categories. Pie charts show percentages of a whole. Study the parts of a chart that are labeled on the column chart below.

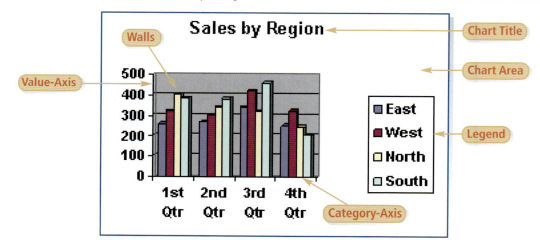

TIP

Another option for inserting a chart is to click **Insert**; **Object**. Then click **Create New tab** and select **Microsoft Graph Chart**.

To create a chart:

1. On the Insert menu click **Picture**, and then click **Chart** to display the default chart.

2. To choose another type of chart, click **Chart** on the menu; then click **Chart Type** to display the list of chart types.

3. Select the type of chart desired and key or modify the data in the datasheet.

4. Click **Chart**, and then click **Chart Options**.

5. Click in the chart title box, and key the title.

6. Click **Legend**, click the **Show Legend** box, and click a placement, such as **Right**.

7. Click outside the chart area when you have completed the chart.

Review

WARMUP

11a
Key each line twice SS (slowly, then faster).

alphabet 1 Zeb had Jewel quickly give him five or six points.

" (quote) 2 Can you spell "chaos," "bias," "bye," and "their"?

y 3 Ty Clay may envy you for any zany plays you write.

easy 4 Did he bid on the bicycle, or did he bid on a map?

| 1 | 2 | 3 | 4 | 5 | 6 | 7 | 8 | 9 | 10 |

SKILLBUILDING

11b Keyboard Reinforcement
Key each line once; repeat the drill to increase fluency.

5 za za zap az az maze zoo zip razz zed zax zoa zone

6 Liz Zahl saw Zoe feed the zebra in an Arizona zoo.

7 yj yj jy jy joy lay yaw say yes any yet my try you

8 Why do you say that today, Thursday, is my payday?

9 xs xs sax ox box fix hex ax lax fox taxi lox sixes

10 Roxy, you may ask Jay to fix any tax sets for you.

11 qa qa aqua quail quit quake quid equal quiet quart

12 Did Enrique quietly but quickly quell the quarrel?

13 fv fv five lives vow ova van eve avid vex vim void

14 Has Vivi, Vada, or Eva visited Vista Valley Farms?

> **TECHNIQUE TIP**
>
> Work for smoothness, not speed.

11c Speed Builder
Key each balanced-hand line twice, as quickly as you can.

15 is to for do an may work so it but an with them am

16 am yam map aid zig yams ivy via vie quay cob amend

17 to do is for an may work so it but am an with them

18 for it|for it|to the|to the|do they|do they|do it

19 Pamela may go to the farm with Jan and a neighbor.

20 Rod and Ty may go by the lake if they go downtown.

| 1 | 2 | 3 | 4 | 5 | 6 | 7 | 8 | 9 | 10 |

Diagrams

The **Insert Diagram or Organization Chart** button is located on the Drawing toolbar and is used to access the Diagram Gallery. The Diagram Gallery at the right illustrates the six types of diagrams that are available. A good way to learn about each of the diagrams is to click on the diagram and read the description explaining its use.

To create a diagram:

1. Click the **Insert Diagram or Organization Chart** button on the Drawing toolbar. (*Option:* On the Insert menu, click **Diagram**.)

2. Select the desired diagram and click **OK** to display the diagram and the Diagram toolbar.

3. Click each box in the diagram to add text; format the text as desired. If text does not fit in the boxes, click **Layout** and then **Scale Organization Chart**. Drag the outside border of the chart to resize the boxes. Then, if necessary to fit the chart on a page, click **Layout** again and then **Fit Organization Chart to Contents**.

4. To add additional boxes, click **Insert Shape** on the Organization Chart toolbar.

5. To change the layout, click **Layout** on the Organization Chart toolbar.

(**Note:** Each diagram has its own toolbar. The toolbars are very similar and accomplish the same purposes.)

D r i l l   1 | **ORGANIZATIONAL CHART**

1. Create the organizational chart shown below.

2. If text does not fit in a box, drag the outside border of the chart to increase the size of the boxes.

3. Save the document as *57c-drill1* and print.

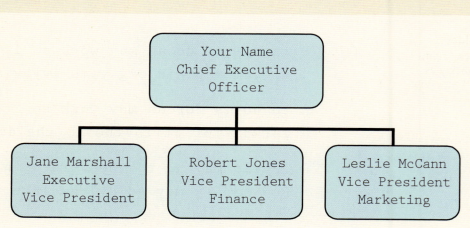

11d Textbook Keying

Key each line once; DS between groups.

enter: key smoothly without looking at fingers

21 Make the return snappily
22 and with assurance; keep
23 your eyes on your source
24 data; maintain a smooth,
25 constant pace as you key.

space bar: use down-and-in motion

26 us me it of he an by do go to us if or so am ah el
27 Have you a pen? If so, print "Free to any guest."

caps lock: press to toggle it on or off

28 Use ALL CAPS for items such as TO: FROM: SUBJECT.
29 Did Kristin mean Kansas City, MISSOURI, or KANSAS?

TECHNIQUE TIP

Tap CAPS LOCK to capitalize several letters. Tap it again to toggle CAPS LOCK off.

11e Speed Check

1. In the Open Screen, key all paragraphs, using wordwrap. Work for smooth, continuous stroking, not speed.
2. Save as *xx-11e*. Substitute your initials for *xx*.
3. Take a 2' writing on all paragraphs. (Key **2** in Variable Setting.)

Goal: 16 *gwam*

To determine gross-words-a-minute (*gwam*) rate for 2':

Follow these steps if you are *not* using the Timer in the Open Screen.

1. Note the figure at the end of the last line completed.

2. For a partial line, note the figure on the scale directly below the point at which you stopped keying.

3. Add these two figures to determine the total gross words a minute (*gwam*) you keyed.

	gwam	2'
Have we thought of communication as a kind	4	31
of war that we wage through each day?	8	35
When we think of it that way, good language	12	39
would seem to become our major line of attack.	17	44
Words become muscle; in a normal exchange or	22	49
in a quarrel, we do well to realize the power of words.	27	54

11f Enrichment

1. Go to Skill Builders 1, Drill 1, page 31. Choose six letters that cause you difficulty. Key each line twice. Put a check mark beside the lines in the book so that you know you have practiced them.

2. Save the drill as *xx-11f*. Substitute your initials for *xx*.

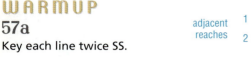

Charts and Diagrams

WARMUP
57a
Key each line twice SS.

adjacent reaches
1 art try pew sort tree position copy opera maker waste three draft
2 sat coil riot were renew forth trade power grope owner score weed

one hand
3 ad null bar poll car upon deed jump ever look feed hill noon moon
4 get hilly are employ save phony taste union versa yummy wedge fad

balanced hand
5 aid go bid dish elan glen fury idle half jamb lend make name slam
6 oak pay hen quay rush such urus vial works yamen amble blame pale

| 1 | 2 | 3 | 4 | 5 | 6 | 7 | 8 | 9 | 10 | 11 | 12 | 13 |

57b Timed Writings
1. Key three 1' writings.
2. Key two 2' writings. Try to maintain your best 1' rate.

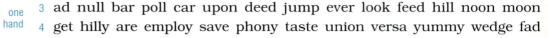

A all letters

	gwam	1'	2'
Good plans typically are required to execute most tasks	11	6	50
successfully. If a task is worth doing, it is worth investing	24	12	56
the time that is necessary to plan it effectively. Many people	37	18	62
are anxious to get started on a task and just begin before they	49	25	69
have thought about the best way to organize it. In the long run,	63	31	75
they frequently end up wasting time that could be spent more	75	37	81
profitably on important projects that they might prefer to tackle.	88	44	88

1' | 1 | 2 | 3 | 4 | 5 | 6 | 7 | 8 | 9 | 10 | 11 | 12 | 13 |
2' | 1 | 2 | 3 | 4 | 5 | 6 |

NEW FUNCTIONS
57c

Create and Modify Diagrams and Charts

Diagrams and charts provide a meaningful way of illustrating data to make it easier for the reader to understand. Diagrams can be created using Drawing tools. Charts can be created using *Microsoft Graph* or other applications such as *Excel* spreadsheets. In this lesson, you will create diagrams with Drawing tools and charts using *Microsoft Graph*.

help keywords

chart, diagram, graph

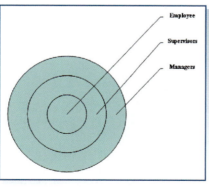

Diagram example

Graph example

Review

WARMUP

12a
Key each line twice SS (slowly, then faster).

alphabet 1 Jack won five quiz games; Brad will play him next.

q 2 Quin Racq quickly and quietly quelled the quarrel.

z 3 Zaret zipped along sizzling, zigzag Arizona roads.

easy 4 Did he hang the sign by the big bush at the lake?

| 1 | 2 | 3 | 4 | 5 | 6 | 7 | 8 | 9 | 10 |

SKILLBUILDING

12b New Key Review
Key each line once; DS between groups; work for smoothness, not speed.

b/f 5 bf bf fab fab ball bib rf rf rib rib fibs bums bee

6 Did Buffy remember that he is a brass band member?

z/y 7 za za zag zig zip yj yj jay eye day lazy hazy zest

8 Liz amazed us with the zesty pizza on a lazy trip.

q/u 9 qa qa quo qt. quit quay quad quarm que uj jug quay

10 Where is Quito? Qatar? Boqueirao? Quebec? Quilmes?

v/m 11 vf vf valve five value mj mj ham mad mull mass vim

12 Vito, enter the words vim, vivace, and avar; save.

all 13 I faced defeat; only reserves saved my best crews.

14 In my opinion, I need to rest in my reserved seat.

all 15 Holly created a red poppy and deserves art awards.

16 My pump averages a faster rate; we get better oil.

12c Textbook Keying
Key each line once; DS between groups. Work for smooth, unhurried keying.

de/ed 17 ed fed led deed dell dead deal sled desk need seed

18 Dell dealt with the deed before the dire deadline.

ol/lo 19 old tolls doll solo look sole lost love cold stole

20 Old Ole looked for the long lost olive oil lotion.

op/po 21 pop top post rope pout port stop opal opera report

22 Stop to read the top opera opinion report to Opal.

we/ew 23 we few wet were went wears weather skews stew blew

24 Working women wear sweaters when weather dictates.

☑ Information technology is creating more customer potential and new demands for the delivery of coursework as well as generating new opportunities for competitors to enter this educational market.

☑ The pace of change is forcing people at all levels of the economy to learn new skills at the same time people are being asked to work harder—and sometimes hold more than one job.

☑ The new school improvement plan has not taken shape as quickly as anticipated, but a move toward mastering skills and testing for proficiencies—not rote knowledge—is gaining momentum.

[56e-d2]
Announcement

TIP

To position the clip art on the same line as the text, right-click the clip art and select **Format Picture**. On the Layout tab, click **Square** wrapping style and left alignment.

1. In a new document, change the page orientation to landscape. Key the heading **Tour of Facilities** as a WordArt of your choice. Click **Format WordArt**; choose an appropriate color and select an attractive pattern.

2. Add two appropriate clip art objects for each paragraph. Under the clip art for soccer, insert a text box and key **State Champions 2004**.

3. Add an AutoShape of your choice. Key the text shown below. Format attractively.

4. Format the document so that it will make a nice announcement that can be posted for guests to read.

5. Save the document as *56e-d2* and print a copy.

Tour of Facilities

Soccer Coaches Eddie Nelson and Susan Hudson invite you to join them for a tour of the new stadium. Tours begin at 2:30, 3:30, and 5:00 p.m. Please join all the soccer coaching staff and players for refreshments in the Captains' Room before or after your tour.

Volleyball Coach Louise Reaves invites you to join her for a tour of the new Practice Facility. Tours begin at 2:00, 3:30, and 4:00 p.m. Please join all the volleyball coaching staff and players for refreshments in the Trophy Room before or after your tour.

Soccer and Volleyball Exhibition Games begin at 6:00 p.m.
Pick up your free tickets at either of the tours.

12d Speed Builder

1. Key each line quickly to build stroking speed.
2. Save as *xx-L12*. (Substitute your initials for *xx*.)

25 a for we you is that be this will be a to and well
26 as our with I or a to by your form which all would
27 new year no order they so new but now year who may

28 This is Lyn's only date to visit their great city.
29 I can send it to your office at any time you wish.
30 She kept the fox, owls, and fowl down by the lake.

31 Harriette will cook dinner for the swimming teams.
32 Annette will call at noon to give us her comments.
33 Johnny was good at running and passing a football.

| 1 | 2 | 3 | 4 | 5 | 6 | 7 | 8 | 9 | 10 |

12e Speed Check

1. In the Open Screen, key both paragraphs, using wordwrap. Work for smooth, continuous stroking, not speed.
2. Save as *xx-12e*. Substitute your initials for *xx*.
3. Take a 1' writing on paragraph 1. Save as *xx-12e-t1*.
4. Repeat step 3 using paragraph 2. Save as *xx-12e-t2*.
5. Set the Timer for 2'. Take a 2' writing on both paragraphs. Save as *xx-12e-t3*.

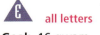 **all letters**

Goal: 16 *gwam*

Copy Difficulty

What factors determine whether copy is difficult or easy? Research shows that difficulty is influenced by syllables per word, characters per word, and percent of familiar words. Carefully controlling these three factors ensures that speed and accuracy scores are reliable—that is, increased scores reflect increased skill.

In Level 1, all timings are easy. Note "E" inside the triangle at left of the timing. Easy timings contain an average of 1.2 syllables per word, 5.1 characters per word, and 90 percent familiar words. Easy copy is suitable for the beginner who is mastering the keyboard.

	gwam	2'
There should be no questions, no doubt, about	5	35
the value of being able to key; it's just a matter	10	40
of common sense that today a pencil is much too slow.	15	45
Let me explain. Work is done on a keyboard	19	49
three to six times faster than other writing and	24	54
with a product that is a prize to read. Don't you	29	59
agree?	30	60

2' | 1 | 2 | 3 | 4 | 5 |

D r i l l 4 | WORDART

1. Open a new document and display the Drawing toolbar. Click the **Insert WordArt** button .

2. Select the first style from the second row of the WordArt Gallery.

3. Key the text **Happy Birthday to you!**

4. Select the text and click the **Format WordArt** button on the WordArt Toolbar. Choose **Pale Blue** color and then choose **Fill Effects**.

5. Click the **Pattern** tab. Apply the fifth patterned effect in the first column of patterns to the foreground.

6. From the Drawing toolbar, apply the first 3-D style.

7. Save the document as *56d-drill4*.

1. In a new document, format the main heading, **Trend Analysis Report**, using the fourth design in the first row of the WordArt Gallery; adjust the size to extend over the line of writing.

2. Create a subheading below the WordArt by keying **Market Trends** using 20-point font and adding black shading to the paragraph.

3. Insert the symbol ☑ from the Wingdings font to each of the items in the body of the report. Use hanging indent to format the paragraphs with 6-point spacing after each paragraph, and key the five paragraphs.

4. Search for clip art using the keyword *academic* and add an appropriate piece of clip art centered below the five paragraphs.

5. Add a horizontal line at the bottom of the page. Above the line, key in 18-point script font **Understanding our community to prepare for the future!**

6. Save the document as *56e-d1* and print a copy.

Trend Analysis Report

Market Analysis

☑ The population in the metropolitan area is growing both in the college's service area and in the demographic segments that represent the greatest market enrollment.

☑ The metropolitan area continues to add employment opportunities at a growth rate of 22 percent, but the area economy suffers from some of the same insecurities about the future as do other areas.

Review

WARMUP

13a
Key each line twice SS (slowly, then faster).

alphabet	1	Bev quickly hid two Japanese frogs in Mitzi's box.
shift	2	Jay Nadler, a Rotary Club member, wrote Mr. Coles.
, (comma)	3	Jay, Ed, and I paid for plates, knives, and forks.
easy	4	Did the amendment name a city auditor to the firm?

| 1 | 2 | 3 | 4 | 5 | 6 | 7 | 8 | 9 | 10 |

SKILLBUILDING

13b Rhythm Builder
Key each line once SS.

word-level response: key short, familiar words as units

5 is to for do an may work so it but an with them am
6 Did they mend the torn right half of their ensign?
7 Hand me the ivory tusk on the mantle by the bugle.

letter-level response: key more difficult words letter by letter

8 only state jolly zest oil verve join rate mop card
9 After defeat, look up; gaze in joy at a few stars.
10 We gazed at a plump beaver as it waded in my pool.

combination response: use variable speed; your fingers will let you feel the difference

11 it up so at for you may was but him work were they
12 It is up to you to get the best rate; do it right.
13 This is Lyn's only date to visit their great city.

| 1 | 2 | 3 | 4 | 5 | 6 | 7 | 8 | 9 | 10 |

13c Keyboard Reinforcement
Key each line once; fingers well curved, wrists low; avoid punching keys with third and fourth fingers.

p	14	Pat appears happy to pay for any supper I prepare.
x	15	Knox can relax; Alex gets a box of flax next week.
v	16	Vi, Ava, and Viv move ivy vines, leaves, or stems.
'	17	It's a question of whether they can't or won't go.
?	18	Did Jan go? Did she see Ray? Who paid? Did she?
.	19	Ms. E. K. Nu and Lt. B. A. Walz had the a.m. duty.
"	20	"Who are you?" he asked. "I am," I said, "Marie."
;	21	Find a car; try it; like it; work a price; buy it.

1. Open *56d-drill2*.

2. Group the five objects so that they can be moved as one object and save the file as *56d-drill3a*.

3. Select the group, click **Copy**, open a new document, and paste the group into the new document.

4. Save the new document as *56d-drill3b* and print.

> **TIP**
>
> WordArt can also be accessed from the Insert menu (**Insert**, **Picture**, **WordArt**) or from the WordArt toolbar.

WordArt

WordArt provides an interesting way to add banners to documents that are formatted in columns, to format casual letterheads, or to add large print to documents such as announcements. Since WordArt is part of the Drawing program, it can be formatted using other drawing features such as colored or textured fills and 3-D effects.

The WordArt Gallery provides a number of shapes and styles for WordArt. The first example shown below was created using the first design in the WordArt Gallery. The second example was created by adding a textured fill color and a 3-D effect to the first banner.

To use WordArt:

1. Display the Drawing toolbar, and click the **Insert WordArt** button. The WordArt Gallery displays.

2. Select the desired style and click **OK** to display the Edit WordArt Text dialog box as shown at the right.

3. Key the text; change the font size or style in this textbox if desired. Click **OK**. Your text is now displayed as WordArt.

4. Select the text to display the WordArt toolbar. Format the WordArt text using the buttons on the WordArt toolbar. You may also use the buttons on the Drawing toolbar.

13d Textbook Keying

Troublesome Pairs:
Key each line once; DS between groups.

t   22 at fat hat sat to tip the that they fast last slat
r   23 or red try ran run air era fair rid ride trip trap
t/r 24 A trainer sprained an arm trying to tame the bear.

m   25 am me my mine jam man more most dome month minimum
n   26 no an now nine once net knee name ninth know never
m/n 27 Many men and women are important company managers.

o   28 on or to not now one oil toil over only solo today
i   29 it is in tie did fix his sit like with insist will
o/i 30 Joni will consider obtaining options to buy coins.

a   31 at an as art has and any case data haze tart smart
s   32 us as so say sat slap lass class just sassy simple
a/s 33 Disaster was averted as the steamer sailed to sea.

e   34 we he ear the key her hear chef desire where there
i   35 it is in tie did fix his sit like with insist will
e/i 36 An expression of gratitude for service is desired.

13e Speed Check

1. In the Open Screen, key the paragraphs once SS.
2. Save as *xx-13e*.
3. Take a 1' writing on paragraph 1. Save as *xx-13e-t1*.
4. Take a 1' writing on paragraph 2. Save as *xx-13e-t2*.
5. Print the better 1' writing.
6. Take a 2' writing on both paragraphs. Start over if time permits.

all letters

Goal: 16 *gwam*

gwam 2'

```
          •              4              •              8
    The questions of time use are vital ones; we      5
  •        12        •         16
miss so much just because we don't plan.              9
          •              4              •              8
    When we organize our days, we save time for      13
  •        12        •         16
those extra premium things we long to do.            17
2' |     1     |     2     |     3     |     4     |     5     |
```

Group Objects

Often multiple drawing objects are used together. The objects can be grouped so that all of them can be moved as one object. They also can be ungrouped so that you can change the formatting of individual objects.

To group objects:

1. Select the first object; then press ctrl and select each of the other objects to be grouped.
2. Click the down arrow on the Draw button `Draw ▾`. Click **Group**.
3. To ungroup objects, select the objects, click the down arrow on the Draw button, and click **Ungroup**.

Drill 2 | INSERT OBJECTS

1. Create the following objects as follows:

Text box

a. Click the **Text Box** button, and insert a text box as shown below. Key the text **Examples of AutoShapes** in 14 point, bold; center-align.

b. Use the **Fill Color** button to add yellow fill to the text box.

c. Click the **Line Style** button and select a 2¼-pt. line.

d. Click the **Shadow Style** button and select the second shadow on the second row (Shadow Style 6).

Rectangle

a. Click the **Rectangle** button, and draw a rectangle approximately 1.5" wide. Use the Horizontal Ruler as a guide.

b. Right-click the rectangle, and key the text **Happy Holidays**. Change the font to Lucida Handwriting (or an alternate font), 16 point, bold. Change the font color to gold and center-align the text in the rectangle.

c. Use the **Fill Color** button to add red fill to the rectangle and the text box.

d. Click the **3-D Style** button and select the third shape in the third row (3-D Style 11).

Smiley Face

a. Click the **AutoShapes** button down arrow. Select **Basic Shapes** and add a smiley face below the rectangle.

b. Change the line color to blue and the fill to yellow.

Oval

a. Draw an oval on the right side of the rectangle; use tan fill and a brown line; add your name to the oval.

b. Change the font color to brown. Center your name in the oval.

Arrow

a. Add the arrow as shown below the oval.

b. Adjust the size so that it is as wide as the oval, and add dark red fill.

2. Save as *56d-drill2*.

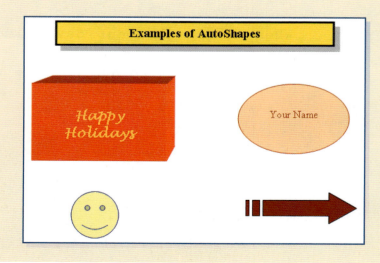

Use the Open Screen for Skill Builders. Save each drill as a separate file.

Drill 1

Goal: to reinforce key locations

Key each line at a comfortable, constant rate; check lines that need more practice; repeat those lines.

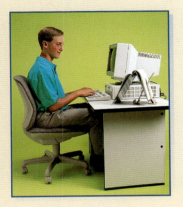

Keep

- your eyes on source copy
- your fingers curved, upright
- your wrists low but not touching
- your elbows hanging loosely
- your feet flat on the floor

A We saw that Alan had an alabaster vase in Alabama.
B My rubber boat bobbed about in the bubbling brook.
C Ceci gave cups of cold cocoa to Rebecca and Rocco.
D Don's dad added a second deck to his old building.
E Even as Ellen edited her document, she ate dinner.
F Our firm in Buffalo has a staff of forty or fifty.
G Ginger is giving Greg the eggs she got from Helga.
H Hugh has eighty high, harsh lights he might flash.
I Irik's lack of initiative is irritating his coach.
J Judge J. J. Jore rejected Jeane and Jack's jargon.
K As a lark, Kirk kicked back a rock at Kim's kayak.
L Lucille is silly; she still likes lemon lollipops.
M Milt Mumm hammered a homer in the Miami home game.
N Ken Linn has gone hunting; Stan can begin canning.
O Jon Soto rode off to Otsego in an old Morgan auto.
P Philip helped pay the prize as my puppy hopped up.
Q Quiet Raquel quit quoting at an exquisite marquee.
R As Mrs. Kerr's motor roared, her red horse reared.
S Sissie lives in Mississippi; Lissa lives in Tulsa.
T Nat told Betty not to tattle on her little sister.
U Ula has a unique but prudish idea on unused units.
V Eva visited every vivid event for twelve evenings.
W We watched as wayworn wasps swarmed by the willow.
X Tex Cox waxed the next box for Xenia and Rex Knox.
Y Ty says you may stay with Fay for only sixty days.
Z Hazel is puzzled about the azure haze; Zack dozes.
alphabet Jacky and Max quickly fought over a sizable prawn.
alphabet Just by maximizing liquids, Chick Prew avoids flu.

| 1 | 2 | 3 | 4 | 5 | 6 | 7 | 8 | 9 | 10 |

1. Search for roses in the clip art gallery, and insert the clip art into a new document.

2. Increase the size of the clip art to approximately double its size. Use the Horizontal and Vertical Rulers to guide you.

3. Move it to the center of the page near the top margin.

4. Create the folder *Module 8 Keys*, and save the document as *56d-drill1* in this folder. Save all exercises for Module 8 in this folder.

---

help keywords

draw

● Drawing Tools

A variety of drawing tools are available in *Word*. These tools can be accessed from the Drawing toolbar (**View, Toolbars, Drawing**). An easy way to become familiar with all of the tools is to display the Drawing toolbar and hold the mouse pointer over each object on the toolbar to display its function. Click the down arrow on each object that has one to display the available options for the tool. A canvas will display when you click a drawing tool to help with the formatting of the object.

To insert an AutoShape:

1. With the Drawing toolbar displayed, click on the desired object such as **Rectangle** or **AutoShapes**. If you choose AutoShapes, a list of various shapes displays. If a triangular arrow appears beside an object, click on it to display the available options.

2. When you choose the desired object, a "canvas" displays with the message "Create your drawing here." The mouse pointer turns into a crosshairs. Drag the mouse to create the object on the canvas.

3. Select the object and format it using the effects such as fill, lines, and 3-D that are available on the Drawing toolbar.

4. To add text to an object such as a rectangle or an oval, right-click the object and select **Add Text** from the drop-down menu. Then key your text.

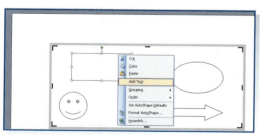

To insert a text box:

1. With the Drawing toolbar displayed, click the **Text Box** button.

2. Click or drag the text box in your document to the desired location.

3. Key the text inside the box.

Drill 2

Goal: to strengthen up and down reaches

Keep hands and wrists quiet; fingers well curved in home position; stretch fingers up from home or pull them palmward as needed.

home position
1 Hall left for Dallas; he is glad Jake fed his dog.
2 Ada had a glass flask; Jake had a sad jello salad.
3 Lana Hask had a sale; Gala shall add half a glass.

down reaches
4 Did my banker, Mr. Mavann, analyze my tax account?
5 Do they, Mr. Zack, expect a number of brave women?
6 Zach, check the menu; next, beckon the lazy valet.

up reaches
7 Prue truly lost the quote we wrote for our report.
8 Teresa quietly put her whole heart into her words.
9 There were two hilarious jokes in your quiet talk.

Drill 3

Goal: to strengthen individual finger reaches

Rekey troublesome lines.

first finger
1 Bob Mugho hunted for five minutes for your number.
2 Juan hit the bright green turf with his five iron.
3 The frigates and gunboats fought mightily in Java.

second finger
4 Dick said the ice on the creek had surely cracked.
5 Even as we picnicked, I decided we needed to diet.
6 Kim, not Mickey, had rice with chicken for dinner.

third/fourth finger
7 Pam saw Roz wax an aqua auto as Lex sipped a cola.
8 Wally will quickly spell Zeus, Apollo, and Xerxes.
9 Who saw Polly? Zoe Pax saw her; she is quiet now.

Drill 4

Goal: to strengthen special reaches

Emphasize smooth stroking. Avoid pauses, but do not reach for speed.

adjacent reaches
1 Falk knew well that her opinions of art were good.
2 Theresa answered her question; order was restored.
3 We join there and walk north to the western point.

direct reaches
4 Barb Nunn must hunt for my checks; she is in debt.
5 In June and December, Irvin hunts in Bryce Canyon.
6 We decided to carve a number of funny human faces.

double letters
7 Anne stopped off at school to see Bill Wiggs cook.
8 Edd has planned a small cookout for all the troop.
9 Keep adding to my assets all fees that will apply.

| 1 | 2 | 3 | 4 | 5 | 6 | 7 | 8 | 9 | 10 |

To insert clip art:

1. Click **Insert** on the menu bar, click **Picture**, and then click **Clip Art**.

2. In the Task Pane Search text box, key the type of clip art to search for, such as rabbit, baseball, or roses, then click **Go**.

3. When the results are displayed, use the scroll bar to view the thumbnail sketches. When you find the desired clip art, point to the image to display a down arrow at the right of the image, click the down arrow, and then click **Insert**. (*Option:* Click the clip art image.)

4. To display a collection of clip art from various places, choose **Organize clips** on the task pane.

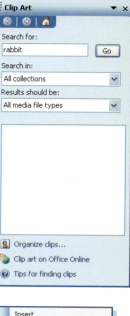

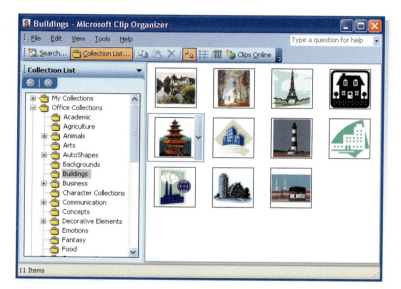

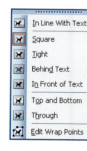

To size clip art:

1. Select the clip art.

2. Position the insertion point over one of the handles. When the pointer turns to a double-headed arrow, drag the lower-right handle down and to the right to increase the size; drag it up and to the left to make it smaller. Drag a corner handle to maintain the same proportion.

To move clip art:

1. Select the clip art.

2. Click the **Text Wrapping** button on the Picture toolbar. Then choose **Tight** (or one of the text-wrapping options) from the drop-down list. The sizing handles change to white.

3. Position the arrow pointer on the clip art until a four-headed arrow displays. Click and drag the clip art to the desired location.

Drill 5

Goal: to improve troublesome pairs

Use a controlled rate without pauses.

```
       1  ad add did does dish down body dear dread dabs bad
  d/k  2  kid ok kiss tuck wick risk rocks kayaks corks buck
       3  Dirk asked Dick to kid Drake about the baked duck.

       4  deed deal den led heed made needs delay he she her
  e/i  5  kit kiss kiln kiwi kick kilt kind six ribs kill it
       6  Abie had neither ice cream nor fried rice in Erie.

       7  fib fob fab rib beg bug rob bad bar bed born table
  b/v  8  vat vet gave five ever envy never visit weave ever
       9  Did Harv key jibe or jive, TV or TB, robe or rove?

      10  aft after lift gift sit tot the them tax tutu tyro
  t/r 11  for far ere era risk rich rock rosy work were roof
      12  In Toronto, Ruth told the truth about her artwork.

      13  jug just jury judge juice unit hunt bonus quiz bug
  u/y 14  jay joy lay you your only envy quay oily whey body
      15  Willy usually does not buy your Yukon art in July.
```

Drill 6

Goal: to build speed

Set the Timer for 1'.
Key each sentence for 1'.
Try to complete each sentence twice (20 *gwam* or more).
Ignore errors for now.

```
  1  Dian may make cocoa for the girls when they visit.
  2  Focus the lens for the right angle; fix the prism.
  3  She may suspend work when she signs the torn form.
  4  Augment their auto fuel in the keg by the autobus.
  5  As usual, their robot did half turns to the right.
  6  Pamela laughs as she signals to the big hairy dog.
  7  Pay Vivian to fix the island for the eighty ducks.
     |  1  |  2  |  3  |  4  |  5  |  6  |  7  |  8  |  9  |  10  |
```

Drill 7

Goal: to build speed

From the columns at the right, choose a *gwam* goal that is two to three words higher than your best rate. Set the Timer for **Variable** and then either **20"** or **30"**. Try to reach your goal.

		words	30"	20"
1	Did she make this turkey dish?		12	18
2	Blake and Laurie may go to Dubuque.		14	21
3	Signal for the oak sleigh to turn right.		16	24
4	I blame Susie; did she quench the only flame?		18	27
5	She turns the panel dials to make this robot work.		20	30

```
     |  1  |  2  |  3  |  4  |  5  |  6  |  7  |  8  |  9  |  10  |
```

gwam 3' | 5'

You may be familiar with the expression that we live in an information age now. People interpret this expression in a host of diverse ways, but most people agree on two key things. The first thing is that a huge amount of information exists today; some even think we suffer from information overload. The second thing is that technology has changed the way we access that huge pool of data.

	4	2
8	5
13	8
17	10
22	13
26	16

Some people are quick to point out that a big difference exists between the quantity and the quality of information. It is very critical to recognize that anyone who has access can simply post information on the Internet. No test exists to screen for junk before something is posted. Some of the data may be helpful and valid. However, much of it must be analyzed quite carefully to judge if it is valid.

30	18
35	21
39	23
43	26
48	29
52	31
53	32

Just how do you judge if the data you have accessed is valid? Some of the same techniques that can be used with print media can be applied with electronic media. A good way to assess material is to examine its source carefully. What do you know about the people who provided this information? Is the provider ethical and qualified to post that information? If you cannot unearth the answer to this question, you should be wary of trusting it.

58	35
62	37
67	40
71	42
75	45
80	48
83	50

3' | 1 | 2 | 3 | 4 |
5' | 1 | 2 | 3 |

new FUNCTIONS 56d

Clip art, pictures, AutoShapes, WordArt, charts, and other images are graphic elements that enhance documents such as announcements, invitations, reports, and newsletters. In this lesson, you will work with clip art, drawing tools, and WordArt.

Clip Art

help keywords

clip art

Microsoft Word (and other applications such as *Excel*, *PowerPoint*, and *Publisher*) provides a collection of pictures, clip art, and sounds that can be added to documents. Additional clips are available online. You can also add your own clips to the collection. The clips are organized into different collections to simplify finding appropriate clip art. The Clip Organizer adds keywords to enable you to search for various types of clip art. You also have the option of selecting the collection and viewing thumbnail sketches (small pictures) of the various clip art available in each category. Once clip art has been inserted into a document, you can size it, copy and paste it, wrap text around it, or drag it to other locations.

D r i l l 8

These writings are available as Diagnostic Writings.

1. Go to the Numeric & Skill Lesson menu and click the **Diagnostic Writing** button in the lower-right corner.
2. Choose the writing and select the length of the timing (1', 3', or 5'). Each timed writing has a one-space or two-space option. The space option refers to the number of times you tap the Space Bar following a period at the end of a sentence.
3. Key the writing. If you finish before time is up, begin again.
4. Review your results.
5. (Optional) Choose **Practice Error Words** from the Edit menu to practice errors in the writing.
6. Click the **Timer** icon at the bottom of the screen to begin your second attempt. Results will be entered in your Summary Report.
7. Print or save the completed Diagnostic Writing (sample filename: *xx-Writing 1-t1*).
8. To return to the program, choose **Exit Diagnostic Writings** from the File menu.

Goal: to build staying power
1. Key each paragraph as a 1' timing.
2. Key a 2' timing on both paragraphs.

Note: The dot above text represents two words.

 all letters

Writing 1: **18 gwam**

gwam 2'

Why spend weeks with some problem when just a few quiet   6

minutes can help us to resolve it.   9

If we don't take time to think through a problem, it will   15

swiftly begin to expand in size.   18

Writing 2: **20 gwam**

We push very hard in our quest for growth, and we all   5

think that only excellent growth will pay off.   10

Believe it or not, one can actually work much too hard,   16

be much too zealous, and just miss the mark.   20

Writing 3: **22 gwam**

A business friend once explained to me why he was often   6

quite eager to be given some new project to work with.   11

My friend said that each new project means he has to   16

organize and use the best of his knowledge and his skill.   22

Writing 4: **24 gwam**

Don't let new words get away from you. Learn how to spell   6

and pronounce new words and when and how finally to use them.   12

A new word is a friend, but frequently more. New words   18

must be used lavishly to extend the size of your own word power.   24

2' | 1 | 2 | 3 | 4 | 5 | 6 |

MODULE 8

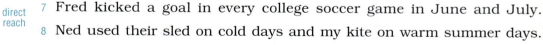

Newsletters and Graphics

OBJECTIVES

- Enhance document format with graphics and WordArt.
- Create diagrams and charts.
- Create multicolumn newsletters.

LESSON 56

Clip Art, Drawing Tools, and WordArt

WARMUP
56a
Key each line twice SS.

alphabet	1	Dixie Vaughn acquired that prize job with a firm just like yours.
figures	2	By May 15 do this: Call Ext. 4390; order 472 clips and 168 pens.
easy/figures	3	The 29 girls kept 38 bushels of corn and 59 bushels of rich yams.
easy	4	The members paid half of the endowment, and their firm paid half.

| 1 | 2 | 3 | 4 | 5 | 6 | 7 | 8 | 9 | 10 | 11 | 12 | 13 |

56b Technique Builder
Key each set of lines three times. Work at a controlled rate.

adjacent reaches	5	Is assessing potential important in a traditional career program?
	6	I saw her at an airport at a tropical resort leaving on a cruise.
direct reach	7	Fred kicked a goal in every college soccer game in June and July.
	8	Ned used their sled on cold days and my kite on warm summer days.
double letters	9	Bobby Lott feels that the meeting at noon will be cancelled soon.
	10	Pattie and Tripp meet at the swimming pool after football drills.
one hand	11	A few treats were served as reserve seats were set up on a stage.
	12	In my opinion, a few trees on a hilly acre created a vast estate.
balanced hand	13	Pam and Jake did go to visit the big island and may fish for cod.
	14	Ken may visit the men he met at the ancient chapel on the island.

Writing 5: **26 *gwam***

We usually get best results when we know where we are   5

going. Just setting a few goals will help us quietly see what   12

we are doing.   13

Goals can help measure whether we are moving at a good   19

rate or dozing along. You can expect a goal to help you find   25

good results.   26

Writing 6: **28 *gwam***

To win whatever prizes we want from life, we must plan to   6

move carefully from this goal to the next to get the maximum   12

result from our work.   14

If we really want to become skilled in keying, we must   19

come to see that this desire will require of us just a little   26

patience and hard work.   28

Writing 7: **30 *gwam***

Am I an individual person? I'm sure I am; still, in a   5

much, much bigger sense, other people have a major voice in   12

thoughts I think and actions I take.   15

Although we are each a unique person, we all work and   21

play in organized groups of people who do not expect us to   26

dismiss their rules of law and order.   30

2' | 1 | 2 | 3 | 4 | 5 | 6 |

Objective Assessment
Answer the questions below to see if you have mastered the content of Module 7.

1. The _____ feature removes text or an image from a document and places it on the Clipboard.

2. To locate and replace existing text with new text in a document, click _____ on the Edit menu.

3. The _____ is a tool that allows you to look up words and replace them with a synonym.

4. To find the word *car* and replace it with *automobile* each time it occurs in a document, click the _____ button in the Find and Replace dialog box.

5. A master copy or a formatting guide for a particular type of document is called a(n) _____.

6. A(n) _____ uses templates and responses to questions to create different types of documents.

7. The two basic types of styles are character and _____ styles.

8. The character effect _____ positions small text above the line of writing.

9. The _____ command is used to copy an object into a document and maintain the ability to format that object.

10. The _____ feature allows you to apply a group of formats automatically to a document.

Performance Assessment

Document 1
Report with Styles

1. Open *sampling plan* from the data files. Make the edits listed below.
2. Save the document as *checkpoint7-d1*.
   - Apply **Title** style to the report title.
   - Apply **Heading 1** style to the next two headings.
   - Apply **Heading 2** style to the last two headings.
   - Search for both *athlete* and *athletes* and replace with, respectively, *student athlete* and *student athletes*.
   - Modify the footer to include your name rather than Student's Name.
   - Apply a paragraph border around the title. Use a 3-point, triple-line box border. Add dark red shading. Place a blank line before and after the title.

Document 2
Memo from Wizard

1. Use the Memo Wizard to prepare a Contemporary style memo. Save the document as *checkpoint7-d2*.
2. Send the message TO: **Student Athletes** FROM: **Jan Marks, Faculty Athletics Representative** DATE: **Current** SUBJECT: **Exit Interview**

In accordance with NCAA bylaws, the enclosed survey is sent to you as a student athlete who has completed your eligibility to compete in college athletics. This survey gives you an opportunity to share your opinions about your experience both as a student and as an athlete.

Please complete the survey and return it to me in the enclosed self-addressed envelope within two weeks. We urge you to be honest with your responses. The information is used to improve the athletics experience for future students. Your coach does not have access to this information, and your responses will be treated confidentially.

We appreciate your sharing your thoughts with us.

MODULE 2

Figure and Symbol Keys

LESSON 14 — 1 and 8

WARMUP

14a
Key each line twice SS.
Line 2: Space once after a series of brief questions within a sentence.

alphabet	1	Jessie Quick believed the campaign frenzy would be exciting.
space bar	2	Was it Mary? Helen? Pam? It was a woman; I saw one of them.
3rd row	3	We were quietly prepped to write two letters to Portia York.
easy	4	Kale's neighbor works with a tutor when they visit downtown.

| 1 | 2 | 3 | 4 | 5 | 6 | 7 | 8 | 9 | 10 | 11 | 12 |

SKILLBUILDING

14b Textbook Keying
The words at the right are from the 100 most used words.

Key each line once; work for fluency.

Top 100

5 a an it been copy for his this more no office please service

6 our service than the they up was work all any many thank had

7 business from I know made more not me new of some to program

8 such these two with your about and have like department year

9 by at on but do had in letter most now one please you should

10 their order like also appreciate that there gentlemen letter

11 be can each had information letter may make now only so that

12 them time use which am other been send to enclosed have will

[55c-d3]
Memo

1. Use the **Professional** memo template to key the memo shown below.
2. Key **Community Park Site Committee** in the *Company Name Here* placeholder.
3. Drag the *Company Name Here* placeholder so that *Community Park Site Committee* is on one line.
4. Send the memo to the **Planning Commission** from the **Community Park Site Committee**. Use the current date, and send a copy of the memo to **Mayor Charles Morgan**.
5. Use the report title from document *55c-d1* as the subject of the memo. Save it as *55c-d3*.

The Community Park Site Committee has completed its assessment of the potential sites for the new park. Our report is attached.

The Committee unanimously recommends that the Westlake site be used for the new park. The Woodcreek site was considered acceptable, but it is not as desirable as the Westlake site. The Southside site was the least desirable of the three sites.

Please contact us if you have any questions.

[55c-d4]
Block Letter

1. Key the following letter in block format. Use the current date and sign your name.
2. Save it as *55c-d4*.

Ms. Margaret C. Worthington
4957 Mt. Elon Church Road
Hopkins, SC 29061-9837

Dear Ms. Worthington

The Planning Commission has authorized me to contact you to discuss the possible purchase of the 120-acre site that we discussed with you for the new Community Park. When we spoke with you yesterday, you indicated that you would be available to meet with us any afternoon next week. If it is still convenient, we would like to meet with you on Wednesday afternoon at 2:00 at the site.

Earlier you indicated that you had a recent survey and an appraisal of the property. We would appreciate it if you could have those documents available for the meeting.

If this time is not convenient, please call my office and leave a message so that I may reschedule the meeting. We look forward to working with you.

Sincerely

www.collegekeyboarding.com

NEW KEYS

14c 1 and 8

Key each line once SS.

Note: The digit "1" and the letter "l" have separate values on a computer keyboard. Do not interchange these characters.

1 Reach *up* with *left fourth* finger.

8 Reach *up* with *right second* finger.

Abbreviations: Do not space after a period within an abbreviation, as in Ph.D., U.S., C.O.D., a.m.

1

13 1 1a a1 1 1; 1 and a 1; 1 add 1; 1 aunt; 1 ace; 1 arm; 1 aye
14 1 and 11 and 111; 11 eggs; 11 vats; Set 11A; May 11; Item 11
15 The 11 aces of the 111th Corps each rated a salute at 1 p.m.

8

16 8 8k k8 8 8; 8 kits; ask 8; 8 kites; kick 8; 8 keys; spark 8
17 OK 88; 8 bags; 8 or 88; the 88th; 88 kegs; ask 88; order 888
18 Eight of the 88 cars score 8 or better on our Form 8 rating.

all figures learned

19 She did live at 818 Park, not 181 Park; or was it 181 Clark?
20 Put 1 with 8 to form 18; put 8 with 1 to form 81. Use 1881.
21 On May 1 at 8 a.m., 18 men and 18 women left Gate 8 for Rio.

SKILLBUILDING

14d Reinforcement

Key each line once; DS between groups. Repeat. Key with accuracy.

figures

22 Our 188 trucks moved 1881 tons on August 18 and December 18.
23 Send Mary 181 No. 188 panes for her home at 8118 Oak Street.
24 The 188 men in 8 boats left Docks 1 and 18 at 1 p.m., May 1.

25 pop was lap pass slaw wool solo swap Apollo wasp load plaque
26 Was Polly acquainted with the equipped jazz player in Texas?
27 The computer is a useful tool; it helps you to perform well.

14e Speed Builder

Set the Timer for 1'. Key each sentence as many times as possible.

Goal: to complete each sentence twice in one minute

28 Did their form entitle them to the land?
29 Did the men in the field signal for us to go?
30 I may pay for the antique bowls when I go to town.
31 The auditor did the work right, so he risks no penalty.
32 The man by the big bush did signal us to turn down the lane.

| 1 | 2 | 3 | 4 | 5 | 6 | 7 | 8 | 9 | 10 | 11 | 12 |

[55c-dl]

Report with Styles

1. Open *site assessment* from the data files, and make the following edits:
   * SS and use 6-point spacing after paragraphs.
   ✱ • Apply **Title** style to the title of the report.
   * Apply **Heading 1** style to all side headings.
   * Use **Paste Special** to add the chart from the data file *Site Costs* at the end of the report.
   * Use **Find and Replace** to find *Theme* and replace it with *Community* each time it occurs.
   * Add a red triple-line box border with sky blue shading to the title of the report. Add a blank line before and after the title.
   * Check the footer to ensure that *Theme* was replaced by *Community*. Change the date format to month/day/year in the footer.

2. Save it as *55c-d1*. Proofread and print.

[55c-d2]

Numbered Outline

1. Key the following numbered outline.
✱ 2. Position the title at approximately 2.1" from the top of the page and apply **Title** style.
3. Use the second outline numbered format (1, 1.1, 1.1.1). Save as *55c-d2a*.
4. Clear the style and apply the first outline numbered format. Save as *55c-d2b*.

✱ **DISCOVER**

Title Style
If Title Style is not available in the Styles box, click **Show All Styles** at the bottom of the Styles and Formatting Task page. Scroll down and select **Title Style**.

	Available formatting
	Formatting in use
	Available styles
	All styles
	Custom...
Show:	All styles

Criteria for Evaluating Sites

1. Site Location
   1.1. The site must be located within ten miles of city center.
   1.2. The site must be easily accessed with good roads—preferably from an Interstate.
2. Site Size
   2.1. The site must be at least 100 acres.
   2.2. The county must not be required to buy more than 150 acres to obtain a site.
   2.3. The terrain must be such that it facilitates the building of the infrastructure needed for the park facilities.
3. Cost
   3.1. The cost of the site including the land and the estimated infrastructure costs must be less than $1,000,000.
4. Other Factors
   4.1. Aesthetic factors should be considered only if a site meets the first three criteria.
      4.1.1. A lake, pond, river, creek, or other body of water must be available.
      4.1.2. At least a portion of the land must be wooded.

5 and 0

WARMUP
15a

Key each line twice SS.

For a series of capital letters, tap CAPS LOCK with the left little finger. Press again to release.

alphabet	1	John Quigley packed the zinnias in twelve large, firm boxes.
1/8	2	Idle Motor 18 at 8 mph and Motor 81 at 8 mph; avoid Motor 1.
caps lock	3	Lily read BLITHE SPIRIT by Noel Coward. I read VANITY FAIR.
easy	4	Did they fix the problem of the torn panel and worn element?

| 1 | 2 | 3 | 4 | 5 | 6 | 7 | 8 | 9 | 10 | 11 | 12 |

15b Technique Reinforcement

Reach up or down without moving your hands. Key each line once; repeat drill.

adjacent reaches

5 as oil red ask wet opt mop try tree open shred operas treaty

6 were pore dirt stew ruin faster onion alumni dreary mnemonic

7 The opened red hydrants were powerful, fast, and very dirty.

outside reaches

8 pop zap cap zag wasp equip lazy zippers queue opinion quartz

9 zest waste paper exist parquet azalea acquaint apollo apathy

10 The lazy wasp passed the potted azalea on the parquet floor.

NEW KEYS
15c 5 and 0

Key each line once SS.

5 Reach *up* with *left first* finger.

0 Reach *up* with *right fourth* finger.

5

11 5 5f f5 5 5; 5 fans; 5 feet; 5 figs; 5 fobs; 5 furs; 5 flaws

12 5 o'clock; 5 a.m.; 5 p.m.; is 55 or less; buy 55; 5 and 5 is

13 Call Line 555 if 5 fans or 5 bins arrive at Pier 5 by 5 p.m.

0

14 0 0; ;0 0 0; skip 0; plan 0; left 0; is below 0; I scored 0;

15 0 degrees; key 0 and 0; write 00 here; the total is 0 or 00;

16 She laughed at their 0 to 0 score; but ours was 0 to 0 also.

all figures learned

17 I keyed 550 pages for Invoice 05, or 50 more than we needed.

18 Pages 15 and 18 of the program listed 150, not 180, members.

19 On May 10, Rick drove 500 miles to New Mexico in car No. 08.

Assessment

WARMUP
55a
Key each line twice SS.

alphabet	1	Max Biqua watched jet planes flying in the azure sky over a cove.
figures	2	Send 105 No. 4 nails and 67 No. 8 brads for my home at 329 Annet.
3rd row	3	We two were ready to type a report for our quiet trio of workers.
easy	4	Pamela owns a big bicycle; and, with it, she may visit the docks.

| 1 | 2 | 3 | 4 | 5 | 6 | 7 | 8 | 9 | 10 | 11 | 12 | 13 |

55b Timed Writings
Take one 3' and one 5'
timing on the paragraphs.

 all letters

gwam   3' | 5'

	3'	5'
Voting is a very important part of being a good citizen.	4	2
However, many young people who are eligible to vote choose not	8	5
to do so. When asked to explain or justify their decision, many	12	7
simply shrug their shoulders and reply that they have no particular	16	10
reason for not voting. The explanation others frequently give is	21	13
that they just did not get around to going to the voting polls.	25	15
A good question to consider concerns ways that we can motivate	29	18
young people to be good citizens and to go to the polls and to vote.	34	21
Some people approach this topic by trying to determine how satisfied	39	23
people are who do not vote with the performance of their elected	43	26
officials. Unfortunately, those who choose not to vote are just as	48	29
satisfied with their elected officials as are those who voted.	52	31
One interesting phenomenon concerning voting relates to the	56	34
job market. When the job market is strong, fewer young people vote	61	36
than when the job market is very bad. They also tend to be less	65	39
satisfied with their elected officials. Self-interest seems to	69	41
be a powerful motivator. Unfortunately, those who do not choose	74	44
to vote miss the point that it is in their best interest to be a	78	47
good citizen.	79	47

3' | 1 | 2 | 3 | 4 |
5' | 1 | 2 | 3 |

[APPLICATIONS]

[55c]
Assessment

→ Continue

✓ Check

With *CheckPro*: When you complete a document, proofread it, check the spelling, and preview for placement. When you are completely satisfied, click the **Continue** button to move to the next document. You will not be able to return to and edit a document once you continue to the next document. Click the **Check** button when you are ready to error-check the test. Review and/or print the document analysis results.

Without *CheckPro*: Key the documents in sequence. When time has been called, proofread all documents again and identify errors.

SKILLBUILDING

15d Textbook Keying
Key each line once; DS between 3-line groups.

improve figures

20 Read pages 5 and 8; duplicate page 18; omit pages 50 and 51.

21 We have Model 80 with 10 meters or Model 180 with 15 meters.

22 After May 18, French 050 meets in room 15 at 10 a.m. daily.

improve long reaches

23 Barb Abver saw a vibrant version of her brave venture on TV.

24 Call a woman or a man who will manage Minerva Manor in Nome.

25 We were quick to squirt a quantity of water at Quin and West.

15e Tab Review
1. Read the instructions to clear and set tabs.
2. Go to the Open Screen. Set a left tab at 4".
3. Practice the lines; tap TAB without watching your keyboard.

PROCEDURE [for Setting and Clearing Tabs in the Open Screen]

Tabs have been preset at .5" intervals in the Open Screen. The preset tabs are not always appropriate for the document you are keying. Sometimes you will need to remove or clear the existing tabs and set new ones. Tabs are displayed on the Ruler. If you do not see your Ruler, click the **View** menu and select **Show Ruler**.

To clear and set tabs:

1. Click the **Format** menu, and then click **Tabs**.

2. Click the **Clear All** button to remove all tabs, and then click the appropriate Alignment button.

3. Key the tab position in the Tab stop position box. Click the **Set** button, and then click **OK**.

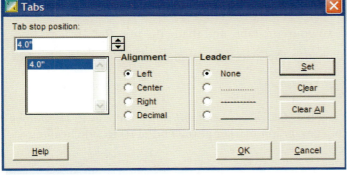

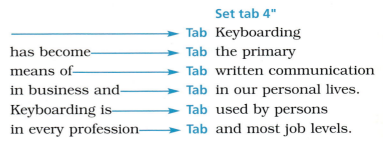

Set tab 4"

	Tab	Keyboarding
has become	Tab	the primary
means of	Tab	written communication
in business and	Tab	in our personal lives.
Keyboarding is	Tab	used by persons
in every profession	Tab	and most job levels.

15f Speed Check
1. In the Open Screen, take two 1' writings on paragraph 2. Note your *gwam*. Do not save the timings.
2. Take two 1' writings on paragraph 1. Try to equal paragraph 2 rate.
3. Take one 2' writing on both paragraphs. Key **2** in Variable Setting.

all letters

	gwam	2'	3'

I thought about Harry and how he had worked for me for — 6 | 4

10 years; how daily at 8 he parked his worn car in the lot; 12 | 8

then, he left at 5. Every day was almost identical for him. 18 | 12

In a quiet way, he did his job well, asking for little 23 | 15

attention. So I never recognized his thirst for travel. I 29 | 19

didn't expect to find all of those maps near his workplace. 35 | 23

APPLICATIONS

[54c-d1]

Report

Follow these steps using the Go To function to facilitate editing a report:

1. Be sure the *meade* data file is open, and go to page 2.
2. Remove the highlighting from *years* and key this citation: **(Snyder, 2005, 6)**.
3. Remove the highlighting from *Metro Analysis Feasibility Study*, and key this citation: **(Emerson, 2005, 8)**.
4. Go to page 3, remove the highlighting from *expenses*, and key this citation: **(Maxey, 2005, 36)**.
5. Go to the top of page 3 and key the table below. Save as *54c-d1* and print.

TABLE 1. BED CAPACITY AND UTILIZATION

Capacity	Roxy	Central	Meade
Number of beds	165	184	385
Hospital utilization average daily census	136	94	326
Medicare utilization average daily census	60	53	104
Full-time equivalent	615	364	1,682

[54c-d2]

Report with Styles

✴ **DISCOVER**

Browse Object Table
1. Click **Select Browse Object** on the scroll bar.
2. Select **Browse by Table**.

Browse by Table

1. Open *meade2* from the data files and save it as *54c-d2*.
2. ✴ Use the **Browse Object** feature to go to the table and shade the first row 10% gray.
3. Select the entire document, and change the spacing to single with 6-point spacing after paragraphs.
4. Delete the tab from the first line of all paragraphs.
5. Change all paragraph headings (such as *Bed capacity and utilization* on page 2; *Word* does not recognize a heading without a paragraph marker at the end of it) to side headings, and apply the style **Heading 3**.
6. Delete the period and spaces after the heading, position the insertion point at the beginning of the sentence, tap ENTER to bring the text back to the margin, and capitalize the main words in each heading. (*Hint:* Format Painter can be used to copy formats.)
7. Modify the footer by substituting your name for Student's Name and using the date feature to add the date in month/day/year format. Update automatically.
8. Check to ensure that all paragraphs begin at the left margin, that heading styles are used on all headings, and that there are no widows and orphans.
9. Print the document, and save again.

[54c-d3]

Title Page

1. Create a title page for the report you prepared for the Strategic Planning Committee in *54c-d2*. Be creative and use a colored border. Use the current date.
2. Save as *54c-d3* and print.

2 and 7

WARMUP
16a
Key each line twice SS.

alphabet 1 Perry might know I feel jinxed because I have missed a quiz.

figures 2 Channels 5 and 8, on from 10 to 11, said Luisa's IQ was 150.

caps lock 3 Ella Hill will see Chekhov's THE CHERRY ORCHARD on Czech TV.

easy 4 The big dog by the bush kept the ducks and hen in the field.

| 1 | 2 | 3 | 4 | 5 | 6 | 7 | 8 | 9 | 10 | 11 | 12 |

NEW KEYS
16b 2 and 7
Key each line once SS.

2 Reach *up* with *left third* finger.

7 Reach *up* with *right first* finger.

2

5 2 2s s2 2 2; has 2 sons; is 2 sizes; was 2 sites; has 2 skis

6 add 2 and 2; 2 sets of 2; catch 22; as 2 of the 22; 222 Main

7 Exactly at 2 on August 22, the 22d Company left from Pier 2.

7

8 7 7j j7 7 7; 7 jets; 7 jeans; 7 jays; 7 jobs; 7 jars; 7 jaws

9 ask for 7; buy 7; 77 years; June 7; take any 7; deny 77 boys

10 From May 7 on, all 77 men will live at 777 East 77th Street.

all figures learned

11 I read 2 of the 72 books, Ellis read 7, and Han read all 72.

12 Tract 27 cites the date as 1850; Tract 170 says it was 1852.

13 You can take Flight 850 on January 12; I'll take Flight 705.

16c Number Reinforcement
Key each line twice SS (slowly, then faster); DS between 2-line groups.

8/1 14 line 8; Book 1; No. 88; Seat 11; June 18; Cart 81; date 1881

2/7 15 take 2; July 7; buy 22; sell 77; mark 27; adds 72; Memo 2772

5/0 16 feed 5; bats 0; age 50; Ext. 55; File 50; 55 bags; band 5005

all 17 I work 18 visual signs with 20 turns of the 57 lenses to 70.

all 18 Did 17 boys fix the gears for 50 bicycles in 28 racks or 10?

Drill 5 | DOCUMENT MAP

1. Open *53b-drill2* and display the document map.

2. Click the heading **Character Style** in the document map.

3. In the last sentence under the Character Style heading, select *Character effects*.

4. From the Format menu, click **Font**, click the **Text Effects** tab, and apply **Marching Black Ants**.

5. In the same sentence, apply the character effects to the words listed, i.e., format the word *subscript* as a subscript, format the words *SMALL CAPS* in small caps, etc.

6. Save as *54b-drill5* and print.

---

help keywords

go to

Go To

The Go To function is used to move quickly to various points within a document, such as a specific page, section, line, footnote, table, graphic, or other location.

To use Go To:

1. Click the **Edit** menu and choose **Go To**. (*Shortcut:* CTRL + G) If Go To is not listed on the menu, click the double down arrows at the bottom of the menu to display more options.

2. In the Go to what box, click the type of item (such as **Page**) you wish to access.

3. Enter the appropriate number in the text box.

4. Click **Go To**; then **Close**.

Find and Replace

| Find | Replace | Go To |

Go to what:

- Page
- Section
- Line
- Bookmark
- Comment
- Footnote
- Endnote

Enter page number:

3

Enter + and – to move relative to the current location. Example: +4 will move forward four items.

Previous   Go To   Close

Drill 6 | GO TO

1. Open *meade* from the data files.

2. Go to line 14. The status line should read *Page 1, Sec 1, 1/5, At 5", Ln 14*.

3. Go to page 3. The status line should read *Page 3, Sec 1, 3/5, At 1"*.

4. Go to heading 4. The heading should read *Development of the Business Plan*.

5. Keep the document open to use in the application activity that follows.

SKILLBUILDING

16d Reach Review

Key each line once; fingers curved and relaxed; wrists low.

3rd/4th
19 pop was lap pass slaw wool solo swap apollo wasp load plaque
20 Al's quote was, "I was dazzled by the jazz, pizza, and pool."

1st/2nd
21 bad fun nut kick dried night brick civic thick hutch believe
22 Kim may visit her friends in Germany if I give her a ticket.

3rd/1st
23 cry tube wine quit very curb exit crime ebony mention excite
24 To be invited, petition the six executive committee members.

16e Textbook Keying

Key each line once; DS between 3-line groups. Do not pause at the end of lines.

words: *think, say,* and *key* words
25 is do am lay cut pen dub may fob ale rap cot hay pay hem box
26 box wit man sir fish also hair giant rigor civic virus ivory
27 laugh sight flame audit formal social turkey bicycle problem

phrases: *think, say,* and *key* phrases
28 is it|is it|if it is|if it is|or by|or by|or me|or me|for us
29 and all|for pay|pay dues and|the pen|the pen box|the pen box
30 such forms|held both|work form|then wish|sign name|with them

easy sentences
31 The man is to do the work right; he then pays the neighbors.
32 Sign the forms to pay the eight men for the turkey and hams.
33 The antique ivory bicycle is a social problem for the chair.
| 1 | 2 | 3 | 4 | 5 | 6 | 7 | 8 | 9 | 10 | 11 | 12 |

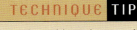

TECHNIQUE TIP

Think and key the words and phrases as units rather than letter by letter.

16f Speed Check

1. Take two 1' writings on paragraph 1. Do not save.
2. Take two 1' writings on paragraph 2.
3. Take one 2' writing on both paragraphs.

gwam 2' | 3'

When choosing a password, do not use one you have already   6 | 4
used. Change to a new one quite often, perhaps every two to 12 | 8
four weeks. Be sure that you combine both letters and numbers. 18 | 12

Know your password; do not write it on paper. If you must 24 | 16
write it down, be sure it's not recognized. Don't let anyone 30 | 20
see you key. Just turn your body or key a little extra.   36 | 24

2' | 1 | 2 | 3 | 4 | 5 | 6 |
3' | 1 | 2 | 3 | 4 |

To modify a header or footer:

1. Click the **View** menu, and then click **Header and Footer**.

2. Click the **Switch Between Header and Footer** button to move to either a header or footer and the **Previous** or **Next** button to view the desired header or footer if the document has more than one header or footer.

3. Make the desired changes; then click **Close**.

Drill 4 | MODIFY HEADERS AND FOOTERS

1. Open *proposed guides* from the data files.

2. Change the header to **Revised Guidelines** (View, Header and Footer).

3. Switch to the footer, change it to **Internal Approval**, and add the date in the right position (click the **Switch Between** button, edit the text; then click the **Date** button).

4. Print the document, and save it as *54b-drill4*.

---

help keywords

document map

Document Map

The document map provides a list of headings within a document. It displays in a separate pane usually at the left side of the document window. The document map provides an effective means for navigating through a document that has been formatted using heading styles. Headings in the document map act as **hyperlinks**—text that you click to go to a specific location. To move to a heading in the document, click on the heading in the document map.

To display and use the document map, click the **View** menu and then **Document Map**, or the **Document Map** button on the Standard toolbar. Click on the desired heading to move to that point in the document.

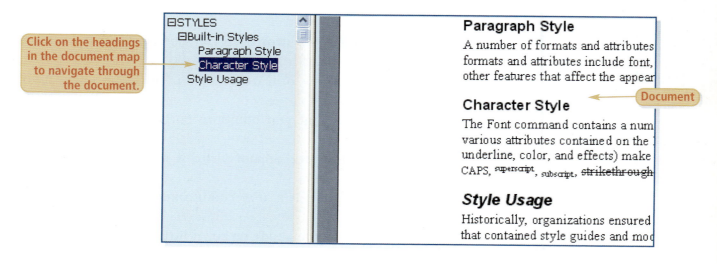

Click on the headings in the document map to navigate through the document.

4 and 9

WARMUP

17a
Key each line twice.

alphabet	1	Bob realized very quickly that jumping was excellent for us.
figures	2	Has each of the 18 clerks now corrected Item 501 on page 27?
shift keys	3	L. K. Coe, M.D., hopes Dr. Lopez can leave for Maine in May.
easy	4	The men paid their own firms for the eight big enamel signs.

NEW KEYS

17b `4` and `9`

Key each line once SS.

4 Reach *up* with *left first* finger.

9 Reach *up* with *right third* finger.

4

5 4 4f f4 4 4 4; if 4 furs; off 4 floors; gaff 4 fish; 4 flags
6 44th floor; half of 44; 4 walked 44 flights; 4 girls; 4 boys
7 I order exactly 44 bagels, 4 cakes, and 4 pies before 4 a.m.

9

8 9 9l l9 9 9 9; fill 9 lugs; call 9 lads; Bill 9 lost; dial 9
9 also 9 oaks; roll 9 loaves; 9.9 degrees; sell 9 oaks; Hall 9
10 Just 9 couples, 9 men and 9 women, left at 9 on our Tour 99.

all figures learned

11 Memo 94 says 9 pads, 4 pens, and 4 ribbons were sent July 9.
12 Study Item 17 and Item 28 on page 40 and Item 59 on page 49.
13 Within 17 months he drove 85 miles, walked 29, and flew 490.

SKILLBUILDING

17c Textbook Keying
Key each line once.

14 My staff of *18* worked *11* hours a day from May *27* to June *12*.
15 There were *5* items tested by Inspector *7* at *4* p.m. on May *8*.
16 Please send her File *10* today at *8*; her access number is *97*.
17 Car *47* had its trial run.   The qualifying speed was *198* mph.
18 The estimated score? *485*. Actual? *190*. Difference? *295*.

D r i l l   2 | OUTLINE NUMBERED LIST

1. Open a new document. Use the same title and format as Drill 1. Key the outline.

2. Format the outline using the first option on the Outline Numbered tab (**Format, Bullets and Numbering, Outline Numbered** tab).

3. Save as *54b-drill2*; preview and print. Compare the outline with *54b-drill1*.

Master Plan for Foundation Properties

1) Coastal Properties
  TAB ──────► a) Marshall Tract
  TAB ──────► i) Overview of land use
      ii) Master plan for development/disposition
  TAB ──────► (1) Short-term plan
      (2) Long-term plan
  SHIFT + TAB ──────► b) Richardson Tract
      i) Overview of land use
      ii) Master plan for development/disposition
          (1) Short-term plan
          (2) Long-term plan
2) Midlands Properties
  a) Wheeler Tract
      i) Overview of land use
      ii) Master plan for development/disposition
          (1) Short-term plan
          (2) Long-term plan
  b) Blossom Tract
      i) Overview of land use
      ii) Master plan for development/disposition
          (1) Short-term plan
          (2) Long-term plan

D r i l l   3 | LIST STYLES

1. Open *54b-drill2* and save it as *54b-drill3a*.

2. Select the outline text (not the title).

3. From the Format menu, select **Bullets and Numbering** and click the **List Styles** tab in the Bullets and Numbering dialog box.

4. Click the first style below **No List** to apply it; format the text (not the title) with 6 points space after; and save.

5. To remove the style, select the text and click **No List**.

6. Save the revised document as *54b-drill3b*; preview and print.

help keywords

change headers or footers

◉ Modify Headers and Footers

Reports often include headers or footers or both. A header consists of text that appears at the top of the pages of a document, and a footer consists of text that appears at the bottom of the pages of the document. Changing the header or footer on one page changes it throughout the document.

17d Technique Reinforcement

Key smoothly; tap the keys at a brisk, steady pace.

first finger

19 buy them gray vent guy brunt buy brunch much give huge vying
20 Hagen, after her July triumph at tennis, may try volleyball.
21 Verna urges us to buy yet another of her beautiful rag rugs.

second finger

22 keen idea; kick it back; ice breaker; decide the issue; cite
23 Did Dick ask Cecelia, his sister, if she decided to like me?
24 Suddenly, Micki's bike skidded on the Cedar Street ice rink.

third/fourth finger

25 low slow lax solo wax zip zap quips quiz zipper prior icicle
26 Paula has always allowed us to relax at La Paz and at Quito.
27 Please ask Zale to explain who explores most aquatic slopes.

17e Speed Builder

1. Key each paragraph in the Open Screen for a 1' writing.
2. Set the Timer for 2'. Key 2 in Variable Setting. Take two 2' writings on all paragraphs. Reach for a speed within two words of 1' gwam.
3. Take a 3' writing on all paragraphs. Reach for a speed within four words of 1' gwam. Print.

all letters

	gwam	2'	3'
• 4 • 8 •			
We consider nature to be limited to those things, such		6	4
12 • 16 • 20			
as air or trees, that we humans do not or cannot make.		11	7
• 4 • 8 •			
For most of us, nature just exists, just is. We don't		17	11
12 • 16 • 20 •			
question it or, perhaps, realize how vital it is to us.		22	15
• 4 • 8 •			
Do I need nature, and does nature need me? I'm really		28	19
12 • 16 • 20 •			
part of nature; thus, what happens to it happens to me.		33	22

2' | 1 | 2 | 3 | 4 | 5 | 6 |
3' | 1 | 2 | 3 | 4 |

17f Speed Builder

TECHNIQUE TIP

Keep hands quiet and fingers well curved over the keys. Do not allow your fingers to bounce.

1. In the Open screen, key the information below at the left margin.

   Your name   **ENTER**

   Current date   **ENTER**

   Skill Builders 1, Drill 2   **ENTER ENTER**

2. Key Drill 2, page 32, from your textbook. Concentrate as you practice on your own, working for good control. Save as *xx-17f*.

1. Open a new document. Center the main heading about 2.1" from the top of the page and apply **Heading 1** style. Switch to **Outline View**.

2. Key each heading shown below and tap ENTER.

3. Click the **Promote** and **Demote** arrows to assign the headings to the level indicated.

4. Add **Short-term plan** and **Long-term plan** as Level 4 headings after each *Master plan for development/disposition* heading (as was done with the *Marshall Tract* heading).

5. Click the **Move Up** arrow to position *Midlands Properties* above *Wheeler Tract*.

6. Save as *54b-drill1*; preview and print.

Master Plan for Foundation Properties

Level 1 →	Coastal Properties
Level 2 →	Marshall Tract
Level 3 →	Overview of land use
Level 3 →	Master plan for development/disposition
Level 4 →	Short-term plan
Level 4 →	Long-term plan
Level 2 →	Richardson Tract
Level 3 →	Overview of land use
Level 3 →	Master plan for development/disposition
Level 2 →	Wheeler Tract
Level 3 →	Overview of land use
Level 3 →	Master plan for development/disposition
Level 2 →	Blossom Tract
Level 3 →	Overview of land use
Level 3 →	Master plan for development/disposition
Level 1 →	Midlands Properties

To create an outline numbered list:

1. Click **Format** on the menu; then click **Bullets and Numbering**.

2. Click the **Outline Numbered** tab, and select the desired style.

3. Key each line of the outline; tap ENTER after each item.

4. To demote an item to a lower level, click **Increase Indent** (or tap TAB). To promote an item to a higher level, click **Decrease Indent** (or press SHIFT + TAB).

TIP

To prepare an outline for someone else to review, an outline numbered list would be preferable.

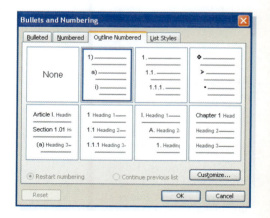

3 and 6

WARMUP

18a
Key each line twice SS.

alphabet	1	Jim Kable won a second prize for his very quixotic drawings.
figures	2	If 57 of the 105 boys go on July 29, 48 of them will remain.
easy	3	With the usual bid, I paid for a quantity of big world maps.

| 1 | 2 | 3 | 4 | 5 | 6 | 7 | 8 | 9 | 10 | 11 | 12 |

NEW KEYS

18b 3 and 6
Key each line once SS.

> Users of ergonomic keyboards will use the "F" finger to key the number 6.

3 Reach *up* with *left second* finger.

6 Reach *up* with *right first* finger.

3

4 3 3d d3 3 3; had 3 days; did 3 dives; led 3 dogs; add 3 dips

5 we 3 ride 3 cars; take 33 dials; read 3 copies; save 33 days

6 On July 3, 33 lights lit 33 stands holding 33 prize winners.

6

7 6 6j 6j 6 6; 6 jays; 6 jams; 6 jigs; 6 jibs; 6 jots; 6 jokes

8 only 6 high; on 66 units; reach 66 numbers; 6 yams or 6 jams

9 On May 6, Car 66 delivered 66 tons of No. 6 shale to Pier 6.

all figures learned

10 At 6 p.m., Channel 3 reported the August 6 score was 6 to 3.

11 Jean, do Items 28 and 6; Mika, 59 and 10; Kyle, 3, 4, and 7.

12 Cars 56 and 34 used Aisle 9; Cars 2 and 87 can use Aisle 10.

SKILLBUILDING

18c Keyboard Reinforcement
Key each line once; DS between 3-line groups.

long reaches

13 ce cede cedar wreck nu nu nut punt nuisance my my amy mystic

14 ny ny any many company mu mu mull lumber mulch br br furbish

15 The absence of receiving my umbrella disturbed the musician.

number review

16 set 0; push 4; Car 00; score 44; jot 04; age 40; Billet 4004

17 April 5; lock 5; set 66; fill 55; hit 65; pick 56; adds 5665

18 Her grades are 93, 87, and 100; his included 82, 96, and 54.

> **TECHNIQUE TIP**
> Make the long reaches without returning to the home row between reaches.

Create Outlines and Edit Reports

WARMUP
54a
Key each line twice SS.

alphabet 1 Jacque Frame and six boys visited a crowded zoo in the long park.

figures 2 I saw 129 geese, 80 birds, 14 deer, 75 squirrels, and 36 rabbits.

one hand 3 Jimmy gave Barbara a free opinion on a decrease in rates at noon.

easy 4 Henry may pay a neighbor to burn the signs and do the field work.

| 1 | 2 | 3 | 4 | 5 | 6 | 7 | 8 | 9 | 10 | 11 | 12 | 13 |

new functions
54b

Create Outlines

An outline is a document formatted in different hierarchical levels. Good writers frequently use an outline to structure long documents before they begin writing. *Word* provides two different types of outlines. One is based on Outline View and the other is an outline numbered list. The outline created in Outline View helps you to organize a document and create an outline from scratch. The Outline Numbered list adds outline numbering to a list to make it easier to read.

Create an Outline from Scratch

You will work in Outline View to create an outline. When you switch to Outline View, the Outlining toolbar displays.

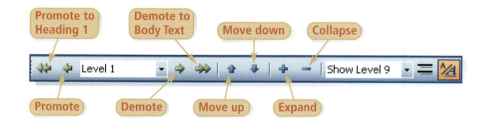

> **TIP**
>
> To outline the report you keyed in *53c-d1* before writing it, use Outline View to create the outline.

To create an outline from scratch:

1. Open a new document; switch to **Outline View**.

2. Key each heading; then tap ENTER.

3. Click in each heading and click either the **Promote** or **Demote** arrow to assign the level.

4. To move headings to different locations, click in the heading and then click the **Move Up** or **Move Down** arrows.

5. After you have arranged all headings, click **Normal View**.

18d Textbook Keying

Key each line once; DS between 2-line groups; repeat.

word response: *think* and *key* words

19 he el id is go us it an me of he of to if ah or bye do so am

20 Did she enamel emblems on a big panel for the downtown sign?

stroke response: *think* and *key* each stroke

21 kin are hip read lymph was pop saw ink art oil gas up as mop

22 Barbara started the union wage earners tax in Texas in July.

combination response: vary speed but maintain rhythm

23 upon than eve lion when burley with they only them loin were

24 It was the opinion of my neighbor that we may work as usual.

18e Diagnostic Writing

Return to the Numeric Lesson menu. Click the **Diagnostic Writings** button. Key the paragraph as a 3' Diagnostic Writing.

Goals: 1', 17–23 *gwam*
2', 15–21 *gwam*
3', 14–20 *gwam*

all letters

	gwam	2'	3'
I am something quite precious. Though millions of people		6	4
in other countries might not have me, you likely do. I have		12	8
a lot of power. For it is I who names a new president every		18	12
four years. It is I who decides if a tax shall be levied.		24	16
I even decide questions of war or peace. I was acquired at		30	20
a great cost; however, I am free to all citizens. And yet,		36	24
sadly, I am often ignored; or, still worse, I am just taken		42	28
for granted. I can be lost, and in certain circumstances I		48	32
can even be taken away. What, you may ask, am I? I am your		54	36
right to vote. Don't take me lightly.		58	39

COMMUNICATION

18f Composition

1. Go to the Open Screen.

2. Introduce yourself to your instructor by composing two paragraphs, each containing about three sentences. Use proper grammatical structure. Do not worry about keying errors at this time.

3. Save the document as *xx-profile*. It is not necessary to print the document. You will open and print it in a later lesson.

The Marshall Tract *Heading style 2*

The Marshall tract consists of over 1,200 acres of environmentally sensitive coastal property. Approximately one-half of the tract consists of wetlands with a conservation and preservation easement on the property. A portion of the remaining property has endangered species, including the red cockaded woodpecker. An eagle nest has also been spotted on the property.

Insert

The master plan calls for the retention of the property because of its potential for research and environmental education. The short-term plans call for the establishment of a system of nature trails and boardwalks and the development of a parking area for visitors. Long-term plans specify the design and construction of a research and learning center.

The Richardson Tract *Heading style 2*

The Richardson tract consists of an entire barrier island that is used for research purposes. The property currently has a very basic research and education center. The gift agreement severely restricts development of facilities on the island; therefore, it is not likely to be highly developed at any point in the future.

Midlands Properties *Heading style 1*

The Midlands portfolio of property consists of more than sixty individual parcels of land. Approximately 60 percent of the land was purchased and 40 percent was received as gifts. The land is valued at $12,650,000.

The Wheeler Tract *Heading style 2*
A decision has been made to sell this property. Currently, the property is being surveyed and a new appraisal has been ordered. The property
placed
will be put on the market as soon as the survey and appraisal have been completed.

The Blossom Tract *Heading style 2*

infrastructure

The Foundation contracted to have work completed before turning the tract over to Midlands University for development.

$ and - (hyphen), Number Expression

WARMUP
19a
Key each line twice SS.

alphabet	1	Why did the judge quiz poor Victor about his blank tax form?
figures	2	J. Boyd, Ph.D., changed Items 10, 57, 36, and 48 on page 92.
3rd row	3	To try the tea, we hope to tour the port prior to the party.
easy	4	Did he signal the authentic robot to do a turn to the right?

| 1 | 2 | 3 | 4 | 5 | 6 | 7 | 8 | 9 | 10 | 11 | 12 |

NEW KEYS
19b $ and -
Key each line once SS;
DS between 2-line groups.

> - = **hyphen**. Use a hyphen in hyphenated words.
> -- = **dash** (tap the hyphen key 2 times). Use a dash in place of a comma.
> Do not space before or after a hyphen or a dash.

$ Shift; then reach *up* with *left first* finger.

- (hyphen) Reach *up* with *right fourth* finger.

$

5 $ $f f$ $ $; if $4; half $4; off $4; of $4; $4 fur; $4 flats

6 for $8; cost $9; log $3; grab $10; give Rolf $2; give Viv $4

7 Since she paid $45 for the item priced at $54, she saved $9.

- (hyphen)

8 - -; ;- - - -; up-to-date; co-op; father-in-law; four-square

9 pop-up foul; big-time job; snap-on bit; one- or two-hour ski

10 You need 6 signatures--half of the members--on the petition.

all symbols learned

11 I paid $10 for the low-cost disk; high-priced ones cost $40.

12 Le-An spent $20 for travel, $95 for books, and $38 for food.

13 Mr. Loft-Smit sold his boat for $467; he bought it for $176.

SKILLBUILDING
19c Keyboard Reinforcement
Key each line once; repeat the drill.

e/d	14	Edie discreetly decided to deduct expenses in making a deed.
w/e	15	Working women wear warm wool sweaters when weather dictates.
r/e	16	We heard very rude remarks regarding her recent termination.
s/d	17	This seal's sudden misdeeds destroyed several goods on land.
v/b	18	Beverley voted by giving a bold beverage to every brave boy.

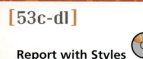

APPLICATIONS

[53c-dl]

Report with Styles

1. Open *master plan* from the data files. Save as *53c-d1*.
2. Increase the spacing after all paragraphs to 6 points.
3. Make the edits shown below. Some of the edits are corrections to the data file. Add text that is in script to the file. Notice that you will be inserting a data file using Paste Special.
4. Add a ½-point black, single-line border and 10% gray shading to all handwritten paragraphs that have been inserted so they can be reviewed carefully.
5. When you finish editing the document, save again. Proofread carefully. Check that you have followed all instructions. Print when you are satisfied.

Master Plan for Foundation Properties ← [Title style]

The Midlands University Foundation properties are categorized into four classifications: Coastal Property, Midlands Property, other in-state property, and out-of-state property. The Foundation acquires property by purchasing it or by accepting gifts from donors desiring to support Midlands University.

Insert → *Generally, the Foundation retains coastal properties for research and environmental education purposes and properties in the Midlands area for future development and use by Midlands University. Usually, properties in the other two categories are held only if they are likely to appreciate significantly; otherwise, they are sold and the proceeds are used to support various University needs. Currently, no out-of-state property is being held.*

Use Paste Special → *Insert Prop Location from the data files here.*

The total value of the property currently held is $34,815,000. The property values are based on the appraisal price.

Coastal Properties Heading style 1

Highlight in yellow → Currently the Foundation owns ~~a number of~~ seven different tracts of land in the Coastal Region valued at $18,325,000. Decisions on the future use of five of the tracts are pending. The master plan contains specific plans for only two of the tracts the Marshall tract and the Richardson tract.
em dash

19d Speed Builder

Key each line once, working for fluid, consistent stroking. Repeat at a faster speed.

easy words

19 am it go bus dye jam irk six sod tic yam ugh spa vow aid dug

20 he or by air big elf dog end fit and lay sue toe wit own got

21 six foe pen firm also body auto form down city kept make fog.

easy phrases

22 it is | if the | and also | to me | the end | to us | if it | it is | to the

23 if it is | to the end | do you wish | to go to | for the end | to make

24 lay down | he or she | make me | by air | end of | by me | kept it | of me

easy sentences

25 Did the chap work to mend the torn right half of the ensign?

26 Blame me for their penchant for the antique chair and panel.

27 She bid by proxy for eighty bushels of a corn and rye blend.

COMMUNICATION

19e Textbook Keying

1. Study the rules and examples at the right.
2. Key the sample sentences 28–33.
3. Change figures to words, as needed, in sentences 34–36.

Spell out numbers:

1. **First word in a sentence.** Key numbers ten and lower as words unless they are part of a series of related numbers, any of which are over ten.

   Three of the four members were present.
   She wrote 12 stories and 2 plays in five years.

2. The **smaller of two adjacent numbers** as words.

   SolVir shipped six 24-ton engines.

3. **Isolated fractions and approximate numbers.** Key as words **large round numbers that can be expressed as one or two words.** Hyphenate fractions expressed as words.

   She completed one-fourth of the experiments.
   Val sent out three hundred invitations.

4. **Preceding "o'clock."**

   John's due at four o'clock. Pick him up at 4:15 p.m.

28 **Six** or **seven** older players were cut from the **37**-member team.

29 I have **2** of **14** coins I need to start my set. Kristen has **9**.

30 Of **nine 24**-ton engines ordered, we shipped **six** last Tuesday.

31 Shelly has read just **one-half** of about **forty-five** documents.

32 The **six** boys sent well over **two hundred** printed invitations.

33 **One** or **two** of us will be on duty from **two** until **six** o'clock.

34 The meeting begins promptly at 9. We plan 4 sessions.

35 The 3-person crew cleaned 6 stands, 12 tables, and 13 desks.

36 The 3d meeting is at 3 o'clock on Friday, February 2.

Drill 7 | PASTE SPECIAL

1. Key the report shown below with double spacing (do not key the chart). Add the title **SALES REPORT** and format it correctly.

2. Open *sales* (the source document) from the data files.

3. Click on the chart to select it, click the **Edit** menu, and then click **Copy**.

4. Switch back to the report and use Paste Special (**Edit, Paste Special**) to embed the chart in your report.

5. Click the chart to select it; then drag it into the correct position.

6. Save as *53b-drill7*.

Sales this year increased significantly. The $3,141,703 sales also exceeded our goals. The first and fourth quarters were strong with total sales in excess of $811,363 and $838,520 respectively. The following chart shows the distribution.

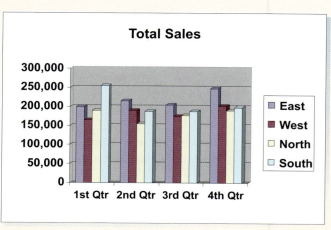

The rankings by regions were: East, South, West, and North. All regions, however, met the sales goals for the year.

Highlight

Text can be highlighted to call attention to it.

To highlight text:

1. Select the text to be highlighted.
2. Click the **Highlight** button on the Formatting toolbar.
3. Click the down arrow on the Highlight button to change colors and select desired color.
4. To remove the highlight, select the highlighted text and click **None**.

Drill 8 | HIGHLIGHT TEXT

Key the sentence below. Highlight the words in yellow and red as shown. Save as *53b-drill8*.

This text illustrates the use of <mark>yellow</mark> and <mark>red</mark> highlights.

and /

WARMUP
20a
Key each line twice SS (slowly, then faster).

alphabet	1	Freda Jencks will have money to buy six quite large topazes.
symbols	2	I bought 10 ribbons and 45 disks from Cable-Han Co. for $78.
home row	3	Dallas sold jade flasks; Sal has a glass flask full of salt.
easy	4	He may cycle down to the field by the giant oak and cut hay.

NEW KEYS
20b # and /
Key each line once SS.

= number sign, pounds
/ = diagonal, slash

Right Shift; then reach *up* with *left second* finger.

/ Reach *down* with *right fourth* finger.

#

5 # #e e# # # #; had #3 dial; did #3 drop; set #3 down; Bid #3

6 leave #82; sold #20; Lyric #16; bale #34; load #53; Optic #7

7 Notice #333 says to load Car #33 with 33# of #3 grade shale.

/

8 / /; ;/ / / /; 1/2; 1/3; Mr./Mrs.; 1/5/94; 22 11/12; and/or;

9 to/from; /s/ William Smit; 2/10, n/30; his/her towels; 6 1/2

10 The numerals 1 5/8, 3 1/4, and 60 7/9 are "mixed fractions."

all symbols learned

11 Invoice #737 cites 15 2/3# of rye was shipped C.O.D. 4/6/95.

12 B-O-A Company's Check #50/5 for $87 paid for 15# of #3 wire.

13 Our Co-op List #20 states $40 for 16 1/2 crates of tomatoes.

SKILLBUILDING

20c Keyboard Reinforcement
Key each line once; work for fluency.
Option: In the Open Screen, key 30" writings on both lines of a pair. Work to avoid pauses.

gwam 30"

14	She did the key work at the height of the problem.	20
15	Form #726 is the title to the island; she owns it.	20
16	The rock is a form of fuel; he did enrich it with coal.	22
17	The corn-and-turkey dish is a blend of turkey and corn.	22
18	It is right to work to end the social problems of the world.	24
19	If I sign it on 3/19, the form can aid us to pay the 40 men.	24

Paragraph Borders and Shading

Borders and shading can be added to paragraphs, pages, or selected text. Various line styles, weights, and colors can be applied to borders. Shading can be applied in a variety of colors and patterns.

> This paragraph illustrates a block border with a 1-point black line. The shading for the paragraph is 10% gray fill.

To apply a paragraph border:

1. Click in the paragraph or select the text to be formatted with a border.

2. Click the **Format** menu, **Borders and Shading**, and then click the **Borders** tab.

3. Select the type of border, line style, color, and width; then click **Apply to Paragraph** and **OK**.

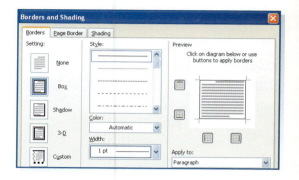

To apply shading:

1. Click in the paragraph or select the text to be shaded.

2. Click the **Format** menu, **Borders and Shading**, and then click the **Shading** tab.

3. Select the fill and pattern, and then apply them to the paragraph.

Drill 6 | BORDERS AND SHADING

Key the paragraph at the right. Then apply a ½-point red, double-line box border and pale blue shading to the paragraph. Save as *53b-drill6.*

> This paragraph is formatted with a ½-point red, double-line box border and pale blue shading.

Paste Special

An **object** (chart, graphic image, or worksheet) created in an *Office* application such as *Microsoft Graph* or *Excel* can be copied to another application such as *Word*. With the **Paste Special** command you can copy an object from one document, called the **source document**, and embed it in another document, called the **destination document**, and modify it. With Copy and Paste, you cannot modify it.

To embed an object in a document:

1. Open the file containing the object to be embedded.

2. Select the object and click **Copy**.

3. Click in the destination document.

4. Click the Edit menu, and then click **Paste Special**.

5. Click the **Paste** radio button in the Paste Special dialog box.

6. Select the format from the As list such as **MS Office Drawing Object**; then click **OK**.

COMMUNICATION

20d Number Usage Review

Key each line once. Decide whether the circled numbers should be keyed as figures or as words and make needed changes. Check your finished work with **19e**, page 47.

```
20 Six or (7) older players were cut from the (37)-member team.
21 I have (2) of 14 coins I need to start my set.  Kristen has (9).
22 Of (9) 24-ton engines ordered, we shipped (6) last Tuesday.
23 Shelly has read just (1) half of about (45) documents.
24 The (6) boys sent well over (200) printed invitations.
25 (1) or (2) of us will be on duty from (2) until (6) o'clock.
```

SKILLBUILDING

20e Speed Builder

1. Go to the Open Screen.
2. Follow the procedures at the right for increasing your speed by taking guided writings.
3. Take a 3' writing without the guide on the complete writing.

all letters

			gwam
1/4'	1/2'	3/4'	1'
4	8	12	16
5	10	15	20
6	12	18	24
7	14	21	28
8	16	24	32
9	18	27	36
10	20	30	40

PROCEDURE [for Guided Writing]

1. In the Open Screen, take a 1' writing on paragraph 1. Note your *gwam*.
2. Add four words to your 1' *gwam* to determine your goal rate.
3. Set the Timer for 1'. Set the Timer option to beep every 15''.
4. From the table below, select from column 4 the speed nearest your goal rate. Note the ¼' point at the left of that speed. Place a light check mark within the paragraphs at the ¼' points.
5. Take two 1' guided writings on paragraphs 1 and 2. Do not save.
6. Turn the beeper off.

	gwam 2'	3'	
Some of us think that the best way to get attention is	6	4	35
to try a new style, or to look quixotic, or to be different	12	8	39
somehow. Perhaps we are looking for nothing much more than	18	12	43
acceptance from others of ourselves just the way we now are.	24	16	47
There is no question about it; we all want to look our	29	19	50
best to impress other people. How we achieve this may mean	35	23	54
trying some of this and that; but our basic objective is to	41	27	58
take our raw materials, you and me, and build up from there.	47	31	62

2' 1 2 3 4 5 6
3' 1 2 3 4

Clear Formatting

The Clear Formatting function clears styles and formatting from selected text. To clear formatting, select the text and click **Clear Formatting** on the Style box on the toolbar or on the Styles and Formatting task pane. To clear formatting and styles from all text, select all text and click **Clear Formatting**.

Drill 4 | **CLEAR FORMATTING**

1. Open *53b-drill3* and select the title (**STYLES**).

2. Click **Clear Formatting** in the Styles and Formatting task pane.

3. Select all text and clear all formatting.

4. Save as *53b-drill4*.

---

help keywords

paragraph spacing

Space After Paragraphs

Double-spaced documents do not need additional space between paragraphs. However, to make single-spaced documents more readable, add additional space after each paragraph. You can add additional space automatically by setting the space after paragraphs to 6 points, the equivalent of one line. Each time you tap ENTER, an additional line is added.

To set spacing after paragraphs:

1. Click the **Format** menu, and then click **Paragraph**.

2. Select the **Indents and Spacing** tab.

3. In the Spacing section of the dialog box, increase spacing in the *After* box from 0 to 6 pt. Click **OK**.

Drill 5 | **PARAGRAPH SPACING**

1. Open *preview* from the data files.

2. Select all of the single-spaced paragraphs.

3. Increase the space after the paragraphs to 6 points.

4. Position the main heading at approximately 2.1"; make it centered, bold, and all caps.

5. Save as *53b-drill5* and print.

% and !

WARMUP
21a
Key each line twice SS.

alphabet 1 Merry will have picked out a dozen quarts of jam for boxing.

fig/sym 2 Jane-Ann bought 16 7/8 yards of #240 cotton at $3.59 a yard.

1st row 3 Can't brave, zany Cave Club men/women next climb Mt. Zamban?

easy 4 Did she rush to cut six bushels of corn for the civic corps?

NEW KEYS
21b % and !
Key each line once SS.

> % = **percent sign:** Use % with business forms or where space is restricted; otherwise, use the word "percent."
> Space twice after the exclamation point!

% Shift; then reach *up* with *left first* finger.

%

5 % %f f% % %; off 5%; if 5%; of 5% fund; half 5%; taxes of 5%

6 7% rent; 3% tariff; 9% F.O.B.; 15% greater; 28% base; up 46%

7 Give discounts of 5% on rods, 50% on lures, and 75% on line.

! reach *up* with the *left fourth* finger

8 ! !a a! ! ! !; Eureka! Ha! No! Pull 10! Extra! America!

9 Listen to the call! Now! Ready! Get set! Go! Good show!

10 I want it now, not next week! I am sure to lose 50% or $19.

all symbols

11 The ad offers a 10% discount, but this notice says 15% less!

12 He got the job! With Clark's Supermarket! Please call Mom!

13 Bill #92-44 arrived very late from Zyclone; it was paid 7/4.

> ### TECHNIQUE **TIP**
> **SPACING TIP**
> - Do not space between a figure and the % or $ signs.
> - Do not space before or after the dash.

21c Keyboard Reinforcement
Key each line once; work for fluency.

all symbols

14 As of 6/28, Jeri owes $31 for dinner and $27 for cab fare.

15 Invoice #20--it was dated 3/4--billed $17 less 15% discount.

16 He deducted 2% instead of 6%, a clear saving of 6% vs. 7%.

combination response

17 Look at my dismal grade in English; but I guess I earned it.

18 Kris started to blend a cocoa beverage for a shaken cowhand.

19 Jan may make a big profit if she owns the title to the land.

Document Properties

Details that help to identify a document are called Document Properties. Document title, author name, document subject, and document statistics are examples of document properties. Some properties must be entered or defined by the author; others are updated automatically. Document properties can be reviewed and modified.

To review and modify document properties:

1. Open the document, click the **File** menu, and select **Properties**.

2. Click each of the four tabs to view the document properties that display.

3. Change information in the document summary by inserting text or selecting text and keying new text. Document statistics are automatically updated.

D r i l l 3 DOCUMENT PROPERTIES

1. Open *53b-drill2*, click the **File** menu, and then click **Properties**.

2. Click the **Statistics** tab and view the information shown. Note that paragraph headings are counted as paragraphs.

3. Click the **Summary** tab and modify it using the information shown at the right.

4. Save as *53b-drill3* and print. Close the document.

5. Reopen the document and note the changes on the Summary and Statistics tabs.

Subject: **Learn About Styles**
Author: Key your name
Manager: Key your instructor's name
Company: Key your school's name
Keyword: **Styles**

SKILLBUILDING

21d Textbook Keying

Key each line once; DS between groups; fingers curved, hands quiet. Repeat if time permits.

1st finger

20 by bar get fun van for inn art from gray hymn July true verb
21 brag human bring unfold hominy mighty report verify puny joy
22 You are brave to try bringing home the van in the bad storm.

2nd finger

23 ace ink did cad keyed deep seed kind Dick died kink like kid
24 cease decease decades kick secret check decide kidney evaded
25 Dedre likes the idea of ending dinner with cake for dessert.

3rd finger

26 oil sow six vex wax axe low old lox pool west loss wool slow
27 swallow swamp saw sew wood sax sexes loom stew excess school
28 Wes waxes floors and washes windows at low costs to schools.

4th finger

29 zap zip craze pop pup pan daze quote queen quiz pizza puzzle
30 zoo graze zipper panzer zebra quip partizan patronize appear
31 Czar Zane appears to be dazzled by the apple pizza and jazz.

21e Speed Runs with Numbers

Take 1' writings; the last number you key when you stop is your approximate *gwam*.

1 and 2 and 3 and 4 and 5 and 6 and 7 and 8 and 9 and 10 and
11 and 12 and 13 and 14 and 15 and 16 and 17 and 18 and 19
and 20 and 21 and 22 and 23 and 24 and 25 and 26 and 27 and

21f Speed Check

Key a 1' and a 2' writing. *Option:* Key a 3' writing.

 **all letters**

	gwam	1'	2'
Teams are the basic unit of performance for a firm.		11	5	42
They are not the solution to all of the organizational needs.		23	12	48
They will not solve all of the problems, but it is known		35	17	54
that a team can perform at a higher rate than other groups.		47	23	60
It is one of the best ways to support the changes needed for		59	30	66
a firm. The team must have time in order to make		71	36	72
a quality working plan.		74	37	74

1' | 1 2 3 4 5 6 7 8 9 10 11 12
2' | 1 2 3 4 5 6

Drill 1 | STYLES

1. Open a new document. View the styles available from the Style box on the Formatting toolbar. Then display the Styles and Formatting task pane and view the styles shown there.

2. Key your name on one line and your address below it. Select your name and apply **Heading 1** style. Select your address and apply **Heading 2** style.

3. Select your name again and apply **Normal**. Then select your name and italicize it. Display the styles list. Notice that Italic has been added as a character style.

4. Close the document without saving.

5. Open *body text* from the data files.

6. Apply the style **Body Text** to the document. Since there is only one paragraph, simply click anywhere within the paragraph and apply the style. The entire paragraph changes to the new style.

7. Save the document as *53b-drill1*.

Drill 2 | STYLES

1. Open *styles* from the data files.

2. Select the first heading (**Styles**); apply the style **Heading 1**. Then center-align the heading.

3. Select the next heading (**Built-in Styles**), and apply the style **Heading 2**.

4. Apply the style **Heading 3** to the next two headings (*Paragraph Style* and *Character Style*).

5. Apply the style **Heading 2** to the last heading (*Style Usage*).

6. Reread the document; note how much easier it is to read a document formatted effectively.

7. Save as *53b-drill2* and print. Your document should be similar to the one shown below.

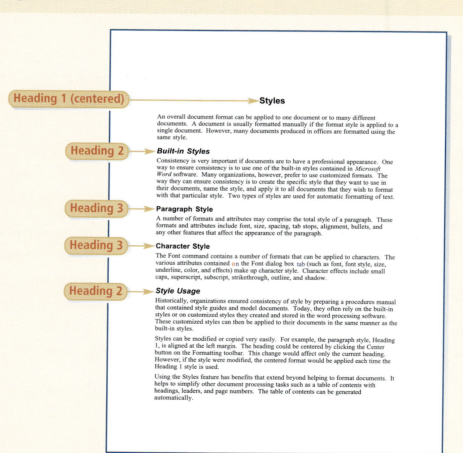

Heading 1 (centered) → **Styles**

An overall document format can be applied to one document or to many different documents. A document is usually formatted manually if the format style is applied to a single document. However, many documents produced in offices are formatted using the same style.

Heading 2 → **Built-in Styles**

Consistency is very important if documents are to have a professional appearance. One way to ensure consistency is to use one of the built-in styles contained in *Microsoft Word* software. Many organizations, however, prefer to use customized formats. The way they can ensure consistency is to create the specific style that they want to use in their documents, name the style, and apply it to all documents that they wish to format with that particular style. Two types of styles are used for automatic formatting of text.

Heading 3 → **Paragraph Style**

A number of formats and attributes may comprise the total style of a paragraph. These formats and attributes include font, size, spacing, tab stops, alignment, bullets, and any other features that affect the appearance of the paragraph.

Heading 3 → **Character Style**

The Font command contains a number of formats that can be applied to characters. The various attributes contained on the Font dialog box tab (such as font, font style, size, underline, color, and effects) make up character style. Character effects include small caps, superscript, subscript, strikethrough, outline, and shadow.

Heading 2 → **Style Usage**

Historically, organizations ensured consistency of style by preparing a procedures manual that contained style guides and model documents. Today, they often rely on the built-in styles or on customized styles they created and stored in the word processing software. These customized styles can then be applied to their documents in the same manner as the built-in styles.

Styles can be modified or copied very easily. For example, the paragraph style, Heading 1, is aligned at the left margin. The heading could be centered by clicking the Center button on the Formatting toolbar. This change would affect only the current heading. However, if the style were modified, the centered format would be applied each time the Heading 1 style is used.

Using the Styles feature has benefits that extend beyond helping to format documents. It helps to simplify other document processing tasks such as a table of contents with headings, leaders, and page numbers. The table of contents can be generated automatically.

(and) and Backspace Key

WARMUP
22a
Key each line twice SS.

alphabet	1	Avoid lazy punches; expert fighters jab with a quick motion.
fig/sym	2	Be-Low's Bill #483/7 was $96.90, not $102--they took 5% off.
caps lock	3	Report titles may be shown in ALL CAPS; as, BOLD WORD POWER.
easy	4	Do they blame me for their dismal social and civic problems?

| 1 | 2 | 3 | 4 | 5 | 6 | 7 | 8 | 9 | 10 | 11 | 12 |

NEW KEYS
22b (and)
(parentheses)
Key each line once SS.

> **( ) = parentheses**
> Parentheses indicate offhand, aside, or explanatory messages.

(Left Shift; then reach *up* with *right third* finger.

) Left Shift; then reach *up* with *right fourth* finger.

5   ((l l((; (; Reach from l for the left parenthesis; as, ((.

6   )); ;))); Reach from ; for the right parenthesis; as,)).

( )

7   Learn to use parentheses (plural) or parenthesis (singular).

8   The red (No. 34) and blue (No. 78) cars both won here (Rio).

9   We (Galen and I) dined (bagels) in our penthouse (the dorm).

all symbols learned

10   The jacket was $35 (thirty-five dollars)--the tie was extra.

11   Starting 10/29, you can sell Model #49 at a discount of 25%.

12   My size 8 1/2 shoe--a blue pump--was soiled (but not badly).

22c Textbook Keying
Key each line once, keeping eyes on copy.

13   Jana has one hard-to-get copy of her hot-off-the-press book.

14   An invoice said that "We give discounts of 10%, 5%, and 3%."

15   The company paid Bill 3/18 on 5/2/97 and Bill 3/1 on 3/6/97.

16   The catalog lists as out of stock Items #230, #710, and #13.

17   Elyn had $8; Sean, $9; and Cal, $7. The cash total was $24.

Edit Reports

WARMUP
53a
Key each line twice SS.

alphabet	1	Dave Cagney alphabetized items for next week's quarterly journal.
figures	2	Close Rooms 4, 18, and 20 from 3 until 9 on July 7; open Room 56.
upward	3	Toy & Wurt's note for $635 (see our page 78) was paid October 29.
easy	4	The auditor is due by eight, and he may lend a hand to the panel.

| 1 | 2 | 3 | 4 | 5 | 6 | 7 | 8 | 9 | 10 | 11 | 12 | 13 |

new functions
53b

Styles

The Styles feature enables you to apply a group of formats to characters and paragraphs in a document automatically. The memo and fax templates in Lesson 49 applied styles to the documents you prepared. As you read the information about styles, note the various styles used on this page. With *Word*, you can apply or create four different types of styles:

1. **Character styles** apply to characters that are selected within a paragraph.

2. **Paragraph styles** include both character styles and other formats that affect paragraph appearance such as alignment, line spacing, tabs, bullets, and numbering.

3. **Table styles** provide consistent appearance to borders, colors, font, shading, and alignment in tables. You applied and modified table styles in Lessons 44–46.

4. **List styles** such as bullets, numbering, and numbered lists present information in a consistent manner.

To apply paragraph styles:

1. Select the text to which you want to apply a style.

2. Select the desired style in the Style box on the Formatting toolbar or in the Styles and Formatting task pane.

> **TIP**
>
> Hold the Mouse pointer over Normal to see the style. The default style (Normal) for regular text is formatted with 12-point Times Roman font and single spacing.

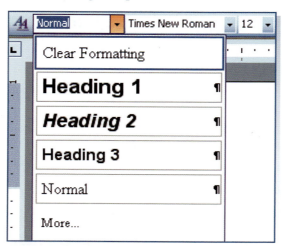

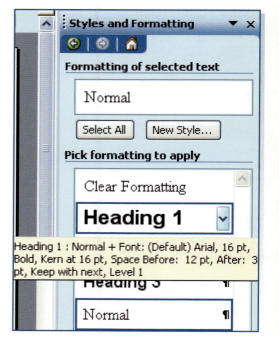

22d BACKSPACE Key

Practice reaching to the BACKSPACE key with your right little finger. Key the sentences, using the BACKSPACE key to correct errors.

18 You should be interested in the special items on sale today.
19 If she is going with us, why don't we plan to leave now?
20 Do you desire to continue working on the memo in the future?
21 Did the firm or their neighbors own the autos with problems?
22 Juni, Vec, and Zeb had perfect grades on weekly query exams.
23 Jewel quickly explained to me the big fire hazards involved.

22e Speed Check

1. Take two 1' timings on each paragraph.
2. Take a 3' timing on all paragraphs. Determine *gwam*.

Goal: 17 *gwam*

all letters

	gwam	1'	3'
Most people will agree that we owe it to our children	10	4	28
to pass the planet on to them in better condition than we	22	7	32
found it. We must take extra steps just to make the quality	34	12	36
of living better.	38	13	37
If we do not change our ways quickly and stop damaging	11	16	41
our world, it will not be a good place to live. We can save	12	21	45
the ozone and wildlife and stop polluting the air and water.	35	25	49

1'	1	2	3	4	5	6	7	8	9	10	11	12
3'		1			2			3			4	

COMMUNICATION

22f Number Expression

1. Study the rules and examples at the right.
2. In the Open Screen, key the information below at the left margin. Tap ENTER as shown.
   Your name ENTER
   Current date ENTER
   Skill Builders 1, Drill 6
   ENTER ENTER
3. Key the sample sentences 24–28. Backspace to correct errors.
4. Save the file as *xx-22f*.

Express as figures

1. **Money amounts** and **percentages, even when approximate.** Spell out cents and percent except in statistical copy.

   The 16 percent discount saved me $145; Bill, 95 cents.

2. **Round numbers expressed in millions or higher with their word modifier.**

   Ms. Ti contributed $3 million.

3. **House numbers** (except house number one) and street names over ten. If a street name is a number, separate it from the house number with a dash (made by keying two hyphens).

   1510 Easy Street   One West Ninth Avenue   1592--11th Street

4. **Date followed by a month.** A date preceding the month or standing alone is expressed in figures followed by "rd" or "th."

   June 9, 2001   4th of July   March 3rd

5. **Numbers used with nouns.**

   Volume 1   Chapter 6

24 Ask **Group 1** to read **Chapter 6** of **Book 11** (**Shelf 19, Room 5**).
25 All **six** of us live at **One Bay Road**, not at **126--56th Street**.
26 At **9 a.m.** the owners decided to close from **12 noon** to **1 p.m.**
27 Ms. Vik leaves **June 9**; she returns the **14th or 15th of July**.
28 The **16 percent** discount saves **$115**. A stamp costs **35 cents**.

[52d-d1]

Research Tool and
Compare and Merge

1. Open *outsourcing* from the data files; save as *outsourcing revised* and turn **Track Changes** on.

✳ 2. Change the subject line text to **Title Case**.

3. SS body with DS between paragraphs.

4. Use the Research Tool to find another term for *GLOBAL* in the subject line. Insert the first or second term in the list you find.

5. Make the changes in the body shown below.

6. Resave and close the document.

7. Open *outsourcing* and use Compare and Merge to compare *outsourcing revised* with the original document. Merge into a new document.

8. Accept all changes except the changes to delete *Monitor* and insert *Supervise* in the third column. (*Tip:* Reject the deletion of *Monitor* and insertion of *Supervise* first; then you can use Accept all changes in Document rather than accepting each change individually.)

9. Save as *52d-d1*.

Most companies in our industry are using worldwide outsourcing to some degree to reduce labor costs. The literature is packed with examples of both successes and failures. The successful companies report considerable savings: labor costs have been reduced from 20 to 60 percent.

The advice the successful companies give is summarized in the table below.

Pilot the Project	Qualifications and Work Specifications	Monitor the Project
Begin with test project Limit what you do Expand if successful	Specify language skills needed Detail knowledge requirements Determine skills needed Establish quality levels Use measurable standards Include all in contract	Manage project Supervise daily Provide feedback early Demand quality results

We look forward to presenting a complete report on this issue.

xx

Deleted: →
Formatted: Line spacing: single
Deleted: cut
Deleted: %.
Deleted: →
Deleted: advise
Formatted: Centered
Deleted: Monitor
Deleted: →

[52d-d2]

Edit Table

1. Open *function coverage* from the data files and save it as *52d-d2*.

2. Delete column 6 (Lesson 53); adjust column widths and row heights according to the Table Format Guides on page 180.

3. Center and bold the title **FUNCTION SUMMARY** a DS above the table.

4. Add a row above *Wizards* and key **Compare and Merge**; place a check in Lesson 52.

5. Center the table horizontally and vertically on the page. Resave and print.

& and : (colon), Proofreaders' Marks

WARMUP
23a
Key each line twice SS.

alphabet	1	Roxy waved as she did quick flying jumps on the trapeze bar.
symbols	2	Ryan's--with an A-1 rating--sold Item #146 (for $10) on 2/7.
space bar	3	Mr. Fyn may go to Cape Cod on the bus, or he may go by auto.
easy	4	Susie is busy; may she halt the social work for the auditor?

| 1 | 2 | 3 | 4 | 5 | 6 | 7 | 8 | 9 | 10 | 11 | 12 |

NEW KEYS
23b & and : (colon)
Key each line once SS.

> **& = ampersand:** The ampersand is used only as part of company names.
> **Colon:** Space twice after a colon except when used within a number for time.

& Shift; then reach *up* with *right first* finger.

: (colon) Left shift; then tap key with *right fourth* finger.

& (ampersand)

5 & &j j& & & &; J & J; Haraj & Jay; Moroj & Jax; Torj & Jones

6 Nehru & Unger; Mumm & Just; Mann & Hart; Arch & Jones; M & J

7 Rhye & Knox represent us; Steb & Doy, Firm A; R & J, Firm B.

: (colon)

8 : :; :: : : :; as: for example: notice: To: From: Date:

9 in stock: 8:30; 7:45; Age: Experience: Read: Send: See:

10 Space twice after a colon, thus: To: No.:   Time: Carload:

all symbols learned

11 Consider these companies: J & R, Brand & Kay, Uper & Davis.

12 Memo #88-89 reads as follows: "Deduct 15% of $300, or $45."

13 Bill 32(5)--it got here quite late--from M & N was paid 7/3.

23c Keyboard Reinforcement
Key each line twice; work for fluency.

double letters

14 Di Bennett was puzzled by drivers exceeding the speed limit.

15 Bill needs the office address; he will cut the grass at ten.

16 Todd saw the green car veer off the street near a tall tree.

figures and symbols

17 Invoice #84 for $672.91, plus $4.38 tax, was due on 5/19/02.

18 Do read Section 4, pages 60-74 and Section 9, pages 198-225.

19 Enter the following: (a) name, (b) address, and (c) tax ID.

Drill 2 | RESEARCH TOOL

1. Key **endowment** in a new document; click in the word.

2. Click the **Tools** menu and click **Research**. Key **endowment** in the Search for box on the Research task pane if it is not shown.

3. Select **All Reference Books** and click the search arrow.

4. Point to **gift** under the Thesaurus options, click the down arrow, and select **Insert**. (*Hint:* Click the plus sign if you do not see any options under Thesaurus.)

5. View the definitions and translation options. Click from **English** to **German**. View the translation.

6. Go to the top of the Research task pane, select **All Research Sites**, and click the search arrow. (This requires Internet access; go to step 9 if you do not have access.)

7. Click the **Read now** button that displays under each article to view a shortened version of the article. In your browser, note the Read the Full Article with Your Free Trial button at the bottom of the article. Fees are charged for the full article.

8. Preview the article and close the Research Pane.

9. Save as *52c-drill2*.

Compare and Merge

Members of writing teams benefit from the Compare and Merge feature as it tracks the differences between two documents. The edited document is compared to the original document. *Word* displays the differences in the two documents in color.

help keywords

compare and merge documents

To compare and merge documents:

1. Open the original copy of the document.

2. Click the **Tools** menu and then click **Compare and Merge Documents**.

3. Select the edited document from the files.

4. Click the down arrow next to the Merge button; select one of these three choices:
   a. **Merge**—to display differences in the orginal document.
   b. **Merge into current document**—to display differences in the edited document.
   c. **Merge into new document**—to display differences in a new document.

Drill 3 | COMPARE AND MERGE

1. Key the following paragraph exactly as shown. Save it as *52c-drill3 original*.

   To avoid copyright infringement, the internet user must be knowledgeable of copyright laws. 2 important laws include The Copyright Law of 1967, and the Digital Millennium Copyright Act, which was enacted in 1998 to update the copyright law.

2. Edit the paragraph keyed in step 1, making the changes indicated as follows. Save it as *52c-drill 3 revised*.

   To avoid copyright infringement, the internet user must be knowledgeable of copyright laws. ②ˢᵖ important laws include The Copyright Law of 1967 and the Digital Millennium Copyright Act, which was enacted in 1998 to update the copyright law —s for the digital age.

3. Compare the two files prepared in steps 1 and 2. Merge into a new document and save it as *52c-drill3*.

SKILLBUILDING

23d Textbook Keying

Key each line once; work for fluency.

20 Jane may work with an auditing firm if she is paid to do so.
21 Pam and eight girls may go to the lake to work with the dog.
22 Clancy and Claudia did all the work to fix the sign problem.
23 Did Lea visit the Orlando land of enchantment or a neighbor?
24 Ana and Blanche made a map for a neighbor to go to the city.
25 Sidney may go to the lake to fish with worms from the docks.
26 Did the firm or the neighbors own the auto with the problem?

| 1 | 2 | 3 | 4 | 5 | 6 | 7 | 8 | 9 | 10 | 11 | 12 |

23e Speed Check

Key two 1' timed writings on each paragraph; then two 3' writings on both paragraphs; compute *gwam*.

Goals: 1', 20–27 *gwam*
3', 17–24 *gwam*

all letters

	gwam	1'	3'
Is how you judge my work important? It is, of course;	11	4	26
I hope you recognize some basic merit in it. We all expect	23	8	30
to get credit for good work that we conclude.	32	11	33
I want approval for stands I take, things I write, and	11	14	36
work I complete. My efforts, by my work, show a picture of	23	18	41
me; thus, through my work, I am my own unique creation.	34	22	44

1' | 1 | 2 | 3 | 4 | 5 | 6 | 7 | 8 | 9 | 10 | 11 | 12 |
3' | 1 | | 2 | | 3 | | 4 |

COMMUNICATION

23f Edit Text

1. Read the information about proofreaders' marks.

2. In the Open Screen, key your name, class, and 23f at the left margin. Then key lines 27–32, making the revisions as you key. Use the BACKSPACE key to correct errors.

3. Save as *xx-23f* and print.

Proofreaders' marks are used to identify mistakes in typed or printed text. Learn to apply these commonly used standard proofreaders' marks.

Symbol	Meaning	Symbol	Meaning
___	Italic	◯ sp	Spell out
﹏	Bold	¶	Paragraph
Cap or ═	Capitalize	#	Add horizontal space
∧	Insert	/ or lc	Lowercase
⟋	Delete	◡	Close up space
⊐	Move to left	∼	Transpose
⊏	Move to right	stet	Leave as originally written

27 We miss 50% in life's rowards by refusing to new try things.

28 do it now--today--then tomorrow's load will be 100%% lighter.

29 Satisfying work--whether it pays $40 or $400--is the pay off.

30 Avoid mistakes: confusing a #3 has cost thousands.

31 Pleased most with a first-rate job is the person who did it.

32 My wife and/or me mother will except the certificate for me.

1. Key the text below, applying the character effects shown.

3. Save as *52c-drill1* and print.

2. Add the text effect Marching Red Ants to the text in small caps in line 1. Add the text effect Shimmer to the second line.

Apply SMALL CAPS to this text.

The symbol for water, H_2O, contains a subscript.

Math formulas often use superscripts, such as $X^2 + Y^3$.

~~Strikethrough~~ is a useful effect in editing text.

Outline and **shadow** change the appearance of text.

Embossed text appears to be raised above the paper.

Engraved text appears to be sunken into the paper.

Research Tool

Word provides a research service that enables you to look up information while you are using *Word*. You can access the Research service by clicking the Research button, by selecting Research on the Tools menu, or by tapping ALT and clicking in a word. The Research task pane is used to look up information.

Options to search for information include:

- *All Reference Books*, which provides definitions, thesaurus, and translations.
- *All Research Sites*, which provides articles on the topic.
- *All Business and Financial Sites*, which provides company profiles and financial information such as stock quotes.

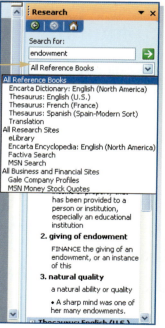

Search Option box

An Internet connection is needed to research topics on Research and Business and Financial sites. Many premium services sites charge fees for those services.

When an article is located, you can click the Read now button to access the article in a full-size window for easy reading.

To use the Research tool:

1. Click the **Tools** menu and click **Research**.
2. Key the topic you wish to research in the Search for box.
3. Click the down arrow in the Search Option box.
4. Select the information you wish to use, click the down arrow, and click **Insert** to position it in the document.

Other Symbols

WARMUP

24a
Key each line twice SS.

alphabet   1   Pfc. Jim Kings covered each of the lazy boxers with a quilt.

figures   2   Do problems 6 to 29 on page 175 before class at 8:30, May 4.

"   3   They read the poems "September Rain" and "The Lower Branch."

easy   4   When did the busy girls fix the tight cowl of the ruby gown?

| 1 | 2 | 3 | 4 | 5 | 6 | 7 | 8 | 9 | 10 | 11 | 12 |

NEW KEYS

24b Textbook Keying

Key each pair of lines once SS;
DS between 2-line groups.

Become familiar with
these symbols:
@   at
<   less than
>   greater than
*   asterisk
+   plus sign (use a
    hyphen for minus and
    x for "times")
=   equals
[ ]   left and right bracket

@   shift; reach *up* with *left third* finger to @

5   @ @s s@ @ @; 24 @ .15; 22 @ .35; sold 2 @ .87; were 12 @ .95

6   You may contact Luke @: LJP@rx.com or fax @ (602) 555-0101.

<   shift; reach *down* with *right second* finger to <
>   shift; reach *down* with *right third* finger to >

7   Can you prove "a > b"? If 28 > 5, then 5a < x. Is a < > b?

8   E-mail Al ajj@crewl.com and Matt mrw10@scxs.com by 9:30 p.m.

*   shift; reach *up* with *right second* finger to *

9   * *k k8* * *; aurelis*; May 7*; both sides*; 250 km.**; aka*

10   Note each *; one * refers to page 29; ** refers to page 307.

+   shift; reach *up* with *right fourth* finger to +

11   + ;+ +; + + +; 2 + 2; A+ or B+; 70+ F. degrees; +xy over +y;

12   The question was 8 + 7 + 51; it should have been 8 + 7 + 15.

=   reach *up* with *right fourth* finger to =

13   = =; = = =; = 4; If 14x = 28, x = 2; if 8x = 16, then x = 2.

14   Change this solution (where it says "= by") to = bx or = BX.

[ ]   reach *up* with *right fourth* finger to [and]

15   Mr. Wing was named. [That's John J. Wing, ex-senator. Ed.]

16   We [Joseph and I] will be in Suite #349; call us @ 555-0102.

Edit Text and Tables

WARMUP
52a
Key each line twice SS.

alphabet	1	Jacky Few's strange, quiet behavior amazed and perplexed even us.
figures	2	Dial Extension 1480 or 2760 for a copy of the 3-page 95-cent book.
double letters	3	Ann will see that Edd accepts an assignment in the school office.
easy	4	If I burn the signs, the odor of enamel may make a toxic problem.

| 1 | 2 | 3 | 4 | 5 | 6 | 7 | 8 | 9 | 10 | 11 | 12 | 13 |

52b Timed Writings
1. Take two 1' timings on each paragraph.
2. Key either a 3' or 5' timing.

all letters

gwam   3'   5'

Who is a professional? The word can be defined in many   4   2   32
ways. Some may think of a professional as someone who is in an   8   5   35
exempt job category in an organization. To others the word can   12   7   37
denote something quite different; being a professional denotes an   17   10   40
attitude that requires thinking of your position as a career, not   21   13   43
just a job. A professional exerts influence over her or his job   25   15   45
and takes pride in the work accomplished.   28   17   47

Many individuals who remain in the same positions for a long   32   19   49
time characterize themselves as being in dead-end positions.   36   22   52
Others who remain in positions for a long time consider them-   40   24   54
selves to be in a profession. A profession is a career to which   45   27   57
you are willing to devote a lifetime. How you view your pro-   49   29   59
fession is up to you.   50   30   60

3' | 1 | 2 | 3 | 4 |
5' | 1 | 2 | 3 |

new functions
52c

Character and Text Effects

Character effects include a number of special attributes that enhance the appearance of text. Commonly used character effects include superscript, subscript, small caps, strikethrough, shadow, and outline. Character effects are available on the Font dialog box (**Format menu, Font**).

help keywords

font

Text Effects include various animations such as a blinking background or a shimmer. Text effects are appropriate for documents that are to be read on screen or online. To access these animations, select the **Text Effects** tab in the Font dialog box. Text effects should be used very judiciously.

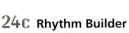

24c Rhythm Builder

In the Open Screen, key each line twice; DS between 2-line groups.

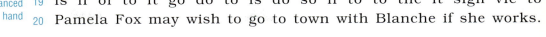

double letters
17 feel pass mill good miss seem moons cliffs pools green spell
18 Assets are being offered in a stuffy room to two associates.

balanced hand
19 is if of to it go do to is do so if to to the it sign vie to
20 Pamela Fox may wish to go to town with Blanche if she works.

one hand
21 date face ere bat lip sew lion rear brag fact join eggs ever
22 get fewer on; after we look; as we agree; add debt; act fast

combination
23 was for|in the case of|they were|to down|mend it|but pony is
24 They were to be down in the fastest sleigh if you are right.

| 1 | 2 | 3 | 4 | 5 | 6 | 7 | 8 | 9 | 10 | 11 | 12 |

24d Edited Copy

1. Key each line, making the corrections marked with proofreaders' marks.
2. Correct errors using the BACKSPACE key.
3. Save as *xx-24d*.

25 Ask Group 1 to read Chater 6 of Book 11 (Shelf 19, Room 5).

26 All 6 of us live at One Bay road, not at 126-56th Street.

27 AT 9 a.m. the owners decided to close form 12 noon to 1 p.m.

28 Ms. Vik leaves June 9; she returns the 14 or 15 of July.

29 The 16 per cent discount saves 115. A stamp costs 35 cents.

30 Elin gave $300,000,000; our gift was only 75 cents.

24e Speed Check

1. Key a 1' writing on each paragraph using wordwrap.
2. Key two 3' writings on both paragraphs. Save the timings if desired (*xx24e-t1* and *xx24e-t2*).

gwam 1' | 3'

Why don't we like change very much? Do you think that — 11 | 4 | 26
just maybe we want to be lazy; to dodge new things; and, as — 23 | 8 | 30
much as possible, not to make hard decisions? — 32 | 11 | 33
We know change can and does extend new areas for us to — 11 | 14 | 36
enjoy, areas we might never have known existed; and to stay — 24 | 18 | 40
away from all change could curtail our quality of life. — 34 | 22 | 44

1' | 1 | 2 | 3 | 4 | 5 | 6 | 7 | 8 | 9 | 10 | 11 | 12 |
3' | 1 | | 2 | | 3 | | 4 |

COMMUNICATION

24f Composition Revision

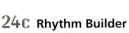

1. In the Open Screen, open the file *xx-profile* that you created in Lesson 18.

2. Position the insertion point at the end of the last paragraph. Tap ENTER twice.

3. Key an additional paragraph that begins with the following sentence:

   Thank you for allowing me to introduce myself.

4. Finish the paragraph by adding two or more sentences that describe your progress and satisfaction with keyboarding.

5. Correct any mistakes you have made. Click **Save** to resave the document. Print.

6. Mark any mistakes you missed with proofreaders' marks. Revise the document, save, and reprint. Submit to your instructor.

[51d-d1]

Make and Accept Changes

1. Open the data file *proposal analysis* from the data files.

2. Click **Original Showing Markup** and activate the **Track Changes** feature.

3. Make the following changes in the document:

   - Use proper format for the date.
   - Change the spelling of Ann to **Anne**.
   - Her new address is **6328 Myrtle Street**.
   - The ZIP Code is **47710-5903**.
   - Delete the header.
   - Find all occurrences of *quotation* and replace it with *proposal*.

4. Switch to **Final Showing Markup** and review the changes made.

5. Accept all changes. Review the final document and make any additional corrections that are needed.

6. Save as *51d-d1* and print.

[51d-d2]

Review and Add Comments

1. Open *proposal price* from the data files.

2. Margaret Shuler received her copy of the memo electronically, and she asked you to review her comments and add your own comments before she sends the memo to Lynn Timmons.

3. Insert the following comment at the end of the last paragraph:

   I agree with Margaret. Shall I set up a meeting to talk about this?

4. Save as *51d-d2* and print.

[51d-d3]

Delete Comments

1. Open document *51d-d2* that you just completed.

2. Delete the three comments.

3. Save as *51d-d3* and print.

[51d-d4]

Review, Change, and Format Letter

1. Open the data file *follow-up*.

2. Review the changes made. Accept all of the changes except the one made by Phillip C. Blackmon.

3. Use the address and closing information from *51d-d1* to format the letter to Ms. Marshall from Mr. Timmons. Add your reference initials and an attachment notation.

4. Save as *51d-d4* and print.

Assessment

WARMUP
25a
Key each line twice SS.

alphabet   1   My wife helped fix a frozen lock on Jacque's vegetable bins.

figures   2   Sherm moved from 823 West 150th Street to 9472--67th Street

double letters   3   Will Scotty attempt to sell his accounting books to Elliott?

easy   4   It is a shame he used the endowment for a visit to the city.

| 1 | 2 | 3 | 4 | 5 | 6 | 7 | 8 | 9 | 10 | 11 | 12 |

25b Reach Review
Key each line once; repeat.

n/y

5   deny many canny tiny nymph puny any puny zany penny pony yen

6   Jenny Nyles saw many, many tiny nymphs flying near her pony.

b/r

7   bran barb brim curb brat garb bray verb brag garb bribe herb

8   Barb Barber can bring a bit of bran and herbs for her bread.

c/e

9   cede neck nice deck dice heck rice peck vice erect mice echo

10   Can Cecil erect a decent cedar deck? He erects nice condos.

n/u

11   nun gnu bun nut pun numb sun nude tuna nub fun null unit gun

12   Eunice had enough ground nuts at lunch; Uncle Launce is fun.

> **TECHNIQUE TIP**
>
> Keep arms and hands quiet as you practice the long reaches.

25c Speed Check
Key two 3' writings.
Strive for accuracy.
Goal: 3', 19–27 *gwam*

all letters

	gwam	3'

The term careers can mean many different things to   3 | 51
different people. As you know, a career is much more than a   8 | 55
job. It is the kind of work that a person has through life.   12 | 59
It includes the jobs a person has over time. It also involves   16 | 63
how the work life affects the other parts of our life. There   20 | 67
are as many types of careers as there are people.   23 | 71

Almost all people have a career of some kind. A career   27 | 74
can help us to reach unique goals, such as to make a living   31 | 79
or to help others. The kind of career you have will affect   35 | 83
your life in many ways. For example, it can determine where   39 | 87
you live, the money you make, and how you feel about yourself.   44 | 91
A good choice can thus help you realize the life you want.   47 | 95

3' | 1 | 2 | 3 | 4 |

Note the differences when Final Showing Markup is selected rather than Original with Markup.

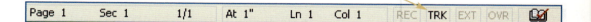

Note that when Track Changes is turned on, TRK on the status bar is activated. It is dimmed when Track Changes is turned off.

To track and accept changes:

1. Open the document that contains the changes and display the Reviewing toolbar.
2. Select **Original Showing Markup** and click the **Track Changes** button.
3. Edit the document and change the Display for Review to **Final Showing Markup**.
4. Select the changed text and click the **Accept Change** button for individual changes, or click the **Accept Change** button drop arrow and accept all changes shown or all changes in the document.

D r i l l   7 | TRACK AND ACCEPT CHANGES

1. Open the data file *track changes*.
2. Display the **Reviewing** toolbar, select **Original Showing Markup,** and click the **Track Changes** button.
3. Edit the document so that it will read as below.
4. Change to **Final Showing Markup** and note the differences. Save as *51c-drill7a*.
5. Accept all changes in the document.
6. Save the revised document as *51c-drill7b*.

> Please make suggested changes and track the changes on this document. First display the Reviewing toolbar and click the Track Changes button. (Options to turn on the Track Changes feature are: Click Tools and then Track Changes or click Tools, Options, and set desired options on the Track Changes tab.) Note how the changes you mark are shown on the screen. If you have not already done so, enter your name and initials in the User Information box.

SKILLBUILDING

25d Textbook Keying

Key each line once; DS between groups; repeat. Key with precision and without hesitation.

13 is if he do rub ant go and am pan do rut us aid ox ape by is

14 it is | an end | it may | to pay | and so | aid us | he got | or own | to go

15 Did the girl make the ornament with fur, duck down, or hair?

16 us owl rug box bob to man so bit or big pen of jay me age it

17 it | it is | time to go | show them how | plan to go | one of the aims

18 It is a shame they use the autobus for a visit to the field.

| 1 | 2 | 3 | 4 | 5 | 6 | 7 | 8 | 9 | 10 | 11 | 12 |

25e Figure Check

In the Open Screen, key two 1' writings and two 3' writings at a controlled speed.

all letters/figures

Goal: 3', 16–24 *gwam*

gwam 3'

Do I read the stock market pages in the news? Yes; and .... 4 | 35

at about 9 or 10 a.m. each morning, I know lots of excited ...... 8 | 39

people are quick to join me. In fact, many of us zip right ..... 12 | 43

to the 3d or 4th part of the paper to see if the prices of ...... 6 | 47

our stocks have gone up or down. Now, those of us who are ...... 19 | 51

"speculators" like to "buy at 52 and sell at 60"; while the ..... 23 | 55

"investors" among us are more interested in a dividend we .... 27 | 59

may get, say 7 or 8 percent, than in the price of a stock. ...... 31 | 62

3' | 1 | 2 | 3 | 4 |

COMMUNICATION

25f Edited Copy

1. Key the paragraphs and make the corrections marked with proofreaders' marks. Use the BACKSPACE key to correct errors.
2. Check all number expressions and correct any mistakes that may exist.
3. Save as *xx-25f*.

www.collegekeyboarding.com

Last week the healthy heart foundation relased the findings of a study that showed exercise diet and if individuals don't smoke are the major controllable factors that led to a healthy heart. Factors such as heredity can not be controlled. The study included 25 to 65 year old males as well as females.

The study also showed that just taking a walk benefits our health. Those who walked an average of 2 to 3 hours a week were more then 30 percent less likely to have problems than those who did no exercise.

Drill 3 | INSERT COMMENT

1. Open *rules* from the data files.

2. Select *player-to-player* and insert the comment shown at the right:

Do you prefer the term man-to-man or player-to-player?

3. Save as *51c-drill3*.

Drill 4 | EDIT COMMENT

1. Open *51c-drill3*.

2. Click in the comment and edit it as follows:

Do you prefer the term man-to-man or player-to-player for the handbook?

3. Save as *51c-drill4*.

Drill 5 | RESPOND TO COMMENT

1. Open *rules2* from the data files.

2. Click in the comment and insert the following response:

I prefer man-to-man because the referees and other coaches use that term.

3. Save as *51c-drill5*.

Drill 6 | DELETE COMMENTS

1. Open *51c-drill5*.

2. You agree with the comment suggested. Make the edit by selecting *player-to-player* and replacing it with *man-to-man*; then delete both Comments.

3. Save as *51c-drill6*.

---

help keywords

track changes; track changes while you edit

Note: Screen tips allow you to see information about a function when you hold the mouse over it. Screen tips must be turned on (**Tools, Customize, Options** tab, check **Show Screen Tips on toolbars**).

Track Changes

The Track Changes feature is used to mark suggested changes in a document without changing the document itself. An author can use this feature to edit a document by marking changes and reviewing them before actually making a change. Usually the feature is used when multiple reviewers make suggestions for revising a document. The changes are color-coded by each person reviewing the document. The Screen Tip feature can also be used to identify the person who made specific changes.

In the previous exercise you used the Reviewing toolbar to work with Comments. In this exercise you will use it to track changes in a document. The first illustration shows the original markup of changes tracked in a document. The Display for Review box is used to determine how the markup is shown. The Show box determines what is shown.

Use the Open Screen for Skill Builders 2. Save each drill as a separate file.

Drill 1

OPPOSITE HAND REACHES

Key at a controlled rate; concentrate on the reaches.

i/e

1 ik is fit it sit laid site like insist still wise coil light
2 ed he ear the fed egg led elf lake jade heat feet hear where
3 lie kite item five aide either quite linear imagine brighter
4 Imagine the aide eating the pears before the grieving tiger.

w/o

5 ws we way was few went wit law with weed were week gnaw when
6 ol on go hot old lot joy odd comb open tool upon money union
7 bow owl word wood worm worse tower brown toward wrote weapon
8 The workers lowered the brown swords toward the wood weapon.

Drill 2

PROOFREADERS' MARKS

Key each sentence. DS after each sentence. Make all the editing (handwritten) corrections. Print. Go on to Drill 3.

≡ Capitalize
/ Change letter
◡ Close up space
ℛ Delete
∧ Insert
lc Lowercase
Space
∾ Transpose

When a writer create the preliminary version of a document, they is are concentrating on conveying the intended ideas. This version of a preliminary document is called a rough draft. After the draft is created the Writer edits/refines the copy. Sometimes proofreader's marks are used to edit the draft. The changes will them be make to the original. editing After the changes have been made, then the Writer reads the copy again. Edit ing and proofreading requires alot of time and effort. An attitute of excellance is required to produce error free message.

Drill 3

PROOFREADING

Compare your printout to this paragraph. How did you do? Then key the paragraph for fluency. Concentrate on keying as accurately as possible.

When a writer creates the preliminary version of a document, he or she is concentrating on conveying ideas. This preliminary version is called a rough draft. After the draft is created, the writer edits or refines the copy. Proofreaders' marks are used to edit the rough draft. The editing changes will be made to the original. Then the writer reads the copy again. Editing requires a lot of time and effort. An attitude of excellence is required to produce an error-free message.

Drill 2 | THESAURUS

1. Key the following words on separate lines:
   generous   data   smart   profit

2. Replace *generous* and *data* with synonyms.

3. Replace *smart* (meaning clever) with a synonym.

4. Key **smart** again (meaning elegant) and replace it with an antonym.

5. Replace *profit* with an antonym.

6. Save the document as *51c-drill2*.

help keywords

insert a comment; modify a comment; delete a comment

TIP

Right-click comment and click **Delete Comment**.
Click **Insert Comment** on Reviewing Toolbar to insert a comment.

Comments

The Comment feature allows reviewers to add notes to selected text. Different individuals who review a document make different comments about the same topic. Comments are displayed in a balloon in the margin of a document or in the Reviewing Pane. In Print Layout View, the balloons containing comments are displayed. If Comments are not visible on the screen, click **View**, **Markup** to view the comments.

To insert a comment in a document:

1. Select the text or item on which you want to comment, or click at the end of the text.

2. Click the **Insert** menu; click **Comment**.

3. Type the comment in the balloon that displays. To edit a comment, click in the balloon and make the desired changes.

All defenses must be player-to-player, but double-teaming is allowed within the three point line. Within the lane, all defenders may go after the ball.

Comment [SHVH1]: Do you prefer the term man-to-man or player-to-player?

To delete comments:

1. Display the Reviewing toolbar (**View, Toolbars, Reviewing**).

2. Click the **Reject Change/Delete Comment** button on the Reviewing toolbar. To delete all comments, click the down arrow on that button and choose **Delete All Comments in Document**.

Final Showing Markup ▾ Show ▾

To respond to a comment, click in the comment; then click **Insert Comment** on the Reviewing toolbar.

All defenses must be player-to-player, but double-teaming is allowed within the three point line. Within the lane, all defenders may go after the ball.

Comment [SHVH1]: Do you prefer the term man-to-man or player-to-player for the handbook?

Comment [CMF2R1]: I prefer man-to-man because the referees and other coaches use that term.

Drill 4
TECHNIQUE BUILDERS
Key each line once; DS between groups; repeat.

TECHNIQUE TIP

Concentrate on keeping hands and fingers quiet. Reach directly from the top to bottom rows.

adjacent keys

1 I saw her at an airport at a tropical resort leaving on a cruise.

2 Is assessing potential important in a traditional career program?

3 The boisterous boys were playing on a trampoline near an airport.

4 Three policemen were cruising down that street in Freeport today.

long, direct reach

5 The brave driver swerved to avoid the RV and the boy on the curb.

6 The umpire must check the Brums for number of pitches in one day.

7 The happy bride and groom decided on nuptials preceded by brunch.

8 The nervous mother decided she must keep Marv at a small nursery.

| 1 | 2 | 3 | 4 | 5 | 6 | 7 | 8 | 9 | 10 | 11 | 12 | 13 |

Drill 5
REACH FOR NEW GOALS

1. From the second or third column at the right, choose a goal 2–3 *gwam* higher than your best rate on either straight or statistical copy.

2. Take 1' writings on that sentence; try to finish it the number of times shown at the top of the goal list.

3. If you reach your goal, take 1' writings on the next line. If you don't reach your goal, use the preceding line.

		1' timing	
	words	6 times *gwam*	5 times *gwam*
Do they blame me for the goal?	6	36	30
The 2 men may enamel 17 oboes.	6	36	30
The auditor may handle the problem.	7	42	35
Did the 4 chaps focus the #75 lens?	7	42	35
She did vow to fight for the right name.	8	48	40
He paid 10 men to fix a pen for 3 ducks.	8	48	40
The girl may cycle down to the dormant field.	9	54	45
The 27 girls paid their $9 to go to the lake.	9	54	45
The ensign works with vigor to dismantle the auto.	10	60	50
Bob may work problems 8 and 9; Sid did problem 40.	10	60	50
The form may entitle a visitor to pay for such a kayak.	11	66	55
They kept 7 panels and 48 ivory emblems for 29 chapels.	11	66	55

| 1 | 2 | 3 | 4 | 5 | 6 | 7 | 8 | 9 | 10 | 11 |

Drill 6
IMPROVE CONCENTRATION
Set a left tab at 3.5" for the addresses. Key the Internet addresses in column 2 exactly as they are listed. Accuracy is critical.

New York City Tourist website	http://www.nycvisit.com
A trip to outer space	http://spacelink.msfc.nasa.gov
Search engine	http://webcrawler.com
Government Printing Office access	http://www.access.gpo.gov
Information Today, Inc	http://www.infotoday.com
Trend Micro virus scan	http://www.antivirus.com

To replace text:

1. Click **Edit** on the menu bar; then click **Replace**.

2. Enter the text you wish to locate in the Find what box.

3. Key the replacement text in the Replace with box.

4. Click **Find Next** to find the first occurrence of the text.

5. Click **Replace** to replace one occurrence or click **Replace All** to replace all occurrences of the text.

✳ **DISCOVER**

Click the **Format** and **Special** buttons in the extended Find and Replace dialog box to learn about search options for formats and other elements.

Find and Replace

Find | Replace | Go To

Find what: Workgroup A
Options: Search Down

Replace with: Team A

Less ✸ | Replace | Replace All | Find Next | Cancel

Search Options
Search: Down
☐ Match case
☐ Find whole words only
☐ Use wildcards
☐ Sounds like (English)
☐ Find all word forms (English)

Replace
Format ▾ | Special ▾ | No Formatting

Drill 1   FIND AND REPLACE

1. Open *restructure* from the data files.

2. Find the word *restructuring* the first place it appears.

3. Find the second and third occurrences of *restructuring*.

4. Find *Workgroup A* and replace it with *Team A*.

5. Edit the document so that the letter is formatted correctly as a block-style letter.

6. Save the document as *51c-drill1*.

✳ 7. Open *meade* from the data files. Search the document for text formatted in Arial. In the Find and Replace dialog box, click **Format**, **Font**, and then select **Arial**. Search again to find all occurrences of highlighting; then close the document without saving any changes.

Thesaurus

The Thesaurus is a tool that enables you to look up words and replace them with synonyms, antonyms, or related words.

To use the Thesaurus:

1. Position the insertion point in the word you wish to replace.

2. Click **Tools** on the menu, click **Language**, and then click **Thesaurus**.

3. If more than one meaning appears, select the appropriate meaning.

4. Point to the desired synonym or antonym, click the down arrow, and then click **Insert**.

TIP

An alternative way to use the Thesaurus is to position the insertion point in a word and right-click the mouse. Select **Synonyms** and then the desired word or **Thesaurus** for more information.

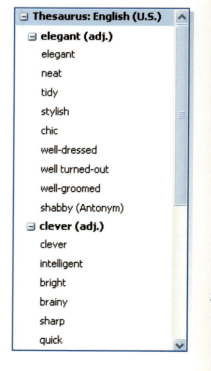

Thesaurus: English (U.S.)
⊟ **elegant (adj.)**
 elegant
 neat
 tidy
 stylish
 chic
 well-dressed
 well turned-out
 well-groomed
 shabby (Antonym)
⊟ **clever (adj.)**
 clever
 intelligent
 bright
 brainy
 sharp
 quick

Thesaurus: English (U.S.)
⊟ **kind (adj.)**
 kind
 liberal   Insert
 bighearte   Copy
 openhan   Look Up

Drill 7

ASSESS SKILL GROWTH

These writings are available as Diagnostic Writings in *Keyboarding Pro.* Access Diagnostic Writings from the Numeric & Skill menu.

OPEN SCREEN OPTION

1. Key 1' writings on each paragraph of a timing. Note that paragraphs within a timing increase by two words.
   Goal: to complete each paragraph
2. Key a 3' timing on the entire writing.

 all letters

To access writings on *MicroPace Pro*, key **W** and the timing number. For example, key **W8** for *Writing 8.*

gwam

| | 1' | 3' |

Writing 8

Any of us whose target is to achieve success in our professional | 13 | 4
lives will understand that we must learn how to work in harmony | 26 | 8
with others whose paths may cross ours daily. | 35 | 12

We will, unquestionably, work for, with, and beside people, just | 13 | 16
as they will work for, with, and beside us. We will judge them, | 26 | 20
as most certainly they are going to be judging us. | 38 | 24

A lot of people realize the need for solid working relations and | 13 | 28
have a rule that treats others as they, themselves, expect to be | 26 | 33
treated. This seems to be a sound, practical idea for them. | 40 | 37

Writing 9

I spoke with one company visitor recently; and she was very | 13 | 4
much impressed, she said, with the large amount of work she had noted | 26 | 9
being finished by one of our front office workers. | 36 | 12

I told her how we had just last week recognized this very person | 13 | 16
for what he had done, for output, naturally, but also because of | 26 | 21
its excellence. We know this person has that "magic touch." | 38 | 25

This "magic touch" is the ability to do a fair amount of work in | 13 | 29
a fair amount of time. It involves a desire to become ever more | 26 | 34
efficient without losing quality--the "touch" all workers should | 39 | 38
have. | 40 | 38

Writing 10

Isn't it great just to untangle and relax after you have keyed a | 13 | 4
completed document? Complete, or just done? No document is | 25 | 8
quite complete until it has left you and passed to the next step. | 38 | 13

There are desirable things that must happen to a document before | 13 | 17
you surrender it. It must be read carefully, first of all, for | 26 | 22
meaning to find words that look right but aren't. Read word for | 39 | 26
word. | 40 | 26

Check all figures and exact data, like a date or time, with your | 13 | 31
principal copy. Make sure format details are right. Only then, | 26 | 35
print or remove the work and scrutinize to see how it might look | 39 | 39
to a recipient. | 42 | 40

1' | 1 | 2 | 3 | 4 | 5 | 6 | 7 | 8 | 9 | 10 | 11 | 12 | 13 |
3' | 1 | 2 | 3 | 4 |

Edit Letters

5la
Key each line twice SS.

1 When Jorg moves away, quickly place five dozen gloves in the box.
2 Flight 372 leaves at 10:46 a.m. and arrives in Omaha at 9:58 p.m.
3 I obtain unusual services from a number of celebrated decorators.
4 She may sign an authentic name and title to amend this endowment.

| 1 | 2 | 3 | 4 | 5 | 6 | 7 | 8 | 9 | 10 | 11 | 12 | 13 |

5lb Timed Writings
1. Key one 3' timing.
2. Key one 5' writing.
   Strive for control.

 all letters

	gwam	3'	5'

Subtle differences exist among role models, mentors, and sponsors. A role model is a person you can emulate, or one who provides a good example to follow. A mentor is one who will advise, coach, or guide you when you need information about your job or your organization. A sponsor is a person who will support you or recommend you for a position or a new responsibility.

One person may fill all three roles, or several people may serve as role models, mentors, or sponsors. These individuals usually have higher ranks than you do, which means they will be able to get information that you and your peers may not have. Frequently, a mentor will share information with you that will enable you to make good decisions about your career.

Line-by-line gwam 3'/5':
4 | 2 | 32
8 | 5 | 35
12 | 7 | 37
16 | 10 | 40
21 | 12 | 42
25 | 15 | 45
30 | 18 | 48
34 | 20 | 50
38 | 23 | 53
42 | 25 | 55
46 | 28 | 58
50 | 30 | 60

3' | 1 | 2 | 3 | 4 |
5' | 1 | 2 | 3 |

new functions

5lc

Find and Replace

Find is used to locate text, formatting, footnotes, graphics, and other items within a document. Replace substitutes new text, formatting, or other items for those that are found.

In the Find and Replace dialog box, click **Highlight all items found in** and select the document to find all occurrences of the text. Clicking the **More** button displays additional search options, such as *Match case* or *Find whole words only*.

To find text:

1. Click the **Edit** menu and click **Find**.
2. Enter text to be located in the Find what box.
3. Click **Find Next** to find the next occurrence.

Find and Replace dialog box:
Find | Replace | Go To
Find what: Workgroup A
☐ Highlight all items found in:
Main Document
More ▾ | Find Next | Close

ASSESS SKILL

To access writings on *MicroPace Pro*, key **W** and the timing number. For example, key **W11** for *Writing 11*.

The writings are available as Diagnostic Writings in *Keyboarding Pro*.

Writing 11

		4		8		12		

Anyone who expects some day to find an excellent job should 4 | 34

begin now to learn the value of accuracy. To be worth anything, 8 | 38

completed work must be correct, without question. Naturally, we 13 | 43

realize that the human aspect of the work equation always raises 17 | 47

the prospect of errors; but we should understand that those same 20 | 51

errors can be found and fixed. Every completed job should carry 26 | 56

at least one stamp: the stamp of pride in work that is exemplary. 30 | 60

Writing 12

No question about it: Many personal problems we face today 4 | 34

arise from the fact that we earthlings have never been very wise 8 | 38

consumers. We haven't consumed our natural resources well; as a 13 | 43

result, we have jeopardized much of our environment. We excused 17 | 47

our behavior because we thought that our stock of most resources 20 | 51

had no limit. So, finally, we are beginning to realize just how 26 | 56

indiscreet we were; and we are taking steps to rebuild our world. 30 | 60

Writing 13

When I see people in top jobs, I know I'm seeing people who 4 | 34

sell. I'm not just referring to employees who labor in a retail 8 | 38

outlet; I mean those people who put extra effort into convincing 13 | 43

others to recognize their best qualities. They, themselves, are 17 | 47

the commodity they sell; and their optimum tools are appearance, 20 | 51

language, and personality. They look great, they talk and write 26 | 56

well; and, with candid self-confidence, they meet you eye to eye. 30 | 60

3' | 1 | 2 | 3 | 4 |

[50c-d1]
Memo from Template

1. Create the following memo using the Professional style memo. Do not use the Memo Wizard.
2. Add the company name **Ocean Springs, Inc.**
3. Add your reference initials.
4. Save as *50c-d1* and print.

To: Richard M. Taylor | From: Dianne Gibson | CC: Bruce Diamond | Date: Current date | Re: Trail Design

Last week, Madilyn signed the contract for the trail design for Phase 1 of our Georgetown property. NatureLink was selected as the contractor. This firm was chosen because of its extensive experience in selecting interpretative sites, designing trails, and installing boardwalks to protect wetlands and environmentally sensitive areas.

The first onsite meeting is scheduled for November 10. We plan to meet at the main entrance at 10:30 a.m. to tour the property and review the procedures that NatureLink plans to use in designing the trails near the red cockaded woodpecker (RCW) habitat. Since the RCW is an endangered species, we want to balance the desires of ecotourists to observe these birds and the need to protect them.

Please let me know if you plan to participate in the initial meeting with NatureLink.

[50c-d2]
Fax Cover Sheet

1. Use the fax template you created in *50b-drill3* to create a fax cover sheet for the memo you created in *50c-d1*.
2. Send the fax to **Richard M. Taylor**; Fax: **846-555-0172**; Telephone: **846-555-0139**. Change the number of pages to 2. (Do not include comments.)
3. Save as *50c-d2*.

✳ Note that recently used templates can be accessed from the list in the New Document task pane.

✳ DISCOVER

Recently Used Templates and Wizards

Templates
Search online for:

[ ] [Go]

Templates on Office Online
On my computer...
On my Web sites...

Recently used templates
49b-drill3
Professional Fax
Memo Wizard
Professional Memo

These writings may be used as Diagnostic Writings.

To access writings on *MicroPace Pro*, key **W** and the timing number. For example, key **W14** for *Writing 14*.

Writing 14

gwam 1' | 3'

What do you expect when you travel to a foreign country? 12 | 4
Quite a few people realize that one of the real joys of 23 | 8
traveling is to get a brief glimpse of how others think, work, 36 | 12
and live. 40 | 12

The best way to enjoy a different culture is to learn as 11 | 16
much about it as you can before you leave home. Then you can 24 | 20
concentrate on being a good guest rather than trying to find 36 | 24
local people who can meet your needs. 44 | 27

Writing 15

gwam 1' | 3'

What do you enjoy doing in your free time? Health experts 12 | 4
tell us that far too many people choose to be lazy rather than 24 | 8
to be active. The result of that decision shows up in our 36 | 12
weight. 37 | 13

Working to control what we weigh is not easy, and seldom 12 | 16
can it be done quickly. However, it is quite important if our 24 | 21
weight exceeds what it should be. Part of the problem results 37 | 25
from the amount and type of food we eat. 44 | 27

If we want to look fit, we should include exercise as a 11 | 31
substantial part of our weight loss plan. Walking at least 23 | 35
thirty minutes each day at a very fast rate can make a big 35 | 39
difference both in our appearance and in the way we feel. 47 | 42

Writing 16

gwam 1' | 3'

Doing what we like to do is quite important; however, 10 | 4
liking what we have to do is equally important. As you ponder 23 | 8
both of these concepts, you may feel that they are the same, 36 | 12
but they are not the same. 41 | 14

If we could do only those things that we prefer to do, the 12 | 18
chances are that we would do them exceptionally well. Generally, 25 | 22
we will take more pride in doing those things we like doing, 37 | 26
and we will not quit until we get them done right. 47 | 29

We realize, though, that we cannot restrict the things 11 | 33
that we must do just to those that we want to do. Therefore, 23 | 37
we need to build an interest in and an appreciation of all the 36 | 41
tasks that we must do in our positions. 44 | 44

1' | 1 | 2 | 3 | 4 | 5 | 6 | 7 | 8 | 9 | 10 | 11 | 12 |
3' | 1 | 2 | 3 | 4 |

Editing Templates

Templates can be edited, customized, and saved as templates so that you do not need to insert repetitive information, such as company name or address, each time you use it. Customized templates are stored under the General tab in the Templates dialog box.

To customize a template:

1. Click the File menu; click **New**; and then click **On my computer** in the task pane.
2. In the Templates dialog box, click the desired tab, such as **Letters & Faxes**.
3. Click **Template** under Create New and then double-click the template icon you wish to customize, such as **Professional Fax**.
4. Complete the company and contact information.
5. Use **Save as** to name and save the template.

To use the customized template:

1. Click the **General** tab in the Templates dialog box.
2. Double-click the template you customized.

D r i l l   3 | **CUSTOMIZE A TEMPLATE**

1. Click the **Letters & Faxes** tab in the Templates dialog box and then select **Professional Fax**.

2. Click **Template** under Create New and click **OK**. Fill in the company information at the top of the template with the following:

Create New
○ Document   ● Template

Ocean Springs, Inc.

2948 Toms Creek Road, Hopkins, SC 29061-5387

Telephone: 803-555-0197 Fax: 803-555-0199

3. Save as *50b-drill3* and print. Close the document.

4. Click the **General** tab in the Templates dialog box. Notice that the file you created, *50b-drill3*, is saved as a template. It can be opened and a message added.

2948 Toms Creek Road, Hopkins, SC 29061-5387
Telephone: 803-555-0197 Fax: 803-555-0199

Ocean Springs, Inc.

Writing 17

gwam 1' | 3'

Many people like to say just how lucky a person is when	11	4	29
he or she succeeds in doing something well. Does luck play a	24	8	33
large role in success? In some cases, it might have a small	36	12	37
effect.	37	13	38
Being in the right place at the right time may help, but	11	16	41
hard work may help far more than luck. Those who just wait for	24	20	46
luck should not expect quick results and should realize luck	36	24	50
may never come.	39	26	51

```
1'  |  1  |  2  |  3  |  4  |  5  |  6  |  7  |  8  |  9  | 10  | 11  | 12  |
3'        |     1     |        2        |        3        |        4        |
```

Writing 18

gwam 1' | 3'

New golfers must learn to zero in on just a few social	11	4	39
rules. Do not talk, stand close, or move around when another	23	8	44
person is hitting. Be ready to play when it is your turn.	35	12	47
Take practice swings in an area away from other people.	11	15	51
Let the group behind you play through if your group is slow.	24	20	55
Do not rest on your club on the green when waiting your turn.	36	23	59
Set your other clubs down off the green. Leave the green	12	27	63
quickly when done; update your card on the next tee. Be sure	24	31	67
to leave the course in good condition. Always have a good time.	37	36	72

```
1'  |  1  |  2  |  3  |  4  |  5  |  6  |  7  |  8  |  9  | 10  | 11  | 12  |
3'        |     1     |        2        |        3        |        4        |
```

Writing 19

gwam 1' | 3'

Do you know how to use time wisely? If you do, then its	11	4	51
proper use can help you organize and run a business better.	24	8	55
If you find that your daily problems tend to keep you from	35	12	59
planning properly, then perhaps you are not using time well.	48	16	63
You may find that you spend too much time on tasks that are	60	20	67
not important. Plan your work to save valuable time.	70	24	70
A firm that does not plan is liable to run into trouble.	12	27	74
A small firm may have trouble planning. It is important	23	31	78
to know just where the firm is headed. A firm may have a	35	35	82
fear of learning things it would rather not know. To say	46	39	86
that planning is easy would be absurd. It requires lots of	58	43	90
thinking and planning to meet the expected needs of the firm.	70	47	94

```
1'  |  1  |  2  |  3  |  4  |  5  |  6  |  7  |  8  |  9  | 10  | 11  | 12  |
3'        |     1     |        2        |        3        |        4        |
```

Drill 1 | MEMO TEMPLATE

1. Create a new document using the Professional memo template.

2. Select **Company Name Here**; key **Ocean Springs, Inc.**

3. Read the instructions on the memo template and then key the heading information provided in the next column. The date is automatically inserted.

To: Richard M. Taylor
From: Dianne Gibson
CC: Bruce Diamond
Date: Current date
Re: Trail Design

4. Save the document as *50b-drill1* and print one copy.

5. Check the folder where your file is saved. The file has the extension *.doc* because it was created as a document.

---

help keywords

wizards

Wizards

Wizards enable you to enter information into different document templates by responding to questions. Many of the tabs in the Template dialog box contain wizards. Note that the format of memos created with templates and wizards may be slightly different from the memos that you have previously created.

To create a new document using a wizard:

1. Click the **File** menu and click **New**.

2. Click **On my computer** in the task pane.

3. In the Templates dialog box, click the desired tab, such as **Memos**.

4. Double-click the **Wizard** icon and follow directions to add information.

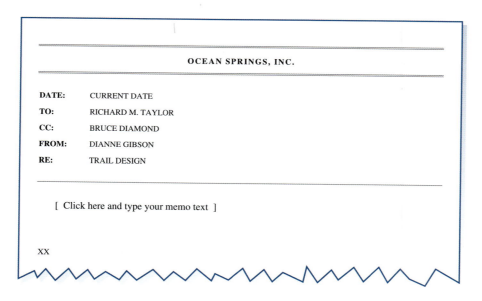

OCEAN SPRINGS, INC.

DATE:	CURRENT DATE
TO:	RICHARD M. TAYLOR
CC:	BRUCE DIAMOND
FROM:	DIANNE GIBSON
RE:	TRAIL DESIGN

[Click here and type your memo text]

XX

Drill 2 | MEMO WIZARD

1. Use the Memo Wizard to create the same memo you did in Drill 1; however select **Elegant** style for this memo.

2. Key **Ocean Springs, Inc.** as the title. Click the **Next** button to move through the various screens to key the necessary information.

3. Leave those fields for which you have no information blank or deselect them. Key your initials as the typist.

4. Click the **Finish** button to view the memo.

5. Save the memo as *50b-drill2* and print.

Writings 20 and 21 are available as Diagnostic Writings.

To access writings on *MicroPace Pro*, key **W** and the timing number. For example, key **W20** for *Writing 20*.

Writing 20

gwam 3' | 5'

If asked, most people will agree that some people have far more creative skills than others, and they will also say that these skills are in great demand by most organizations. A follow-up question is in order. Are you born with creative skills or can you develop them? No easy answer to that question exists, but it is worth spending a bit of time pondering.

If creative skills can be developed, then the next issue is how can you develop these skills. One way is to approach each task with a determination to solve the problem and a refusal to accept failure. If the normal way of doing a job does not work, just keep trying things never tried before until you reach a good solution. This is called thinking outside the box.

3'	5'
4	2 · 21
8	5 · 34
12	7 · 37
17	10 · 39
21	13 · 42
24	15 · 44
28	17 · 46
32	19 · 49
37	22 · 51
41	25 · 54
45	27 · 56
49	29 · 58

```
3' | 1       2       3       4    |
5' |     1         2         3     |
```

Writing 21

gwam 1' | 3'

Figures are not as easy to key as many of the words we use. Balanced-hand figures such as 16, 27, 38, 49, and 50, although fairly easy, are slower to key because each one requires longer reaches and uses more time per stroke.

Figures such as 12, 45, 67, and 90 are even more difficult because they are next to one another and each uses just a single hand to key. Because of their size, bigger numbers such as 178, 349, and 1,220 create extra speed losses.

1'	3'
12	4 · 36
25	8 · 40
37	12 · 44
45	16 · 46
12	20 · 50
25	25 · 54
39	29 · 59
45	32 · 61

```
1' | 1 | 2 | 3 | 4 | 5 | 6 | 7 | 8 | 9 | 10 | 11 | 12 | 13 |
3' |   1   |     2     |     3     |     4     |
```

Drill 8
SKILL TRANSFER

1. Set the Timer for 2'. Take a 2' writing on paragraph 1. Do not save.
2. Set the Timer for 2'. Take a 2' writing on paragraph 2. Do not save.
3. Take two or more 2' writings on the slower paragraph. Do not save.

gwam 1' | 2'

Few people attain financial success without some kind of planning. People who realize the value of prudent spending and saving are those who set up a budget. A budget helps individuals determine just how much they can spend and how much they can save so that they will not squander their money recklessly.

Keeping records is a crucial *vital* part of a budget. Complete *A detailing* records of *all* income and expenses *ditures* over a period of a number of *several* months will help to determine what bills, as water *like utilities* or rent, are static *fixed* and which are flexible. To get the most out of your income, pay *focus* attention to *on* the items that you can modify *be changed*.

1'	2'
11	6
24	12
36	18
49	24
61	31
12	6
24	12
37	18
49	25
61	30

```
1' | 1 | 2 | 3 | 4 | 5 | 6 | 7 | 8 | 9 | 10 | 11 | 12 |
2' |   1   |   2   |   3   |   4   |   5   |   6   |
```

Memo Templates and Wizards

WARMUP
50a
Key each line twice SS.

alphabet 1 Jacki might analyze the data by answering five complex questions.

figures 2 Memo 67 asks if the report on Bill 35-48 is due the 19th or 20th.

double letters 3 Aaron took accounting lessons at a community college last summer.

easy 4 Hand Bob a bit of cocoa, a pan of cod, an apricot, and six clams.

| 1 | 2 | 3 | 4 | 5 | 6 | 7 | 8 | 9 | 10 | 11 | 12 | 13 |

NEW FUNCTIONS
50b

Templates

A template is a master copy of a set of predefined styles for a particular type of document. Templates are available for formatting documents such as a memo, fax, or letter. A template can be used exactly as it exists, or it can be modified or customized and saved as a new template. The tabs on the Templates dialog box indicate the variety of templates that *Word* has available. You can also attach a template to a document.

help keywords

templates

To use an existing template:

1. Click the **File** menu and click **New**.

2. In the New Document task pane, click **On my computer**.

3. In the Templates dialog box, click the desired tab, such as **Memos**.

4. Select the desired memo style, such as **Contemporary**, **Elegant**, or **Professional**.

5. Click **OK**. Follow the directions on the template to key the desired document.

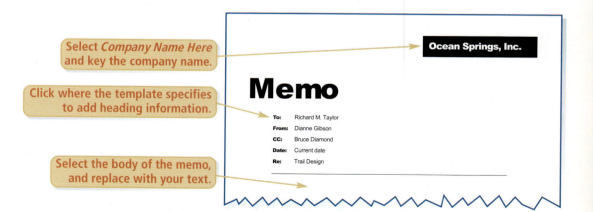

Select *Company Name Here* and key the company name. → **Ocean Springs, Inc.**

Click where the template specifies to add heading information.

Memo

To: Richard M. Taylor
From: Dianne Gibson
CC: Bruce Diamond
Date: Current date
Re: Trail Design

Select the body of the memo, and replace with your text.

ACTIVITY 1
Open Web Browser

Know Your Browser

The browser provides you with tools to use the Internet. It will display a toolbar that allows you to save information, print, and navigate the Internet. Commonly used browsers are Internet Explorer, Netscape Navigator, and America Online.

To activate the Web browser:

If you see an icon on the Windows screen for the Web browser, double-click it. If the icon is not on the windows screen, click the **Start** button, then **Programs**. A Web browser should be listed in the Programs menu. Click the Web browser to open it.

Drill 1

1. Follow the steps above to activate your Web browser.
2. Continue reading below.

Open Website

With the Web browser open, click **Open** or **Open Page** from the File menu (or click the **Open** button if it is available on your browser's toolbar). Key the Web address (e.g., http://www.weather.com) and click **OK** or **Open**. The website displays.

Open Page

Enter the World Wide Web location (URL) or specify the local file you would like to open:

`http://www.weather.com`   Choose File...

Open location or file in: ○ Composer
                           ● Navigator   Open   Cancel   Help

(*Shortcut*: Click inside the Location or Address entry box, key the Web address, and press ENTER.)

Bookmarks   Go to: `http://www.weather.com`

A **Web address**—commonly called the URL or Uniform Resource Locator—consists of four parts:

1. The transfer protocol used to transport the file
2. The domain name of the computer on which the file resides
3. The pathname of the folder or directory in which the file resides
4. The name of the file

The domain name contains an extension, which includes a period followed by three letters. The extension identifies the type of organization to which the website belongs.

.com	Business and other commercial enterprises
.edu	Educational institution
.gov	Government agency, bureau, or department
.mil	Military unit or agency
.org	Charitable or nonprofit organization

[49d-d1]

Memo

1. Key and edit the memo below. Use plain paper; position heading at approximately 2.1".
2. Save as *49d-d1* and print.
3. Cut the last sentence of paragraph 2.
4. Use drag-and-drop editing to move the first paragraph below the second paragraph; adjust spacing, if necessary.
5. Open *punctuality* from the data files. Copy this paragraph to *49d-d1* as the final paragraph.
6. Proofread, save as *49d-d1a*, and print.

TO: All Employees
FROM: Taylor Westfield
DATE: Current date
SUBJECT: Punctuality—Does It Really Matter?

What message does ~~being late~~ *lateness* convey to others. *?* This question perhaps is the most important one. The message conveyed to ~~some~~ *most* people is that you think your time is more important than ~~there~~ *ir* time. It conveys rudeness and lack of care about others. It also convey*s* that you are not organized and ⟨can't⟩ *write out* get things done in a timely manner. Being tardy ~~also~~ forces you to make embarrassing excuses for not being on time or not having work done on time. Most people give little credibility to lame excuses, especially if you have a reputation for being tardy. These messages clearly are not in anybody's best interest. Punctuality really does matter!

Just how important is punctuality? What difference do a few minutes one way or the other make? A local newspaper sports headline recently read, "Punctuality—Not Performance—determines Outcome!" A defending champion hurdler, and by all accounts one who was unbeatable and assured to repeat the title, was a few minutes late for the championship meet because of traffic problems and missed the 110-meter hurdle event. At least this young athlete learned the ~~price~~ *cost* of being late early in life. The question is, have we learned our lesson yet?

[49d-d2]
E-mail

1. Compose an e-mail to your instructor. Indicate that you are sharing an interesting memo that the training manager of the company where you are employed part-time sent to all employees. Be sure to tell your instructor that you asked permission to share the e-mail with your instructor and class. Make one or two comments about the content of the memo.
2. Attach *49d-d1a*. Print a copy of the e-mail.

D r i l l   2

Identify the domain name for each site. Identify the filename in #3 and #4.

1. http://fbla-pbl.org_____

2. http://www.army.mil_____

3. http://www.dhs.gov/dhspublic_____

4. http://www.cnn.com/TRAVEL_____

Explore the Browser's Toolbar

The browser's toolbar is very valuable when surfing the Internet. Become familiar with your browser's toolbar by studying the screen. Browsers may vary slightly.

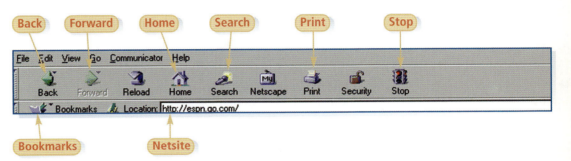

Netsite entry box	Displays the active URL or website address.
Back	Moves to websites or pages visited since opening the browser.
Forward	Moves forward to sites visited prior to using the Back button. (The Forward button is ghosted if the Back button has not been used.)
Print	Prints a Web page.
Home	Returns to the Web page designated as the Home or Start Page.
Stop	Stops the computer's search for a website.
Search	Opens one of the Internet search engines.
Bookmarks	Moves to the list of websites marked for easy access.

D r i l l   3

1. Open the following websites:

   a. http://www.nike.com

   b. http://www.realage.com

   c. http://www.mapquest.com

   d. A site of your choice

2. Click the **Back** button twice. The_____website displays.

3. Click the **Forward** button once. The_____website displays.

4. Print the active Web page.

Drill 3 | CLIPBOARD

1. Open *effective pres* from the data files.

2. Display the Office Clipboard (**Edit, Office Clipboard**) and clear all items from it.

3. Select the heading **Opening** and the paragraph that follows, and cut them.

4. Select the heading **Presentation Body** and the paragraph that follows, and cut them.

5. Select the heading **Closing** and the paragraph that follows, and cut them.

6. Place the insertion point a DS below the paragraph with the heading *Planning and Preparing Presentations* and paste all items on the Clipboard at once; adjust line spacing, if necessary.

7. Save as *49c-drill3* and print the document.

Drag-and-Drop Editing

Another way to edit text is to use the mouse. With drag and drop, you can move or copy text using the mouse. To move copy, you must first select the text, then hold down the left mouse button, and drag the text to the desired location. The mouse pointer displays a rectangle indicating that copy is being moved. Release the mouse button to "drop" the text into the desired location.

Follow a similar procedure to copy (or duplicate) text. Hold down the left mouse button and the CTRL key, and drag the text to the desired location. A plus sign indicates the text is being copied.

Drill 4 | DRAG AND DROP

1. Open *effective pres* from the data files.

2. Use drag and drop to make the same changes that you made in *49c-drill3*.

3. Save the document as *49c-drill4* and print it.

Drill 5 | COPY AND PASTE

1. Open *49c-drill4* and then open *effective pres 2* from the data files.

2. Copy the three paragraphs with the headings *Opening*, *Presentation Body*, and *Closing* from *49c-drill4* and paste the paragraphs under the heading *Planning and Preparing Presentations* in the *effective pres2* file.

3. Adjust the line spacing, if necessary.

4. Save the document as *49c-drill5*.

Bookmark a Favorite Website

When readers put a book aside, they insert a bookmark to mark the place. Internet users also add bookmarks to mark their favorite websites or sites of interest for browsing later.

To add a bookmark:

1. Open the desired website.

2. Click **Bookmarks** and then **Add Bookmark** or **Favorites** and then **Add to Favorites**.

To use a bookmark:

1. Click **Bookmarks** (or **Communicator**, **Favorites**, or **Window Bookmarks**).

2. Select the desired bookmark. Click or double-click, depending on your browser. The desired website displays.

D r i l l   4

1. Open these favorite websites and bookmark them on your browser.

   a. http://www.weather.com

   b. http://www.cnn.com

   c. http://ask.com

   d. Key the Web address of a city you would like to visit (http://www.destin.com).

2. Use the bookmarks to go to the following websites to find answers to the questions shown.

   a. The Weather Channel—What is today's temperature in your city?_____

   b. CNN—What is today's top news story?_____

   c. Ask Jeeves. Ask a question; then find the answer. _____

   d. City website you bookmarked—Find one attraction in the city to visit._____

ACTIVITY 2

Set Up E-mail Addresses

Electronic Mail

Electronic mail or **e-mail** refers to electronic messages sent by one computer user to another computer user. To be able to send or receive e-mail, you must have an e-mail address, an e-mail program, and access to the Internet or an intranet (in-house network).

Many search engines such as Excite, Google, Lycos, Hotbot, and others provide free e-mail via their websites. These e-mail programs allow users to set up an e-mail address and then send and retrieve e-mail messages. To set up an account and obtain an e-mail address, the user must (1) agree to the terms of agreements, (2) complete an online registration form, and (3) create an e-mail name and password.

D r i l l   1

1. Click the **Search** button on the browser's toolbar. Find a search engine that offers free e-mail.

2. Click **Free E-mail** or **Mail**. (Terms will vary.)

3. Read the Terms of Agreement and accept.

4. Enter an e-mail name. This name will be the login-name portion of your e-mail address.

5. Enter a password for your e-mail account. For security reasons, do not share your password, do not leave it where others can use it, and avoid choosing pet names or birth dates.

6. Review the entire registration form and submit it. You will be notified immediately that your e-mail account has been established. (If your e-mail name is already in use by someone else, you may be instructed to choose a different name before your account can be established.)

Drill 2 | CUT AND PASTE BETWEEN DOCUMENTS

1. Open *resume* from the data files.

2. Open *job objective* from the data files.

3. Click **resume** on the Windows taskbar. Note that you can move from one document to the other by clicking the document name on the taskbar.

4. With *resume* displayed on the screen, click the **Window** menu and select **job objective**.

5. Select the second job objective and click **Copy**.

6. Click **resume** on the Windows taskbar and check to see that the insertion point is positioned a DS below the heading at the left margin. Click **Paste**.

7. Save as *49c-drill2* and print.

help keywords

office clipboard

Office Clipboard

The **Clipboard** can store up to 24 items that have been cut or copied. The Clipboard displays in the side pane. If it is not displayed, click **Edit** on the menu bar and then **Office Clipboard** to display it. Note that each item on the Clipboard is displayed for easy reference. All items on the Clipboard can be pasted at once by clicking **Paste All**. A single item can be pasted by clicking on the item and selecting **Paste** from the drop-down menu.

All items on the Clipboard can be removed by clicking the **Clear All** button. A single item can be removed by clicking the item and selecting **Delete** from the drop-down menu.

When an item is pasted into a document, the Paste button smart tag provides options for formatting the text that has been pasted.

Office Clipboard

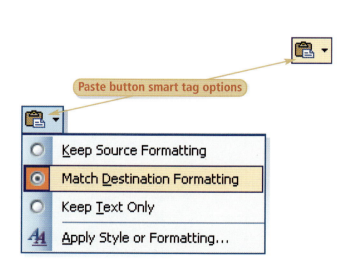

Paste button smart tag options

To format the text using the same format as the new document, click **Match Destination Formatting**. To format the text using the same format as the document from which the text was copied, click **Keep Source Formatting**.

Send E-mail Message

To send an e-mail message, you must have the address of the computer user you want to write. Business cards, letterheads, directories, etc., now include e-mail addresses. Often a telephone call is helpful in obtaining e-mail addresses. An e-mail address includes the user's login name followed by @ and the domain (sthomas@yahoo.com).

Creating an e-mail message is quite similar to preparing a memo. The e-mail header includes TO, FROM, and SUBJECT. Key the e-mail address of the recipient on the TO line, and compose a subject line that concisely describes the theme of your message. Your e-mail address will automatically display on the FROM line.

D r i l l   2

1. Open the search engine used to set up your e-mail account. Click **E-mail** or **Mail**. (Terms will vary.)

2. Enter your e-mail name and password when prompted.

E-mail Message 1

3. Enter the e-mail address of your instructor or another student. Compose a brief message describing the city you would like to visit. Mention one of the city's attractions (from Activity 1, Drill 4). Include a descriptive subject line. Send the message.

E-mail Message 2

4. Enter your e-mail address. The subject is **Journal Entry for March 29, 20--**. Compose a message to show your reflections on how keyboarding is useful to you. Share your progress in the course and your plan for improving this week. Send the message.

Respond to Messages

Replying to e-mail messages

Reading one's e-mail messages and responding promptly are important rules of netiquette (etiquette for the Internet). However, avoid responding too quickly to sensitive situations.

Forwarding e-mail messages

Received e-mail messages are often shared or forwarded to other e-mail users. Be sure to seek permission from the sender of the message before forwarding it to others.

D r i l l   3

1. Open your e-mail account if it is not open.

2. Read your e-mail messages and respond immediately and appropriately to any e-mail messages received from your instructor or fellow students. Click **Reply** to answer the message.

3. Forward the e-mail message titled *Journal Entry for March 29, 20--* to your instructor.

4. Delete all read messages.

Attach a Document to an E-mail Message

Electronic files can be attached to an e-mail message and sent to another computer electronically. Recipients of attached documents can transfer these documents to their computers and then open them for use.

D r i l l   4

1. Open your e-mail account if it is not open.

2. Create an e-mail message to your instructor that states your homework is attached. The subject line should include the specific homework assignment (**xx-profile**, for example).

3. Attach the file by clicking **Attach**. Use the browser to locate the homework assignment. (E-mail programs may vary.)

4. Send the e-mail message with the attached file.

Cut, Copy, and Paste

The Cut feature removes text or an image from a document and places it on the Office Clipboard. The Copy feature places a copy of text or an image from a document on the Clipboard. The Paste feature transfers a copy of the text or image from the Clipboard to a document.

To move text to a new location:

1. Select the text to be copied. Click **Cut** on the Standard toolbar.
2. Move the insertion point to the new location. Click **Paste**.

To copy text to a new location:

1. Select the text to be copied. Click **Copy** on the Standard toolbar.
2. Move the insertion point to the new location. Click **Paste**.

D r i l l   1   CUT AND PASTE

1. Open *cut and paste* from the data files.
2. Select **Cut and** in the first heading and cut it so the heading is *Paste*.
3. Select the heading **Paste** and the paragraph that follows it.
4. Move the selected copy below the last paragraph.
5. Key a line across the page.
6. Copy both paragraphs and paste them below the line.
7. Create the folder *Module 7 Keys* and save the document as *49c-drill1* in this folder. Save all documents for Module 7 in this folder.

Copy and Paste Between Documents

Multiple documents can be opened at the same time. Each document is displayed in its own window. To move from one document to another, click **Window** on the menu; then click the document name. You may also just click the document name on the Windows taskbar. Text can then be copied and pasted between documents.

To copy and paste between documents:

1. Open both documents.
2. Select the text you wish to copy in the source document; click the **Copy** button.
3. Move to the destination document and click the **Paste** button.

formatting Business Documents

2

Keyboarding
- To key about 40 *wam* with good accuracy.

Document Design Skills
- To format accurately business letters, memos, reports, and tables.
- To apply basic design skills to newsletters and announcements.

Word Processing Skills
- To learn the basic word processing competencies (Core).
- To create, edit, and format documents efficiently.

Communication Skills
- To apply proofreaders' marks and revise text.
- To compose simple e-mails and other documents.

MODULE 7

OBJECTIVES

- Edit memos and e-mail.
- Edit business letters.
- Edit tables.
- Edit reports.
- Build keying skill.
- Apply communication skills.

Editing Documents

Edit Memos and E-mail

WARMUP
49a
Key each line twice SS.

alphabet 1 Zack worked on five great projects and quickly became the expert.

figures 2 Kimberly sold 294 copies of the 518-page book at $37.60 per book.

double letters 3 Jeff's committee will add all the career books to that list soon.

easy 4 Pam may go with me to town to work for the auditor if he is busy.

| 1 | 2 | 3 | 4 | 5 | 6 | 7 | 8 | 9 | 10 | 11 | 12 | 13 |

49b Technique Builders
Key each line twice SS.

adjacent keys

5 were pool fast join tree guy trait cruise walk fare port trio buy

6 mere try career trade polka excite joint report revere riot quiet

7 Polly and Guy were trying to prepare a joint report very quickly.

long, direct reach

8 braced munch decide jumped many brave curve numb young hunt brunt

9 jungle nut glum bun precede muck break junk must plum nerve bunch

10 Cecilia munched on junk food while she hunted for her cat, Brent.

| 1 | 2 | 3 | 4 | 5 | 6 | 7 | 8 | 9 | 10 | 11 | 12 | 13 |

MODULE 3

Memos and E-mail

OBJECTIVES

- Open, create, save, preview, and print documents.
- Format text.
- Edit text.
- Create memos.
- Create e-mail.
- Apply communication skills.

LESSON 26

Get Started

NEW FUNCTIONS
26a

Start Word

You are about to learn the leading word processing package available today. *Microsoft Word®* accounts for more than 90 percent of all word processing use. *Word* is one of the applications in the *Microsoft Office 2003®* suite. At the same time, you will continue to develop your keyboarding skills. You will use *Word* to create and format professional-looking documents. *Word* will make keying documents such as memos, letters, tables, and reports easy and fun.

When you first start *Word*, the screen appears with two windows. The left area is a blank document screen where you can enter text. The right area, which is shown in this illustration, is called the **task pane**. The contents of the task pane change depending on the task you are performing at the time.

Note that this task pane gives you options to:

- Connect to Microsoft Online
- Open documents
- Create a new document

ACTIVITY 5

Map a Trip

Determining the route to your destination city is most important in ensuring a pleasant journey. The printed atlas is a valuable tool for mapping a trip; however, with today's technology, we can map our trips electronically using the Maps hyperlinks provided by several search engines. This invaluable site will search for the specific route you identify and provide you an overview map and turn-by-turn maps with text.

Drill

1. Open a search engine and locate the hyperlink for *Maps*. Your destination city is Asheville, North Carolina. Enter your city and state as the starting point. Search for a turn-by-turn map with text. Print the directions.

   What is the total distance? _____ What is the estimated time? _____

2. You are having a party and would like to include a map to your house with the invitation. Use your search engine to access Mapquest. Key your address in Mapquest to generate a map of your location.

3. Zoom in or out as needed so that the map will show adequate streets in the area for guests to locate your home. Print the map and trim it to fit in the invitation.

4. Use *Maps* from the AltaVista search engine to create a map of your city. (*Hint:* Click **More** if you don't see the Maps link.) Use the *SmartView* feature to display the Food and Dining establishments in your city. Click **Printable Version** to display the name, address, and telephone number of each restaurant and then print the information. You may wish to narrow the list to include only specific types of restaurants if you have a lot of them in your city.

ACTIVITY 6

Using Meta-Search Tools

It is time consuming to have to perform searches in several search engines. Meta-search tools are available that allow you to search several search engines simultaneously. ProFusion is an example of a meta-search tool that uses several search engines. After identifying the topic that you are researching, ProFusion will display a search screen listing some of the sources that it searches. In some cases, you can select which sources you would like searched.

Drill

1. Open the ProFusion website (http://www.profusion.com). Review the list of search groups and the related categories displayed, and then click the **Career** link.

   a. Key **MCSE** in the Search for box. (MCSE stands for Microsoft Certified Systems Engineer).

   b. Place a check mark in the High-Tech Jobs box and tap ENTER.

   c. Print the first page of the job listings, and then return to the ProFusion home page.

2. You can select from a list of search groups or key the topic in the Search box.

   a. Key **weather** in the Search box and tap ENTER. Select a link and find your current weather.

   b. Key **area code** in the Search box and tap ENTER. Use one of the links to find the area code for Jackson, Mississippi and Cincinnati, Ohio.

3. ProFusion allows you to select the links to be included in the meta-search.

   a. Select the category **Headline News** from the ProFusion home page.

   b. Place a check in BBC News, CNN, Time, and USNews boxes. Deselect other boxes that may be selected.

   c. Key **peace** in the Search for box and tap ENTER.

   d. Select an article and print it.

1. Turn on the computer and the monitor. When the *Windows* Log On screen displays, key your password and click **OK** to display the *Windows* desktop.

2. Click the **Start** button at the bottom of the screen. Point to **Programs** to display the Programs menu; then click **Microsoft Office Word 2003** to display the *Microsoft Word* document screen.

3. If the program does not fill the entire screen, you will need to maximize the window. You will learn about the Maximize button in the next section.

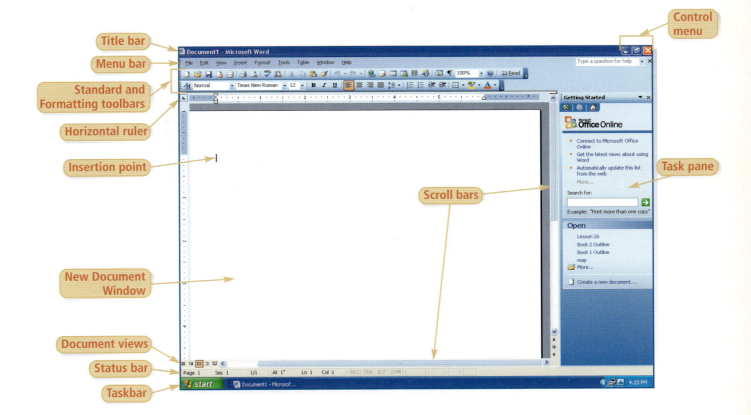

Title bar	Displays the name of the application and document that are currently open.
Control menu	Buttons that size (enlarge or shrink) and close a window. Buttons include Maximize/Minimize, Restore, and Close.
Menu bar	Displays drop-down menus from which commands can be selected.
Standard toolbar and Formatting toolbar	Display buttons that provide access to common commands. The name of each button displays when you point to it.
Horizontal ruler	Displays the margins, tabs, and indents. To change the display of the Ruler, choose **Ruler** from the View menu. A vertical ruler displays in Print Layout View.
New Document window	A blank area on the screen where you can enter text.
Task pane	Displays options for opening files and creating new documents.
Insertion point	Blinking vertical line that shows where the text you key will appear. Moving the pointer with the mouse does not move the insertion point until you click the mouse.
Document views	Display documents in five views: Normal, Web Layout, Print Layout, Outline, and Reading Layout.
Scroll bars	Enable you to move rapidly through documents.
Status bar	Displays information about the document such as page number and position of the insertion point.
Taskbar	Displays the Start button and whatever programs are currently running.

ACTIVITY 3

Explore Search Engines

Search engines will help you locate specific information on the World Wide Web (WWW). There are many search engines available, such as Yahoo, Google, AltaVista, Excite, AskJeeves, etc. Search engines will use different methods to search for your request, so the results you receive from them may differ. Because of this, you should use several search engines in order to obtain more complete results.

Go to a search engine by clicking the **Search** button on your Web browser or by keying the search engine URL in the Address box.

Drill

1. Click the **Search** button on your browser toolbar. Key **Yahoo** in the Search box to display the browser Yahoo.

2. Browse the hyperlinks available such as Weather, News, Sports, Maps, Movies, Music, etc.

3. Conduct the following search using Dogpile, a multithreaded search engine that searches multiple databases:

   a. Open the website for Dogpile (http://www.dogpile.com).

   b. In the Search entry box, key the keywords **American Psychological Association publications**; click **Go Fetch**.

4. Pick two of the following topics and search for each using three different search engines. Look over the first ten results you get from each search. Which search engine gave you the greatest number of promising results for each topic?

aerobics	antivirus software	career change
censorship	college financing	fighting terrorism

ACTIVITY 4

Search Yellow Pages

Searching the Yellow Pages for information on businesses and services is commonplace, both in business and at home. Let your computer do the searching for you the next time. Several search engines provide a convenient hyperlink to the Yellow Pages.

Drill

1. Open the MetaCrawler website (http://www.metacrawler.com). Browse the various categories on the page.

2. Click the **Yellow Pages** tab at the top of the Web page.

   a. Click the **Business by Type** button.

   b. Key **Department Store** in the Business Type box.

   c. Key your city, select your state from the drop list, and then click the **Search** button.

   d. Categories of department stores may display, such as *Department Stores* and *Outlet Malls*. Click each category to display the full list. Print.

3. Open the Yahoo website. Determine a city that you would like to visit. Assume you will need overnight accommodations. Use the Yellow Pages to find a listing of hotels in this city.

4. Your best friend lives in (*you provide the city*); you want to send him/her flowers. Find a listing of florists in this city.

Enter Text

When you key text, it is entered at the insertion point (the blinking vertical bar). When a line is full, the text automatically moves to the next line. This feature is called **wordwrap**. To begin a new paragraph, tap ENTER. To indent the first line of a paragraph to the first default tab, tap the TAB key.

To change or edit text, you must move the insertion point around within the document. You can move to different parts of the document by using the mouse or the keyboard. To use the mouse, move the I-beam pointer to the desired position and click the left mouse button. You can also use the arrow keys on the keyboard to move the insertion point to a different position.

Drill 2 | ENTER TEXT

1. If the opening *Word* screen does not fill your entire screen, click the **Maximize** button on the Control menu.

2. Key the text that follows using wordwrap. Tap ENTER twice only at the ends of paragraphs to DS between paragraphs. Ignore any red and green wavy lines that may appear under the text as you key.

3. Using the mouse, move the insertion point immediately before the *S* at the beginning of the document.

4. Key your name. Tap ENTER four times. Notice that paragraph 1 moves down four lines.

5. Use the Right arrow key to move the insertion point to the left of the *h* in *homework*. Key the word **new**, followed by a space. Notice that the text moves to the right.

6. Keep the document on the screen for the next drill.

Serendipity, a homework research tool from Information Technology Company, is available to subscribers of the major online services via the World Wide Web. **(Tap ENTER two times.)**

Offered as a subscription service aimed at college students, Serendipity is a collection of tens of thousands of articles from major encyclopedias, reference books, magazines, pamphlets, and Internet sources combined into a single searchable database.

Serendipity puts an electronic library right at students' fingertips. The program offers two browse-and-search capabilities. Users can find articles by entering questions in simple question format or browse the database by pointing and clicking on key words that identify related articles. For more information, call 800-555-0174 or address e-mail to lab@serendipity.com.

Menu Bar Commands

The commands available in *Word* are listed in menus located on the menu bar at the top of your screen. The names of the menus indicate the type of commands they contain. You can execute all commands using the proper menu. When you click an item on the menu bar, a menu cascades or pulls down and displays the available commands. Note that common shortcuts, including toolbar buttons and keyboard commands, are provided when appropriate. The File menu that follows illustrates the main characteristics of pull-down menus.

Drill 2

Key the sentences, correcting the errors in pronoun case. Save as *pronoun-drill2*.

1. Marie and me have volunteered to work on the committee. _I_
2. Give the assignment to George and I. _me_
3. It is she who received the free airline ticket. _ok_
4. It was not me who sent in the request. _I_
5. She has more time available than me for handling this project. _I_
6. Did you see Cheryl and he at the opening session? _him_

Drill 3

Key the sentences, correcting the errors in pronoun and antecedent agreement. Save as *pronoun-drill3*.

1. Each student must have their own data disk. _his_
2. Several students have his or her own computer. _theres_
3. Some of the employees were happy with their raises. _ok_
4. The company has not decided whether they will make profit sharing available. _it_
5. All candidates must submit his or her resume. _there_
6. Napoleon organized their armies. _his_

APOSTROPHE GUIDES

Apostrophes:

1. Add *'s* to a singular noun not ending in *s*.
2. Add *'s* to a singular noun ending in *s* or *z* sound if the ending *s* is pronounced as a syllable.

     Sis's lunch, Russ's car, Buzz's average

3. Add *'* only if the ending *s* or *z* is awkward to pronounce.

     series' outcome, ladies' shoes, Delibes' music, Cortez' quest _no_

4. Add *'s* to a plural noun that does not end in *s*. _pluar_

     men's notions, children's toys, mice's tracks _men's_ _mice's_ _ou_

5. Add only *'* after a plural noun ending in *s*.

     horses' hooves, lamps' shades

6. Add *'s* after the last noun in a series to show joint possession of two or more people.

     Jack and Judy's house; Peter, Paul, and Mary's song

7. Add *'s* to each noun to show individual possession of two or more persons.

     Li's and Ted's tools, Jill's and Ed's races. _ading 's_   _singular poseriv._

Drill 4

Key the sentences, correcting all errors in apostrophes. DS between items. Save as *apostrophes-drill4*.

our instructor

1. Mary Thomas, my neighbors sister, will take care of my son.
2. The assistant gave him the instructors telephone number.
3. The announcers microphone is never shut off.
4. His father-in-laws home will be open for touring next week.
5. Two hours time is not sufficient to set up the exhibit.
6. Someones car lights have been left on.

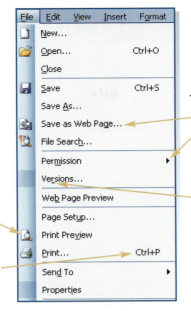

ze form cos jest jeszcze: otter option (handwritten note)

Ellipsis (...): indicates dialog box will display.

Arrow: indicates additional commands are available.

Bold: indicates the command can be used.

Dimmed command: indicates the command cannot be used.

Underlined letter: activates a command when keyed.

Bottom arrow: shown at the bottom of a partial menu indicates additional commands are available.

Toolbar button: indicates button to click to activate a command.

Keyboard shortcut: activates a command when keys are pressed.

Toolbar Commands

Frequently-used commands also can be accessed using the buttons on the Standard and Formatting toolbars. Whenever you use *Word*, make sure that both toolbars are displayed, with the Standard toolbar on top of the Formatting toolbar. If either toolbar is missing or other toolbars are displayed, change the display, following these steps. ✳ See the Discover box at the left.

✳ **DISCOVER**

If the Standard and Formatting toolbars do not display on separate lines:
- Click the **Toolbar Options** button at the right of the toolbar.
- Click the option **Show Buttons on Two Rows**.

Option: Click **Customize** on the toolbar menu. On the Options tab, a check mark should display beside **Show Standard and Formatting Toolbars on Two Rows**.

Toolbar Options button

To display or hide a toolbar:

1. Position the mouse pointer over any toolbar and click the right mouse button; a shortcut menu appears listing all of the toolbars that are available. (*Option:* Click **View** on the menu bar; then click **Toolbars**.)

2. Click to the left of **Standard** or **Formatting**, placing a check mark next to its name. The toolbar is displayed. If toolbars other than the Standard or Formatting toolbars are displayed, click the toolbar name to remove the check mark and hide the toolbar.

3. If task pane is checked, click to the left of it to close the window. You can also close the task pane by clicking the Close button at the upper right of the task pane.

Drill 3 | COMMANDS

1. Check that the Standard and Formatting toolbars are the only ones that are displayed and that they each display on a separate row.

2. Point to several buttons on the Standard and Formatting toolbars. Notice the name of each button as it displays.

3. Click **File** on the menu bar. Point to the arrow at the bottom of the File menu and click the left mouse button to display additional commands. If there is no arrow at the bottom of the File menu, then your entire menu is already displayed.

4. Click **Edit** on the menu bar. Note that *Cut* is dimmed. A dimmed command is not available; making it available requires another action.

5. Click **File** on the menu bar again. Note that the Save As command is followed by an ellipsis (...). Click **Save As** to display the Save As dialog box. Click **Cancel** to close it.

6. Click each of the different View buttons on the status bar. Notice that a button is highlighted when that view is active. Return to Normal view.

PRONOUN GUIDES

Pronoun Case:

Use the **nominative case** (*I, you, we, she, he, they, it, who*):

1. When the pronoun acts as the **subject of a verb**.

> Jim and *I* went to the movies.
> Mike and *she* were best friends.

2. When the pronoun is used as a **predicate pronoun**. (The verb *be* is a linking verb; it links the noun/pronoun to the predicate.)

> It was *she* who answered the phone.
> The person who objected was *I*.

Use the **objective case** (*me, you, us, her, him, them, it, whom*):

3. When the pronoun is used as a **direct** or **indirect object**.

> Jill invited *us* to the meeting.
> The printer gave Bill and *me* tickets to the game.

4. When the pronoun is an **object of the preposition**.

> I am going with **you** and **him**.
> This issue is between **you** and **me**.

Pronoun-Antecedent Agreement:

1. The **antecedent** is the word in the sentence that the pronoun refers to. In the examples, the antecedent is bold and the pronoun is in italics.

> **Players** must show *their* birth certificates.
> The *boy* lost **his** wallet.

2. The antecedent must agree with the pronoun in **person** (first, second, third).

> **I** am pleased that *my* project placed first. (Both are first person.)
> **You** must stand by *your* display at the science fair. (Both are second person.)
> **He** has lost *his* watch. (Both are third person.)

3. The antecedent must agree with the pronoun in **gender** (neuter when gender of antecedent is unknown).

> **Gail** said that *she* preferred the duplex apartment.
> The adjustable **chair** sits firmly on *its* five-leg base.
> The **dog** looked for *its* master for days.

4. The antecedent must agree with the pronoun in **number**. If the antecedent of a pronoun is singular, use a singular pronoun. If the antecedent is plural, use a plural pronoun.

> All **members** of the class paid *their* dues.
> **Each** of the Girl Scouts brought **her** sleeping bag.

Drill 1 | PRONOUN CHOICE

1. Open *pronoun* from the data files. Save it as *pronoun-drill1*.

2. Follow the specific directions provided in the data file. Save again and print.

Save/Save As

Saving a document preserves it so that it can be used again. If a document is not saved, it will be lost once the computer is shut down. It is a good idea to save a document before printing. The first time you save a document, you must give it a filename. Filenames should accurately describe the document. In this course, use the exercise number as the filename (for example, *26a-drill4*).

The Save As command on the File menu is used to save a new document or to rename an existing one. The Save As dialog box contains a Save In list box, a File Name list box, and a Files of Type list box. The Save As dialog box may either be blank or display a list of files that have already been saved.

Word makes it easy to create a new folder when saving a file. A folder can be created for storing related files. The Create New Folder button is located near the top of the Save As dialog box.

✳ DISCOVER

Renaming a Folder
- Click the **Open** button.
- Click the down arrow on the Look in box and click the drive or folder that contains the folder you want to rename.
- Right-click the folder and click **Rename**.
- Type the new name and press ENTER.

To save a new document:

1. Click the **Save** button on the Standard toolbar. (*Option:* Click **File** on the menu; then click **Save As**.) The Save As dialog box displays.

2. If necessary, change the folder or the drive in the Save In box. Use the down arrow to locate the desired drive.

3. To save the document in a new folder, click the **Create New Folder** button at the top of the dialog box. Key the folder name (for example, **Module 3**).

4. Key the filename in the File Name text box.

5. Click the **Save** button or tap ENTER. *Word* automatically adds the file extension *.doc* to the filename. This extension identifies the document as a *Word* document.

Objective Assessment
Answer the questions below to see if you have mastered the content of Module 6.

1. A vertical list of information within a table is referred to as a(n) _COLUMNS_.
2. To move to the next cell in a table, tap the _TAB_ key.
3. A quick way to select an entire table is by clicking on the _TABLE MOVE HANDLE_.
4. To center a table horizontally on the page, use the _TABLE BAR PROPERTIES_ option.
5. Preformatted styles can be applied to tables by using the _AUTO FORMAT_ feature.
6. A row can be added at the end of the table by clicking the insertion point in the last cell and tapping _TAB ov ENTER_.
7. Text from a document can be converted to a table if it is separated by _CONVERT_, _PARAGRAPHS_, or _TABS_.
8. Increase _ROWS HIGHTS_ to place more blank space between rows.
9. Documents saved in _PLAIN TEXT_ format saves the text but not the formats.
10. Documents saved as a Web page are stored in _HMTML_ or _MHTML_ format.

Performance Assessment

Document 1
Table with Hyperlink

1. Key the table below. Increase the height of row 1 to 0.45". Center the column heads vertically in the cells.
2. Right-align column B; set a decimal tab in column C to align numbers approximately centered.
3. Change the height of rows 3–9 to 0.3" and center the text vertically in the cells.
4. Center the table vertically on the page. Add a hyperlink to *College of Business* that will link it to http://www.unevada.edu/colleges/cba.
5. Save as *checkpoint6-d1*. Print.

Document 2
Revise Table

1. Delete row 4, *Communication*. Add a row for **Information Technology** that has 8,756 majors and a 14.5% growth rate. Position in alphabetical order.
2. Delete column B. Insert a new column to the right of the table. Insert the following data in the new column: **Enrollment | 1,328 | 642 | 715 | 537 | 2,005 | 1,610 | 789**. *Tip:* The new column will contain a decimal tab. Select all the cells in the column and delete the decimal tab.
3. Save as *checkpoint6-d2* and print. Convert the document to plain text format and print.

UNIVERSITY OF NEVADA
College of Business

Department	Majors	Growth Rate
Accounting	945	3.65%
Banking, Finance, and Insurance	1,021	2.17%
Communication	326	-2.5%
Economics	453	1.4%
International Business	620	14.74%
Management Science	1,235	11.8%
Marketing	1,357	10.38%

D r i l l 4 | SAVE A FILE

1. The document you keyed in Drill 2 should be displayed. If you are saving your files to a floppy disk, insert a disk into Drive A.

2. Click the **Save** button. The Save As dialog box displays.

3. Click the arrow in the Save In list box to locate the drive you will use. Point to the drive on which you wish to save the file, such as A, C, or D, to highlight it; then click the left mouse button to select it.

4. Click the **Create New Folder** button. The New Folder dialog box displays. Key the name **Module 3 Solutions** in the text box; then click **OK**.

5. With the insertion point in the File name text box, key *26a-drill4* as the filename.

6. Check to see that the default (*Word Document*) is displayed in the Save as type list box. If not, click the down arrow and select **Word Document**.

7. Click the **Save** button or tap ENTER to close the dialog box and return to the document window.

8. Rename the folder **Module 3 Keys**.

9. Keep the document on the screen for the next drill.

Print Preview

Print Preview enables you to see how a document will look when it is printed. Use Print Preview to check the layout of your document, such as margins, line spacing, and tabs, before printing.

To preview a document:

1. Click **Print Preview** on the Standard toolbar. A full-page version of the document displays. Print Preview displays the page where the insertion point is located.

2. Click **Close** to return to the document screen.

In Print Preview, a special toolbar displays with additional options for viewing the document. For example, when you click the Magnifier button, the mouse pointer changes to a magnifying glass. When you click the magnifying glass on the page, you can see a portion of the document at 100%.

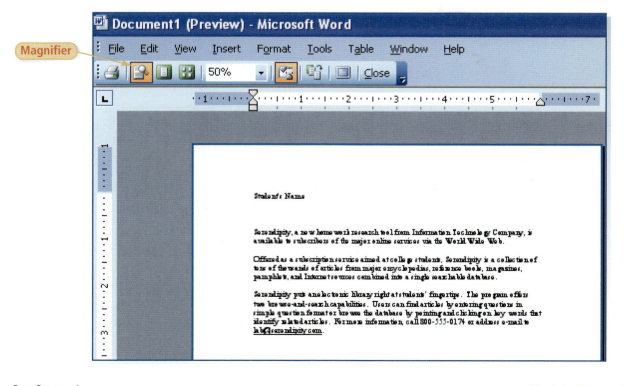

[48c-d3]
Insert and Delete Columns and Rows

1. Open *48c-d2* and save it as *48c-d3*.
2. Delete column D (*Unit Price*). Insert a new column between columns A and B.
3. Key the text below in the new column.

   Publisher
   Bodwin
   American
   TWSS
   Bodwin
   TWSS

4. Insert a new row above *Pommery Mountain* and add the information below.

   Sound of Trumpets   **American**   **2005**   **9,675.00**

5. Add a double-line border around all the cells. Save.

[48c-d4]
Convert Text to Table in Memo

1. Key the following text as shown. Tap ENTER at the end of each line.

   Test, Healthy Levels
   Cholesterol, under 200 mg/dL
   Triglycerides, under 150 mg/dL
   Blood pressure, under 120/80 mm/HG
   Blood sugar, under 120 mg/dL

2. Convert the text to a two-column table. Format it according to Table Format Guides on page 180.
3. Key the following text for a memo above and below the table. Format the memo properly. Insert a hyperlink that will link *Health Center* to http://www.cmc.com/healthcenter.
4. Save it as *48c-d4* and print.

TO: CMC Employees | **FROM:** Angela Rachett, Facility RN | **DATE:** Current date | **SUBJECT:** Staying Healthy

CMC Corporation is encouraging all employees to stop at the Health Center for free health check screenings every six months. The following is a list of routine tests performed by our nursing staff.

Center table here. →

Call extension 722 to schedule your free testing today.

xx

Print

You can print a document by clicking Print on the File menu or by clicking the Print button on the Standard toolbar. Clicking the Print button immediately prints the document using all of the default settings. To view or change the default settings, click **Print** on the File menu or use the keyboard shortcut CTRL + P to display the Print dialog box.

D r i l l   5 | **PREVIEW AND PRINT**

1. The document *26a-drill4* should be displayed on your screen.

2. Click the **Print Preview** button to view your document.

3. Change the magnification to **75%**; then change it to **Whole Page**.

4. Click the **Close** button to return to Normal view.

5. Check to be sure that your printer is turned on and has paper.

6. Click **File** on the menu bar and then click **Print**. Compare your dialog box with the one above. Your printer name may differ, but other choices should be the same. Verify that you will print one copy and then click **OK**.

Help

Help provides you with quick access to information about commands, features, and screen elements, as well as available online resources. If you are connected to the Internet, you can get online help while you are working in *Word*. You can access Help in several ways:

Type a question for help provides answers to questions such as How do I print a document?

Click the **Help** button on the menu bar and then click **Microsoft Office Word Help** to display the Help task pane. Click **Table of Contents** to display the Help Table of Contents. Click one of the topics, such as Printing, to display the information available.

D r i l l   6 | **HELP**

1. Document *26a-drill4* should be displayed on your screen. Click **Help** on the menu bar; then click **Microsoft Office Word Help**.

2. Key **print a document** in the Search for box; click the arrow to start searching.

3. Click **Print a document** from the list of results and view the directions for printing a document.

4. Click the **Microsoft Office Word Help Close** button to return to your document.

5. Leave the document on the screen for the next drill.

[48c-dl]
Table Without Borders

1. Set 1" side margins. Key the main heading on line 2.1".
2. Create a three-column, five-row table. Change the width of column A to approximately 2", and column B to 0.25". Key the text in columns A and C. Column B will be blank. Bold the items in column A. Insert a blank row after each row except the last. Do not print the borders. (*Hint:* Choose **None** in the Borders and Shading dialog box.) Save it as *48c-d1*.
3. Resave it as a Web page and preview it in your Web browser.

NOTEBOOK SECURITY GUIDELINES

Choose an easy-to-use security system.		Select a security system that is easy to use. If the security system is difficult to use and requires complicated steps, users will either not use it or look for ways to defeat it.
Assign someone to be in charge of notebook security.		One or more persons in the company should be responsible for monitoring the hardware and software on notebook computers. This person needs to be in charge of disseminating security rules and making sure that the rules are followed.
Apply several levels of security.		Different levels of security should be applied to different levels of employees. A CEO or an engineer working in the company's R & D department may be working with data that will require a higher level of security than someone in the art department. Don't bog down the artist with the high level of security needed for the CEO.
Most laptop/notebook thefts are opportunistic.		Train users to be alert and to keep an eye on their computers at all times. Remind them to use extra caution when passing through airports and staying in hotels.
Hold users responsible for their computers.		Encourage users to take precautions, and punish those who are careless by taking away laptop privileges.

[48c-d2]
Table with AutoFormat

1. Key the table. Center column B; set decimal tabs for columns C and D, resulting in the numbers appearing centered within the columns.
2. Apply **Table List 4** style. Format the table according to the Table Format Guides on page 180. Center table vertically and horizontally and save it as *48c-d2*.

OXFORD LEARNING SYSTEMS

Book Title	Publication	Sales	Unit Price
The Mice in the Dice	2005	478,769.00	37.85
Tale of Five Cities	2004	91,236.00	32.50
Horrell Hill Adventures	2004	89,412.00	29.00
Pommery Mountain	2004	104,511.00	34.80
Tom Creek's Adventures	2005	194,137.50	36.50

Close

Close clears the screen of the document and removes it from memory. You will be prompted to save the document before closing if you have not saved it or to save your changes if you have made any to the document since the previous save. It is necessary to close each document that is open.

To close a document, do one of the following:
- Click **File** on the menu bar; then click **Close**.
- Click the **Close** button at the top right side of the document title bar.

New

When all documents have been closed, *Word* displays a blank screen. To create a new document, click the **New Blank Document** button on the Standard toolbar.

Open

Any documents that have been saved can be opened and used again. When you open a file, a dialog box displays the names of folders or files within a folder. You can also select files saved on a floppy disk.

To open a document:
1. Click **Open** on the File menu. (*Option:* Click the **Open** button on the Standard toolbar.) The Open dialog box displays.
2. In the Look In box, click the down arrow; then click the drive in which your files are stored (Drive A).
3. If necessary, double-click the folder name to display the filenames. Click the desired filename; then click **Open**.

Exit

Exit saves all documents that are on the screen and then quits the software. When you exit *Word*, you close both the document and the program window. You will be prompted to save before exiting if you have not already saved the document or if you have made changes to it since last saving. Click the **Close** button in the title bar (top bar) to exit *Word*.

D r i l l   7   **CLOSE AND OPEN A DOCUMENT**

1. Close the file *26a-drill4* that you saved in Drill 4.

2. Click **New Blank Document** on the Standard toolbar.

3. Close the blank document.

4. Click **Open** on the Standard toolbar and open the file *26a-drill4*.

5. Click **Save As** on the File menu. In the Save As dialog box, save the file again as *26a-drill4a*. Close the document and exit *Word*.

WARMUP
48a
Key each line three times SS.

alphabet	1	Jacob Kazlowski and five experienced rugby players quit the team.
figures	2	E-mail account #82-4 is the account for telephone (714) 555-0108.
double letters	3	Anne will meet with the committee at noon to discuss a new issue.
easy	4	The men may pay my neighbor for the work he did in the cornfield.

| 1 | 2 | 3 | 4 | 5 | 6 | 7 | 8 | 9 | 10 | 11 | 12 | 13 |

48b
Timed Writing
Assess Straight-Copy Skill
Take two 3' timings. Strive to key with control and fluency.

all letters

	gwam	3'	5'
Whether any company can succeed depends on how well it fits		4	2
into the economic system. Success rests on certain key factors		8	5
that are put in line by a management team that has set goals for		13	8
the company and has enough good judgment to recognize how best to		17	10
reach these goals. Because of competition, only the best-organized		21	13
companies get to the top.		23	14
A commercial enterprise is formed for a specific purpose:		27	16
that purpose is usually to equip others, or consumers, with		31	19
whatever they cannot equip themselves. Unless there is only one		36	21
provider, a consumer will search for a company that returns the		40	24
most value in terms of price; and a relationship with such a		43	27
company, once set up, can endure for many years.		47	28
Thus our system assures that the businesses that manage to		51	31
survive are those that have been able to combine successfully an		56	33
excellent product with a low price and the best service—all in a		60	36
place that is convenient for the buyers. With no intrusion from		64	39
outside forces, the buyer and the seller benefit both themselves		69	41
and each other.		70	42

```
3' |    1    |    2    |    3    |    4    |
5' |      1      |      2      |      3      |
```

[APPLICATIONS]

[48c]
Assessment

→ Continue

✓ Check

With *CheckPro*: When you complete a document, proofread it, check the spelling, and preview for placement. When you are completely satisfied with the document, click the **Continue** button to move to the next document. You will not be able to return to and edit a document once you continue to the next document. Click the **Check** button when you are ready to error-check the test. Review and/or print the document analysis results.

Without *CheckPro*: On the signal to begin, key the documents in sequence. When time has been called, proofread all documents again and identify errors.

You may choose to use *CheckPro* for Lesson 26. To complete the remaining exercises in *CheckPro*, open the software and choose Lesson 26. See the directions on page xxii for further instruction. Your opening screen will be different than the example shown here.

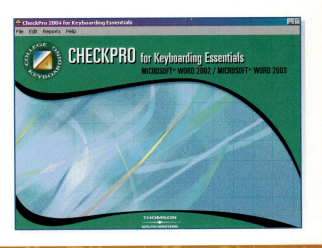

[26b-d1]
Create a New Document

1. Start *Microsoft Word.*
2. Create a document by keying the text below. DS between paragraphs.
3. Save the document as *26b-d1*. Print; then close the document.

In Lesson 26, I have learned the basic operations of my word processing software. Today I opened the word processor, created a new document, saved the document, printed the document, closed the document, and exited the software. This new document that I am creating will be named 26b-d1. I will save it so that I can use it in the next lesson to open an existing document.

(Tap ENTER two times)

Help is available online for me at all times. If I get stuck on a test, and I cannot use my textbook or solicit the help of my teacher or classmates, I can still rely on using the Microsoft Office Word Help.

[26b-d2]
Create a New Document

1. Open a new blank document and key the text below. Tap TAB to indent the first line of each paragraph. DS between paragraphs.
2. Save the document as *26b-d2* and print. Close the document. Then exit *Word.*

As the man says, "I have some good news and some bad news." Let me give you the bad news first.

Due to a badly pulled muscle, I have had to withdraw from the Eastern Racquetball Tournament. As you know, I have been looking forward to the tournament for a long time, and I had begun to hope that I might even win it. I've been working hard.

That's the bad news. The good news is that I have been chosen to help officiate, so I'll be coming to Newport News anyway. In fact, I'll arrive there a day earlier than I had originally planned.

So, put the racquet away, but get out the backgammon board. I'm determined to win something on this trip!

[47c-d4]
Table

1. Key the table below. Save as *47c-d4a* and print.
2. Convert the table to text, using tabs to separate text. Save as *47c-d4b* and print.

Form	Name of File	Path and Subdirectory
Invoice	Invoice	C:\Busforms
Purchase Order	Purchord	C:\Busforms
Medical Leave of Absence	Medleav	C:\HR\Medical
Cash Reimbursement	Reimburs	C:\HR\Forms
Dental Insurance	Dental	C:\HR\Medical

[47c-d5]
Memo with Table

1. Open *47c-d4b* and save it as *47c-d5*. Key the following text above and below the converted table and format it as a memo.
2. Save and print.

TO:	Royal Canadian Employees
FROM:	Mary Nottingham, Administrative Assistant
DATE:	Current date
SUBJECT:	Company Forms

The IT Department has downloaded the most widely used forms onto the hard drive of your computer. Below is a list of the forms, the filename under which the form is stored, and the path and subdirectory in which the form is stored.

> The table converted to text in *47c-d4b* should display here.

If you need additional help in retrieving these forms, please call me at extension 617.

xx

[47c-d6]
Convert Text to Table

1. Open the data file *malware*.
2. Select the text and convert it to a two-column table. Click **AutoFit to window** and select the **Table Colorful 2** AutoFormat style.
3. Center the text in column A horizontally in the cells.
4. Format the table according to the Table Format Guides on page 180.
5. Save as *47c-d6* and print.

[47c-d7]
Convert Document to Different Formats

1. Open *47c-d6* and save it as *47c-d7a* in RTF format. Open *47c-d6* and save it as *47c-d7b* in TXT format.
2. Open *47c-d6* and save it as a Web page named *47c-d7c*.

Format Text

Navigate in a Document

The document window displays only a portion of a page at one time. There are several ways to move quickly through a document to view it.

Keyboard

To move through a document using the keyboard, study the following shortcuts.

To move	Press
Next word	CTRL + ← or → arrow key
One paragraph up or down	CTRL + ↑ or ↓ arrow key
To beginning of line	HOME
To end of line	END
Up one screen	PgUp
Up one page	ALT + CTRL + PgUp
To beginning of document	CTRL + HOME
To end of document	CTRL + END

Scroll bars

To move through the document using the mouse, use the scroll bars. The vertical scroll bar enables you to move up and down through a document. The horizontal scroll bar enables you to move left and right across a line. Scrolling does not change the position of the insertion point, only your view of the document.

To scroll	Click
Up or down	Scroll bar and drag or click up and down arrows
Up one screen	Above the scroll box
Down one screen	Below the scroll box
To a specific page	Drag the vertical scroll box and watch for page number
Left or right	Scroll bar and drag or click arrows

Select Text

To make any formatting changes to existing text, you must first select the text you want to change. Selected text is highlighted in black. You can select text using either the mouse or the keyboard. To deselect text, click anywhere outside of the selected text.

To select text with the mouse:

To select	Do this
Any amount of text	Click at the beginning of the text and drag the mouse over the text.
A word	Double-click the word.
A line	Click in the area left of the line.
Multiple lines	Drag in the area left of the lines (selection bar).
A paragraph	Double-click in the selection bar next to the paragraph or triple-click anywhere in the paragraph.

CONVERT TABLES TO DIFFERENT FORMATS

1. Open the data file *insert rows*.

2. Save the file as *47b-drill2a* in RTF format. Close the file.

3. Open the data file *insert rows* again.

4. Save the file as *47b-drill2b* in TXT format; when the File Conversion dialog box displays, click **OK**. Close the file. Reopen *47b-drill2b*; click **OK** at the File Conversion dialog box. Notice that the table format has been removed.

5. Open the data file *web page*. Create a new folder called *Web Pages*.

6. Save the file as a Web page in the new *Web Pages* folder. Name the file *web table.htm*. View the file in Web Layout View. Drag the graphic back to the center of the page. Save again.

7. Choose **Web Page Preview** to view the file in your Web browser.

[APPLICATIONS]

[47c-d1]
Convert Text to Table

1. Key the document at the right SS. Tap ENTER at the end of each line except the last.

2. Select the text beginning with *Account, Amount*.

3. Convert the text to a two-column table. Separate the text at commas. Click **OK**.

4. Apply the **Table Colorful 3** AutoFormat style and then format according to Table Format Guides on page 180.

5. Save it as *47c-d1* and print.

JUNE EXPENSES

Account, Amount

Office Supplies, 125.75

Telephone Expenses, 380.00

Electricity, 943.00

Petty Cash, 75.00

Rent, 995.00

[47c-d2]
Key Text with Tabs

1. Set a left tab at position 3.5".

2. Key the copy shown below SS. Key the first column at the left margin; tab before keying the second column.

3. Save it as *47c-d2* and print.

ROYAL CANADIAN, INC.
Board of Directors

Position	Name
President	Lawrence T. Buckingham
Vice President	Alexandria C. Devonshire
Vice President	Lillian M. Patel
Treasurer	Robert C. Lindahl
Secretary	Calvin H. Ayers

[47c-d3]
Convert Table to Text

1. Open *47c-d2* and save it as *47c-d3*.

2. Convert the text to a table. Click the **AutoFormat** button in the Convert Text to Table dialog box and apply **Table Grid 1** style. Deselect **Last Row** to remove the italics from the last row.

3. Shade the first row 15%. Format the table according to the Table Format Guides on page 180. Center the table vertically and horizontally on the page.

4. Save and print.

To select text with the keyboard:

To select	Do this
One character to left or right	SHIFT + Left or Right arrow
Beginning or end of word	CTRL + SHIFT + Right or Left arrow
End of line	SHIFT + END
Beginning of line	SHIFT + HOME

Drill 1 | NAVIGATE AND SELECT TEXT

1. Open the file you created in Lesson 26, *26b-d1*.

2. Move to the end of the document (CTRL + END).

3. Move to the top of the document (CTRL + HOME).

4. Select the first sentence; then deselect it.

5. Move to the last sentence and select the word **Microsoft**.

6. Move to the beginning of the line (HOME) and select the first sentence.

7. Move to the top of the document (CTRL + HOME) and key your name followed by a DS.

8. Save the document as *27a-drill1*; then close it.

Character Formats

Character formats apply to letters, numbers, and punctuation marks and include such attributes as bold, underline, italic, fonts, and font sizes. The Formatting toolbar provides an efficient way to apply character formats. Formatting toolbar buttons also make it easy to align text.

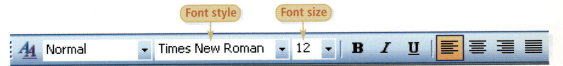

To apply character formats as you key:

1. Click the appropriate format button and key the text to be formatted.

2. When you finish keying the formatted text, click the same button again to turn off the format. Notice that a format button is highlighted when the feature is on.

To apply character formats to existing text:

1. Select the text.

2. Click the appropriate format button.

Font Size and Styles

Word's default font is 12-point Times New Roman. Font size is measured in points. One vertical inch equals 72 points. Most text is keyed in a 10-, 11-, or 12-point font, although a larger font may be used to emphasize headings. *Word* has a variety of font styles available.

To change font size:

1. Select the text to be changed.

2. Click the **Font Size** down arrow.

3. Scroll through the list of available sizes and click the desired font size.

> **TIP**
>
> You can also change font size and formats by choosing Format on the menu bar and then choosing Fonts to display the Font dialog box.

Convert Documents to Different Formats

There may be times when you will need to save a *Word* document in a different format. If the document needs to be opened in another program, you will have to save or convert it to **RTF** or **TXT** format. Choose the format that best suits your needs.

- **Rich Text Format (RTF)** Saving a file in RTF format will save the formatting along with the text.
- **Plain Text (TXT)** Saving the file in TXT format saves the text but not the formats.

To save a file in **RTF** or **TXT** format:

1. Open the *Word* document. Click the **File** menu and choose **Save As**.
2. Click the **Save as type** drop list arrow and choose **Rich Text Format (*.rtf)** or **Plain Text (*.txt)**.

Save a Word Document as a Web Page

help keywords

create a Web page from an existing Microsoft Word *document*

about ways to view a Word *document*

preview a document as a Web page

To distribute a *Word* document on the World Wide Web, you must first convert it to HTML format by saving it as a Web page document. When you save a *Word* document as a Web page, *Word* automatically inserts the HTML codes. Pages may appear different when displayed in a Web browser than they do when they are displayed as a *Word* document. To view the new Web document as it will appear online, choose **Web Layout View**. Make formatting alterations as needed so that the page displays as desired on the Web. Finally, preview the Web document in your Web browser. **Note:** Using *Internet Explorer* will reduce formatting differences.

To save a *Word* document as a Web page:

TIP

Single File Web Page (.mht; *.mhtml)* displays as the default Web page format. This format saves the entire website, graphics, and text as one file. However, you must use *Internet Explorer 4.0* or a later version to view your file. You cannot view it using another browser or an earlier version of *Internet Explorer*.

1. Click the **File** menu and click **Save as Web Page**. Click the **Save as type** drop list arrow and choose **Web Page** (see TIP).
2. Select the drive and folder where you wish to save the file. (*Hint:* Save Web files in a folder created for that purpose.)
3. In the File name box, key the filename or accept the name provided. *Word* automatically adds the file extension *.htm*.
4. Click **Save**.

To view a document as a Web page:

1. Click the **View** menu and click **Web Layout**. Make any necessary formatting revisions (e.g., reposition graphics). **Note:** As a shortcut, click the **Web Layout View** button on the status bar.
2. Click the **File** menu and click **Web Page Preview** to view the page in the Web browser.

To change font style:

1. Select the text to be changed.
2. Click the **Font** down arrow.
3. Scroll through the list of available styles and click the desired style.

Drill 2 | **CHARACTER STYLES**

1. Open a new blank document.
2. Key your name and press ENTER.
3. Key the document name *27a-drill2* and press ENTER four times.
4. Key the sentences that follow, applying the formats as you key.
5. Save the document as *27a-drill2*.

This sentence is keyed in bold.

This sentence is keyed in italic.

This sentence is underlined.

This sentence is keyed in bold and italic and underlined.

This sentence is keyed in 14-point Times New Roman.

This sentence is keyed in 12-point Arial.

Paragraph Formats

Paragraph formats apply to an entire paragraph and can be applied before or after a paragraph has been keyed. Each time you press ENTER, *Word* inserts a paragraph mark and starts a new paragraph. Thus, a paragraph may consist of a single line followed by a hard return (¶ mark) or several lines that wrap and are followed by a hard return. In order to apply paragraph formats such as line spacing or alignment, you must be able to see where paragraphs begin and end. Show/Hide displays hard returns as a paragraph mark (¶).

Show/Hide

¶ Click the **Show/Hide** button on the Standard toolbar to display all nonprinting characters such as hidden text paragraph markers (¶) and spaces (··). The Show/Hide button appears highlighted or depressed when it is active. To turn nonprinting characters off, click the **Show/Hide** button again.

Hidden Text

Text within a document can be hidden and then displayed again when desired. Hidden text is not visible on the screen unless the Show/Hide feature is active. Hidden text will not print unless the Hidden Text option is selected in the Include with Document option for printing.

To hide text:

1. Select the text to be hidden.
2. Click **Font** on the Format menu.
3. Click the **Hidden** box in the Effects section.

Convert Documents

WARMUP

47a

Key each pair of lines twice at a controlled rate.

1st and 2nd fingers	1	Mickey teaches golf three times this month to young children.
	2	Jenny might meet her husband at the new stadium before the match.
3rd and 4th fingers	3	Wallace was so puzzled over the sizable proposal due in six days.
	4	Paula will wash, wax, and polish Polly's old, aqua car quite soon.
direct	5	Kilgore, located in a low-lying area, was destroyed by the flood.
reach	6	Dennie framed the ball to help the Jupiter pitcher earn a strike.

| 1 | 2 | 3 | 4 | 5 | 6 | 7 | 8 | 9 | 10 | 11 | 12 | 13 |

NEW FUNCTIONS

47b

Convert Text to Table

You can convert text in a document to table format by using a comma, tab, or other indicator of where a new column should begin. Likewise, you can select a table or rows of a table and convert it to regular text format.

To convert text to a table:

1. Select the text to be converted to a table.
2. Click the **Table** menu, point to **Convert**, and click **Text to Table**. The Convert Text to Table dialog box displays.
3. Indicate the number of columns for the table.
4. Indicate whether the columns are to be a fixed width or whether to use Autofit.
5. Click the **AutoFormat** button to select a style, if appropriate.
6. Indicate how the text is currently separated.

To convert a table to a text document:

1. Select the table to be converted to text.
2. Click the **Table** menu, point to **Convert**, and click **Table to Text**.
3. Indicate how the columns are to be separated. Click **OK**.

Drill 1 | CONVERT TEXT TO TABLE

1. Key the text shown at the right. Turn on Show/Hide.

2. Select only the text; do not select any ¶ markers above or below the text.

3. Convert the text to a two-column table using fixed column width. Change row height to 0.3". Save as *47b-drill1a* and print.

4. Select the table and convert it to text, separating the text at tabs. Save as *47b-drill1b* and print.

Employee, Department

Louise C. Harrington, Accounting

Justin A. Rodriguez, Information Technology

Douglas M. Anderson, Project Planning

Irma J. Stevenson, Human Resources

D r i l l 3 | HIDE TEXT

1. Key the three lines at the right.

2. Select the second line and hide the text.

3. View the text with the second line hidden; then click **Show/Hide** to view the hidden text. Turn off Show/Hide.

4. Save as *27a-drill3*.

Hidden text is not visible on the screen.
Select and hide this line.
Click the Show/Hide button to view the hidden text.

Alignment

Alignment refers to the way in which the text lines up. Text can be aligned at the left, center, right, or justified (lined up with both margins). Use the Alignment buttons on the Formatting toolbar to quickly align paragraphs.

To align existing text:

1. Place the insertion point in the paragraph to be changed. If more than one paragraph is affected, select the paragraphs to be aligned.

2. Click the appropriate **Align** button.

To align text as you key:

1. Click the appropriate **Align** button.

2. Key the text. This alignment will remain in effect until you click the button again.

D r i l l 4 | ALIGNMENT

1. Open a new blank document and center **USING ALIGNMENTS** in 14 point and bold. Tap ENTER twice to create a DS.

2. Change to left alignment and 12 point to key the first paragraph, using wordwrap.

3. Apply the formatting and alignment as shown in the following document.

4. Turn on **Show/Hide** and check to see that no hard returns (¶) appear except in paragraph 2.

5. Save the document as *27a-drill4* and print a copy.

USING ALIGNMENTS

Left alignment is used for this first paragraph. When left alignment is used, each line in the paragraph begins at the same position on the left side. The right margin will be uneven.

Center alignment
Center titles and short lines.
Use for invitations, announcements, and other documents.

Right alignment is used for this third paragraph. When right alignment is used, each line in the paragraph ends at the same position on the right side. The left side will be uneven.

Justify is used for this fourth paragraph. When justification is used, all lines (except the last line of a paragraph) begin and end at the same position at the left and right margins. Extra spaces are automatically inserted to achieve this look.

1. Create the table below. Key the text in the cells using wordwrap. Do not change the row height.

2. Change the width of column A to approximately 2" and bold the text.

3. After keying the table, change the height of row 1 to 1.25"; row 2, 1.5"; row 3, 1.5"; and row 4, 1". Align the text in the cells by clicking the **Align Center Left** button on the Tables and Borders toolbar.

4. Add hyperlinks to the bulleted items in B4 as follows:

   http://www.americancomnet.com

   http://www.speedybp.com

   http://www.viceroy.net

5. Save as *46d-d4* and print.

BENEFITS OF DSL SERVICE

Improves productivity and eliminates frustration	• Never a busy tone; always on, ends busy signals and dropped calls. • High-speed Internet access; greatly reduces wait time when uploading or downloading files.
Saves money	• Unlimited Internet access for one affordable flat rate. • One dedicated connection; no extra costs for network of multiple users. • No additional telephone company fees or usage charges.
Maximizes growth potential	• Increased bandwidth enables you to fully take advantage of the Internet. • Scalable enhanced services and applications that can accommodate change and growth with your business needs.
DSL providers	• American Communications Network • Speedy Broadband Providers • Viceroy Royal Networks

Line Spacing

Word's default line spacing is single. When paragraphs are single-spaced, the first line of the paragraph normally is not indented. However, a blank line is inserted between paragraphs to distinguish them and to improve readability. Double spacing leaves a blank line between every keyed line. Therefore, it is necessary to indent the first line of each double-spaced paragraph to indicate the beginning of the paragraph. To indent the first line of a paragraph, tap the TAB key. The default indention is 0.5". Choosing multiple line spacing allows you to specify the percentage by which the line spacing is increased or decreased. For instance, changing line spacing to 1.3 will increase the line spacing 30 percent.

To change line spacing:

1. Position the insertion point in the paragraph in which you want to change the line spacing. If more than one paragraph is to be changed, select all the paragraphs.

2. Click **Format** on the menu bar; then click **Paragraph**.

3. Select the **Indents and Spacing** tab.

4. Click the arrow in the Line Spacing box; then click **Double**. Click **OK**.

Line spacing can also be changed using the Formatting toolbar. Place the cursor in the paragraph in which the spacing will be changed. Click the **Line Spacing** button; click the down arrow; then click the desired line spacing such as 2.0. If the Line Spacing button is not displayed, click the **Toolbar Options** button at the right of the toolbar to display additional formatting options.

Drill 5 | LINE SPACING

1. Open *27a-drill4*.

2. Click in the first paragraph and change the line spacing to double.

3. Select **Center Alignment** and the two lines below it in the second paragraph. Change the line spacing to 1.5. Note

that the spacing change affects only paragraph 2—the paragraph you selected.

4. Click in the third paragraph and change the line spacing to Multiple. Accept the default number in the At box. Save as *27a-drill5* and close the document.

APPLICATIONS

[27b-dl]
Apply Character Formats

1. Key the following lines; format as shown or as directed in each line; leave a blank line between each line.

2. Save the document as *27b-d1* and print the document.

Key your name on the first line; then bold it; tap Enter twice and key this line.

Key this line using a 14-point script font with bold applied.

Key this line in 10-point Arial Black font; and then hide it.

Key this line and apply **bold**, *italic*, and underline as shown.

Key this line; then click the Show/Hide button. View the hidden line (3rd line).

Key the 3rd line again as directed; then modify the format to Arial, 14-point font. Modify the sentence to reflect these changes. (Key this line in 14-point Arial font; then hide it.)

[46d-d1]
Table with Grid Border

1. Key the table according to the Table Format Guides on page 180. Key the main heading at approximately 2.1".
2. Use red, double lines to apply a Grid border to the table. Shade the first row 15%.
3. Save as *46d-d1* and print.

SAFETY AWARDS

Award Winner	Department	Amount
Lorianna Mendez	Accounting	2,500
William Mohammed	Marketing	2,000
Marjorie Adams	Engineering	1,500
Charles Drake	Purchasing	500

[46d-d2]
Insert Column and Rows

1. Open *46d-d1* and make the following changes:
   a. Insert a row after Lorianna Mendez and add the following information:
      Robert L. Ruiz, Research, 2,250
   b. Insert a row at the end of the table, and add the following information:
      Franklin T. Cousins, Security, 500
   c. Delete the row for William Mohammed.
   d. Insert a new column between columns B and C and add the following information: Align the text in the new column vertically and horizontally in the cells.
      Year
      2001
      2002
      2003
      2004
      2005
2. Save as *46d-d2* and print.

[46d-d3]
Letter with Hyperlink and Table
Communication Activity

1. Compose a letter to your instructor requesting office supplies. Key the list of office supplies in table format.
2. Access an office supply website and obtain the prices for the items requested. Insert the unit price in the third column of the table.
3. Include a hyperlink in your letter to the website.
4. Format the letter in block letter style with open punctuation.

Office supplies requested:

Quantity	Description	Unit Cost
1 box	File folders, 1/3 cut tabs	
3 each	2" presentation binders	
1 each	Electric pencil sharpener	

[27b-d2]
Apply Paragraph Formats

1. Key your name; right-align and bold it; then tap ENTER three times.
2. Key **PARAGRAPH FORMATS** as the title. Use 14-point bold font, center-align it, and then tap ENTER two times.
3. Key the following two paragraphs; format as shown or as directed in each paragraph. Save the document as *27b-d2* and print.

Key this paragraph using single spacing and align the paragraph using justify. Note that justify has even margins on both the right and the left sides. To cause the margins to be even, additional spaces are added between words. Reports are often typed using this alignment. It is normally not used for letters or memos. Always leave a blank line between single-spaced paragraphs.

Key this paragraph using double spacing and left alignment.

Remember that the first line of paragraphs that are double-spaced should be indented. As shown, the default for indenting is .5". Note that you have used all four different alignments in the activity. Your name is right-aligned. The title, PARAGRAPH FORMATS, is center-aligned. The first paragraph is justified, and this paragraph is left-aligned. You have also used both single and double spacing.

27c Technique Builder
Key at a controlled rate.

n/u
1 nun nut unbolt null unable nudge under nurture thunder numb shunt
2 Uncle Hunter runs with me to hide under the bed when it thunders.

c/e
3 ecru cell echo ceil check cedar pecan celery secret receive price
4 Once Cecilia checked prices for acceptable and special offerings.

b/r
5 brag barb brown carbon brain marble break herb brace gerbil brick
6 Bradley will try to break the unbroken brown brood mare bareback.

n/y
7 many bunny irony grainy granny sunny phony rainy runny zany funny
8 Aunt Nanny says rainy days are for funny movies and many candies.

Align Text in Cells

You can align text both vertically and horizontally in cells by using the Align button on the Table and Borders toolbar. If the same alignment is to be applied to more than one cell, select the cells first. Click the **Align** button drop list arrow to display the alignment choices, and then click the alignment of your choice.

help keywords

create a hyperlink

Hyperlinks

Hyperlinks enable an online reader to move quickly from place to place in the same document or to another file such as a spreadsheet or Web page. Hyperlinked text is usually displayed in a different color than the body text of the document. Images such as clip art, charts, and other graphics may contain hyperlinks. In this lesson you will learn to create a hyperlink to an existing file or Web page.

To create a hyperlink to an existing file or Web page:

1. Select the text or object to be displayed as a hyperlink.
2. Click the **Insert Hyperlink** button.
3. Click **Existing File or Web Page**.
4. Select the filename or Web page by using either of the following methods:
   a. Key the filename or Web address in the Address entry box.
   b. Select a file from the displayed list. Click the category tabs (**Current Folder, Browsed Pages**, and **Recent Files**) to display various files.
5. Click **OK**.

To go to the hyperlinked location:

1. Point to the hyperlinked text or object.
2. Tap the CTRL key and click on the hyperlinked text or object. **Note:** When the *Word* document is saved as a Web page, just click on the hyperlinked text or object.

Drill 4   ALIGN CELLS AND INSERT HYPERLINK

1. Open *align cells* and save it as *46c-drill4*.

2. Select row 1 and change the height to 0.5". Click the **Align** button on the Borders and Tables toolbar and select the **Align Center** button (vertical and horizontal center).

3. Select rows 2–4 and change the row height to 0.3".

4. Select cells A2–A4 and click the **Align Center** button.

5. Select cells B2–B4 and select the **Align Center Left** button.

6. Select cells C2–C4 and select the **Align Center Right** button.

7. Insert a hyperlink for each item in the description to http://www.pcproducts.com.

8. Save and print.

Create an Interoffice Memo

new functions
28a

Spelling and Grammar

When you key, *Word* places a red wavy line under misspelled words and a green wavy line under potential grammar errors. Clicking the right mouse button in a marked word displays a shortcut menu with suggested replacement words that you can use to correct the error.

The Spelling and Grammar Status button on the status bar also informs you if there is an error in the document.

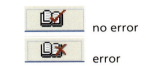

no error

error

To manually check a document, click the Spelling and Grammar button on the Standard toolbar to start the checking process.

When *Word* locates a possible error, the Spelling and Grammar dialog box displays. You can change words marked as errors or ignore them. You can click the Add button to add correct words not recognized by *Word* to the dictionary. If you choose Ignore All and Change All, the marked words will either be ignored or changed throughout the entire document.

Spelling and Grammar: English (U.S.)

Not in Dictionary:
The **softwore** places a red wavy line under misspelled words and an green wavy line under potential grammar errors.

Suggestions:
software
soft wore

- Ignore Once
- Ignore All
- Add to Dictionary
- Change
- Change All
- AutoCorrect

☑ Check grammar

Options... | Undo | Cancel

AutoCorrect

As you key, common errors are automatically corrected. For example, if you key *teh*, the AutoCorrect feature automatically corrects the spelling to *the*. When this feature is enabled, *Word* automatically replaces errors using the spell checker's main dictionary. You can customize or add words to the software's dictionary by accessing AutoCorrect Options on the Tools menu. Additional AutoCorrect options enable you to format text and automatically insert repetitive text as you key.

Drill 1 | **SPELLING AND GRAMMAR AND AUTOCORRECT**

1. On the Tools menu, select **AutoCorrect Options**. Note the available options and then scroll through the list of replacement words (you can add additional words). Click **Cancel** to close the AutoCorrect dialog box.

2. Key the following sentences exactly as they are shown; include the misspellings and abbreviations. Note that many errors are automatically corrected as you key.

3. In the last sentence, tap ENTER to accept the AutoText entry at the beginning of the sentence.

4. Right-click on the words marked with a wavy red line and correct the errors.

5. Proofread the lines to find two unmarked errors.

6. Save the document as *28a-drill1*. Print and close the document.

i beleive a lot of dissatisfied customers will not return.

a seperate committee was formed to deal with the new issues.

please includ a self-addressed stamped envelope with you letter.

To Whom It May Concern: If you don't receive a repsonse to you e-mail messige, call Robbins and Assocaites at 555-0106.

D r i l l 2   INSERT COLUMN

1. Open *46c-drill1*.

2. Click the insertion point in cell B1 and insert a column to the right.

3. Key the data at the right. Left-align the column data. Adjust the column widths so that all copy fits on one line.

4. Center the text vertically in the cells for the new column. Save as *46c-drill2* and print.

Office

Wilshire

Toledo

Lake Forest

Tampa

Las Vegas

Boston

Chicago

San Francisco

Change Table Borders and Lines

You can change the appearance of a table by changing the style, width (thickness), and color of the lines. You also can apply different borders to different parts of the table. To apply changes to the entire table, be sure that *Table* is displayed in the Apply to list box. To change a cell, select the cell, click the down arrow in the Apply to list box, and choose **Cell**.

When working with borders, keep in mind the difference between gridlines and borders. **Gridlines** are light gray lines that show the structure of a table; **borders** are solid lines over the gridlines. Gridlines do not print, but borders do.

To change table borders:

1. Click in the table, click the **Format** menu, and choose **Borders and Shading**.

2. If necessary, click the **Borders** tab, and choose an appropriate setting.

   a. **None:** No borders on cells; gridlines display but do not print.
   b. **Box:** Borders only on the outside of the table; gridlines display but do not print.
   c. **All:** Borders on all cells.

3. To change the border style, scroll through the Style list and choose a border.

4. To change the color, click the **Color** down arrow and select a border color.

5. To change the border width (thickness), click the **Width** down arrow and select a width.

D r i l l 3   TABLE BORDERS

1. Open the data file *insert rows*.

2. Click anywhere in the table. In the Borders and Shading dialog box, change the border setting to **None**. Print.

3. Click the **Undo** button to restore the original table. Change the border setting to **Box**, and then print. Undo and repeat with the setting changed to **All**.

4. Change the border settings of the table to **Grid**. Change the border style to a double line and change the color to red. Save as *46c-drill3a*. Print.

5. Open the data file *insert rows*. Select only row 1. Display the Borders and Shading dialog box; notice that the Apply to box displays Cell. Change the border color to red and the width to 2¼ pt. Save the file as *46c-drill3b*. Print.

Date and Time

The current date and time can be inserted into documents using the **Date and Time** command from the Insert menu.

1. Choose **Date and Time** from the Insert menu.

2. Choose a format from the Available Formats box. Standard business format is the month-day-year format.

Note: The date is inserted as text and will not change. To update the date each time the document is opened, click the **Update Automatically** checkbox.

D r i l l   2 | INSERT DATE

1. Open *27b-d2*. Position the pointer at the right margin on the line below your name.

2. Insert the date using the day/month/year format; then tap ENTER.

3. Spell-check the document and make corrections, if necessary.

4. Save as *28a-drill2*.

Undo/Redo

To reverse the most recent action you have taken (such as inserting or deleting text, formatting in bold or underline, changing line spacing, etc.), click the **Undo** button. To reverse several actions, click the down arrow beside Undo to display a list of recent actions. Then click the action you wish to reverse. Note, however, that all actions you performed prior to the action you select also will be reversed. Commands such as Save and Print cannot be undone this way.

Redo reverses the last Undo and can be applied several times to redo the past several actions. Click on the down arrow beside Redo to view all actions that can be redone.

D r i l l   3 | UNDO/REDO

1. Open *28a-drill2*. Change the line spacing in paragraph 1 to 1.5 and indent the first line.

2. Underline PARAGRAPH FORMATS in the last paragraph.

3. Undo the line spacing and the indent in paragraph 1.

4. Undo the underline on PARAGRAPH FORMATS.

5. Redo the line spacing and the indenting in paragraph 1. Key the following sentence at the end of paragraph 1:

   Line spacing in this paragraph is now 1.5". *dovad*

6. Save as *28a-drill3*.

Edit Text

Once text is keyed, it often needs to be corrected or changed. *Word* automatically corrects some text as you key it and provides various other methods for editing text. These methods are described below.

Insert: Insert mode is the *Word* default. To insert text, click or move the insertion point where the new text is to appear and key the text. Existing text moves to the right.

Delete: Delete is used to remove text that is no longer wanted. To delete a single character, click the insertion point to the left of the character and press DELETE. To delete a word, double-click the word and press DELETE.

Overtype: Overtype replaces existing text with new text that is being keyed. To turn on Overtype, double-click **OVR** on the status bar. To return to Insert mode, double-click **OVR** again.

> **TIP**
>
> Tap the Insert key to change from Insert mode to overtype mode. Tap the Insert key again to change to Insert mode.

Revise Tables

WARMUP
46a
Key each line twice SS.

alphabet	1	Jakob will save the money required for your next big cash prizes.
fig/sym	2	I saw Vera buy 13 7/8 yards of #240 cotton denim at $6.96 a yard.
3rd/4th	3	Zone 12 is impassable; quickly rope it off. Did you wax Zone 90?
easy	4	Did an auditor handle the formal audit of the firms for a profit?

| 1 | 2 | 3 | 4 | 5 | 6 | 7 | 8 | 9 | 10 | 11 | 12 | 13 |

46b
Technique Builder
Key each line twice SS.

caps	5	James Carswell plans to visit Austin and New Orleans in December.
	6	Will Peter and Betsy go with Mark when he goes to Alaska in June?
	7	John Kenny wrote the book Innovation and Timing—Keys to Success.
double letters	8	Jeanne arranges meeting room space in Massey Hall for committees.
	9	Russell will attend to the bookkeeping issues tomorrow afternoon.
	10	Todd offered a free book with all assessment tools Lynette sells.
balanced hand	11	Jane, a neighbor and a proficient auditor, may amend their audit.
	12	Blanche and a neighbor may make an ornament for an antique chair.
	13	Claudia may visit the big island when they go to Orlando with us.

NEW FUNCTIONS
46c

Insert and Delete Columns and Rows

Columns can be added to the left or right of existing columns. Rows can be added above or below existing rows. A row also can be added at the end of the table by clicking the insertion point in the last cell and tapping TAB.

To insert rows or columns in a table:

1. Click the insertion point where the new row or column is to be inserted. If several rows or columns are to be inserted, select the number you want to insert.
2. Click the **Table** menu and choose **Insert**.
3. Choose **Rows Above** or **Rows Below** to insert rows. Choose **Columns to the Left** or **Columns to the Right** to insert columns.

To delete rows or columns in a table:

1. Click the insertion point in the row or column to be deleted. If you want to delete more than one row or column, you must first select them.
2. Click the **Table** menu, choose **Delete**, and then choose **Rows** or **Columns**.

Drill 1 | INSERT ROWS

1. Open the data file *insert rows* and add the sales representatives' names in alphabetical order.
2. Delete the row containing *Heil, Clinton*.
3. Save the document as *46c-drill1*, and leave it open.

Connors, Margaret	**South**	**87,560**
Roberts, George	**East**	**97,850**
Zales, Laura	**West**	**93,500**

Drill 4 | EDIT TEXT

1. Open the document *26a-drill4*.

2. Edit the document as indicated by the proofreaders' marks below. Use the most efficient method to move within the document to make the changes.

3. Change the line spacing to double. If necessary, delete any extra hard returns between paragraphs.

4. Tab to indent the first line of each paragraph.

5. Print the document and then save it as *28a-drill4*.

Serendipity, a ~~new homework~~ research tool from Information Technology Company, is available to subscribers of ~~the major~~ online services via the World Wide Web.

Offered as a subscription service aimed at ~~college~~ students, Serendipity is a collection of tens of thousands of articles from ~~major~~ encyclopedias, reference books, magazines, pamphlets, and Internet sources combined into a single searchable database. *with just a computer and a modem*

Serendipity puts an electronic library right at students' fingertips. The program offers two browse-and-search capabilities. Users can find articles by entering questions in simple question format or browse the database by pointing and clicking on key words that identify related articles. For more information, call 800-555-0174 or address e-mail to lab@serendipity.com. *on just about any subject*

DOCUMENT DESIGN • DOCUMENT DESIGN • DOCUMENT DESIGN • DOCUMENT DESIGN • DOCUMENT DESIGN • DOCUMENT DESIGN

» DOCUMENT DESIGN
28b

Interoffice Memorandums

Messages sent to employees within an organization are called **memorandums** (memos for short). Memos may be keyed on plain paper, on letterhead, or on forms.

Position first line about 2.1" from top of page.

2.1" (Tap ENTER six times.)

Use double spacing, bold, and all caps for memo headings. Typically, titles are not used.

Use default side margins.

SS the body of the memo. DS between paragraphs.

Key notations a DS below the body.

TO: All Employees
    ↓2
FROM: Lee Marks
    ↓2
DATE: Insert current date
    ↓2
SUBJECT: Holiday Schedule
    ↓2

As you know, we celebrate our Founder's Day on Friday. The luncheon begins at noon. All offices will close at 11:45 a.m. and reopen on Monday.

We hope you enjoy the luncheon and free afternoon.
    ↓2
xx

[45d]
Build Staying Power

Take two 3' writings on all paragraphs.

all letters

In a recent show, a young skater gave a great performance. 12 | 4 | 69
Her leaps were beautiful, her spins were impossible to believe, 25 | 8 | 74
and she was a study in grace itself. But she had slipped during 38 | 13 | 78
a jump and had gone down briefly on the ice. Because of the high 51 | 17 | 82
quality of her act, however, she was given a third-place medal. 64 | 21 | 87

Her coach, talking later to a reporter, stated his pleasure 12 | 25 | 91
with her part of the show. When asked about the fall, he said 25 | 30 | 95
that emphasis should be placed on the good qualities of the per- 37 | 34 | 99
formance and not on one single blemish. He ended by saying that 50 | 38 | 104
as long as his students did the best they could, he would be 63 | 42 | 108
satisfied. 65 | 43 | 108

What is "best"? When asked, the young skater explained she 12 | 47 | 112
was pleased to have won the bronze medal. In fact, this perfor- 25 | 51 | 117
mance was a personal best for her; she was confident the gold 37 | 55 | 121
would come later if she worked hard enough. It appears she knew 50 | 60 | 125
the way to a better medal lay in beating not other people, but her 64 | 64 | 130
own personal best. 67 | 65 | 131

```
1' | 1 | 2 | 3 | 4 | 5 | 6 | 7 | 8 | 9 | 10 | 11 | 12 | 13 |
3' |     1     |      2      |      3      |      4      |
```

Timely Topics

safely shopping online

Shopping online is easy and convenient; you can shop 24 hours a day, seven days a week. You can do comparison shopping and look for your best bargain without leaving your chair. Just like shopping in a mall or by mail, Internet shopping has its dangers. Protect yourself by shopping with companies with a good reputation. Almost anyone can set up shop anytime on the Internet. Read the company's refund and return policy before making your purchase. Obtain all the details about the item, such as detailed description, cost for shipping, tax, and delivery time. Use a credit card to make your purchase. By doing so, you can dispute your charges, and if there is unauthorized use of the card, you are only held liable for the first $50 in charges. Do not supply information that is not necessary for the purchase, such as your social security number or bank account numbers. Always print a copy of the sales transaction, which should include a confirmation number. Being "cyber smart" will make your online shopping experiences safer and more enjoyable.

Sterling Design Consultants

2.1" (Tap ENTER six times.)

Heading

TO:　　　　Students　↓2

FROM:　　　Roger C. Westfield　↓2

DATE:　　　Current date　↓2

SUBJECT:　A New Perspective on Memos　↓2

Body

Your instructor has asked that I prepare a memo for you describing the changing role of memos and the importance of formatting memos effectively. Sterling uses its logo and company name on the top of its memos. First, you will learn to prepare memos on plain paper. Later you will learn to use templates for them. A template is a stored document format that would contain the company logo and name as well as the memo headings.

The format does not differ regardless of whether plain paper or a template is used. The headings are positioned about 2" from the top of the paper, and default side margins are used. Headings are keyed in all caps, bold, and double-spaced. The body is single-spaced with a blank line between each paragraph. Notations such as reference initials, enclosures, or copies are keyed a double space below the body. Some companies adopt slightly different styles; however, this style is very commonly used.

Often a memo is sent electronically. It can either be in the form of an e-mail or as an attachment to an e-mail. Memos were designed to be documents that stayed within a company. However, e-mail is changing the role of memos. E-mails, even though they are formatted as memos, are frequently sent outside of companies. Some companies use e-mail to deliver a document but attach a letter or a memo to it.

Reference Initials → xx

[45c-d3]
Table with AutoSum

1. Key the table and apply **Table List 8** style; deselect **Last row** and **Last column** under Apply special formats to. Format the table according to the Table Format Guides on page 180.
2. Center column B and align column C in the approximate center with a decimal tab.
✳ 3. Total the figures in column C using AutoSum from the Tables and Borders toolbar. Center the table vertically and horizontally.
4. Save the document as *45c-d3a* and print.
✳ 5. Change the price of dinner rolls to $20. Recalculate the total. Save as *45c-d3b* and print again.

✳ DISCOVER

Σ With the insertion point in the correct cell, click **AutoSum** to total a column.

To recalculate a total when any numbers have been changed, tap F9.

QUEEN'S BAKERY AND PASTRIES

Catering Invoice

Item	Quantity	Total Price ($)
Cherry nut muffins	3 dozen	25.75
Dinner rolls	4 dozen	18.50
Whole wheat breadsticks	2 dozen	10.00
Brownies	2 dozen	16.00
Assorted pastries	3 dozen	24.00
Total		

[45c-d4]
Table with AutoFormat

1. Display the Tables and Borders toolbar. Click the **Insert Table** button. Set the number of columns and rows needed to create the table below.
2. Click the **AutoFormat** button and select **Table List 1** style. Deselect **Last row**. This removes the horizontal line above the last row. Click **Apply**.
3. Select the numbers in column D and set a decimal tab that aligns the numbers so they appear centered in the column. Center-align column A.
4. Change the row height and center the text vertically in the cells. Center the table vertically and horizontally on the page. Save as *45c-d4a* and print. Apply **Table Grid** style; recenter the text vertically in the cells. Save as *45c-d4b* and print.

INTERNATIONAL FINANCIAL SYSTEMS

Collection Status Report

Client Number	Last Name	First Name	Current Balance
1002	Castillo	Robert	2,861.63
1003	Aguirre	Janna	115.02
1007	Perez	Linda	1,194.30
1008	Nieto	Victor	1,746.80
1009	Plate	Sharon	1,352.00
1011	Mau	Marianne	942.25

Proofread and Finalize a Document

Before documents are complete, they must be proofread carefully for accuracy. Error-free documents send the message that you are detail-oriented and capable. Apply these procedures when processing all documents:

1. Use Spelling and Grammar to check spelling when you have completed the document.
2. Proofread the document on screen to be sure that it makes sense.
3. Preview the document and check the overall appearance.
4. Save the document and then print it.
5. Compare the document to the source copy (textbook) and check that text has not been omitted or added. Revise, save, and print, if necessary.

Drill 5 | FORMAT MEMO

1. Key the short memo in 28b on page 89; do not key the memohead.

2. Proofread on the screen and make any necessary corrections.

3. Save as *28b-drill5*.

APPLICATIONS

1. Key the following paragraphs DS *Double Space* and make the revisions shown.
2. Save the document as *28c-d1*. Print the document.

[28c-d1]
Rough Draft

The World Wide Web (www) and Internet Usenet News groups are electronic fan clubs that offers users a ways to exchange views and information on just about any topic imaginable with people all around the world.

World Wide Web screens contain text, graphic*s* and pictures*, and often audio and video*. Simple pointing and clicking on the pictures and links (underlined words) bring users to new pages or sites of information.

[28c-d2]
Memo

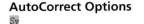
1. Read the memo illustrated on page 90 carefully. Key this memo on plain paper; do not key the memohead.
2. Use the Date and Time feature to insert the current date.
3. If the first letter of your reference initials is automatically capitalized, point to the initial until the AutoCorrect Options button appears. Click the button; then choose **Undo Automatic Capitalization**.
4. Proofread the memo carefully and make any changes that are necessary.
5. Save as *28c-d2* and print the document.

1. Open *45b-drill2* and click the insertion point in the table.

2. Apply a style of your choice. **Note:** When a new AutoFormat style is applied, the text moves back to the top of the cell. Recenter the text vertically in the cells (**Table, Table Properties, Cell**). Print.

3. Apply the **Table Grid** style to the table to return it to its original state. **Note:** The shading applied in *45b-drill2* has been removed. Recenter the text vertically in the cells.

4. Save the document as *45b-drill3*.

APPLICATIONS

[45c-d1]

Memo with Table with Decimal Tabs

1. Key the following memo to **Robert May**, from **Marcia Lewis**. The subject is **Purchase Order 5122**.

2. Center the data in column A, set a decimal tab to align column C in the approximate center of the column, apply 15% shading to row 1, adjust the columns widths, and center the table horizontally.

3. DS after the table and add your reference initials. Save it as *45c-d1*.

The items that you requested on Purchase Order 5122 are in stock and will be shipped from our warehouse today. The shipment will be transported via Romulus Delivery System and is expected to arrive at your location in five days. ↓2

Item Number	Description	Unit Price
329	Lordusky locking cabinet	212.00
331	Anchorage heavy-duty locking cabinet	265.00
387	Lordusky locking cabinet (unassembled)	99.00

[45c-d2]

Table with Shading

1. Key the table. Then set a decimal tab to align columns B and C in the approximate center of the column and apply 15% shading to row 1.

2. Adjust the column widths, center the table horizontally, and center the page vertically. Save the table as *45c-d2*.

LOS ALTOS DRY CLEANING SPECIALS

Garment	Regular Price	Special Price
Wool sweater	6.50	5.00
Men's two-piece suit	8.00	6.75
Women's two-piece suit	8.00	6.75
Leather jacket	45.00	40.00
Leather pants	37.00	30.50
Slacks	4.50	3.75
Skirt	4.00	3.00
Blazer	5.00	3.75
Silk shirt/blouse	5.00	4.25

Create E-mail and Memos

WARMUP
29a
Key each line twice.

Use *CheckPro*, if available, for this lesson.

alphabet 1 Which oval-jet black onyx ring blazed on the queen's prim finger?

figures 2 Cy will be 19 on May 4; Jo, 27 on May 6 or 8; Mike, 30 on June 5.

adjacent 3 We acquire few rewards for walking short treks to Union Terminal.

easy 4 To augment and enrich the visual signal, I turn the right handle.

| 1 | 2 | 3 | 4 | 5 | 6 | 7 | 8 | 9 | 10 | 11 | 12 | 13 |

29b Rhythm Builder
Key lines 5–10 twice.

Balanced-hand words, phrases, and sentences

5 if me to so he is us do go or sod fir for pen may big dig got fix

6 dog jam sit men lap pay cut nap tug lake worn make torn turn dock

7 he is | it is | of it | is it | go to | to go | is he | he is it | for it | she can

8 did he | pay them | she may | is it torn | it is worn | he may go | the lake

9 He may also go with them to the dock or down to the lake with us.

10 Did she go with Keith to the lake, or can she go to town with us?

NEW FUNCTIONS
29c

AutoText

The AutoText feature enables you to store text that is used often and to insert it without keying it. For example, you probably key your full name frequently. Once you key and store your name, a screen tip appears as you start to key it. You can insert it by tapping ENTER or by selecting the name of your AutoText from the entries listed.

To create AutoText:

1. Select the text you want to store as AutoText.
2. Click **AutoText** on the Insert menu.
3. Select **New** to display the Create AutoText name box.
4. Key a name and click **OK**.

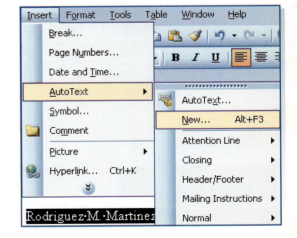

Tables and Borders Toolbar

You can change the appearance of tables by adding shading, borders, patterns, and color. You can use Table AutoFormat to apply a preformatted design to the table or to display the Tables and Borders toolbar, which provides you with many formatting options. To display this toolbar, click the **View** menu, click **Toolbars**, and then click **Tables and Borders**.

Shading Cells

Shading can be applied to cells for emphasis. Normally, shading is applied to emphasize headings, totals, or divisions and sections of a table.

To add shading to cells:

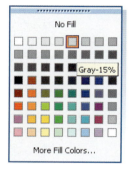

1. Select the cells to be shaded and click the **Shading Color** drop list arrow on the Tables and Borders toolbar.

2. Choose a color or shade of gray. If you are applying shading over text, choose 20% gray or lighter.

Option: Click the **Format** menu, choose **Borders and Shading**, and then click the **Shading** tab. Under Style, click the down arrow to change *Clear* to *15%* (row 1, item 5); then click **OK**.

D r i l l   2   SHADING

1. Open *45b-drill1*.

2. Display the Table and Borders toolbar (**View menu, Toolbars**).

3. Select row 1 and apply 15% shading.

4. Save as *45b-drill2*. Print.

Table AutoFormat

AutoFormat enables you to apply one of *Word's* many attractive preformatted styles to tables. Choose a style based on the information in the table. For example, a style with shading in the last row is well suited to a table with totals. The table can be restored to its original style by clicking the **Undo** button or by choosing the **Table Grid** AutoFormat.

To use AutoFormat:

1. Create the table and key the table data without formats.

2. Click the insertion point in the table and then click the **AutoFormat** button on the Tables and Borders toolbar.

3. In the Table AutoFormat dialog box, check to see that All table styles is displayed in the Category list box; then choose a style from the Table styles list box.

4. Click **Apply** to apply the style and return to the table.

5. If you wish to restore the table to its original state, choose **Table Grid** from the Table styles list box.

To insert AutoText:

1. Click **AutoText** on the Insert menu.

2. Next, click **AutoText** and scroll down to find the name of the AutoText you wish to enter.

3. Click **Insert**.

Note: If you check the Show AutoComplete suggestions box, a screen tip will display the AutoText once you key the first four letters in a document. Tap ENTER and the text will be inserted.

D r i l l   1   **CREATE AND INSERT AUTOTEXT**

1. Create AutoText for your full name.

2. Use **My Name** as the name for the AutoText.

3. Enter your name at the top of a new document by inserting AutoText; check the Show AutoComplete suggestions box.

4. Position the insertion point several lines below your name; key the first four letters of your name. Tap ENTER when your name appears in a screen tip.

5. Save as *29c-drill1*.

DOCUMENT DESIGN • DOCUMENT DESIGN • DOCUMENT DESIGN • DOCUMENT DESIGN • DOCUMENT DESIGN • DOCUMENT DESIGN

>> DOCUMENT DESIGN
29d

Electronic Mail

Electronic mail (or **e-mail**) is a message sent by one computer user to another computer user. E-mail was originally designed as an informal, personal way of communicating. However, it is now used extensively in business. For business use, e-mail should not be casual or informal.

Using e-mail requires an e-mail program, an e-mail address, and access to the Internet. If you cannot meet these requirements, format all e-mail in this text as memos.

Address e-mail carefully. Key and check the address of the recipient and always supply a subject line. Also, key the e-mail address of anyone who should receive a copy of the e-mail.

Format the body of an e-mail SS; DS between paragraphs. Do not indent paragraphs. Limit the use of bold, italics, and uppercase. For business use, avoid abbreviations and emoticons (e.g., :- for wink or BTW for by the way).

Format Tables

alphabet	1	Gay expected to solve the jigsaw puzzle more quickly than before.
	2	Extra awards given by my employer amazed Jo, the file clerk.
figures	3	Jane opened Rooms 16, 20, and 39 and locked Rooms 48, 53, and 57.
	4	I will be on vacation June 4-7, October 3, 5, 8, and December 6-9.
shift	5	Ted and I spent April in San Juan and May in St. Paul, Minnesota.
	6	Sue, May, Al, Tom, and Jo will meet us at the Pick and Save store.

| 1 | 2 | 3 | 4 | 5 | 6 | 7 | 8 | 9 | 10 | 11 | 12 | 13 |

new FUNCTIONS
45b

Decimal Tabs

Decimal **tabs** are used to align numbers at their decimal points when numbers have varying lengths of decimal places. Dollar amounts and other numbers should be aligned at the right.

Tab Alignment button

Left-aligned   **Center-aligned**   **Right-aligned**   **Decimal-aligned**

Employee	Position	Identification	Rating
Ralph Marshall	Associate	486028776	564.333
Janice Goodman	Manager	3495075	87654.01

To set a decimal tab:

1. Display the Horizontal Ruler (**View menu, Ruler**).
2. Select the column or cells to be aligned (do not include the column heading). The numbers in the cells should be left-aligned.
3. Click the **Tab Alignment** button at the far left of the Horizontal Ruler and change the tab type to a decimal tab.
4. Click the **Horizontal Ruler** to set a decimal tab.

Drill 1 | DECIMAL TABS

1. Create and key the table.
2. Follow the Table Format Guides on page 180 for headings and row height.
3. Select column B and center-align it. Right-align column C.
4. Select cells D2–D5 and set a decimal tab at about 5.4" to align the numbers near the center of the column.
5. Save the document as *45b-drill1*. Keep the document displayed on your screen.

Employee	Position	Identification	Rating
Ralph Marshall	Associate	486028776	564.333
Janice Goodman	Manager	3495075	87654.01
Frank Wiley	Associate	9376	157.198
Dinh Lee	Manager	732	96.52

Using Word to Create E-mail

Landscape Plan - Message

File   Edit   View   Insert   Format   Tools   Table   Window   Help   Type a question for help

Normal   Times New Roman   12   **B** *I* U

Options...   HTML

To...   Les.Grenzeback@sterlingtech.edu

Cc...   wdinkins@krider.com

Subject: Landscape Plan

Attach...   Landscape Plan.doc (24 KB)   Attachment Options...

The landscape plan for your new building has been completed, and a reduced version is attached. Three full-size copies will be delivered to your office tomorrow morning. If you need additional copies, please e-mail me today.

To create e-mail using *Word*:

1. Click **New** on the File menu.
2. Click **E-mail** message on the task pane that displays; note that the form contains lines for To, Cc, and Subject.
3. Key the e-mail addresses for the recipient(s) and anyone else who is to receive a copy of the e-mail.
4. Key a subject in the appropriate box.
5. If you wish to attach a file, click the **Attach** button. The Attach box is added to the e-mail form. Next, browse for the name of the file you wish to insert and double-click it.
6. Click the **Send** button or key ALT + S to send the e-mail. (Note that you must be connected to the Internet to send the e-mail.)

To create e-mail using another system:

1. Click the **Write** button or a similarly named button on your system.
2. Fill in the addresses for the To and Copy boxes. Add a subject line and key the message.
3. Click the **Attach** button if a file is to be attached; then click the **Send** button.

1. Center the two-line main heading SS on approximately line 2.1". Tap ENTER twice.
2. Change to left-align and turn off bold. Use the Table button to create the table. Key the table. Center column B.
3. Select row 1 and bold and center-align the column headings. Adjust column widths and center the table horizontally.
4. Select the table and change the row height to .3"; center the text vertically in the cells. Save as *44d-d2*.

COMPARISON OF CIVILIAN
AND MILITARY TIMES

Civilian Time	Military Time
1:00 a.m.	0100
2:00 a.m.	0200
4:15 a.m.	0415
Noon	1200
2:20 p.m.	1420
6:00 p.m.	1800
Midnight	2400

Center this column.

1. Key and format the table: Center and bold column heads; adjust column widths; change row height to .3". Center the text vertically in the cells.
2. Center the table vertically and horizontally on the page. Check to see that you have followed the Table Format Guides on page 180. Save as *44d-d3*.

STAGES OF LIFE SPAN DEVELOPMENT

Stage	Approximate Age
Infancy	Birth to 1 year
Toddler	1 to 3 years
Preschool	3 to 5 years
School age	6 to 12 years
Adolescence	13 to 19 years
Early adulthood	20 to 39 years
Middle adulthood	40 to 65 years
Late adulthood	65 years and over

Using Another E-mail System (AOL®) to Create E-mail

Write Mail

Send To: Les.Grenzeback@sterlingtech.edu   Copy To: wdinkins@krider.com

Send Now

Subject: Landscape Plan

Arial   10   B I U A A ≡ ☺ ♥ Extras ▾

Send Later

The landscape plan for your new building has been completed, and a reduced version is attached. Three full-size copies will be delivered to your office tomorrow morning. If you need additional copies, please e-mail me today.

Address Book

Print

📄 Landscape Plan.doc (23 KB)

[Attach File] [Detach File]   ☐ Request "Return Receipt" [Spell Check] [Signatures ▾]

APPLICATIONS

Follow these directions for completing all e-mail applications in this text:

- *Without Internet access:* Complete all documents as memos.
- *With an e-mail address:* Complete the documents in your software and send them.
- *With Internet access but no e-mail address:* Your instructor will assist you in setting up a free e-mail account and address.

[29e-d1]

E-mail

1. Prepare the e-mail below to your instructor; copy a classmate.
2. Attach the file *28c-d2* that you prepared in the last lesson.
3. Print and send the e-mail. If you cannot send it, key it as a memo and save the file as *29e-d1*.

Subject: Preparing E-mails

The guides that Sterling Design Consultants prepared for memos are good advice for preparing business e-mails as well. I have attached a copy of the memo from Mr. Westfield for your review.

Be sure to proofread and edit e-mails carefully. Making e-mails error free is as important as making any other document error free.

Drill 3 | ADJUST COLUMN WIDTH AND CHANGE ROW HEIGHT

1. Open *44b-drill2*. Use the mouse to adjust the width of the columns so they look attractive.

2. Change the row height to .3". Center the text vertically in the cell.

3. Center the table horizontally on the page.

4. Save the table as *44b-drill3* and print.

DOCUMENT DESIGN • DOCUMENT DESIGN • DOCUMENT DESIGN • DOCUMENT DESIGN • DOCUMENT DESIGN • DOCUMENT DESIGN

» DOCUMENT DESIGN
44c

Table Format Guides

1. Key the main heading on approximately line 2.1", or center the table vertically on the page.

2. **Headings:** Center, bold, and key the main heading in all caps. Key the secondary heading a DS below the main heading in bold and centered; capitalize main words. Center and bold all column headings.

3. Adjust column widths attractively, and center the table horizontally.

4. Select the table, change the row height to .3", and then center the text vertically in the cells.

5. Align text within cells at the left. Align numbers at the right. Align decimal numbers of varying lengths at the decimal point.

6. When a table appears within a document, DS before and after the table.

[APPLICATIONS]

[44d-d1]
Table

1. Center the main heading on approximately line 2.1". Center the secondary heading.

2. Tap ENTER twice. Change the alignment to left and turn off bold. Create a three-column, six-row table.

3. Key the table. Right-align the numbers in column C. Center column heads.

4. Adjust column width, change row height to .3", and center text vertically in the cells. Center the table horizontally on the page.

5. Check to see that you have followed the Table Format Guides above. Save as *44d-d1*. Print.

COOK OFFICE PRODUCTS

20-- Sales

Sales Agent	Territory	Amount of Sale
Stephanie Acosta	Northwest	$1,157,829
George Cunningham	Central	$4,245,073
Angel Izadi	Southwest	$6,301,625
Joseph Viceroy, Jr.	Midwest	$99,016
Lauren Zimmerman	East	$82,479

[29e-d2]
Memo

1. Key and format the following memo.
2. Use the Date and Time feature to insert the current date. Check the spelling.
3. Proofread and correct all errors, following the steps under *Proofread and Finalize a Document* on page 91. Remember to add your reference initials.
4. Save as *29e-d2* and print.

▼2.1"

TO: All Laurel Aircraft Employees

FROM: Melvin Galvez, Manager

DATE: *Insert current date*

SUBJECT: New Production Center

Laurel Aircraft is pleased to announce the completion of our new production center, located in B-107. Our center is able to produce high-resolution digital imaging for both color and black-and-white documents. You can bring us your PC or Mac files on disk, CD-ROM, or Zip disk, or you can e-mail them directly to our center.

Our staff is here to serve you and help you with all your in-house graphic needs from conception through completion. Stop by and visit our new center.

[29e-d3]
E-mail

1. Prepare an e-mail to your instructor using an appropriate subject line; attach the file *29e-d2* to it.
2. Print and send the e-mail. If you cannot send it, key it as a memo and save the file as *29e-d3*.

My internship will be in the new Production Center. I thought you might be interested in the attached memo about it.

I am excited about this opportunity.

29f Timed Writings

1. Take two 1' timings; key as rapidly as you can.
2. Take one 2' timing. Try to maintain your 1' rate.

 all letters

	gwam	1'	2'
The value of an education has been a topic discussed many	12	6	48
times with a great deal of zest. The value is often measured in	25	12	54
terms of costs and benefits to the taxpayer. It is also judged	37	19	61
in terms of changes in the individuals taking part in the	49	24	67
educational process. Gains in the level of knowledge, the	61	30	72
development and refinement of attitudes, and the acquiring of	73	36	79
skills are believed to be crucial parts of an education.	84	42	84

```
1' |  1  |  2  |  3  |  4  |  5  |  6  |  7  |  8  |  9  |  10 |  11 |  12 |  13 |
2' |     1     |     2     |     3     |     4     |     5     |     6     |
```

Column marker

COLLEGE·SPORTS·PR

Fall·Events□		Winter·Events□
Football□		Basketball□
Soccer□		Gymnastics□
Volleyball□		Swimming□

Adjust Column Widths

Tables are created with equal column widths. Since text in the columns may vary in length, the table may be more attractive if columns are adjusted to accommodate the text in them. Column widths can be changed manually using the mouse or automatically using AutoFit. Using the mouse enables you to adjust the widths as you like. Once the width of the columns has been changed, you will need to recenter the table horizontally.

To adjust column widths using the mouse:

1. Position the mouse over the right border of the column that is to be adjusted. When the pointer changes to ✛, drag the border to the left to make the column narrower or to the right to make it wider.

2. Adjust the column width so that there is approximately 0.5" to 0.75" between the longest line and the column border. Use the Horizontal Ruler as a guide. Display the width of the columns by pointing to a column marker on the Ruler, holding down the ALT key, and clicking the left mouse button.

To center a table horizontally:

1. With the insertion point in the table, click the **Table** menu and choose **Table Properties**.

2. Click the **Table** tab, if necessary.

3. Choose the **Center** option in the Alignment box and click **OK**.

Change Row Height

Tables can be made to look more attractive and easier to read by inserting some blank space above and below the text; this can be done by increasing the row height. After increasing the row height, center the text vertically in the cell.

To increase the row height and center the text vertically in the cell:

1. Create and key the table. Turn on **Show/Hide**.

2. Select only the table; be careful not to select any ¶ markers outside the table. Click the **Table** menu and select **Table Properties**.

3. Click the **Row** tab. Click the **Specify Height** checkbox. Use the spin arrows to select a row height.

4. Click the **Cell** tab. Choose **Center Alignment** so the text will display in the middle of the cell. Click **OK**.

Review Memos and E-mail

WARMUP
30a
Key each line twice.

alphabet	1	Buddy Jackson is saving the door prize money for wax and lacquer.
figures	2	I have fed 47 hens, 25 geese, 10 ducks, 39 lambs, and 68 kittens.
one hand	3	You imply Jon Case exaggerated my opinion on a decrease in rates.
easy	4	I shall make hand signals to the widow with the auditory problem.

| 1 | 2 | 3 | 4 | 5 | 6 | 7 | 8 | 9 | 10 | 11 | 12 | 13 |

30b Rhythm Builder
Key lines 5–8 twice.
Take two 30" timings on lines 9 and 10.

Balanced-hand words, phrases, and sentences

5 am an by do go he if is it me or ox or so for and big the six spa

6 but cod dot dug eye end wit vie yam make also city work gage them

7 is it| is it| is it he| is it he| for it| for it| paid for it| it is she

8 of it| pay due| pay for| paid me| paid them| also make| such as| may end

9 Sue and Bob may go to the zoo, and he or she may pay for the gas.

10 Jim was sad; Ted saw him as we sat on my bed; we saw him get gas.

| 1 | 2 | 3 | 4 | 5 | 6 | 7 | 8 | 9 | 10 | 11 | 12 | 13 |

FUNCTION REVIEW
30c

1. Key and format the following paragraphs SS; justify alignment; make all edits marked.
2. Right-align your name a DS below the last line.
3. Insert the current date in month/date/year format a DS directly below your name.
4. Proofread and correct errors. Run Spelling and Grammar Check.
5. Print and save as *30c*.
6. Reformat the two paragraphs; DS and indent paragraphs; use left alignment; hide the date; save as *30c-2*.

GOOD COMMUNICATION SKILLS — bold, center-align, 14 pt. font

Documents that are formatted correctly and that are free of errors create a good impression. Creating a good impression is as important on internal documents such as memos and e-mail as it is on external documents.

When people read your documents that are not formatted appropriately and that contain errors they think your communications skills are lacking or that you do not care. Either way, the result could be harmful to your career. The time you spend editing documents will pay big dividends. Good communication skills are critical for success in virtually every job.

Format Table, Rows, Columns, or Cells

If you wish to apply a format such as bold, alignment, or line spacing to the table, you must first select the table. Likewise, to format a specific row, column, or cell, you must select the table parts and then apply the format. Editing features such as delete and undo work in the usual manner. Follow these steps to select various parts of the table:

To select	Move the insertion point:
Entire table	Over the table and click the table move handle in the upper left of the table. (*Option:* **Table menu, Select, Table**). To move the table, drag the table move handle to a new location.
Column	To the top of the column until a solid down arrow appears; click the left mouse button.
Row	To the left area just outside the table until the pointer turns to an open arrow (⬦); then click the left mouse button.

Note: You can also select rows and columns by selecting a cell, column, or row, and dragging across or down.

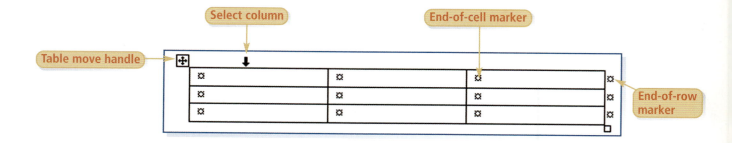

D r i l l 2   **CREATE TABLES**

1. Center-align and key the main heading in bold; tap ENTER twice.

2. Change the alignment to left and turn bold off.

3. Create a three-column, four-row table.

4. Key the table shown below; tap TAB to move from cell to cell.

5. Select row 1; then bold and center-align the column headings. Row 1 is called the **header row** because it identifies the content in each column.

6. Create the folder *Module 6 keys* and save the table as *44b-drill2* in this folder.

COLLEGE SPORTS PROGRAM

Fall Events	Winter Events	Spring Events
Football	Basketball	Golf
Soccer	Gymnastics	Baseball
Volleyball	Swimming	Softball

new functions

30d

Tabs

Tabs are used to indent paragraphs and align text vertically. Tapping the TAB key aligns text at the **tab stop**. *Word* has five types of tabs, which are listed below. The left, right, and center tabs are similar to paragraph alignment types.

⌞	**Left tab**	Aligns text at the left.
⌟	**Right tab**	Aligns text at the right.
⊥	**Center tab**	Aligns text evenly on either side of the tab stop.
⊥	**Decimal tab**	Aligns numbers at the decimal point.
I	**Bar tab**	Aligns text to the right of a vertical bar.

Tabs can be set and cleared on the Horizontal Ruler. The numbers on the Ruler indicate the distance in inches from the left margin. The small gray lines below each half-inch position are the default tab stops. The Tab Alignment button at the left edge of the Ruler indicates the type of tab. To change the tab type, click the Tab Alignment button.

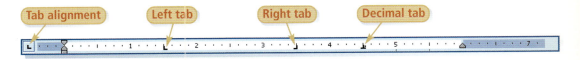

To set a tab:	Click the **Tab Alignment** button, and choose the desired tab type. Click the Horizontal Ruler where you want to set the tab.
To delete a tab:	Click the tab marker and drag it straight down off the Ruler.
To move a tab:	Click the tab marker and drag the tab to the new location.

Tabs can also be set in the Tab dialog box (**Format** menu, **Tabs**). The Tab dialog box provides more options and allows you to set precise settings.

Drill 1 | SET AND MOVE TABS

1. Display the Horizontal Ruler, if necessary (**View** menu, **Ruler**).

2. Set these tabs: left 1.5", right 3.5", and decimal 4.5".

3. Key the first three lines of the drill at these tab stops.

4. Move the left tab to 1", the right tab to 3", and the decimal tab to 5". Key the last three lines. Save it as *30d-drill1*.

Left tab 1.5"	Right tab 3.5"	Decimal tab 4.5"
Schneider	5,000	100.503
Langfield	17,200	98.9
Almich	9,500	.0198

Left tab 1"	Right tab 3"	Decimal tab 5"
McCoy	12,000	12.1
Buswinka	198,250	.98
Oritz	500	1.345

You can create tables using the Table menu or the Table button on the Standard toolbar. Either method produces the same results. Position the insertion point where you want the table to appear in the document before you begin.

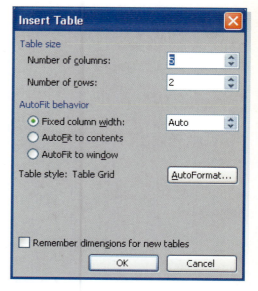

To create a table using the Table menu:

1. Click the **Table** menu and choose **Insert**; then **Table**. The Insert Table dialog box displays. The default setting of AutoFit is set to create a table with a fixed width. The columns will be of equal width and spread across the writing line.

2. Click the up or down arrows to specify the number of rows and columns. Click **OK**. The table displays.

Notice that column widths are indicated by column markers on the Ruler.

To create a table using the Insert Table button:

1. Click the **Insert Table** button on the Standard toolbar. A drop-down grid displays.

2. Click the left mouse button and drag the pointer across to highlight the number of columns in the table and down to highlight the number of rows in the table. The table displays when you release the left mouse button.

2 x 3 Table

Move Within a Table

When a table is created, the insertion point is in cell A1. To move within a table, use the TAB key or simply click within a cell using the mouse. Refer to this table as you learn to enter text in a table:

Press	Movement
TAB	To move to the next cell. If the insertion point is in the last cell, tapping TAB will add a new row.
SHIFT + TAB	To move to the previous cell.
ENTER	To increase the height of the row. If you tap ENTER by mistake, tap BACKSPACE to delete the line.

Drill 1 | CREATE TABLES

1. Create a two-column, five-row table using the Table menu.

2. Turn on **Show/Hide** and notice the marker at the end of each cell and each row. Hold down the ALT key, and click on one of the column markers on the Ruler. Notice that the width of the column is displayed in inches (2.93").

3. Close the table without saving it.

4. Create a four-column, four-row table using the Table button on the Standard toolbar.

5. Move to cell B3. Move to cell B2.

6. Move to cell A1 and tap ENTER.

7. Move to cell D4 and tap TAB.

8. Close the table without saving it.

Leader tabs

A leader tab displays a series of dots that leads the eye to the next column. Leaders can be combined with a left, center, right, or decimal tab. Leaders are often used in documents such as a table of contents, agendas, and financial statements. Leader tabs can only be set from the Tab dialog box.

To set a leader tab:

1. Click **Tabs** on the Format menu to display the Tab dialog box.
2. Enter the position of the tab in the Tab Stop Position box.
3. Choose the **Alignment** type.
4. Choose the **Leader** style, for example, 2; click **Set**; then click **OK**.

Drill 2 | LEADER TABS

1. In the Tabs dialog box, set a right leader tab at 6" using Leader style 2.

2. Set line spacing at 2.0.

3. Key the first name at the left margin and tap TAB. Note that the leaders extend to the right margin.

4. Key the title. Notice that it aligns at the right tab stop.

5. Complete the drill and save it as *30d-drill2*.

John Sneider . . . . President

JoAnn Rouche . . . . Vice President, Education

Janice Weiss . . . . Vice President, Membership

Lotus Fijutisi . . . . Chief Financial Officer

Loretta Russell . . . . Recording Secretary

Drill 3 | UNDERLINE TAB

1. In the Tabs dialog box, set a right underline tab (#4) at 6".

2. Set line spacing at 2.0.

3. Save as *30d-drill3* and print.

Name _____

Title _____

Company _____

MODULE 6

Table Basics

LESSON 44

Create Tables

WARMUP

44a

Key each line twice SS.

alphabet	1	Jim Daley gave us in that box the prize he won for his quick car.
figures	2	At 7 a.m., I open Rooms 18, 29, and 30; I lock Rooms 4, 5, and 6.
adjacent reaches	3	As Louis said, few questioned the points asserted by the porters.
easy	4	Did he vow to fight for the right to work as the Orlando auditor?

| 1 | 2 | 3 | 4 | 5 | 6 | 7 | 8 | 9 | 10 | 11 | 12 | 13 |

NEW FUNCTIONS

44b

help keywords

tables; create a table

Create Tables

Tables consist of columns and rows of data—either alphabetic, numeric, or both.

Column: Vertical list of information labeled alphabetically from left to right.

Row: Horizontal list of information labeled numerically from top to bottom.

Cell: An intersection of a column and a row. Each cell has its own address consisting of the column letter and the row number (cell A1).

Use Show/Hide to display end-of-cell marks in each cell and end-of-row marks at the end of each row. End-of-cell and end-of-row markers are useful when editing tables. Use Print Layout View to display the table move handle in the upper left of the table and the sizing handle in the lower right of the table.

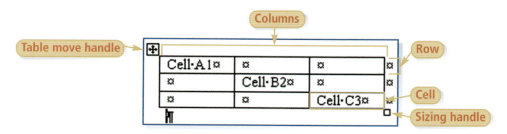

[30e-d1]
Memo with Leader and Right Tabs

1. Set a left leader tab using Leader style 2 at 5.25". Set a right tab at 5.75".

2. Key the name at the left margin; tap TAB to insert the leaders; tap TAB again and key the numbers.

3. DS memo headings; SS memo; change line spacing for the table with tabs to 1.5. Save as *30e-d1*.

TO:	David McGee, Principal
FROM:	Mike Odom, Coach
DATE:	Current
SUBJECT:	New Lineup

We have made changes in our lineup for Friday's game. We think that this lineup will improve our performance significantly, and we look forward to seeing the results.

5.25" tab   5.75" tab

Matt Hart, small forward 145
Josh McBride, power forward... 169
Carlos Goner, center 203
Rolando Powell, point guard 99
Marcus Boynton, shooting guard 127

xx

[30e-d2]
Compose E-mail

1. Compose an e-mail to your instructor indicating that you are attaching a copy of the new lineup for Friday's game. Tell your instructor that you think this will be a great improvement and that you are optimistic that the Sky Hawks will win the game. Use an appropriate subject line; attach *30e-d1*.

2. Save it as *30e-d2* if you can't send e-mail. Print the e-mail or memo.

[30e-d3]
Memo with Tabs

1. Set a left tab at .5", a right tab at 4.25", and a decimal tab at 5.0".

2. DS memo headings; SS the body.

3. Proofread carefully, save as *30e-d3*, and print.

TO:	Jane Lawrence
FROM:	Mary Bradford
DATE:	Current
SUBJECT:	Stock Transaction Completed

Today I completed the purchase of the stocks that you requested. The prices were all within the range specified. I think you will be pleased with the selections we made.

The name of the stock and symbol, the number of shares, and the price per share are listed below.

0.5" tab   4.25" tab   5.0" tab

Krider Technology (KTEC)	475	147.5
RCT Mines (RCTM)	150,875	0.875
Chrisman Pharmaceuticals (CPHAR)	1,396	89.36

xx

Drill 1
SUBJECT/VERB AGREEMENT

1. Review the rules and examples on the previous page.
2. Open *subjectverb1* from the data files. Save it as *subjectverb-drill1*.
3. Follow the specific directions provided in the data file.
4. Save again and print.

Drill 2
SUBJECT/VERB AGREEMENT

1. Open *subjectverb2* from the data files. Save it as *subjectverb-drill2*.
2. Follow the specific directions provided in the data file.
3. Save and print.

Drill 3
SUBJECT/VERB AND CAPITALIZATION

1. Key the ten sentences at the right, choosing the correct verb and applying correct capitalization.
2. Save as *subjectverb-drill3* and print.

1. both of the curies (was/were) nobel prize winners.
2. each of the directors in the sales department (has/have) given us approval.
3. mr. and mrs. thomas funderburk, jr. (was/were) married on november 23, 1936.
4. my sister and her college roommates (plan/plans) to tour london and paris this summer.
5. our new information manager (suggest/suggests) the following salutation when using an attention line: ladies and gentlemen.
6. the body language expert (place/places) his hand on his cheek as he says, "touch your hand to your chin."
7. the japanese child (enjoy/enjoys) the american food her hosts (serve/serves) her.
8. all of the candidates (was/were) invited to the debate at boston college.
9. the final exam (cover/covers) chapters 1–5.
10. turn south onto interstate 20; then take exit 56 to bossier city.

Drill 4
EDITING SKILLS

1. Key the paragraph, correcting all errors in grammar and capitalization.
2. Save as *editing-drill4*.

This past week I visited the facilities of the magnolia conference center in isle of palms, south carolina, as you requested. bob bremmerton, group manager, was my host for the visit.

magnolia offers many advantages for our leadership training conference. The prices are reasonable; the facilities is excellent; the location is suitable. In addition to the beachfront location, tennis and golf packages are part of the group price.

Assessment

31a
Key each line twice.

alphabet 1 I quickly explained to two managers the grave hazards of the job.

figures 2 All channels—16, 25, 30, and 74—reported the score was 19 to 8.

shift 3 Maxi and Kay Pascal expect to be in breezy South Mexico in April.

easy 4 Did the man fight a duel, or did he go to a chapel to sign a vow?

| 1 | 2 | 3 | 4 | 5 | 6 | 7 | 8 | 9 | 10 | 11 | 12 | 13 |

31b Timed Writing
Take two 3' timings.

all letters

gwam   3'

Hard work is required for job success. Set high goals and   4 | 43

devote time to the exact things that will help you succeed. Work   8 | 47

hard each day and realize you must be willing to make sacrifices.   13 | 51

Avoid being like the loser who says, "It may be possible, but   17 | 55

it's too difficult." Take on the attitude of the winner who says,   21 | 59

"It may be difficult, but it's possible." Count on working hard.   26 | 64

Also, seek mentors to pilot you in your long road to success.   30 | 69

They will encourage you and will challenge you to reach for higher   34 | 73

dreams even when you are very happy with where you are.   39 | 77

| 1' | 1 | 2 | 3 | 4 | 5 | 6 | 7 | 8 | 9 | 10 | 11 | 12 | 13 |
| 3' | | 1 | | 2 | | 3 | | 4 | |

[31c]
Assessment

➜ Continue

✓ Check

General Instructions: Format the memos and e-mail. Position the memos about 2" from the top of the page. DS memo headings, SS the body, and DS between paragraphs. Add your reference initials to the memos. Check the spelling, preview for placement, and carefully proofread each document before proceeding to the next one.

With *CheckPro*: *CheckPro* will keep track of the time it takes you to complete the entire production test, to compute your speed and accuracy rate on each document, and to summarize the results. When you complete a document, proofread it, check the spelling, and preview for placement. When you are completely satisfied with the document, click the **Continue** button to move to the next document. You will not be able to return and edit a document once you continue to the next one. Click the **Check** button when you are ready to error-check the test. Review and/or print the document analysis results.

Without *CheckPro*: On the signal to begin, key the documents in sequence. When saving documents, name them in the usual manner (for example, *31c-d1*). When time has been called, proofread all documents again and identify errors.

SUBJECT/VERB AGREEMENT

Use a singular verb:

1. With a **singular subject**. (The singular forms of *to be* include: am, is, was. Common errors with *to be* are: you was, we was, they was.)

> She monitors employee morale.
> You are a very energetic worker.
> A split keyboard is in great demand.

2. With most **indefinite pronouns**: *another, anybody, anything, everything, each, either, neither, one, everyone, anyone, nobody*.

> Each of the candidates has raised a considerable amount of money.
> Everyone is eager to read the author's newest novel.
> Neither of the boys is able to attend.

3. With singular subjects joined by *or/nor, either/or, neither/nor*.

> Neither your grammar nor punctuation is correct.
> Either Jody or Jan has your favorite CD.
> John or Connie has volunteered to chaperone the field trip.

4. With a **collective noun** (*family, choir, herd, faculty, jury, committee*) that acts as one unit.

> The jury has reached a decision.
> The council is in an emergency session.
> But:
> The faculty have their assignments. (Each has his/her own assignments.)

5. With words or phrases that express **periods of time**, **weights**, **measurements**, or **amounts of money**.

> Fifteen dollars is what he earned.
> Two-thirds of the money has been submitted to the treasurer.
> One hundred pounds is too much.

Use a plural verb:

6. With a **plural subject**.

> The students sell computer supplies for their annual fund-raiser.
> They are among the top-ranked teams in the nation.

7. With **compound (two or more) subjects** joined by *and*.

> Headaches and backaches are common worker complaints.
> Hard work and determination were two qualities listed by the references.

8. With *some, all, most, none, several, few, both, many*, and *any* when they refer to more than one of the items.

> All of my friends have seen the movie.
> Some of the teams have won two or more games.

[31c-d1]
Memo with Leader Tabs

1. Set a left leader tab at 3.5" and a right tab at 6". Use 1.5 spacing for the names and addresses.
2. Save as *31c-d1* and print.

TO: Javier Devarez
FROM: Miyoko Suno
DATE: Current
SUBJECT: E-mail Addresses

We have received new e-mail addresses from several customers. Please change these addresses in your printed directory. The changes have already been made in our database.

3.5" Leader tab   *6" Right tab*

Jordan, Brenda...................................... bjordan@alexander.jones.com
Maillet, Zachary.................................... Zachary.Maillet@twestwood.com
Peterson, Lynn...................................... lpeterson@rentswellsupplies.com

New printed directories will be available in about 90 days.

[31c-d2]
E-mail with Attachment

1. Send an e-mail to your instructor from you.
2. Attach *31c-d1*.

SUBJECT: E-mail Addresses

Today I received new e-mail addresses for three of our customers. I know that you also communicate with these three individuals; therefore, I am sending you their new e-mail addresses in the attached memo.

[31c-d3]
Memo with Tab

1. Key the following memo in correct format.
2. After keying the second paragraph, tap ENTER twice. Set a tab at 2.5" and key the last several lines. Save the document as *31c-d3*.

TO: All Sunwood Employees
FROM: Julie Patel, Human Relations
DATE: Current date
SUBJECT: Eric Kershaw Hospitalized

We were notified by Eric Kershaw's family that he was admitted into the hospital this past weekend. They expect that he will be hospitalized for another ten days. Visitations and phone calls are limited, but cards and notes are welcome.

A plant is being sent to Eric from the Sunwood staff. Stop by our office before Wednesday if you wish to sign the card. If you would like to send your own "Get Well Wishes" to Eric, send them to:

Left tab 2.5" → Eric Kershaw
County General Hospital
Room 401
Atlanta, GA 38209-4751

Objective Assessment
Answer the questions below to see if you have mastered the content of Module 5.

Part A:

1. Margins for unbound reports are _____ side margins, _____ top margin (first page), _____ top margin (second page), and _____ bottom margin.

2. To set margins, choose _____ from the _____ menu.

3. Use _____ -point font for main headings. Use _____ -point font for side headings.

4. To insert a footnote, choose _____ from the _____ menu.

5. To prevent a side heading from printing at the bottom of a page, apply _____.

6. To number the pages of a multipage report, choose _____ from the _____ menu. Numbers are positioned at the _____.

7. To prevent the middle initial in the name Thomas J. Swenson from being separated from the first name, insert a _____ after the first name.

8. Use the _____ View to read a document with minimum eyestrain and the _____ View to edit headers and footers.

Part B: Study each format below. Circle the correct format.

9. Which of the following illustrates a hanging indent format?

   A   Bruce, Lawrence A. *The Report Guide: Selected Form and Style*. Boise:
         State of Idaho Press, 2000.

   B   Bruce, Lawrence A. *The Report Guide: Selected Form and Style*. Boise:
   State of Idaho Press, 2000.

10. Which of the following illustrates use of the right indent feature?

    A   E-mail is a popular and effective means of communication that is being used by both companies and individuals.

    B   E-mail is a popular and effective means of communication that is being used by both companies and individuals.

Performance Assessment

Document 1
Edit Report

1. Open *checkpoint5* from the data files. Make the edits below and save as *checkpoint5-d1*.
   a. Position the main heading and format it correctly; insert an em dash to replace the two hyphens.
   b. Format the side headings correctly.
   c. Format the report as a DS, unbound report.
   d. Format correctly the two long quotations that are displayed in red font. Change the red text to black.
   e. Format the references in hanging indent format. Begin references on a separate page. Position the first line correctly.
   f. Create a header for page numbers. Suppress the number on the first page.

Document 2
Prepare Title Page

1. Prepare a creative title page for *checkpoint5-d1*. You may use page borders, horizontal lines, or a design of your choice. Save as *checkpoint5-d2*.

   Prepared for
   Mr. Derrick Novorot, President
   Altman Corporation
   388 North Washington Street
   Starkville, MS 39759

   Prepared by
   Your Name, Communication Consultant
   Your Street Address
   Your City, State ZIP Code

Objective Assessment
Answer the questions below to see if you have mastered the content of Module 3.

1. *Microsoft Word* inserts a paragraph each time you tap _ENTER & TAB_ PAGE 74
2. Which menu provides you with the option to display toolbars on your screen? _VIEW 75_
3. An ellipsis following a command on a pull-down menu indicates that a(n) _____ will display. *elipsis z kropekami* 75 page
4. A(n) _No ARROW_ *niemą strzałką zaznaczenie kolor* command on a menu indicates that it is not available for use. 75 page
5. The _Open / Open a File._ command is used to bring a previously stored document to the screen. 79 page *File*
6. The _zmienic styl pisania_ *character format* command on the Standard toolbar displays all nonprinting characters 82
7. Text can be hidden by clicking the Hidden box in the _FONT_ /cos *zeby y zaslonc* dialog box. 83 page . *zeby wrdaito spowrotem* DIALOG BOX *zeby nik niewidział*
8. Use the _PREVIEW_ command to see how the document will look before it is printed.
9. _MEMO_ are messages sent to persons within the organization. They contain a heading, a body, and one or more notations. 89 page
10. _E-mails_ are messages sent by one computer user to another via the Internet.

Performance Assessment *page 55*

Document 1
Rough Draft Memo
1. Key the memo at the right. Make corrections as marked.
2. Save as *checkpoint3-d1*, proofread, and print.

TO: J. Ezra Bayh   4
FROM: Greta Sangtree   8
DATE: August 14, 20--   13
SUBJECT: Letter-Mailing Standards   20

DS   *, because of the delay,*

chk sp
Recently the post office delivered late a letter that   35
caused us some *embarassment*. To avoid recurrence, please   47
ensure that all administrative assistants and mail person-   58
nel follow postal service guidelines.   67
U.S.

Perhaps a refresher seminar on correspondence guidelines is   79
in in order. Thanks, or you help.   86
(for your

words

Document 2
Edit memo

1. Open *checkpoint3-d1*. Save as *checkpoint3-d2*.
2. Select the four-line heading and delete it.
3. Bold U.S. Postal Service guidelines.
4. Change the spacing of paragraphs 1 and 2 to double. Delete the hard return between paragraphs 1 and 2. Indent each paragraph using TAB.
5. Key your name at the top of the document (not the top of the page). Tap ENTER twice below your name.
6. Format your name in 14-point bold. Key the filename below your name. Align it at the left.
7. Save the document again and print.

1. Locking up data by disabling the printing function and removing the cut, copy, and paste functions.
2. Placing digital watermarks on an image that identify the source.
3. Requiring a password from the copyright owner for users to gain access to copyrighted material.

Insert the data file summary here.

Order appropriately.

REFERENCES

Weatherford, Byron F. "Enforcing the Copyright Law." *Technology Journal,* Spring 2004. http://www.tj.edu/enforcelaw.htm (26 December 2004).

Morgan, Allison. "Know the Copyright Law?" *Digital Journal,* Vol. 26, No. 2, February 2005, 20–25.

[43c-d2]

Unbound Report

1. Open *present* from the data files. Save it as *43c-d2*.
2. Convert this leftbound report to an unbound report.
3. Format main and side headings correctly. Position the main heading on the correct line.
4. Be alert to a widow line on page 1.
5. Insert a footnote after the word *Garrin* in the sixth paragraph. Key the following footnote text:

    [1]William Garrin, *Speaking Skills for Your Success Today.* (Los Angeles: Waltman Publishers, 2005), p. 92.

6. Prepare the header as shown below; suppress it on the first page.

Effective·Presentations	→	→	Page·2·of·2

7. Prepare the references page. Key the following reference:

    Garrin, William. *Speaking Skills for Your Success Today.* Los Angeles: Waltman Publishers, 2005.

[43c-d3]

Title Page for Leftbound Report

1. Prepare a title page for the leftbound report created in *43c-d1*.
2. The report is prepared for **Webb & Morse Company Employees** by **Your Name, Information Technology Manager**.
3. Expand character spacing in the title, add a page border, and change the font color.
4. Save the document as *43c-d3*.

www.collegekeyboarding.com

Skill Builder Lesson A

1. Open *Keyboarding Pro*, Skill Builder module. The Skill Builder section includes 20 lessons of increasing difficulty that will help you build keying speed and improve control.

2. You can choose to emphasize speed or accuracy as you complete a lesson. Choose **Speed**. Click **Emphasis** displayed at the bottom of the Lesson menu to toggle between Speed and Accuracy. (Not available if preferences are locked.) Or use the Preferences option before you choose a lesson to change the emphasis (choose **Edit** from the menu bar).

3. Complete Lesson A or the first lesson that you have not completed. A red check mark will display to the left of any lesson completed.

4. Print your Lesson Report if requested by your instructor.

Skill Builder

Lesson A	Lesson K
Lesson B	Lesson L
Lesson C	Lesson M
Lesson D	Lesson N
Lesson E	Lesson O
Lesson F	Lesson P
Lesson G	Lesson Q
Lesson H	Lesson R
Lesson I	Lesson S
Lesson J	Lesson T

Click **Emphasis** to change to **Accuracy** → Emphasis: Speed

---

Drill 1

SKILL TRANSFER PARAGRAPHS

1. Key a 1' writing on each paragraph. Compare your *gwam*. Type additional 1' writings on the slower timing.

2. Repeat these steps for 2'.

   To save timings in the Open Screen, use a filename that identifies the timing such as *xx-sb3-drill1-t1* (your initials-Skill Builder 3-Drill1-Timing1).

	gwam	1'	3'

There are many qualities which cause good employees to stand out in a group. In the first place, they keep their minds on the task at hand. Also, they often think about the work they do and how it relates to the total efforts of the project. They keep their eyes, ears, and minds open to new ideas.

12	6
25	13
38	19
52	26
60	30

Second, good workers may be classed as those who work at a steady pace. Far too many people work by fits and pieces. They begin one thing, but then they allow themselves to be easily taken away from the work at hand. A lot of people are good starters, but fewer of them are also good finishers.

13	6
25	13
39	19
52	26
59	29

```
1' | 1 | 2 | 3 | 4 | 5 | 6 | 7 | 8 | 9 | 10 | 11 | 12 | 13 |
3' |   1   |     2     |     3     |     4     |
```

Leftbound Report

1. Key this leftbound report with DS.
2. Number the pages in a header at the top right; suppress the header on the first page.
3. Add a footer using the title of the report.
4. Insert the data files *copyright* and *summary* where indicated in the report.
5. Key the references on a separate references page at the end of the report.
6. Save the report as *43c-d1*.

COPYRIGHT LAW IN THE INTERNET AGE

Copyright owners continue to face copyright challenges as technology advances more rapidly than ever before. History shows us that copyright infringements occur at the introduction of each new invention or emerging technology. Examples include the phonograph and tape recorder and mimeograph and copy machines. Today, the Internet age provides Internet users the ease of copying and distributing electronic files via the Internet.

Insert the data file *copyright* here.

Copyright Laws

To avoid copyright infringement, the Internet user must be knowledgeable about copyright law. Two important laws include The Copyright Law of 1976 and the Digital Millennium Copyright Act, which was enacted in 1998 to update the copyright law for the digital age. Morgan (2005, 22) explains that under the Copyright Law of 1976:

> Original works are protected by copyright at the moment they are first originated—printed, drawn, captured, or saved to a digital storage area. The copyright protection is automatic when the original work is first established in this real medium of expression.

With an understanding of the copyright laws, users now realize that materials placed on a website may be copyrighted and are not available for downloading or copying and pasting into other documents. Sound advice is always to seek permission from the original copyright owner before using the material. Purchasing royalty-free content is another excellent way to avoid any question of copyright infringement.

Technology

Understanding the copyright laws and awareness of all types of copyrighted material are important as copyright owners fight against infringement. Interestingly, technology is and will continue to be a key player in the policing of copyright offenders. Weatherford (2004) shares the following ways technology is currently being used:

Skill Builder Lesson B

1. Open *Keyboarding Pro*, Skill Builder module. Complete Lesson B with Speed Emphasis. If you have already completed Lesson B, go on to the next uncompleted lesson.

2. Print your Lesson Report if requested by your instructor.

Drill 2
BALANCED-HAND COMBINATIONS
Practice the reaches for fluency.

1 to today stocks into ti times sitting until ur urges further tour
2 en entire trend dozen or order support editor nd and mandate land
3 he healthy check ache th these brother both an annual change plan
4 nt into continue want of office softer roof is issue poison basis

5 My brother urged the editor to have an annual health check today.
6 The manager will support the change to order our stock annually.
7 The time for the land tour will not change until further notice.
8 Did the letter mention her position or performance in the office?

| 1 | 2 | 3 | 4 | 5 | 6 | 7 | 8 | 9 | 10 | 11 | 12 | 13 |

Drill 3
SKILL TRANSFER PARAGRAPHS
Follow the directions for Drill 1 on page 104.

To save timings, use a filename that identifies the timing such as *xx-sb3-drill3-t1* (your initials-Skill Builder 3-Drill3-Timing1).

gwam 1' | 3'

Most of us, at some time, have had a valid reason to complain— 12 | 6
about a defective product, poor service, or perhaps being tired of 26 | 13
talking to voice mail. Many of us feel that complaining, however, 39 | 20
to a firm is an exercise in futility and don't bother to express 52 | 26
our dissatisfaction. We just write it off to experience and 64 | 32
continue to be ripped off. 70 | 35

Today, more than at anytime in the past consumers are taking some 12 | 6
steps to let their feelings be known—and with a great amount of 25 | 13
success. As a result, firms are becoming more responsive to 38 | 19
the needs of the consumer. complaints from customers alert firms 51 | 26
to produce or service defect and there by cause action to be taken 65 | 33
for their benefit. 70 | 35

| 1' | 1 | 2 | 3 | 4 | 5 | 6 | 7 | 8 | 9 | 10 | 11 | 12 | 13 |
| 3' | | 1 | | | 2 | | | 3 | | | 4 | | |

Assessment

43a

Key each pair of lines three
times at a controlled rate.

direct	1	June and my brother, Bradly, received advice from junior umpires.
reaches	2	My bright brother received minimum reward for serving many years.
adjacent	3	Clio and Trey were sad that very few voters were there last week.
reaches	4	Western attire was very popular at the massive auction last week.
double	5	Tommie Bennett will go to a meeting in Dallas tomorrow afternoon.
letters	6	Lee will meet Joanne at the swimming pool after accounting class.

| 1 | 2 | 3 | 4 | 5 | 6 | 7 | 8 | 9 | 10 | 11 | 12 | 13 |

43b Timed Writing

Key one 3' timing; then key
one 5' timing.

all letters

	gwam	3'	5'
How is a hobby different from a business? A very common way	4	2	32
to describe the difference between the hobby and the business is	8	5	35
that the hobby is done for fun, and the business is done as work	13	8	38
which enables people to earn their living. Does that mean that	17	10	40
people do not have fun at work or that people do not work with their	22	13	43
hobbies? Many people would not agree with that description.	26	15	45
Some people begin work on a hobby just for fun, but then they	30	18	48
realize it has the potential to be a business. They soon find out	34	21	51
that others enjoy the hobby as well and would expect to pay for	39	23	53
the products or services the hobby requires. Many quite successful	43	26	56
businesses begin as hobbies. Some of them are small, and some grow	48	29	59
to be large operations.	49	30	60

3' | 1 | 2 | 3 | 4 |
5' | 1 | 2 | 3 |

[APPLICATIONS]

[43c]

Assessment

→ Continue

✓ Check

With CheckPro: *CheckPro* will keep track of the time it takes you to complete the entire production test and will compute your speed and accuracy rate on each document and summarize the results. When you complete a document, proofread it, check the spelling, and preview for placement. When you are completely satisfied with the document, click the **Continue** button to move to the next document. You will not be able to return and edit a document once you continue to the next document. Click the **Check** button when you are ready to error-check the test. Review and/or print the document analysis results.

Without CheckPro: On the signal to begin, key the documents in sequence. When time has been called, proofread all documents again and identify errors.

Skill Builder Lesson C

1. Open *Keyboarding Pro*, Skill Builder module. Complete Lesson C with the Speed Emphasis. If you have already completed Lesson C, go on to the next uncompleted lesson.

2. Print your Lesson Report if requested by your instructor.

Drill 4
BALANCED-HAND COMBINATIONS
Practice the reaches for fluency.

1 an anyone brand spans th their father eighth he head sheets niche
2 en enters depends been nd end handle fund or original sport color
3 ur urban turns assure to took factory photo ti titles satin still
4 ic ice bicycle chic it item position profit ng angle danger doing

5 I want the info in the file on the profits from the chic bicycle.
6 The original of the color photo she took of the factory is there.
7 Assure them that anyone can turn onto the road to the urban area.
8 The color of the title sheet depends on the photos and the funds.

Drill 5
TIMED WRITING
1. Take a 1' writing on each paragraph.
2. Take a 3' writing on both paragraphs.

Option: Key the timing as a Diagnostic Writing in *Keyboarding Pro 4* or from *MicroPace Pro.*

Filename *SB3-T5*

	gwam	1'	3'
Practicing basic health rules will result in good body condi-		12	4
tion. Proper diet is a way to achieve good health. Eat a variety		26	9
of foods each day, including some fruit, vegetables, cereal pro-		38	13
ducts, and foods rich in protein, to be sure that you keep a bal-		51	17
ance. Another part of a good health plan is physical activity,		64	21
such as running.		67	22
Running has become popular in this country. A long run is a		12	27
big challenge to many males and females to determine just how far		26	31
they can go in a given time, or the time they require to cover a		38	35
measured distance. Long runs of fifty or one hundred miles are on		52	40
measured courses with refreshments available every few miles.		64	44
Daily training is necessary in order to maximize endurance.		76	48

1'	1	2	3	4	5	6	7	8	9	10	11	12	13
3'		1			2			3			4		

1. Open the data file *authors' top 10*. Save it as *42d-drill3*.

2. Point to the split box at the top of the vertical scroll bar. Drag the split bar and drop just before #3.

3. In the bottom pane, scroll to #9.

4. In the top pane, select the second numbered item. *Hint:* Do not select the automatic number 2.

5. Drag the selection across the split bar. Drop to the left of the bold word *fewer* (Item #9). **Note:** If you did not drop the text correctly, you may have to make minor spacing and numbering adjustments.

6. Double-click the split bar, save the changes, and close the file.

[APPLICATIONS]

[42e-d1]
View Report

1. Open *41d-d3*.

2. View in the following views: Normal, Print Layout, and Outline.

3. View in Reading Layout. Click **View Multiple Pages** button. Tap PgDn to scroll to the bottom of the report. Close Reading Layout.

4. In Print Layout View, hide the white space. View the document.

5. Zoom out to 150%. Zoom in to 75%. Return to 100%.

6. View in Full Screen view and then close that view. Keep this document open for the next application.

[42e-d2]
Split Panes in a Report

1. With *41c-d3* open, split the window into two panes. Drop the split bar at the beginning of the references page.

2. In the top pane, position the insertion point at the superscript for the first reference. Scroll down to the bottom of page 1 and verify the footnote text for the first footnote, Catledge. In the bottom pane, verify that the first footnote, Catledge, appears in the references list.

3. Repeat step 2 for verifying the remaining footnotes.

4. Double-click the split bar to return to a single pane.

[42e-d3]

Leftbound Report

1. Open *benefits* from the data files. Save it as *42e-d3*.

2. Format the main and side headings; set margins for a leftbound report.

3. Insert page numbers; suppress page number on first page. Check that no headings are left alone at the bottom of the page.

4. Insert the following footnote at the end of paragraph 1.

    [1]Lynn M. Adams, *Managing Employee Benefits Effectively*. (New Haven: Quorum Books, 2005), p. 26.

5. Prepare the References page. Key the following reference in hanging indent style.

    Adams, Lynn M. *Managing Employee Benefits Effectively*. New Haven: Quorum Books, 2005.

6. Save and print.

Skill Builder Lesson D

1. Open *Keyboarding Pro*, Skill Builder module. Complete Lesson D with the Speed Emphasis.

2. Print your Lesson Report if requested by your instructor.

Drill 6
ADJACENT KEY REVIEW

Key each row once; strive for accuracy. Repeat.

1 nm many enmity solemn kl inkling weekly pickle oi oil invoice join
2 iu stadium medium genius lk milk talk walks uy buy buyer soliloquy
3 mn alumni hymn number column sd Thursday wisdom df mindful handful
4 me mention comment same fo found perform info le letter flew files

5 The buyer sent his weekly invoices for oil to the group on Thursday.
6 Mindful of the alumni, the choirs sang a hymn prior to my soliloquy.
7 An inmate, a fogger, and a genius joined the weekly talks on Monday.
8 They were to join in the talk shows to assess regions of the Yukon.

| 1 | 2 | 3 | 4 | 5 | 6 | 7 | 8 | 9 | 10 | 11 | 12 | 13 |

Drill 7
TIMED WRITINGS

1. Take a 1' writing on each paragraph.
2. Take a 3' writing on both paragraphs.

Option: Key the timing as a Diagnostic Writing in *Keyboarding Pro 4* or from *MicroPace Pro.*

Filename *SB3-T7*

	gwam	1'	3'
All people, in spite of their eating habits, have two major		12	4
needs that must be met by their food. They need food that		24	8
provides a source of energy, and they need food that will fill		37	12
the skeletal and operating needs of their bodies. Carbohydrates,		50	17
fats, and protein form a major portion of the diet. Vitamins and		63	21
minerals are also necessary for excellent health.		72	24
Carbohydrates make up a major source of our energy needs.		12	28
Fats also serve as a source of energy and act as defense against		25	32
cold and trauma. Proteins are changed to amino acids, which are		38	37
the building units of the body. These, in turn, are utilized to		51	41
make most body tissue. Minerals are required to control many		64	46
body functions, and vitamins are used for normal growth and aid		78	50
against disease.		79	51

1' | 1 | 2 | 3 | 4 | 5 | 6 | 7 | 8 | 9 | 10 | 11 | 12 | 13 |
3' | 1 | 2 | 3 | 4 |

Splitting and Arranging Panes

In long documents it can be very useful to be able to view two parts of the document at the same time. To do so, you must first split the window into two panes. Each pane will have its own ruler bar and scroll bars.

To split panes:

1. Point to the split box at the top of the top vertical scroll bar. The pointer changes to a resize pointer.

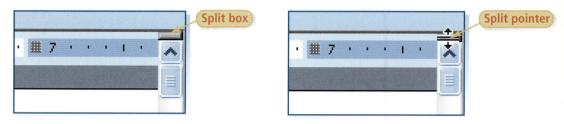

2. Drag the split bar to the desired position in the document. Note that you have two panes with each having a ruler bar and scroll bars.

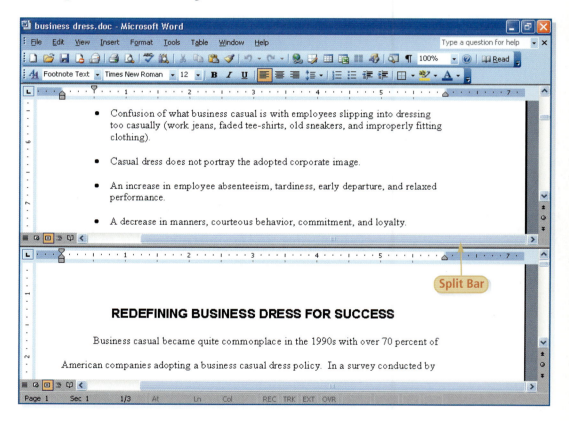

Once the screen is split, you can arrange the panes by dragging the split bar to any desired location. The pane becomes active when you click in it. Position the insertion point at one part in the document. Then click in the second pane and position the insertion point at another position. If you want to move or copy text or a graphic from one pane to another, just select and drag the text or graphic across the split bar.

To return to a single window, double-click the split bar.

Skill Builder Lesson E

1. Open *Keyboarding Pro*, Skill Builder module. Complete Lesson E with the Speed Emphasis.
2. Print your Lesson Report if requested by your instructor.
3. Complete the Skill Builder lessons on your own or as directed by your instructor.

Drill 8
WORD BEGINNINGS
In the Open Screen, key each row once; strive for accuracy. Repeat.

br
1 bright brown bramble bread breath breezes brought brother broiler
2 In February my brother brought brown bread and beans from Boston.

exe
3 exercises exert executives exemplify exemption executed exemplary
4 They exert extreme effort executing exercises in exemplary style.

bt
5 doubt subtle obtains obtrusion subtracts indebtedness undoubtedly
6 Extreme debt will cause more than subtle doubt among my creditors.

ny
7 tiny funny company nymph penny nylon many anyone phony any brainy
8 Anyone as brainy and funny as Penny is an asset to their company.

| 1 | 2 | 3 | 4 | 5 | 6 | 7 | 8 | 9 | 10 | 11 | 12 | 13 |

Drill 9
TIMED WRITINGS
1. Take a 1' writing on each paragraph.
2. Take a 3' writing on both paragraphs.

Option: Key the timing as a Diagnostic Writing in *Keyboarding Pro 4* or from *MicroPace Pro.*

Filename *SB3-T9*

gwam 1' | 3'

Many people believe that an ounce of prevention is worth a   12 | 4
pound of cure. Care of your heart can help you prevent serious   25 | 8
physical problems. The human heart is the most important pump ever   38 | 13
developed. It constantly pushes blood through the body tissues.   51 | 17
But the layers of muscle that make up the heart must be kept in   64 | 23
proper working order. Exercise can help this muscle to remain in   77 | 26
good condition.   84 | 27

Another important way of keeping a healthy heart is just to   12 | 31
avoid habits that are considered detrimental to the body. Food   25 | 35
that is high in cholesterol is not a good choice. Also, use of   38 | 39
tobacco has quite a bad effect on the function of the heart. You   51 | 44
can minimize your chances of heart trouble by avoiding these bad   64 | 48
health habits.   67 | 49

1' | 1 | 2 | 3 | 4 | 5 | 6 | 7 | 8 | 9 | 10 | 11 | 12 | 13 |
3' | 1 | 2 | 3 | 4 |

Show/Hide White Space

When in Print Layout View, the white space at the top and bottom of each page and the gray space between pages can be hidden using the Show/Hide White Space feature. This saves screen space as you are viewing a document.

To hide white space, move the insertion point to the top or bottom of the page and click the **Hide White Space** button. To show the white space again, click the **Show White Space** button.

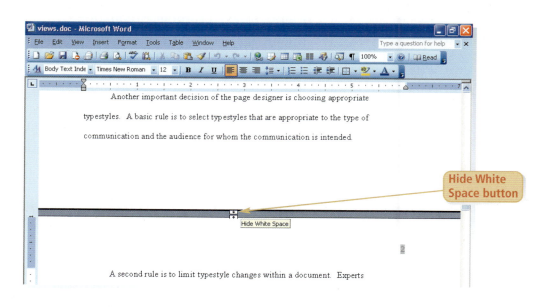

Hide White Space button

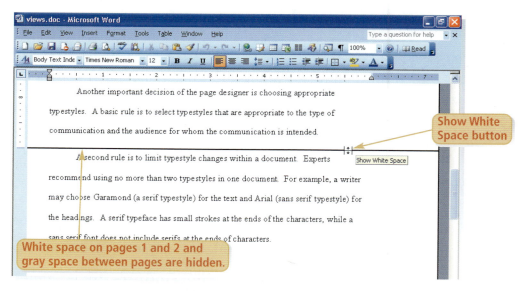

Show White Space button

White space on pages 1 and 2 and gray space between pages are hidden.

D r i l l   2 | **SHOW/HIDE WHITE SPACE**

1. Open the data file *views* that you used earlier.

2. Move the insertion point to the bottom of the first page. Click the **Hide White Space** button. The white space at the bottom of page 1 and the top of page 2 and the gray space are hidden.

3. Move the insertion point to the same position and click the **Show White Space** button. The white space and gray space are now displayed.

Business Letter Formats

OBJECTIVES

- Format block and modified block business letters.
- Create envelopes and labels.
- Send documents as e-mail attachments.
- Improve keying speed and accuracy.

LESSON 32

Block Letter Format

WARMUP

32a

Keep fingers curved, hands quiet, as you key each line twice.

1st finger
1 My 456 heavy brown jugs have nothing in them; fill them by May 7.
2 The 57 bins are numbered 1 to 57; Bins 5, 6, 45, and 57 are full.

2nd finger
3 Ed decided to crate 38 pieces of cedar decking from the old dock.
4 Mike, who was 38 in December, likes a piece of ice in cold cider.

3rd finger
5 Polly made 29 points on the quiz; Wex 10 points. Did they pass?
6 Sall saw Ezra pass 200 pizza pans to Sean, who fixed 20 of them.

| 1 | 2 | 3 | 4 | 5 | 6 | 7 | 8 | 9 | 10 | 11 | 12 | 13 |

32b Timed Writing

Take two 3' timings.

 all letters

	gwam	3'

So now you are operating a keyboard and don't you find it   4 | 38
amazing that your fingers, working with very little visual help,   8 | 43
move easily and quickly from one key to the next, helping you to   13 | 47
change words into ideas and sentences. You just decide what you   17 | 51
want to say and the format in which you want to say it, and your   21 | 56
keyboard will carry out your order exactly as you enter it. One   26 | 60
operator said lately that she sometimes wonders just who is most   30 | 64
responsible for the completed product—the person or the machine.   34 | 69

3' | 1 | 2 | 3 | 4 | 5 |

new FUNCTIONS
42d

help keywords

about ways to view a Word document

Views

Depending on your task, you may choose from several different ways to get a good "view" of your work in a document. Click **View** on the Standard toolbar, and then choose from one of the views (or use toolbar buttons if available). Study the descriptions below.

Normal—Work in Normal View when you want keying and editing to be done quickly.

Web Layout—Work in Web Layout View when you are creating a Web page or any document that will be viewed on screen. Web Layout View shows you how your document would look in a browser.

Print Layout—Work in Print Layout View when you need to see how headers, footers, columns, etc., will display when printed. You may also edit these items easily in Print Layout View.

Outline—Work in Outline View when you want to identify the document headings. Restructuring the document is easy. Simply select the heading (if heading styles have been applied) and then copy or move that section. You will learn about styles in a later lesson.

Reading Layout—View the document in Reading Layout when you need to read a document with minimum eyestrain. *Shortcut:* Click the **Read** button on the Standard toolbar. Click the **Allow Multiple Pages** button on the Reading toolbar to view more pages. Click **Page Up** or **Page Down** or scroll arrows to move in the document. Click **Close** when finished.

Zoom—For a close-up view of the document, you "zoom in" on it. To see more of the page, you "zoom out" and see a reduced document on the screen. To change the zoom on documents, click the arrow next to the Zoom box on the Standard toolbar and select the desired zoom setting.

Full Screen—This view shows a full screen without toolbars. Click **Close Full Screen** when finished.

Optional: You may also use the view buttons at the bottom left of the window.

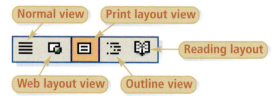

D r i l l   1   VIEWS

1. Open the data file *views*.

2. Click **View, Normal** to display in Normal *View*.

3. Change to Printout Layout View. Note that you can see the page number on page 2.

4. Change to Outline View. Click on the plus to the left of the heading *White Space* to highlight the entire section. Note

that this section could be easily deleted, moved, or copied. *Note:* Heading styles had been applied in the data file.

5. Change to Full Screen. Click **Close Full Screen**.

6. Zoom out to 75%, then 150%, and then 100%.

7. Change to Reading Layout. Click **Close**.

Center Page

The Center Page command centers a document vertically on the page. If extra hard returns (¶) appear at the beginning or end of a document, these are also considered to be part of the document. Be careful to delete extra hard returns before centering a page.

To center a page vertically:

1. Position the insertion point on the page to be centered.
2. From the File menu, select **Page Setup**. The Page Setup dialog box displays.
3. Click the **Layout** tab.
4. Click the **Vertical alignment** down arrow. Select **Center**; then click **OK**.

Drill 1 | CENTER PAGE

1. Open *27a-drill4*, which you created in the last module. Create the folder **Module 4 Keys** and save the file as *32c-drill1* in this folder. Save all files for Lessons 32–36 in the **Module 4 Keys** folder.

2. On the File menu, click **Page Setup**; then center the page vertically.

3. Click **Print Preview** to view the entire document and notice that there is equal space at the top and bottom of the page.

4. Return to Normal View and save the document.

DOCUMENT DESIGN · DOCUMENT DESIGN · DOCUMENT DESIGN · DOCUMENT DESIGN · DOCUMENT DESIGN · DOCUMENT DESIGN

>> DOCUMENT DESIGN
32d

Business Letters

Business letters are used to communicate with persons outside of the business. Business letters carry two messages: the first one is the tone and content; the second is the appearance of the document. Appearance is important because it creates the critical first impression. Stationery, use of standard letter parts, and placement should convey that the writer is intelligent, informed, and detail minded.

Stationery

Letters should be printed on high-quality (about 24-pound) letterhead stationery. Standard size for letterhead is 8½" x 11". Envelopes should match the letterhead in quality and color.

Document Views and Report Review

WARMUP
42a
Key the entire drill working at a controlled rate. Repeat.

adjacent key
1 her err ire are cash free said riot lion soil join went wean news
2 sat coil riot were renew forth weed trade power grope owner score

one hand
3 him bear joy age kiln loup casts noun loop facet moon deter edges
4 get hilly are fear imply save phony taste union versa yummy wedge

balanced hand
5 oak pay hen quay rush such burp urus vial works yamen amble blame
6 cot duty goal envy make focus handy ivory lapel oriel prowl queue

| 1 | 2 | 3 | 4 | 5 | 6 | 7 | 8 | 9 | 10 | 11 | 12 | 13 |

42b Technique Builder
Key each line once; fingers curved and relaxed; wrists low.

third row
7 query were pure wipe wept you tort twirp report rip tire weep tip
8 Perry required two types of paper, a protractor, and four rulers.

3rd/home
9 we tattle wayward pepper rattle eloped require your yellow queasy
10 Patty wrote poetry, took art, and worked two jobs this past year.

1st/3rd
11 minimum box zip zinc bomb ripen corner mine cure woven zoo winner
12 Merv and Robert were to turn a valve to terminate the water flow.

| 1 | 2 | 3 | 4 | 5 | 6 | 7 | 8 | 9 | 10 | 11 | 12 | 13 |

42c Timed Writing
Key a 3' and a 5' writing.

	gwam	3'	5'
As you read copy for keyboarding, try to read at least a word	4	2	44
or, better still, a word group ahead of your actual keyboarding	8	5	46
point. In this way, you will be able to recognize the keystroking	13	8	49
pattern needed as you learn to keyboard balanced-hand, one-hand,	17	10	51
or combination word sequences. The adjustments you make in your	22	13	54
speed will result in the variable rhythm pattern needed for expert	26	16	57
keyboarding. It is easy to read copy correctly for keyboarding	30	18	59
if you concentrate on the copy.	32	19	60
When you first try to read copy properly for keyboarding, you	36	22	63
may make more errors, but as you learn to concentrate on the copy	41	25	66
being read and begin to anticipate the keystroking pattern needed,	45	27	68
your errors will go down and your keyboarding speed will grow. If	50	30	71
you want to increase your keyboarding speed and reduce your errors,	54	33	74
you must make the effort to improve during each and every practice	59	35	76
session. If you will work to refine your techniques and to give a	63	38	79
specific purpose to all your practice activities, you can make the	68	41	82
improvement.	69	41	82

3' | 1 | 2 | 3 | 4 |
5' | 1 | 2 | 3 |

Letter Parts and Block Letter Format

Businesspeople expect to see standard letter parts arranged in the proper sequence. Letters consist of three main parts: the opening lines to the receiver (letter address and salutation), the body or message, and the writer's closing lines. Standard letter parts are illustrated below.

Block letter style is a typical business letter format in which all letter parts are keyed at the left margin. For most letters, use open punctuation, which requires no punctuation after the salutation or the complimentary closing.

Letterhead: Preprinted stationery that includes the company name, logo, address, and other optional information such as telephone number and fax number

Dateline: Date the letter is prepared

- Position at about 2.1" or use the **Center Page** command.
- Be sure to begin at least 0.5" below the letterhead.

Letter address: Complete address of letter recipient

- Begin QS (four lines) below the date.
- Generally includes receiver's name, company name, street address, city, state (one space after state), and ZIP code.
- Include a personal title, e.g., *Mr.*, *Ms.*, *Dr.*
- Capitalize the first letter of each word.

Salutation (or greeting):

- Begin DS below the letter address.
- Include courtesy title with person's name, e.g., *Dear Mr. Smith*.
- Use *Ladies and Gentlemen* when addressing a company.

Body:

- Begin DS below the salutation.
- SS paragraphs; DS between paragraphs.

Complimentary closing:

- Begin DS below the body.
- Capitalize only the first letter of the closing.

Writer's name and title:

- Begin four lines below the complimentary closing.
- Include a personal title to designate gender only when the writer's name is not gender specific, such as Pat or Chris, or when initials are used, such as J. A. Moe.
- Key the name and title on either of two lines, whichever gives better balance. Use a comma to separate name and title if on one line.

Reference initials:

- Begin DS below the writer's name and title.
- Key reference initials, e.g., **xx**, in lowercase. Replace *xx* with your initials.

E-Market Firm
10 East Rivercenter Boulevard
Covington, KY 41016-8765

Current date   ↓4

Mr. Ishmal Dabdoub
Professional Office Consultants
1782 Laurel Canyon Road
Sunnyvale, CA 94085-9087   ↓2

Dear Mr. Dabdoub   ↓2

Have you heard your friends and colleagues talk about obtaining real-time stock quotes? What about real-time account balances and positions, NASDAQ Level II quotes, or extended-hours trading? If so, then they are among the three million serious investors who have opened an account with E-Market Firm.   ↓2

We believe that the best decisions are informed decisions that are made in a timely manner. E-Market Firm has an online help desk that provides information for all levels of investors, from beginners to the experienced serious trader. You can learn basic tactics for investing in the stock market, avoiding common mistakes, and picking up some advanced strategies.   ↓2

Stay on top of the market and your investments! Please visit our website at http://www.emarketfirm.com to learn more about our banking and brokerage services and to access our online help desk. E-Market Firm is the premier site for online investing.   ↓2

Sincerely   ↓4

Margaritta Gibson
Marketing Manager   ↓2

xx

Block Letter Style with Open Punctuation

[41d-d2]
Title Page

1. Prepare a title page for the leftbound report created in *41d-d1*.

2. Prepare the title page for **Donovan National Bank Employees** by **Tara Field, Administrative Management Specialist**. (List Tara's name and title on two lines.)

3. Use bold and 14 point for all lines. Change the font color.

4. Center the page vertically, and save the file as *41d-d2*.

[41d-d3]
Unbound Report

1. Reformat report *41d-d1* as an unbound report.

2. Change the numbered list to a bulleted list.

3. Change the heading font to Arial. (Use Format Painter.)

4. Preview the document for correct pagination; then save it as *41d-d3*.

[41d-d4]
Delete Footnote

1. Open *41d-d3* and save it as *41d-d4*.

2. Delete the first footnote. Edit the second sentence of the first paragraph as follows:

   Today approximately half of the employees are allowed to dress casually, while over 90 percent are allowed to dress casually occasionally.

3. Delete the reference from the references page.

4. Save and print.

© Getty/PhotoDisc

Timely Topics

on e-mail privacy

Is e-mail private? The answer is definitely not. In some companies, the e-mail administrator is able to read any and all e-mail messages. Some companies actually monitor employee e-mail wanting to ensure that employees are not spending time on personal activities or leaking confidential company information. Also remember that most companies back up their systems on a regular basis so that information is not lost (including e-mail).

Occasionally, e-mail software malfunctions, causing your e-mail to be delivered to the wrong person or you to receive e-mail intended for someone else. In addition, there are many hackers who, if they try hard enough, can bypass security measures and read your e-mail. So remember, e-mail is not private. Don't send anything by e-mail that you would not want to find on the company bulletin board.

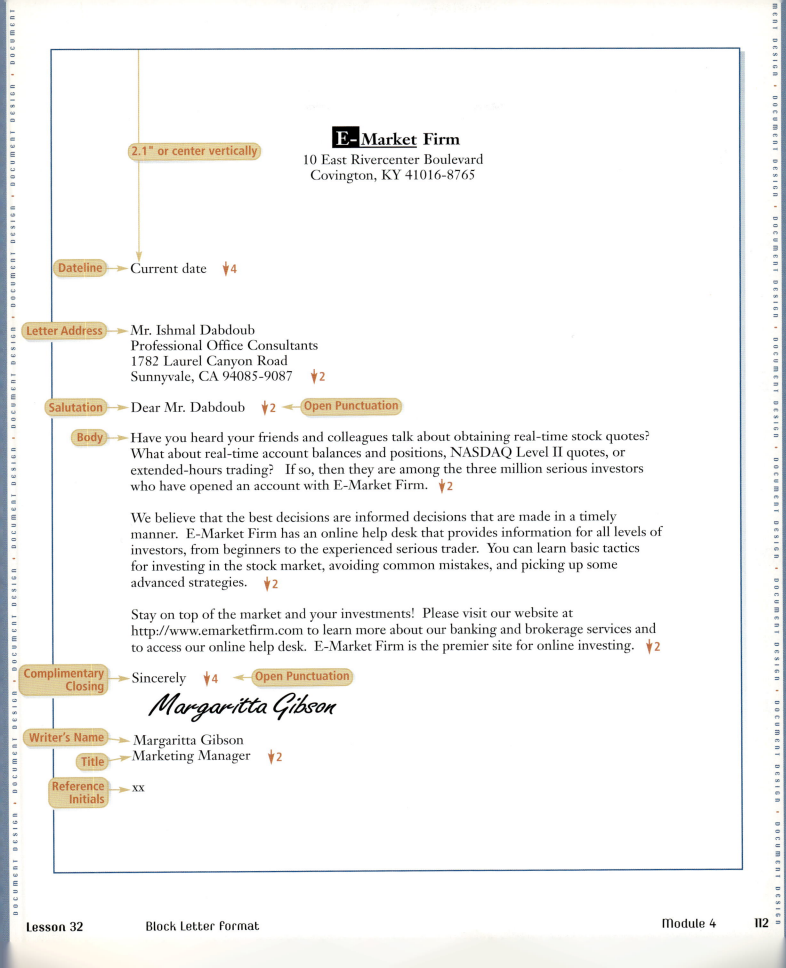

E-Market Firm

10 East Rivercenter Boulevard
Covington, KY 41016-8765

2.1" or center vertically

Dateline → Current date ↓4

Letter Address → Mr. Ishmal Dabdoub
Professional Office Consultants
1782 Laurel Canyon Road
Sunnyvale, CA 94085-9087 ↓2

Salutation → Dear Mr. Dabdoub ↓2 ← **Open Punctuation**

Body → Have you heard your friends and colleagues talk about obtaining real-time stock quotes? What about real-time account balances and positions, NASDAQ Level II quotes, or extended-hours trading? If so, then they are among the three million serious investors who have opened an account with E-Market Firm. ↓2

We believe that the best decisions are informed decisions that are made in a timely manner. E-Market Firm has an online help desk that provides information for all levels of investors, from beginners to the experienced serious trader. You can learn basic tactics for investing in the stock market, avoiding common mistakes, and picking up some advanced strategies. ↓2

Stay on top of the market and your investments! Please visit our website at http://www.emarketfirm.com to learn more about our banking and brokerage services and to access our online help desk. E-Market Firm is the premier site for online investing. ↓2

Complimentary Closing → Sincerely ↓4 ← **Open Punctuation**

Margaritta Gibson

Writer's Name → Margaritta Gibson
Title → Marketing Manager ↓2

Reference Initials → xx

employers realize that many positions, often hi-tech, creative positions, do not require traditional business dress, and those individuals perhaps are more productive in a more flexible environment. However, when communicating with clients, these individuals must dress professionally to create the necessary corporate image.

Guidelines for Business Dress

Interestingly, companies are employing image consultants to teach employees what is appropriate business casual and to plan the best business attire to project the corporate image. Laura Thorn,[3] the author of *A Guidebook to Business Casual*, provides the following useful tips on how to dress casually:

Do not wear any clothing that is designed for recreational or sports activities, e.g., cargo pants or pants with elastic waist. Invest the time in pressing shirts and pants or pay the price for professional dry cleaning. Wrinkled clothing does not enhance one's credibility. Be sure clothing fits properly, avoiding baggy clothes or clothes that are too tight.

In summary, energetic employees working to climb the corporate ladder will need to plan their dress carefully. If the company dress policy allows business casual, observe your colleagues in higher rank and consult the experts on business casual for advice on projecting a powerful image.

Footnote text:

[1]Rachel Catledge, "Your Business Wardrobe Decisions Are Important Decisions," *Business Management Journal*, January 2005, p. 10.

[2]Shondra Diaz, "Business Dress Codes Are Shifting," *Business Executive*, April 2005, p. 34.

[3]Laura T. Thorn, "Business Casual Dress," http://www.casualbusiness.com, 21 November 2004.

Reference text: (order alphabetically)

Thorn, Laura T. "Business Casual Dress." http://www.casualbusiness.com (21 November 2004).

Diaz, Shondra. "Business Dress Codes Are Shifting." *Business Executive*, April 2005, 34–35.

Catledge, Rachel. "Your Business Wardrobe Decisions Are Important Decisions." *Business Management Journal*, January 2005, 10–12.

[32e-d1]
Block Letter

`At 2.1"    Ln 7    Col 1`

1. Key the model letter on page 112 in block format with open punctuation. Assume you are using letterhead stationery.
2. Tap ENTER to position the dateline at about 2.1" (see the status bar). The position will vary depending on the font size.
3. Insert the current date using the Date and Time feature (**Insert, Date and Time**).
4. Include your reference initials. If the first letter of your initials is automatically capitalized, point to the initial until the AutoCorrect Option button appears, click the button, and then choose **Undo Automatic Capitalization**.
5. Follow the proofreading procedures outlined in Lesson 28. Use **Print Preview** to check the placement.
6. Use **Show/Hide** to view paragraph markers to confirm that you have correct spacing between letter parts. Save as *32e-d1* and print.

[32e-d2]
Block Letter

1. Key the letter below in block format with open punctuation. Use **Date and Time** to insert the current date. Add your reference initials in lowercase letters.
2. Proofread; use **Print Preview** to check the document. Save it as *32e-d2* and print.

↓2.1"

Current date ↓4

Ms. Alice Ottoman
Premiere Properties, Inc.
52 Ocean Drive
Newport Beach, CA 92660-8293 ↓2

Dear Ms. Ottoman ↓2

Internet Solutions has developed a new technique for you to market your properties on the World Wide Web. We can now create 360-degree panoramic pictures for your website. You can give your clients a virtual spin of the living room, kitchen, and every room in the house. ↓2

Call today for a demonstration of this remarkable technology. Give your clients a better visual understanding of the property layout—something your competition doesn't have. ↓2

Sincerely ↓4

Ms. Lee Rodgers
Marketing Manager ↓2

xx

[32e-d3]
Block Letter and Center Page

1. Open *32e-d2* and save it as *32e-d3*.
2. Replace the letter address with the one below, using proper format.
   Ms. Andrea Virzi, J P Personnel Services, 2351 West Ravina Drive, Atlanta, GA 30346-9105
3. Supply the correct salutation. Turn on **Show/Hide (¶)**. Delete the six hard returns above the dateline. Align the page at vertical center (**File, Page Setup**). Proofread and save. Use **Print Preview** to view placement. Note that a short letter looks more attractive centered on the page rather than positioned at 2.1".

[41d-d1]
Leftbound Report

1. Key the following leftbound report DS. SS the long quotation, and indent it 0.5".
2. Create a header to number the pages at the top right; suppress it on the first page.
3. Key the references on a references page at the end of the report.
4. Switch to Print Layout View to verify the page numbers and ensure there are no widows or orphans.
5. Save the report as *41d-d1*.

REDEFINING BUSINESS DRESS FOR SUCCESS

Business casual became quite commonplace in the 1990s, with over 70 percent of American companies adopting a business casual dress policy. In a survey conducted by Image, Inc., 58 percent of employees surveyed were allowed to dress casually for work every day, while 92 percent of the companies allowed employees to dress casually occasionally.[1] Over a decade later, managers are considering the issues related to business dress and developing appropriate guidelines for business dress.

Trend Shifts

According to Shondra Diaz,[2] the trend to dress casually is shifting. What accounts for this change in companies' philosophy on business dress? Several reasons may include:

1. Confusion of what business casual is with employees slipping into dressing too casually (work jeans, faded tee-shirts, old sneakers, and improperly fitting clothing).

2. Casual dress does not portray the adopted corporate image.

3. An increase in employee absenteeism, tardiness, early departure, and relaxed performance.

4. A decrease in manners, courteous behavior, commitment, and loyalty.

Understanding the advantages and disadvantages of business casual dress, managers are now publishing well-defined dress codes, often written with feedback from clients and employees. Employers realize that when presenting to highly sophisticated corporate clients, a professional image is important and casual dress is viewed as unacceptable. On the other hand,

LESSON 33 — Modified Block Letter Format

WARMUP
33a
Key each line twice.

alphabet 1 Johnny Willcox printed five dozen banquet tickets for my meeting.

fig/sym 2 Our check #389 for $21,460—dated 1/15/01—was sent to O'Neil & Co.

1st finger 3 It is true Greg acted bravely during the severe storm that night.

easy 4 In the land of enchantment, the fox and the lamb lie by the bush.

| 1 | 2 | 3 | 4 | 5 | 6 | 7 | 8 | 9 | 10 | 11 | 12 | 13 |

33b Timed Writings
Take two 3' timings.

 all letters

gwam 3'

Many young people are quite surprised to learn that either 4 | 48
lunch or dinner is included as part of a job interview. Most of 8 | 52
them think of this part of the interview as a friendly gesture from 13 | 56
the organization. 15 | 58

The meal is not provided just to be nice to the person. The 18 | 62
organization expects to use that function to observe the social 22 | 66
skills of the person and to determine if he or she might be effective 27 | 71
doing business in that type of setting. 30 | 73

What does this mean to you if you are preparing for a job 33 | 77
interview? The time spent reading about and learning to use good 38 | 81
social skills pays off not only during the interview but also after 42 | 86
you accept the job. 44 | 87

1' | 1 | 2 | 3 | 4 | 5 | 6 | 7 | 8 | 9 | 10 | 11 | 12 | 13 |
3' | 1 | 2 | 3 | 4 |

FUNCTION REVIEW
33c

Left Tabs

1. Set a 3.0" left tab by clicking the ruler bar. Key the date and closing lines. Tap TAB to align the text.
2. Click **Format** and then click **Tabs**; set left tabs at 0.15" and 0.9" and key the special notations. Save as *33c*.

Left tab 3.0" → Current date
Sincerely

Your Name, Student

Left tab 0.9"

Enclosures: Check #831
Left tab 0.15" Order Form

c Lanya Jenkins
   W. C. Quarrels

? Where would you set a tab to begin keying text at the centerpoint of the paper? Find the answer on the next page.

TIP
Click the **Undo** button after keying the copy notation (c) to lowercase the letter *c*.

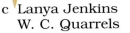

>> DOCUMENT DESIGN

41c

Footnotes and References

When another person's work is used in a report, insert a superscript number to mark the text (…story[1]) and then at the bottom of the page list the corresponding footnote number with full information about where to locate the full reference (whether a book, journal article, or Internet location).

Insert the superscript footnote number in the text by using the footnote feature. The detailed footnote is then keyed at the "foot" or bottom of the page where the footnote is referenced in the report body. Remember to key footnotes in 12 point.

Study the report and references page below that illustrates the correct formatting of Footnote 1. Note the following:

- Superscript [1] in the first paragraph to mark text
- Detailed footnote [1] at the bottom of the page
- Corresponding reference on the references page listed in alphabetical order by author's last name

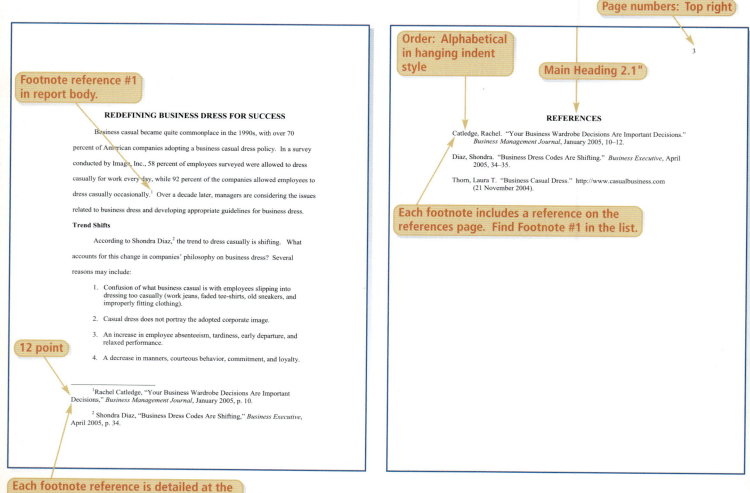

Page numbers: Top right

Order: Alphabetical in hanging indent style

Main Heading 2.1"

Footnote reference #1 in report body.

REDEFINING BUSINESS DRESS FOR SUCCESS

Business casual became quite commonplace in the 1990s, with over 70 percent of American companies adopting a business casual dress policy. In a survey conducted by Image, Inc., 58 percent of employees surveyed were allowed to dress casually for work every day, while 92 percent of the companies allowed employees to dress casually occasionally.[1] Over a decade later, managers are considering the issues related to business dress and developing appropriate guidelines for business dress.

Trend Shifts

According to Shondra Diaz,[2] the trend to dress casually is shifting. What accounts for this change in companies' philosophy on business dress? Several reasons may include:

1. Confusion of what business casual is with employees slipping into dressing too casually (work jeans, faded tee-shirts, old sneakers, and improperly fitting clothing).
2. Casual dress does not portray the adopted corporate image.
3. An increase in employee absenteeism, tardiness, early departure, and relaxed performance.
4. A decrease in manners, courteous behavior, commitment, and loyalty.

12 point

[1]Rachel Catledge, "Your Business Wardrobe Decisions Are Important Decisions," *Business Management Journal*, January 2005, p. 10.

[2] Shondra Diaz, "Business Dress Codes Are Shifting," *Business Executive*, April 2005, p. 34.

REFERENCES

Catledge, Rachel. "Your Business Wardrobe Decisions Are Important Decisions." *Business Management Journal*, January 2005, 10–12.

Diaz, Shondra. "Business Dress Codes Are Shifting." *Business Executive*, April 2005, 34–35.

Thorn, Laura T. "Business Casual Dress." http://www.casualbusiness.com (21 November 2004).

Each footnote includes a reference on the references page. Find Footnote #1 in the list.

Each footnote reference is detailed at the "foot" or bottom of the page where it was referenced. See Footnote #1.

>> DOCUMENT DESIGN
33d

Modified Block Format

In the modified block format, the dateline and the closing lines begin at the center point of the page.

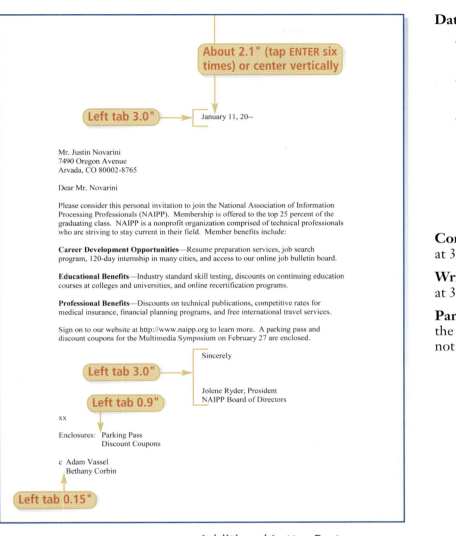

About 2.1" (tap ENTER six times) or center vertically

Left tab 3.0"

January 11, 20--

Mr. Justin Novarini
7490 Oregon Avenue
Arvada, CO 80002-8765

Dear Mr. Novarini

Please consider this personal invitation to join the National Association of Information Processing Professionals (NAIPP). Membership is offered to the top 25 percent of the graduating class. NAIPP is a nonprofit organization comprised of technical professionals who are striving to stay current in their field. Member benefits include:

Career Development Opportunities—Resume preparation services, job search program, 120-day internship in many cities, and access to our online job bulletin board.

Educational Benefits—Industry standard skill testing, discounts on continuing education courses at colleges and universities, and online recertification programs.

Professional Benefits—Discounts on technical publications, competitive rates for medical insurance, financial planning programs, and free international travel services.

Sign on to our website at http://www.naipp.org to learn more. A parking pass and discount coupons for the Multimedia Symposium on February 27 are enclosed.

Sincerely

Left tab 3.0"

Jolene Ryder, President
NAIPP Board of Directors

Left tab 0.9"

xx

Enclosures: Parking Pass
Discount Coupons

c Adam Vassel
Bethany Corbin

Left tab 0.15"

Dateline:

- Position at about 2.1" or use Center Page Command.

- Begin at least 0.5" below the letterhead.

- Set a left tab at 3.0". Determine the position of the tab by subtracting the side margins from the center of the paper.

	4.25"	Center of the paper
−	1.25"	Margins
	3.0"	Tab setting

Complimentary closing: Begin keying at 3.0".

Writer's name and title: Begin keying at 3.0".

Paragraphs: May be blocked or indented to the first tab stop; however, it is more efficient not to indent paragraphs.

Additional Letter Parts

In Lesson 32 you learned the standard letter parts. Listed below are optional letter parts.

Enclosure notation: If an item is included with a letter, key an enclosure notation a DS below the reference initials. Tap TAB to align the enclosures or set a left tab at 0.9" for more precise spacing.

Left tab at 0.9" or use default

Enclosures: Check #831
Order form
Enclosures: 2

Copy notation: A copy notation (c) indicates that a copy of the document has been sent to the person/s listed. Key the copy notation a DS below the reference initials or enclosure notation (if used). Tap TAB to align the names or set a left tab at 0.15" for more precise spacing. Click the **Undo** button after keying the copy notation to lowercase the letter *c*.

 Click Undo

c Larry Qualls

5. Move the insertion point before the reference number, and tap TAB to indent it. Then move the insertion point beyond the number and key the footnote in 12-point font. (Note the default font is 10 point.) Click Close to return to the document text. **Note:** If you are in Print Layout View, click anywhere above the footnote divider line to return to the document.

6. To edit a footnote, double-click on the reference number in the text. Edit the footnote text in the Footnote Pane.

7. To delete a footnote, select the reference number in the text and tap DELETE.

Drill 1   FOOTNOTES

1. Key the paragraph in Drill 2 DS, and add the three footnotes.

2. Format footnotes in 12 point and DS between them.

3. Include all three sources on a separate references page in proper reference format. Select the title **References** and format it in 14 point, bold, centered.

4. Save as *41b-drill1* and print.

Drill 2   DELETE FOOTNOTES

1. Open *41b-drill1*. Delete the second footnote. Update the references page.

2. Save as *41b-drill2* and print.

Payton Devaul set the school record for points in a game—50.[1] He holds six statewide records. This makes him one of the top ten athletes in the school's history.[2] He expects to receive a basketball scholarship at an outstanding university.[3]

Footnotes

Book → [1]Marshall Baker, *High School Athletic Records*. (Seattle: Sports Press, 2004), p. 41.

Online Journal → [2]Lori Guo, "Top Ten Athletes," *The Sports Journal*, Spring 2005, http://www.tsj.edu/athletes/topten.htm, 25 June 2005.

E-mail → [3]Payton Devaul, pdevaul@mail.com. "Basketball Scholarship." E-mail to Kirk Stennis, kstennis@umt.edu, 15 April 2005.

References

Baker, Marshall. *High School Athletic Records*. Seattle: Sports Press, 2004.

Devaul, Payton. pdevaul@mail.com. "Basketball Scholarship." E-mail to Kirk Stennis, kstennis@umt.edu. 15 April 2005.

Guo, Lori. "Top Ten Athletes." *The Sports Journal*, Spring 2005. http://www.tsj.edu/athletes/topten.htm (25 June 2005).

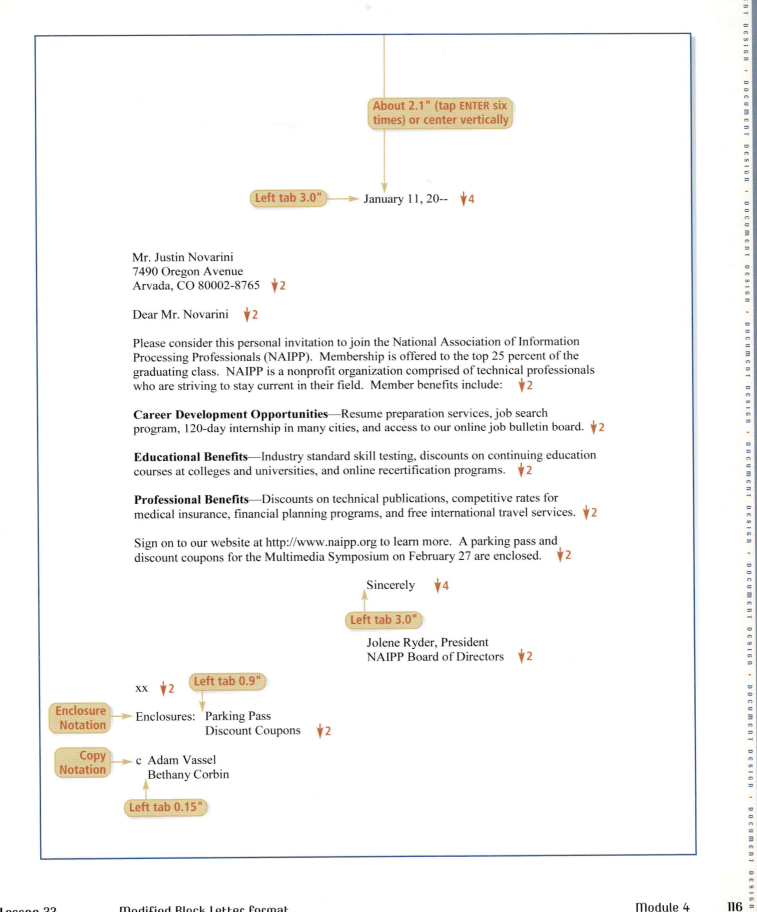

About 2.1" (tap ENTER six times) or center vertically

Left tab 3.0" → January 11, 20-- ↓4

Mr. Justin Novarini
7490 Oregon Avenue
Arvada, CO 80002-8765 ↓2

Dear Mr. Novarini ↓2

Please consider this personal invitation to join the National Association of Information Processing Professionals (NAIPP). Membership is offered to the top 25 percent of the graduating class. NAIPP is a nonprofit organization comprised of technical professionals who are striving to stay current in their field. Member benefits include: ↓2

Career Development Opportunities—Resume preparation services, job search program, 120-day internship in many cities, and access to our online job bulletin board. ↓2

Educational Benefits—Industry standard skill testing, discounts on continuing education courses at colleges and universities, and online recertification programs. ↓2

Professional Benefits—Discounts on technical publications, competitive rates for medical insurance, financial planning programs, and free international travel services. ↓2

Sign on to our website at http://www.naipp.org to learn more. A parking pass and discount coupons for the Multimedia Symposium on February 27 are enclosed. ↓2

Sincerely ↓4

Left tab 3.0"

Jolene Ryder, President
NAIPP Board of Directors ↓2

xx ↓2   Left tab 0.9"

Enclosure Notation → Enclosures: Parking Pass
                                  Discount Coupons ↓2

Copy Notation → c Adam Vassel
                   Bethany Corbin

Left tab 0.15"

Report with Footnotes and References

alphabet	1	Jim Ryan was able to liquefy frozen oxygen; he kept it very cold.
figures	2	Flight 483 left Troy at 9:57 a.m., arriving in Reno at 12:06 p.m.
direct reaches	3	My brother served as an umpire on that bright June day, no doubt.
easy	4	Ana's sorority works with vigor for the goals of the civic corps.

| 1 | 2 | 3 | 4 | 5 | 6 | 7 | 8 | 9 | 10 | 11 | 12 | 13 |

NEW FUNCTIONS
41b

help keywords

insert footnote

Footnotes

References cited in a report are often indicated within the text by a superscript number (… story.[1]) and a corresponding footnote with full information at the bottom of the same page where the reference was cited.

Word automatically numbers footnotes sequentially with Arabic numerals (1, 2, 3), positions them at the left margin, and applies 10-point type. After keying footnotes, select them and apply 12-point type to be consistent with the report text. Indent the first line of a footnote 0.5" from the left margin. Footnotes are automatically SS; however, DS between footnotes.

To insert and edit footnotes:

1. Switch to Normal view and position the insertion point where you want to insert the footnote reference.

2. On the menu, click **Insert**, **Reference**, and then **Footnote**. The Footnote and Endnote dialog box displays.

3. Be sure Footnotes is selected and Bottom of page (the default location) is displayed. Then click **Insert**.

4. The reference number and the insertion point appear in the Footnote Pane.

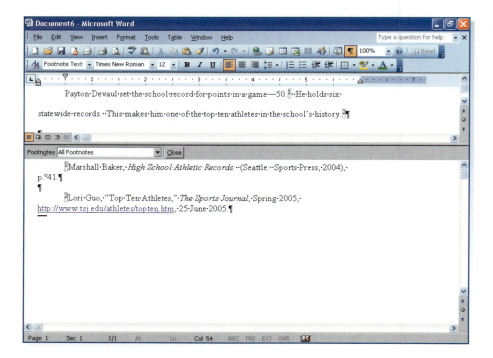

[33e-dl]
Modified Block Letter

1. Open a new document and set a left tab at 3.0". Tap TAB and insert the current date at about line 2.1".

2. Key the letter on the previous page in modified block letter format. Check spelling and correct errors.

3. Before keying the enclosure notation, set a left tab at 0.9". Before keying the copy notation, set a left tab at 0.15".

4. Save the letter as *33e-d1*, preview the document for attractive placement, and print it when you are satisfied.

[33e-d2]
Modified Block Letter

1. Key the following letter in modified block letter format with open punctuation. Add your reference initials and a copy notation to your instructor. Set appropriate tabs. *Hint:* When keying the writer's initials, space once after the period: **Ms. J. E. Mitchell**—not **Ms. J.E. Mitchell**.

2. Center the letter vertically. Proofread carefully, save the letter as *33e-d2*, and print.

Current date ↓4

Ms. Abbie Welborn
One-Stop Printing Co.
501 Madison Road
Cincinnati, OH 45227-6398 ↓2

Dear Ms. Welborn ↓2

Do you know that more and more people are opting to go on a shopping spree on the Internet rather than the mall? Businesses, ranging from small mom-and-pop stores to global multinational corporations, are setting up shop on the Web if they haven't already. They are selling goods, services, and themselves! ↓2

Consumers expect businesses to have a website. Those that don't will give their business to their competitors. ↓2

E-Business, Inc. has helped hundreds of businesses nationwide establish their business on the Internet. May we help you integrate your online and offline sales strategies? Call us today at 800-555-0100 and arrange for one of our outstanding consultants to analyze your e-commerce strategies to increase your volume. ↓2

Sincerely ↓4

Ms. J. E. Mitchell
Marketing Manager ↓2

Timely Topics

© Getty/PhotoDisc

on e-mail etiquette

Keep your messages short and to the point. Limit the amount of punctuation, especially exclamation points at the ends of sentences. Use a single font; don't try to be fancy. Use only commonly understood abbreviations. Avoid the use of emoticons (symbols used to convey the writer's emotions, such as a smiley face). Do not send any e-mail message that you would not want anyone else to read. Do not use your company computer for personal e-mail.

will be quick to include all these references in a report without verifying their credibility. Just as writers verify the value of printed sources, experienced writers check electronic sources as well.

Using a Style Manual

Three popular style manuals are the *MLA Handbook, The Chicago Manual of Style,* and the *Publication Manual of the American Psychological Association.* After selecting a style, carefully study the acceptable formats for citing books, magazines, newspapers, brochures, online journals, e-mail messages, and other sources. Use the style manuals and other electronic resources made available to assist writers in this important task.

With the availability and volume of excellent electronic resources, writers are including a number of electronic citations along with printed journals, books, and newspapers. Sarah Quattlebaum (2004, 159) writes:

> Electronic citations may include online journal articles or abstracts, articles on CD-ROM, e-mail messages, discussion list messages, etc. To format references for documents retrieved electronically, include the author (if given), date of publication, title of article and name of publication, URL, and date document was retrieved from the Internet.

Summary

Experienced writers understand the importance of selecting credible resources, documenting references in the report, and applying the exact reference style required for the report. Learning to document your references accurately is an important step toward becoming an experienced writer.

[40e-d2]
References Page

1. Open *40e-d1*. Save it as *40e-d2*.
2. Position the insertion point at the end of the report. Tap CTRL + ENTER to begin a new page. Key **REFERENCES** approximately 2.1" from the top of the page.
3. Key the references in hanging indent style. (*Hint:* Try the shortcut, CTRL + T.)

Millsaps, John. *Report Writing Handbook: An Essential Guide.* Columbus, OH: Wellington Books, 2005.

Quattlebaum, Sarah. "Apply Reference Styles Correctly." http://www.reportwriting.com (15 December 2004).

[40e-d3]
Leftbound Report

Convert the unbound report *40e-d2* to a leftbound report. Save the report as *40e-d3*.

Block Letter with Envelope

---

alphabet	1	Perhaps Max realized jet flights can quickly whisk us to Bolivia.
fig/sym	2	Send 24 Solex Cubes, Catalog #95-0, price $6.78, before April 31.
1st finger	3	The boy of just 6 or 7 years of age ran through the mango groves.
easy	4	The auditor did sign the form and name me to chair a small panel.

| 1 | 2 | 3 | 4 | 5 | 6 | 7 | 8 | 9 | 10 | 11 | 12 | 13 |

COMMUNICATION
34b

Salutations and Complimentary Closings

The salutation, or greeting, consists of the person's personal title (*Mr.*, *Ms.*, or *Mrs.*) or professional title (*Dr.*, *Professor*, *Senator*, *Honorable*), and the person's last name. Do not use a first name unless you have a personal relationship. The salutation should agree in number with the addressee. If the letter is addressed to more than one person, the salutation is plural.

	Receiver	Salutation
To individuals	Dr. Alexander Gray	Dear Dr. Gray
	Dr. and Mrs. Thompson	Dear Dr. and Mrs. Thompson
To organizations	TMP Electronics, Inc.	Ladies and Gentlemen
Name unknown	Advertising Manager	Dear Advertising Manager

Choose a complimentary closing that reflects the relationship with the receiver. Use *Sincerely* to show a neutral relationship, *Cordially* for a friendly relationship, and *Respectfully* when requesting approval.

D r i l l   1 | **PRACTICE LETTER PARTS**

1. Review block letter format on page 112 for correct placement of letter parts.

2. Key the letter parts for each activity, spacing correctly between parts. In the first exercise, tap ENTER six times to begin the dateline at 2.1"; use the Date and Time feature.

3. Tap ENTER five times between drills. Do not save the drills.

4. Take a 2' timing on each drill. Repeat if you finish before time is up.

A Current date

Ms. Joyce Bohn, Treasurer
Citizens for the Environment
1888 Hutchins Avenue
Seattle, WA 98111-2353

Dear Ms. Bohn

B Please confirm our lunch date.

Sincerely

James D. Bohlin
District Attorney

xx

---

1. Key the unbound report that follows.

2. Tap ENTER to leave an approximate 2.1" top margin. SS the two-line main heading as shown. DS the report.

3. Create a header with the page number that tracks the number of pages in the report displaying at the right. Suppress the header on the first page.

4. Create a footer that includes **Writing 101 Manual** in the left position and **Module 1-1** in the right position. Suppress the footer on the first page.

5. Check for side headings alone at the bottom of the page and correct.

6. Save the report as *40e-d1*.

DOCUMENTING REFERENCES: AN ESSENTIAL STEP IN REPORT WRITING

Preparing a thorough and convincing report requires excellent research, organization, and composition skills as well as extensive knowledge of documenting referenced materials. The purpose of this report is to present the importance of documenting a report with credible references and the techniques for creating accurate citations.

Documenting with References

For a report to be credible and accepted by its readers, a thorough review of related literature is essential. This background information is an important part of the report and provides believability of the writer and of the report. When sharing this literature in the body of the report, the report writer understands the following basic principles of report documentation:

- All ideas of others must be cited so that credit is given appropriately.
- The reader will need to be able to locate the material using the information included in the reference citation.
- Format rules apply to ideas stated as direct quotations and ideas that are paraphrased.
- A thorough list of references adds integrity to the report and to the report writer.

Good writers learn quickly how to evaluate the many printed and electronic references that have been located to support the theme of the report being written. Those references judged acceptable are then cited in the report. Writer John Millsaps (2005, 12) shares this simple advice:

Today writers can locate a vast number of references in very little time. Electronic databases and Internet web pages are very easy to locate and provide a multitude of information. The novice writer

Envelopes

The envelope feature can insert the delivery address automatically if a letter is displayed; postage can even be added if special software is installed. The default is a size 10 envelope (4⅛" by 9½"); other sizes are available by clicking the Options button on the Envelope tab. The common practice is to use initial cap style on envelopes because scanners can read this format easily and the process is more efficient. An alternative style for envelope addresses is uppercase (ALL CAPS) with no punctuation.

Ms. Alice Ottoman
Premiere Properties, Inc.
52 Ocean Drive
Newport Beach, CA 92660-8293

To generate an envelope:

1. With the letter you have created displayed, click **Tools** on the menu and then **Letters and Mailings**. Click **Envelopes and Labels**, and if necessary, click the **Envelopes** tab. The mailing address is automatically displayed in the Delivery address box. (To create an envelope without a letter, follow the same steps, but key the address in the Delivery address box.)

2. If you are using business envelopes with a preprinted return address (assume you are), click the **Return address Omit** box. To include a return address, do not check the Omit box; click in the **Return address** box and enter the return address.

   Note: To format a letter address on the envelope in all caps, click **Add to Document** to attach the envelope to the letter and then edit the address.

Change Case

Change Case enables you to change the capitalization of text that has already been keyed.

Sentence case capitalizes the first letter of the first word of a sentence.

Lowercase changes all capital letters to lowercase letters.

Uppercase changes all letters to uppercase.

Title case capitalizes the first letter of each word.

Toggle case changes all uppercase letters to lowercase and vice versa.

To change case, select the text to be changed, choose **Change Case** from the Format menu, and then choose the appropriate option.

Drill 2 | **CREATE ENVELOPE**

1. Open a blank document. Key the letter address in Drill 1.

2. Create an envelope.

3. Attach the envelope to the blank document.

4. Save the document as *34c-drill2* and print it. Your instructor may have you print envelopes on plain paper.

Drill 3 | **ADD ENVELOPE**

1. Open *32e-d2*. Create and attach an envelope to the letter.

2. Select the entire address and convert it to uppercase. Delete the punctuation.

3. Save the document as *34c-drill3* and print it.

>> DOCUMENT DESIGN

Internal Citations

Internal citations are an easy and practical method of documentation. The last name of the author(s), the publication date, and the page number(s) of the cited material are shown in parentheses within the body of the report (Crawford, 2005, 134). This information cues a reader to the name Crawford in the reference list included at the end of the report. When the author's name is used in the text to introduce the quotation, only the year of publication and the page numbers appear in parentheses: "Crawford (2005, 134) said that . . . ."

Short, direct quotations of three lines or fewer are enclosed within quotation marks. Long quotations of four lines or more are indented 0.5" from the left margin and SS. A DS or one blank line comes before and after the long quotation. The first line is indented an additional 0.5" if the quotation is the beginning of a paragraph.

If a portion of the text that is referenced is omitted, use an ellipsis (. . .) to show the omission. An ellipsis is three periods, each preceded and followed by a space. If a period occurs at the end of a sentence, include the period or punctuation.

---

deserves more attention that it gets. "Successful businesses have long known the importance of good verbal communication." (Catlette, 2000, 29)

Short Quotation

Probably no successful enterprise exists that does not rely for its success upon the ability of its members to communicate:

> Make no mistake; both written and verbal communication are the stuff upon which success is built . . . . Both forms deserve careful study by any business that wants to grow. Successful businesspeople must read, write, speak, and listen with skill. (Schaefer, 1999, 28)

Long Quotation

References Page

References cited in the report are listed at the end of the report in alphabetical order by authors' last names. The reference list may be titled REFERENCES or BIBLIOGRAPHY. Study the formatting guidelines shown below.

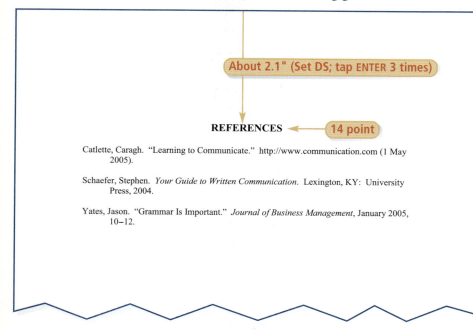

About 2.1" (Set DS; tap ENTER 3 times)

REFERENCES ← 14 point

Catlette, Caragh. "Learning to Communicate." http://www.communication.com (1 May 2005).

Schaefer, Stephen. *Your Guide to Written Communication.* Lexington, KY: University Press, 2004.

Yates, Jason. "Grammar Is Important." *Journal of Business Management,* January 2005, 10–12.

Main Heading: About 2.1". Tap ENTER three times to position the insertion point on approximately 2.1". Apply 14 point, bold.

Page numbers: Numbered at top right

New page: Start references on a new page (CTRL + ENTER).

References:

- List alphabetically by authors' last names
- SS references
- Hanging indent style
- DS between references

[34d-d1 and 34d-d2]
Block Letter and Envelope

1. Key the following letter in block style with open punctuation. Use the Date feature to insert the current date. Proofread and check the spelling.
2. Center the page vertically. Preview the letter and check the placement before printing. Save the letter as *34d-d1* and print one copy.
3. Add an envelope to the letter and save it as *34d-d2*. Print.
4. Study the illustration in the Reference Guide on folding and inserting letters in an envelope. Fold the letter for a large envelope (#10).

Current date | Mr. Trace L. Brecken | 4487 Ingram Street | Corpus Christi, TX 78409-8907 | Dear Mr. Brecken

We have received the package you sent us in which you returned goods from a recent order you gave us. Your refund check, plus return postage, will be mailed to you in a few days.

We are sorry, of course, that you did not find this merchandise personally satisfactory. It is our goal to please all of our customers, and we are always disappointed if we fail.

Please give us an opportunity to try again. We stand behind our merchandise, and that is our guarantee of good service.

Sincerely | Margret Bredewig | Customer Service Department | xx

[34d-d3 and 34d-d4]
Block Letter and Envelope

1. Follow the directions for *34d-d1*.
2. Save the letter as *34d-d3* and print one copy.
3. Add an envelope to the letter. Convert text to uppercase and delete punctuation. Save it as *34d-d4* and print.
4. Fold the letter for a large envelope (#10).

Current date | Mrs. Rose Shikamuru | 55 Lawrence Street |Topeka, KS 66607-6657 | Dear Mrs. Shikamuru

Thank you for your recent letter asking about employment opportunities with our company. We are happy to inform you that Mr. Edward Ybarra, our recruiting representative, will be on your campus on April 23, 24, 25, and 26 to interview students who are interested in our company.

We suggest that you talk soon with your student placement office, as all appointments with Mr. Ybarra will be made through that office. Please bring with you the application questionnaire the office provides.

Within a few days, we will send you a company brochure with information about our salary, bonus, and retirement plans. You will want to visit our website at http://www.skylermotors.com to find facts about our company mission and accomplishments as well as learn about the beautiful community in which we are located. We believe a close study of this information will convince you, as it has many others, that our company builds futures as well as small motors.

If there is any way we can help you, please e-mail me at mbragg@skylermotors.com.

Yours very truly | Myrtle K. Bragg | Human Services Director | xx

Footer with Number of Pages Field

The Footer function places information at the bottom of each page in a document. Footers print 0.5" from the bottom edge of the paper. If necessary, select the footer to apply 12-point type. Footers can only be viewed from Print Layout View.

In legal documents such as wills and corporate minutes, it is necessary to print on each page the total number of pages in a document, e.g., Page 1 of 10. This feature can be used in either the header or the footer.

To create a footer to track the number of pages in a document:

1. Choose **View** from the menu and then choose **Header and Footer**. This will display the Header and Footer toolbar and a grid area.

2. Click **Switch Between Header and Footer** to move to the footer area. **Note:** The footer also has three positions: left, center, and right.

Insert auto text — Switch between header and footer button

3. Tap TAB to move to the right position of the footer.

4. Click the **Insert AutoText** down arrow; then choose **Page X of Y**.

5. Click **Close**. View the footer in Print Layout View.

Drill 6   FORMAT FOOTER

1. Open *will* from the data files. Save it as *40c-drill6*.

2. Create the footer shown below. Do not suppress the footer on the first page.

3. Position the insertion point in the heading Article I. Double-click **Format Painter**, and format Articles II through VII.

4. Use the Keep with next feature to keep Article V with its paragraph.

5. View the footer in Print Layout View. Save your changes and close the file.

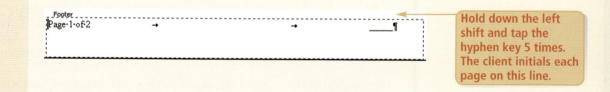

Hold down the left shift and tap the hyphen key 5 times. The client initials each page on this line.

DOCUMENT DESIGN · DOCUMENT DESIGN · DOCUMENT DESIGN · DOCUMENT DESIGN · DOCUMENT DESIGN · DOCUMENT DESIGN

» DOCUMENT DESIGN
40d

Report Documentation

Reports must include the sources of all information used in the report. Documentation gives credit for published material, whether electronic or printed, that is quoted or closely paraphrased by the writer. The writer may document sources by using footnotes, endnotes, or internal citations. In this module, you will use internal citations and footnotes.

At the end of the report, the writer provides the reader with a complete alphabetical listing of all references. With this complete information provided in the references, the interested reader may locate the original source. Study the information on the next page about internal citations (both short and long quotations) and learn how to list those references on the references page at the end of the report.

[34d-d5]
Rough-Draft Letter
Block Style

1. Key the following letter in block style with mixed punctuation. Apply what you have learned about correct letter placement and letter parts.
2. Save the document as *34d-d5* and print one copy.
3. Fold the letter for a small envelope.

Mr. John Crane

5760 Sky Way

Seattle, WA 98108-0321

Would you like to invest in a company that will provide you with a 180% return on your investment? Consider investing in a ~~company~~ firm, that specializes in importing and exporting with China. China's gross domestic product (GDP) is expected to be over a trillion dollars.

Ameri-Chinois *(bold & italic)* has made a significant number of business arrangements with key organizations in China to source goods and to participate in global two-way trade. Trade between China and ~~other countries~~ the rest of the world is expected to grow over 20% this year. China's exports are expected to rise to $244 billion in the year 2006. Imports ~~will~~ are expected to grow to $207 billion.

Contact Lawrence Chen at Century Investments to learn how you can be an investor in the growing company of Ameri-Chinois. The current price is per share $0.52; the targeted price is $9.00. Call today!

Sincerely

800-555-0134

Lawrence Chen

[34d-d6]
Edit Block Letter

1. Open *34d-d5* and save it as *34d-d6*. Select the letter address and then delete it.
2. Address the letter to: **Mr. Tom K. Onehawk, 139 Via Cordoniz, Evansville, IL 62242-3277**. Supply an appropriate salutation. Change the letter to open punctuation.
3. Add **Please study the enclosed portfolio and then** at the beginning of paragraph 3. Be sure to change the *c* in contact to lowercase.
4. Add an enclosure notation.

[34d-d7]
Label

✳ DISCOVER

Tools, Letters and Mailings, Envelopes and Labels, Labels tab, Options. Choose a label style; click OK, click **Single label**, click **Print**.

✳ 1. Open the letter to Mr. Onehawk (*34d-d6*). Prepare a label to send the portfolio in a larger envelope. Create an Avery 5160 address label. **Note:** Once you click the Options button on the Labels tab, select **Avery standard** in the Label products. Then select **5160 – Address** from the Product number list box.

2. Open document *34d-d1*, and create and print an address label for this letter as well. Choose an **Avery 5168** label.

help keywords

hanging indent;
paragraph; about text
alignment and spacing

Hanging Indent

Hanging indent places the first line of a paragraph at the left margin and indents all other lines to the first tab. It is commonly used to format bibliography entries, glossaries, and lists. Hanging indent can be applied before text is keyed or after.

To create a hanging indent:

1. Display the Horizontal Ruler (click **View**; then **Ruler**).

2. From the Horizontal Ruler, drag the hanging indent marker to the position where the indent is to begin.

Hanging indent

3. Key the paragraph. The second and subsequent lines are indented beginning at the marker. (*Shortcut:* CTRL + T, then key the paragraph; or select the paragraphs to be formatted as hanging indents, and press CTRL + T.)

D r i l l   3 | HANGING INDENT

1. Drag the hanging indent marker 0.5" to the right; then key the references that follow.

2. Turn Hanging Indent off by dragging the hanging indent marker back to the left margin.

3. Save the document as *40c-drill3*.

Fuller, G. Ronald and Watkins, Janet T. *Internet Security*. Boston: Jones-Flynt Publishers, 2004.

Osaji, Allison. "Know the Credibility of Electronic Citations." *Graduate Education Journal*, April 2004, 45–51.

Van Straaten, Linda J. "Conforming to APA Style." *APA Monitor Online*, (2005): http://www.apa.org/monitor/jan05/conf.html (10 March 2005).

Walters, Daniel S. dswalters2@umt.edu. "Final Report Available on Intranet." E-mail to Stephen P. Cobb, spcobb@umt.edu (14 September 2004).

D r i l l   4 | FORMAT TEXT WITH HANGING INDENT

1. Open *references* from the data files and save it as *40c-drill4*.

2. Select the references, and format them with a hanging indent. (*Hint:* Try the shortcut.) Save the file again.

D r i l l   5 | FORMAT TEXT WITH HANGING INDENT

1. Open *glossary* from the data files and save it as *40c-drill5*.

2. Select all the glossary entries and format them with a hanging indent. Save the file again.

Electronic Distribution of Letters

WARMUP
35a
Key each line twice.

alphabet	1	Dave Cagney alphabetized items for next week's quarterly journal.
figures	2	Close Rooms 4, 18, and 20 from 3 until 9 on July 7; open Room 56.
up reaches	3	Toy & Wurt's note for $635 (see our page 78) was paid October 29.
easy	4	The auditor is due by eight, and he may lend a hand to the panel.

| 1 | 2 | 3 | 4 | 5 | 6 | 7 | 8 | 9 | 10 | 11 | 12 | 13 |

COMMUNICATION
35b

Divide into groups of four and assign a recorder to key your answers to the following questions.

1. Does the letter recipient form an opinion of the business letter writer by reading the letter?
2. Does the attractiveness of the letter format affect the evaluation? Why or why not?
3. What factors might the recipient use as criteria for evaluating the letter and letter writer?
4. The following signs were actually posted for the public's eye. Identify the error in each sign and correct it. Add at least two realistic examples you have noticed.

   a. Store window sign   Turkeys' are in the meat department.
   b. Locker room sign   Gentlemens' Locker Room
   c. Door at ballpark   Employees' Only
   d. Store door   Personal Only
   e. Ice cream shop sign   Only cash/checks excepted.

FUNCTION REVIEW

35c Format Review and Data Files

Letters

The CD-ROM in the back of your textbook contains data files you will use in this course. They are organized by module. Your instructor may already have installed these files for classroom use. *CheckPro* users: the software will open these files automatically.

Ask your instructor how to access the files, or install the files on the hard drive following the instructions on the CD-ROM. When the files are installed, locate the data path or folder where these files are stored. (The default path is *c:\College Keyboarding L1-60 Data*. Double-click the **Module 4** folder to open it.)

Drill 1   LETTER

1. Open the data file *decker* and save it as *35c-drill1*.
2. Correct the spacing between the letter parts. Set a left tab at the center of the paper. Position letter parts appropriately for a modified block letter.
3. Position the letter vertically on the page so that it looks attractive.
4. Preview the letter to check placement, resave, and print.

Drill 2   APPROPRIATE LETTER PARTS

1. Open the data file *letter parts* and save it as *35c-drill2*.
2. Key the appropriate salutation and complimentary closing. (Tap TAB to move between parts of the table.) Resave.

increase the left indent of an entire paragraph

Increase Indent

Decrease Indent

To indent text from the left margin:

1. Click the **Increase Indent** button on the toolbar. (*Shortcut:* CTRL + M)

2. Key the paragraph and tap ENTER. The left indent will continue until you click the **Decrease Indent** button. (*Shortcut:* CTRL + SHIFT + M)

Indent can also be applied to text that has already been keyed by selecting the text and then clicking **Increase Indent**.

To indent text from the right margin:

1. Display the Horizontal Ruler (click **View**; then **Ruler**).

2. On the Horizontal Ruler, drag the right indent marker to the position where the right indent is to begin.

Right indent

3. Key the paragraph. The text will wrap to the next line when the right indent marker is reached.

D r i l l   1   INDENT

1. Key the copy below. DS paragraph 1; tap TAB to indent the paragraph.

2. To format paragraph 2, at the left margin, click **Increase Indent**. Change to SS. Tap TAB, and then key paragraph 2.

3. For paragraph 3, click **Decrease Indent**; change to DS.

4. Save as *40c-drill1*. Leave the document open for Drill 2.

However, the trend to use e-mail almost exclusively is causing a tremendous challenge for both e-mail recipients and companies. ↓2

Tab → With the convenience of electronic mail resulting in its widespread use, many users are forsaking other forms of Indent → communication—face-to-face, telephone (including voice mail), and printed documents. Now companies are challenged to create clear e-mail policies and to implement employee training on effective use of e-mail (Ashford, 2005, 2). ↓2

Communication experts have identified problems that may occur as a result of misusing e-mail. Two important problems include information overload (too many messages) and inappropriate form of communication.

D r i l l   2   INDENT FROM BOTH MARGINS

1. Save *40c-drill1* as *40c-drill2*.

2. Click in paragraph 2.

3. Drag the right indent marker to 5.5" (or to the left 0.5").

4. Save the document again.

NEW FUNCTIONS
35d

Send Document as an E-mail Attachment

The **Mail Recipient (as Attachment)** command provides an easy way to send documents to colleagues via e-mail. The command automatically generates an e-mail message and attaches the *Word* document to the e-mail message. The user may edit the default e-mail message and attach additional files. **Note:** To use this command, the user must be using an e-mail program compatible with Messaging Application Programming Interface (MAPI).

1. With the document to be reviewed open, click **File**, **Send To**, and **Mail Recipient (as Attachment)**. A new e-mail message box displays.

2. In the To box, key the recipient's e-mail address. If you wish to copy this e-mail to another recipient, key that recipient's e-mail address in the Cc box.

3. In the Subject box, key an appropriate subject or accept the default subject.

4. Click **Send**.

Drill 3 — SEND DOCUMENT AS ATTACHMENT

1. Open the data file *ottoman*.

2. Click **File**, **Send To**, and **Mail Recipient (as Attachment)**.

3. In the To box, key your instructor's e-mail address.

4. Edit the Subject line to read **Drill 3 Document as Attachment (ottoman.doc)**.

5. Edit the message by adding the following sentence:

   The attached document illustrates the block letter style with open punctuation.

6. Click **Send**. **Note:** If your e-mail program is not compatible, tap PRINT SCREEN, and then open a blank document and click **Paste**. Save the document as *35d-drill3*. You have made a copy of the e-mail message screen.

Drill 4 — SEND ADDITIONAL ATTACHMENTS

1. Open the data file *ottoman*. In an e-mail message, attach this document to your instructor, as you did in Drill 3.

2. Then, click the **Attach** button and select *brackmun* from the browser.

3. Edit the Subject line to read **Block Letter Model Documents**.

4. In the e-mail message, key the following message:

   The attached documents illustrate the block letter style with open punctuation. Please print and add to your procedures manual.

5. Click **Send**. **Note:** If your e-mail program is not compatible, follow the directions in step 6 of Drill 3 and save the document as *35d-drill4*.

WARMUP
40a
Key each line twice.

one-hand

sentences

1 In regard to desert oil wastes, Jill referred only minimum cases.

2 Carra agrees you'll get a reward only as you join nonunion races.

3 Few beavers, as far as I'm aware, feast on cedar trees in Kokomo.

4 Johnny, after a few stewed eggs, ate a plump, pink onion at noon.

5 A plump, aged monk served a few million beggars a milky beverage.

| 1 | 2 | 3 | 4 | 5 | 6 | 7 | 8 | 9 | 10 | 11 | 12 | 13 |

COMMUNICATION
40b

1. Compose a short letter to your teacher that illustrates 6 of the 11 capitalization rules shown on page 131. Format it as a block letter with open punctuation.

2. Bold the capitalized word and key the rule number in parentheses. For example:

   Report (Rule #1) to **Unit** 1 (Rule #8).

   If your letter contains more than one example of a rule, only bold one of them.

3. Save as *40b*.

NEW FUNCTIONS
40c

Indent

When a writer paraphrases or quotes material longer than three lines from another source, the writer must set off the long quote from the rest of the report. Quoted material is set off by indenting it 0.5" from the left margin.

The Indent feature moves all lines of a paragraph to the next tab. In contrast, TAB moves only the first line of a paragraph to the next tab. Indent is a paragraph command. The Indent feature enables you to indent text from either the left or right margin or from both margins.

Tab ——→ Curtis Ward (2005, 34) states that his company perceives the benefits of virtual e-learning as follows:

        Tab ——→ Virtual e-learning seminars are led by experienced trainers and
Indent ——→ last only 3 hours per day. Time out of the office is quite minimal, and no travel costs are incurred. We consider virtual e-learning the top choice as it combines the best of live instruction and online learning.

Send Document in Body of an E-mail Message

The **Mail Recipient** command is similar to the Mail Recipient (as Attachment) command. The document, however, is inserted in the body of the e-mail message. The writer simply keys an introduction at the beginning of the e-mail message to explain the document that follows.

1. Click **File**, **Send To**, and **Mail Recipient**.
2. Key the recipient's e-mail address in the To box.
3. In the Introduction box, key text to give the recipient instructions about the document that follows in the e-mail message.
4. Click **Send a Copy**.

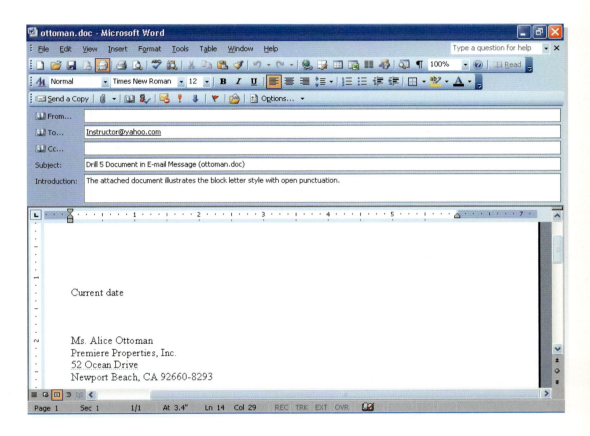

D r i l l 5 | **SEND DOCUMENT IN BODY OF E-MAIL MESSAGE**

1. Open the data file *ottoman*.

2. Click **File**, **Send To**, and **Mail Recipient**.

3. In the To box, key your instructor's e-mail address.

4. Edit the Subject line to read **Drill 5 Document in E-mail Message (ottoman.doc)**.

5. Key the following text as an introduction at the beginning of the e-mail message:

   The attached document illustrates the block letter style with open punctuation.

6. Click **Send a Copy**. **Note:** If your e-mail program is not compatible, follow the directions in step 6 of Drill 3. Save the document as *35d-drill5*. You have made a copy of the e-mail message screen.

[39d-d1]

Two-Page Leftbound Report

1. Key the model two-page report on pages 149–150.
2. Create the header to number the pages; suppress the page number on the first page.
3. Format the bulleted list SS with a DS between items.
4. Apply **Keep with next** to protect the side heading from being left alone at the bottom of the first page.
5. Switch to Print Layout View to verify page numbers.
6. Save as *39d-d1*. Check the spelling and print the document.

[39d-d2]

Title Page

1. Create a title page for the leftbound report prepared in *39d-d1*. Set the left margin at 1.5".
2. Prepare the title page for **XYZ Employees by Jennifer Schoenholtz, Office Manager**.
3. Expand character spacing, add a page border, and change the font color.
4. Save the title page as *39d-d2*.

[39d-d3]

Unbound Report

✳ DISCOVER

Insert file—Position insertion point where file is to be inserted. On the Insert menu, click **File**; select the desired file; click **Insert**.

1. Convert the leftbound report in *39d-d1* to an unbound report.
2. Insert the data file *writing* below the first paragraph. **Note:** Be sure to position the insertion point where you want the text to appear before inserting the file.
3. Switch to Print Layout View. Verify page numbers and check that no lines are left alone at the bottom of the page.
4. Save the report as *39d-d3*.

Timely Topics

© Getty/PhotoDisc

on cell phones

Are cell phones dangerous to your health? Studies are being conducted to determine whether or not cell phones can cause serious health problems such as brain tumors and high blood pressure. So far, there is no conclusive evidence to support this theory. However, it is true that cell phones have caused an increased number of automobile crashes. The Cellular Telecommunications Industry has issued some cell phone safety tips. Use a hands-free device when possible. Try to place calls while you are not moving. Do not engage in stressful conversations that could divert your attention from the road. Never try to take notes or look up phone numbers while driving.

Send Document in E-Mail for Review

The **Mail Recipient (for Review)** command also generates an e-mail message and attaches the *Word* document to the e-mail message. When the recipient receives the document via e-mail, he/she finds the *Word* reviewing tools are already enabled in the document. You will learn about reviewing tools in a later module, but the reviewing tools help the recipient accept or reject changes in the document.

Note: To use this command, the user must be using an e-mail program compatible with Messaging Application Programming Interface (MAPI).

1. With the document to be reviewed open, click **File, Send To**, and **Mail Recipient (for Review)**. A new e-mail message box displays.

2. In the To box, key the recipient's e-mail address. If you wish to copy this e-mail to another recipient, key that e-mail address in the Cc box.

3. In the Subject box, key an appropriate subject or accept the default subject. In the message area, accept the default message or key one of your own.

4. Click **Send**.

D r i l l   6 | **SEND FILE FOR REVIEW**

1. Open *35c-drill1*.

2. Click **File, Send To**, and **Mail Recipient (for Review)**.

3. In the To box, key your instructor's e-mail address.

4. Edit the message by adding the following sentence:

   This document illustrates the modified block letter style with open punctuation.

5. Click **Send**.

   Note: If your e-mail program is not compatible, tap PRINT SCREEN; open a blank document and click **Paste**. Save the document as *35d-drill6*.

DOCUMENT DESIGN · DOCUMENT DESIGN · DOCUMENT DESIGN · DOCUMENT DESIGN · DOCUMENT DESIGN · DOCUMENT DESIGN

>> **DOCUMENT DESIGN**
35e

Mixed Punctuation Style

Although most letters are formatted with open punctuation, some businesses prefer mixed punctuation. To format a letter using mixed punctuation, key a colon after the salutation and a comma after the complimentary closing.

Dear Dr. Hathorn:

Sincerely,

Mixed Punctuation

Ensuring Correct Format

The effective writer understands the importance of using technology to create an attractive document that adheres to correct style rules. Review the list below to determine your use of technology in the report writing process.

- Number preliminary pages of the report with small Roman numerals at the bottom center of the page.

- Number the report with Arabic numbers in the upper-right corner.

- Create attractive headers or footers that contain helpful information for the reader.

- Suppress headers, footers, and page numbering on the title page and on the first page of the report.

- Invoke the widow/orphan protection feature to ensure that no lines display alone at the bottom or top of a page.

- Use the keep with next command to keep side headings from appearing alone at the bottom of the page.

- Format references using the hanging indent feature.

- Use typographic or special symbols to enhance the report. Examples include ¶ for paragraph, ™ for trademark, ® for registered, ≠ for not equal to, and ✂ to indicate cut along this line.

Writers also take advantage of the online thesaurus for choosing the most appropriate word and the spelling and grammar features for ensuring spelling and grammar correctness. Additionally, electronic desk references and style manuals are just a click away.

These simple steps will assist you in your goal to create well-written and attractive reports. The next step is to practice, practice, and practice.

[35f-d1]
Modified Block Letter

1. Format the letter in modified block style with mixed punctuation. Insert the current date at 2.1".
2. Supply the correct salutation, a complimentary closing, and your reference initials. Add an enclosure line and a copy notation to **Laura Aimes, Sales Representative**.
3. Proofread carefully. Preview for good placement. Save as *35f-d1*. Print.
4. Attach an envelope to the letter, and save it again as *35f-d2*. Print.

[35f-d2]
Envelope

Ms. Mukta Bhakta
9845 Buckingham Road
Annapolis, MD 21403-0314

Thank you for your recent inquiry on our electronic bulletin service. The ABC BBS is an interactive online service developed by All Business Communication to assist the online community in receiving documents via the Internet.

All Business Communication also provides a *Customer Support Service* and a *Technical Support Team* to assist bulletin board users. The Systems Administrators will perform various procedures needed to help you take full advantage of this new software.

For additional information call:

Customer and Technical Support
Telephone: 900-555-0112
9:00 a.m.-5:00 p.m., Monday-Friday, Eastern Time

Please look over the enclosed ABC BBS brochure. I will call you within the next two weeks to discuss any additional questions you may have.

Alexis Zampich, Marketing Manager

[35f-d3]
Edit Letter

1. Open *35c-drill1* and save it as *35f-d3*.
2. Change the letter style to block letter style.
3. Change the punctuation style to mixed punctuation. Save and print.

[35f-d4]
Send Document for Review

1. Open *35f-d1*. Send this document to your instructor for review.
2. Use the default subject line and e-mail message.
3. Send the e-mail. If the e-mail program is not compatible, tap PRINT SCREEN, paste the image in a blank *Word* document, and save it as *35f-d4*.

[35f-d5]
Send Document as Attachment

1. Open *35f-d3*. Send this document as an attachment to your instructor. Compose an appropriate subject line and message.
2. Send the e-mail. If the e-mail program is not compatible, tap PRINT SCREEN, paste the image in a blank *Word* document, and save it as *35f-d5*.

About 2.1" (Set DS; tap ENTER 3 times)

THE REVISED REPORT IS THE FINAL REPORT   14 point

Being able to communicate effectively in a clear, concise, and logical manner continues to be one of the most demanded work skills. Employees who know effective revision skills are far ahead of their counterparts who have the mind-set that the first draft is the final draft. This report details effective revision skills as it relates to report writing.

Revising the Draft

After a first draft of a report is completed, the writer is ready to refine or polish the report. The writer must be objective when revising the report draft and cultivate a mind-set for improving the report by always considering the draft as a draft.

First, read the draft for content. This might mean rewriting sections of the report or adding information to areas that appear weak in this review. In this evaluative review, the writer may realize that one section would fit more logically after another section.

When the writer is satisfied with the content, it is time to verify that all style rules have been followed. For example, check all headings to ensure they are "talking" headings. Do the headings describe the content of the section? Also, be sure all headings are parallel. If the writer chooses the side heading *Know Your Audience*, other side headings must also begin with a verb.

[35f-d6 and 35f-d7]
Letter and Envelope

New Address

General | Note

Name

Last name: Goralsky

First name: Arthur

Title: Dr.

Company: Global Enterpises, Inc.

Address

Street: 2000 Corporate Way

City: Lake Oswego

State: OR

Zip: 97035

Country:

1. Open *32e-d1* and save it as *35f-d6*. Edit the letter address using the recipient's information shown in the PDA (Personal Digital Assistant) screen at the left.
2. Compose an appropriate salutation and complimentary closing.
3. Center the letter vertically. Use **Show/Hide** to remove any extra paragraph markers (¶) at the beginning and end of the document.
4. Edit the body of the letter and the writer's name, as shown below. Keep the reference initials at the end of the document. Save and print. Add an envelope and save it as *35f-d7*.

Have you heard your friends and colleagues ~~talk about~~ *discuss* obtaining real-time stock quotes? What about real-time account balances and positions, NASDAQ Level II quotes, or extended-hours trading? If so, then they are among the ~~three~~ *four* million serious investors who have opened ~~an~~ account*s* with E-Market Firm.

Our investors know
~~We believe that~~ the best decisions are informed decisions ~~that are~~ made in a timely manner. E-Market Firm has an online help desk that provides infor-mation for all levels of investors, from beginners to the experienced serious trader. You can learn basic ~~tactics~~ *strategies* for investing in the stock market, *for* avoiding common mistakes, and *for* picking up some advanced strategies.

Stay on top of the market and your investments! Please visit our *award-winning* website at http://www.emarketfirm.com to learn more about our banking and brokerage services and to access our online help desk. E-Market Firm is the premier site for online investing.

Keisha Knight
~~Margaritta Gibson~~
Marketing Manager

[35f-d8]
Send Document as Attachment

1. Open *35f-d7*. Use the Mail Recipient (as Attachment) command to send this document to your instructor for review.
2. Edit the subject line as follows: **Block Letter Review (35f-d7.doc)**
3. Add the following sentence to the e-mail message:
   This document illustrates the block letter style with open punctuation and the envelope added to the document. You may convert the envelope text to uppercase by using Word's Change Case feature.
4. Send the e-mail or follow the directions in step 6 of Drill 3 to print the screen and then save the document as *35f-d8*.

[35f-d9]
Send Document in E-mail Message

1. Open *33e-d1*. Send this document to your instructor in the body of an e-mail.
2. Compose a subject line and an appropriate introduction that explains that a model of a modified block letter with open punctuation follows in the e-mail message.
3. Send the e-mail or follow the directions in step 6 of Drill 3 to print the screen and then save the document as *35f-d9*.

» DOCUMENT DESIGN

39c

Two-Page Reports

Report Format Guidelines

Reports are widely used in various environments. Review the guidelines for formatting a one-page unbound report on page 135 and then study the information that follows:

Side margins: Default side margins for an unbound report. Set the left margin at 1.5" for a leftbound report.

Top margin: Approximately 2.1" for first page of report, preliminary pages, and Reference page; 1" on other pages.

Page numbers: Include page numbers for the second and succeeding pages of a report. Position at the top of the page (header), right alignment.

Single lines: Avoid single lines at the top or bottom of a report (called *widow/orphan lines*). Do not separate a side heading from the paragraph that follows between pages.

To format a report:

1. At the top of the document, change the line spacing to double. Tap ENTER three times to position the insertion point to leave an approximate 2" top margin.

2. Check that the font size is 12 point.

3. Insert page numbers. Suppress the page number on the first page.

4. Key the main heading in ALL CAPS. Tap ENTER; then select the heading and apply 14 point and bold. Center-align the heading.

5. Move the insertion point to below the heading, and begin to key the report.

6. Position the references on a new page. If necessary, insert a manual page break. Format the title REFERENCES in 14 point, bold, at approximately 2.1".

7. Protect side headings that may get separated from the related paragraph with the Keep with next feature.

8. View the report using Print Layout View.

Assessment

36a

Practice each line; repeat the drill.

alphabet	1	The explorer questioned Jack's amazing story about the lava flow.
fig/sym	2	I cashed Cartek & Bunter's $2,679 check (Check #3480) on June 15.
1st/2nd finger	3	Hugh tried to go with Katrina, but he did not have time to do so.
easy	4	The eighty firms may pay for a formal audit of their field works.

| 1 | 2 | 3 | 4 | 5 | 6 | 7 | 8 | 9 | 10 | 11 | 12 | 13 |

36b Timed Writings

Take two 3' timings.

LA all letters

	gwam	1'	3'

Have simple things such as saying please, may I help you, and 12 | 4

thank you gone out of style? We begin to wonder when we observe 25 | 8

front-line workers interact with customers today. Often their bad 39 | 13

attitudes shout that the customer is a bother and unimportant. But 52 | 17

we know there would be no business without the customer. So what 66 | 22

can be done to prove to customers that they really are the king? 79 | 26

First, require that all your staff train in good customer 12 | 30

service. Here they must come to realize that their jobs exist for 25 | 35

the customer. Also, be sure workers feel that they can talk to 38 | 39

their bosses about any problem. You do not want workers to talk 51 | 43

about lack of breaks or schedules in front of customers. Clients 64 | 48

must always feel that they are kings and should never be ignored. 77 | 52

1' | 1 | 2 | 3 | 4 | 5 | 6 | 7 | 8 | 9 | 10 | 11 | 12 | 13 |
3' | 1 | 2 | 3 | 4 |

APPLICATIONS

[36c]

Assessment

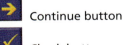

→ Continue button

✓ Check button

General Instructions: Format the letters in the style indicated; add additional letter parts if necessary. Use the Date and Time feature for the current date. Add a proper salutation and your reference initials for all letters. Check spelling, preview for proper placement, and carefully proofread each letter before proceeding to the next document.

With *CheckPro*: *CheckPro* will keep track of the time it takes you to complete the entire production test, compute your speed and accuracy rate on each document, and summarize the results. When you complete a document, proofread it, check the spelling, and preview for placement. When you are completely satisfied with the document, click the **Continue** button to move to the next document. You will not be able to return and edit a document once you continue to the next document. Click the **Check** button when you are ready to error-check the test. Review and/or print the document analysis results.

Without *CheckPro*: On the signal to begin, key the documents in sequence. When saving documents, name them in the usual manner (for example, *36c-d1*). When time has been called, proofread all documents again and identify errors.

D r i l l 3 LINE AND PAGE BREAKS

1. Open *report* from the data files. Save it as *39b-drill3*.

2. Create a header for page numbers. Suppress the header on the first page.

3. Select the heading **In Conclusion** and the paragraph that follows. Apply **Keep with next**.

4. Position the main heading at about 2.1".

5. Format all headings correctly.

6. Change to Print Layout View to verify the page numbers and the top margin.

7. Save and print. Compare your document to the model on page 148.

---

help keywords

insert a symbol; insert a special character

Symbols and Special Characters

Symbols and special characters can be printed using the Symbol command even though they do not appear on the keyboard. Symbols that you use frequently can be assigned to a shortcut key. (See Help, Insert Symbol or Character.) Examples of symbols and special characters include:

Em dash —   En dash –   Copyright ©   Registered ®   Trademark™

To insert symbols or special characters:

1. Position the insertion point where the symbol or special character is to be inserted.

2. Click **Insert** on the menu, and then click **Symbol**.

3. Click the **Symbols** tab to insert a symbol or click the **Special characters** tab to insert a special character. You may also select from the Recently used symbols box.

4. Select the symbol or special character to be inserted. When selecting symbols, you may also want to select a different font to display various symbols, e.g., Wingdings, Wingdings2, and Wingdings3.

5. Click **Insert** and **Close**. (*Hint:* To increase the size of the symbol, select and enlarge font size.)

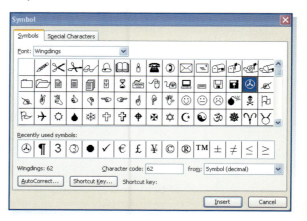

D r i l l 4 SYMBOLS

1. Key the following lines as a numbered list. Do not key the headings or the text in parentheses.

2. Insert the symbols and special characters shown.

3. Save it as *39b-drill4*.

Special Characters

1. Parker House—Best Dining (em dash)
2. Pages 13–25 (en dash)
3. July 20 (nonbreaking space)
4. 92° F (degree and nonbreaking space)
5. Revise ¶3.

Symbols

6. ☺ Have a nice day.
7. ⇨ Room 253.
8. ✍ Sign here.
9. ✓ Yes, send today.
10. ❑ Yes ❑ No

[36c-d1]
Block Letter

1. Key the letter shown below in block letter style with open punctuation. Supply an appropriate salutation.
2. Center the letter vertically on the page.
3. Send a copy to Philip Gilbert and Leigh Browning. Remember to set tabs for enclosures and copy notations. Save as *36c-d1*.

Current date | AMASTA Company, Inc. | 902 Greenridge Drive | Reno, NV 89505-5552

We sell your videocassettes and have since you introduced them. Several of our customers now tell us they are unable to follow the directions on the coupon. They explain that there is no company logo on the box to return to you as you requested.

What steps should we take? A copy of the coupon is enclosed, as is a Super D Container. Please read the coupon, examine the box, and then let me know your plans for extricating us from this problem.

Sincerely | John J. Long | Sales Manager | Enclosures: 2

[36c-d2]
Modified Block Letter

1. Key the letter below in modified block style with mixed punctuation.
2. Center the letter vertically on the page. Save it as *36c-d2*.
3. Add an envelope to the letter. Save it as *36c-d3* and print.

[36c-d3]
Envelope

Current date | Mr. John J. Long, Sales Manager | The Record Store | 9822 Trevor Avenue | Anaheim, CA 92805-5885

With your letter came our turn to be perplexed, and we apologize. When we had our refund coupons printed, we had just completed a total redesign program for our product boxes. We had detachable logos put on the outside of the boxes, which could be peeled off and placed on a coupon.

We had not anticipated that our distributors would use back inventories with our promotion. The cassettes you sold were not packaged in our new boxes; therefore, there were no logos on them.

I'm sorry you or your customers were inconvenienced. In the future, simply ask your customers to send us their sales slips, and we will honor them with refunds until your supply of older containers is depleted.

Sincerely | Bruna Wertz | Sales and Promotions Dept. | xx

[36c-d4]
Edit Letter

1. Open *brackmun* from the data files. Save it as *36c-d4*.
2. Send the letter to: **Vidadex Corporation, 3945 Alexandria Boulevard, Detroit, MI 48230-9732**. Replace the salutation.
3. Change the letter from block to modified block format with mixed punctuation.

www.collegekeyboarding.com

1. Open *header2*. Save it as *39b-drill2*.

2. Create the header shown below for the two-page report and suppress the header on the first page.

3. Key the report title at the left position.

4. Tab to the right position. Key **Page** and space once; then insert the page number.

✳ 5. Use the Border button on the Formatting toolbar to create a bottom border under the header.

6. View the header.

7. Make the revisions shown below to the report.

8. Close the document and save your changes.

> Header
> Basic Tips for Designing Attractive Brochures   Page 2

Summary (Use Format Painter to format)

Remember to plan your page layout ~~with~~ *keeping* the three ~~basic~~ elements of effective page design, *in mind* Always include sufficient white space to give an uncluttered appearance. Learn to add bold when emphasis is needed, *add italic when required.* and do consider your audience when choosing typestyles. ~~Finally, use typestyles to~~ add variety to your *page* layout, but ~~remember, no more than~~ *limit it to* two typestyles ~~in a document~~.

Line and Page Breaks

Pagination or breaking pages at the appropriate location can easily be controlled using two features: Widow/Orphan control and Keep with next.

Widow/Orphan control prevents a single line of a paragraph from printing at the bottom or top of a page. A check mark displays in this option box indicating that Widow/Orphan control is "on" (the default).

Keep with next prevents a page break from occurring between two paragraphs. Use this feature to keep a side heading from being left alone at the bottom of a page. To use Keep with next:

1. Select the side heading and the paragraph that follows.

2. Click **Format**; then **Paragraph**.

3. From the Line and Page Breaks tab, select **Keep with next**. Click **OK**. The side heading moves to the next page.

Paragraph [?] [X]

| Indents and Spacing | Line and Page Breaks |

Pagination
- ☑ Widow/Orphan control
- ☐ Keep lines together
- ☑ Keep with next
- ☐ Page break before

Objective Assessment

Answer the questions below to see if you have mastered the content of Module 4.

1. When a business letter is addressed to a company, the correct salutation is _____.

2. From the dateline, tap ENTER _____ times before keying the letter address.

3. Use 1.25" or _____ side margins for a business letter.

4. Letters are positioned vertically on the page by using the _____ command.

5. When keying a modified block letter, set a tab at the center point of the page, which is _____".

6. When an item is included with a letter, a(n) _____ notation is keyed a DS below the reference initials.

7. Envelopes and labels are accessed from the _____ menu.

8. From the File menu, click _____ to e-mail a document to another user.

9. Use the Mail Recipient (_____) command to e-mail a document for review to another user.

10. The _____ notation is used to indicate that a copy of the letter is being sent to another person.

Performance Assessment

Document 1

Block Letter with Envelope

1. Key the letter in block format with open punctuation. The letter is from Darin Parson, Marketing Manager. Add the necessary letter parts.

2. Save as *checkpoint4-d1*. Proofread and print when you are satisfied.

Document 2

Envelope

With Document 1 open, add an envelope to the letter. Save it as *checkpoint4-d2* and print.

Ms. Lucy Marino | 2155 Mack Avenue | Los Angeles, CA 90015-0989

The keynote speaker for our annual sales conference this year will be Dr. Helen McBride, from the University of Southern California. She will be giving her opening speech at 2:00 p.m. on Tuesday, May 25, 20--.

Dr. McBride, a well-known psychologist who has spent a lot of time researching and writing on employee productivity, will address "Stress Management." I am sure you will find her speech to be both informative and entertaining.

A copy of Dr. McBride's resume is enclosed for use in preparing news releases and announcements for the sales conference.

Document 3

Edit Letter

1. Open *checkpoint4-d1*.

2. Select the date and closing lines; set a tab appropriate for a modified block letter. Format the document in modified block with mixed punctuation.

3. Delete the letter address. Send this letter to **Mr. Joseph Rodrigues, 55 La Brea Avenue, Santa Monica, CA 90405-9876**. Perform all necessary changes to make this a mailable business letter.

4. Save as *checkpoint4-d3*. Print.

Two-Page Reports

WARMUP

39a

Key each line twice.

alphabet	1	Jayne Cox puzzled over workbooks that were required for geometry.
figures	2	Edit pages 308 and 415 in Book A; pages 17, 29, and 60 in Book B.
shift	3	THE LAKES TODAY, published in Akron, Ohio, comes in June or July.
easy	4	The town may blame Keith for the auditory problems in the chapel.

| 1 | 2 | 3 | 4 | 5 | 6 | 7 | 8 | 9 | 10 | 11 | 12 | 13 |

new functions

39b

Header and Footer

The Header feature enables you to place information at the top of each page in a document. The default header allows for three lines, but this space may be increased or decreased. Headers print 0.5" from the top edge of the paper. Headers can only be viewed in Print Layout View.

help keywords

create a header or footer

To create a header for page numbers:

1. Click **View** on the menu bar, and then click **Header and Footer**. This will display the Header and Footer toolbar and a grid area in which you will key the header.

2. The header has three positions: left margin, center, right margin. Tap the TAB key twice to move the insertion point to the right margin position.

3. Click the **Insert Page Number** button to insert the page number.

4. Click the **Page Setup** button on the Header and Footer toolbar and click the **Layout** tab. Choose **Different First Page**; then click **OK** to suppress the header on first page.

5. Choose **Close** on the Header and Footer toolbar. View the header in Print Layout View (View menu).

Drill 1 | HEADER

1. Open *header* from the data files. Save it as *39b-drill1*.

2. Create the header to number the pages in the top right position for the two-page report.

3. Choose **Different First Page** to suppress the header on the first page.

4. View the document by clicking the View menu and then clicking **Print Layout**.

5. Save your changes and close the document.

CAPITALIZATION GUIDES

Capitalize:

1. **First word of a sentence and of a direct quotation.**

   We were tolerating instead of managing diversity.
   The speaker said, "We must value diversity, not merely recognize it."

2. **Proper nouns**—specific persons, places, or things.

   Common nouns: continent, river, car, street
   Proper nouns: Asia, Mississippi, Buick, State St.
   Exception: Capitalize a title of high distinction even when it does not refer to a specific person (e.g., President of the United States).

3. **Derivatives** of proper nouns and **geographical** names.

   Derivatives: American history, German food, English accent, Ohio Valley
   Geographical nouns: Tampa, Florida, Mount Rushmore

4. **A personal or professional title** when it precedes the name; capitalize a title of high distinction without a name.

   Title: Lieutenant Kahn, Mayor Walsh, Doctor Welby
   High distinction: the President of the United States

5. **Days of the week, months of the year, holidays, periods of history, and historic events.**

   Monday, June 8, Labor Day, Renaissance

6. **Specific parts of the country** but not compass points that show direction.

   Midwest   the South   northwest of town   the Middle East

7. **Family relationships** when used with a person's name.

   Aunt Carol   my mother   Uncle Mark

8. **A noun preceding a figure** except for common nouns such as line, page, and sentence.

   Unit 1   Section 2   page 2   verse 7   line 2

9. **First and main words of side headings, titles of books, and works of art.**
   Do not capitalize words of four or fewer letters that are conjunctions, prepositions, or articles.

   Computers in the News   *Raiders of the Lost Ark*

10. **Names of organizations and specific departments** within the writer's organization.

    Girl Scouts   our Sales Department

11. **The salutation of a letter and the first word of the complimentary closing.**

    Dear Mr. Bush   Ladies and Gentlemen: Sincerely yours,
    Very cordially yours,

[38e-d1]
Leftbound Report

1. Key the leftbound report on page 143. Save the report as *38e-d1*.

2. To create the bulleted list, key the items; then select the items and apply bullets.

3. With the items selected, click the **Increase Indent** button to align the bullets with the paragraph indent.

4. Save and print.

[38e-d2]
Title Page

1. Create a title page for the leftbound report prepared in Document 1. Set the left margin at 1.5".

2. Prepare the title page for **John E. Swartsfager, Marketing Director**, by you as the **Information Technology Manager**. (Place the Marketing Director's name and title on two lines.)

3. Expand character spacing by 1.5 points in the report title.

✳ 4. Add a dark red page border and change the text font color to dark red.

5. Save the document as *38e-d2*.

✳ **DISCOVER**

Font Color—Click drop-down arrow; choose color.

[38e-d3]
Leftbound Report

1. Open *37e-d2* and format the document as a leftbound report.

2. Add the last paragraph shown below, and save the document as *38e-d3*.

Summary (Use Format Painter to format)

　　Remember to plan your page layout with the three basic elements of effective page design. Always include sufficient white space to give an uncluttered appearance. Learn to add bold when emphasis is needed, and do consider your audience when choosing typestyles. Finally, use typestyles to add variety to your layout, but remember, no more than two typestyles in a document.

Drill 1

CAPITALIZATION

Review the rules and examples on the previous page. Then key the sentences, correcting all capitalization errors. Number each item and DS between items. Save as *capitalize-drill 1*.

1. according to one study, the largest ethnic minority group online is hispanics.
2. the american author mark twain said, "always do right; this will gratify some people and astonish the rest."
3. the grand canyon was formed by the colorado river cutting into the high-plateau region of northwestern arizona.
4. the president of russia is elected by popular vote.
5. the hubble space telescope is a cooperative project of the european space agency and the national aeronautics and space administration.
6. the train left north station at 6:45 this morning.
7. the trademark cyberprivacy prevention act would make it illegal for individuals to purchase domains solely for resale and profit.
8. consumers spent $7 billion online between november 1 and december 31, 2004, compared to $3.1 billion for the same period in 2003.
9. new students should attend an orientation session on wednesday, august 15, at 8 a.m. in room 252 of the perry building.
10. the summer book list includes *where the red fern grows* and *the mystery of the missing baseball*.

Drill 2

CAPITALIZATION

1. Open the file *capitalize2* from the data files and save it as *capitalize-drill2*.
2. Follow the specific directions provided in the data file. Remember to use the correct proofreaders' marks:

   ≡ Capitalize   <u>sincerely</u>

   lc Lowercase   My ₰ear Sir

3. Resave and print. Submit the rough draft and final copy to your instructor.

Drill 3

CAPITALIZATION OF LETTER PARTS

Key the letter parts using correct capitalization. Number each item and DS between each. Save as *capitalize-drill3*.

1. dear mr. petroilli
2. ladies and gentlemen
3. dear senator kuknais
4. very sincerely yours
5. dear reverend Schmidt
6. very truly yours
7. cordially yours
8. dear mr fong and miss landow
9. respectfully yours
10. sincerely
11. dear mr. and mrs. Green
12. dear service manager

Drill 4

CAPITALIZATION

1. Open the file *capitalize4* from the data files. Save it as *capitalize-drill4*.
2. This file includes a field for selecting the correct answer. You will simply select the correct answer. Follow the specific directions provided in the data file.
3. Resave and print.

About 2.1"

PLANNING A SUCCESSFUL PRESENTATION

Presenters realize the need to prepare for a successful presentation. Two areas of extensive preparation are the development of a thorough audience analysis and a well-defined presentation purpose.

Audience Analysis

The presenter must conduct a thorough audience analysis before developing the presentation. The profile of the audience includes the following demographics.

1.5"   1.25"

- Age and gender
- Education
- Ethnic group
- Marital status
- Geographic location
- Group membership

Interviews with program planners and organization leaders will provide insight into the needs, desires, and expectations of the audience. This information makes the difference in preparing a presentation that is well received by the audience.

Purpose of the Presentation

After analyzing the audience profile, the presenter has a clear focus on the needs of the audience and then writes a well-defined purpose of the presentation. With a clear focus, the presenter confidently conducts research and organizes a presentation that is on target. The presenter remembers to state the purpose in the introduction of the presentation to assist the audience in understanding the well-defined direction of the presentation.

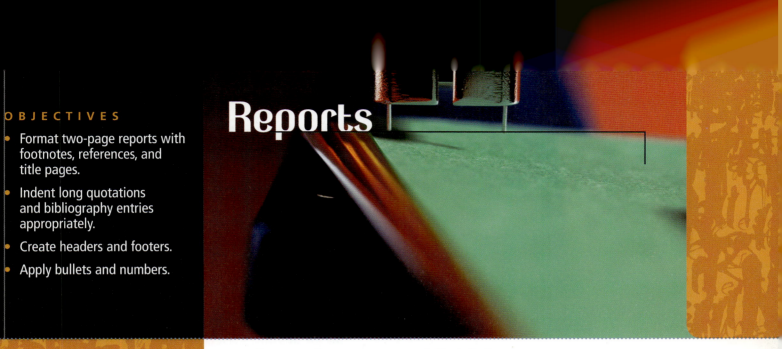

Reports

OBJECTIVES

- Format two-page reports with footnotes, references, and title pages.
- Indent long quotations and bibliography entries appropriately.
- Create headers and footers.
- Apply bullets and numbers.

LESSON 37 — Unbound Report with Title Page

WARMUP
37a
Key each line twice.

alphabet	1	Two exit signs jut quietly above the beams of a razed skyscraper.
figures	2	Send 345 of the 789 sets now; send the others on August 1 and 26.
direct reach	3	I obtain many junk pieces dumped by Marvyn at my service centers.
easy	4	Enrique may fish for cod by the dock; he also may risk a penalty.

| 1 | 2 | 3 | 4 | 5 | 6 | 7 | 8 | 9 | 10 | 11 | 12 | 13 |

SKILLBUILDING
37b
Timed Writings
Key a 1' timing on each paragraph and a 3' timing on all paragraphs.

all letters

gwam 1'   3'

Does a relationship exist between confidence and success? If you think it does, you will find that many people agree with you. However, it is very hard to judge just how strong the bond is.

When people are confident they can do a job, they are very likely to continue working on that task until they complete it correctly. If they are not confident, they give up much quicker.

People who are confident they can do something tend to enjoy doing it more than those who lack confidence. They realize that they do better work when they are happy with what they do.

	1'	3'
	12	4	42
	26	9	46
	38	13	50
	12	17	54
	24	21	58
	38	25	63
	12	29	67
	25	34	71
	37	37	75

1' | 1 | 2 | 3 | 4 | 5 | 6 | 7 | 8 | 9 | 10 | 11 | 12 | 13 |
3' | 1 | 2 | 3 | 4 |

Drill 2 | BULLETS

1. Key the text below in one column.

2. Apply bullets to the list by selecting the text to be bulleted and clicking the **Bullets** button.

3. Convert the bullets to numbers. Select the bulleted items and click the **Numbering** button.

4. Add **Roll Call** as the second item.

5. Delete the number before *Next Meeting*.

6. Save the document as *38c-drill2* and print it.

- Call to Order
- Reading and Approval of the Minutes
- Announcements
- Treasurer's Report

- Membership Committee Report
- Unfinished Business
- New Business
- Adjournment
- Next Meeting: November 3, 20--

Drill 3 | BULLETS

1. Open *bullets* from the data files.

2. Select the bulleted items, and convert them to numbers.

3. Add a blank line between each numbered item without adding an additional number by pressing SHIFT + ENTER at the end of each item.

4. Save as *38c-drill3*.

DOCUMENT DESIGN · DOCUMENT DESIGN · DOCUMENT DESIGN · DOCUMENT DESIGN · DOCUMENT DESIGN · DOCUMENT DESIGN

>> DOCUMENT DESIGN
38d

Leftbound Report

Reports prepared with binders are called leftbound reports. The binding usually takes 0.5" of space. Therefore, set the left margin to 1.5" to accommodate a left binding. Study the illustration below to note the 1.5" left margin required for leftbound reports. Then review the other report formats that are the same for unbound and leftbound reports. A full-page model is shown on page 143.

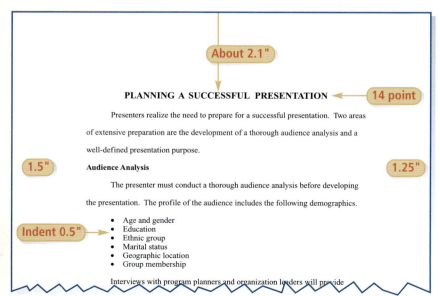

Left margin: 1.5"

Right margin: Default (1.25") or 1"

Bottom margin: Approximately 1"; last page may be deeper

Font: 12 point for body of report

Main Heading:

- Key main heading in ALL CAPS.
- Position at about 2.1". (Tap ENTER three times if report is set as DS; tap ENTER six times if report is set as SS.)
- Apply 14 point, bold.
- Center-align.
- Tap ENTER twice after heading if report is set as SS.

nEW FUNCTIONS
37c

Format Painter

Use Format Painter to copy paragraph and character formats to other text in a document. The Format Painter button is located on the Standard toolbar.

To copy paragraph formats:

1. Click the **Show/Hide** button to display the paragraph marker (¶). Select the entire paragraph, including the paragraph marker.

2. Click the **Format Painter** button once to apply the format to a single paragraph. Double-click the **Format Painter** button to apply the format to more than one paragraph.

3. Click in the paragraph(s) to be reformatted.

4. If the Format Painter button is still active, click it again to turn it off.

To copy character formats:

1. Place the insertion point in the text with the formatting to be copied.

2. Click **Format Painter**. (Double-click **Format Painter** if the formatting will be applied in more than one location.)

3. Select the text to be reformatted.

4. If Format Painter is still active, click the button again to turn it off.

Drill 1 | APPLY FORMATS

1. Open *functions* from the data files. In this drill, you will use Format Painter to apply the format of the first term and definition to the remaining items in the document.

2. Click **Show/Hide** to display tabs and paragraph markers. Select the word **Bullets**.

3. Double-click the **Format Painter** button. Click each of the remaining functions in the first column to apply the format; then click the **Format Painter** button off.

4. Select the paragraph that defines the first function and the paragraph marker following it. Use Format Painter to format the remaining definitions.

5. Create the folder *Module 5 Keys*, and save the document as *37c-drill1* in this folder.

Drill 2 | APPLY FORMATS

1. Open *design* from the data files.

2. Bold the first side heading, *White Space*, and change its font to Arial.

3. Use Format Painter to format the other side headings (*Attributes* and *Typestyles*).

4. Save the document as *37c-drill2* in the *Module 5 Keys* folder.

D r i l l   1   MARGINS

1. Set 1" side margins. Key the paragraph below. Save as *38c-drill1*; then preview the document.

2. Position the insertion point at the beginning of sentence 4. Tap ENTER twice. (Use Show/Hide to delete the two extra spaces before the paragraph marker at the end of sentence 3.)

3. With the insertion point in paragraph 2, change the top and side margins to 2". Preview the document.

4. At the end of sentence 4, tap ENTER twice. Key and complete this sentence with the better response, (a) or (b).

The margin command affects the appearance of the (a) entire document (b) paragraph containing the insertion point.

5. Save the document again.

6. Change the left, right, and top margins to 1.5". Apply margin settings to the whole document.

7. Save the document as *38c-drill1b*.

Attractive document layout begins with margins set an equal distance from the left and right edges of the paper. When margins are equal, the document appears balanced. One exception to the equal-margin rule is in the formatting of reports bound at the left. To ensure the appearance of equal left and right margins in a leftbound report, you must add extra space to the left margin to allow for the binding.

help keywords

bullets; numbering

Bullets   Numbering

Numbered and bulleted lists are commonly used to emphasize information in reports, newspapers, magazine articles, and overhead presentations. Use numbered items if the list requires a sequence of steps or points. Use bullets or symbols if the list contains an unordered listing. *Word* automatically inserts the next number in a sequence if you manually key a number.

Single-space bulleted or numbered items if each item consists of one line. If more than one line is required for any item, single-space the list and double-space between each item. Study the illustrations shown below.

- Spelling and grammar
- Center page
- Bullets and numbering
- Borders and shading
- Page numbers

1. Turn right on Elm Street.

2. Take second left on Lynn Lane.

3. Take first right on Fifth Avenue.

To create bullets or numbers:

1. Key the list without bullets or numbers. Select the list and click the **Bullets** or **Numbering** button on the Formatting toolbar. If a double space is required between items, press SHIFT + ENTER at the end of each line.

2. To add or remove bullets or numbers, click the **Bullets** or **Numbering** button.

3. To convert bullets to numbers or vice versa, select the items to change and click either the **Bullets** or **Numbering** button.

›› DOCUMENT DESIGN
37d

Unbound Report Format

Reports prepared without binders are called unbound reports. Unbound reports may be attached with a staple or paper clip in the upper-left corner. Study the illustration below to learn to format a one-page unbound report. A full-page model is shown on page 137.

Main heading → **ELECTRONIC MAIL GUIDELINES** ← **14-point bold**

2.1"

Electronic mail, a widely used communication channel, clearly has three major advantages—time effectiveness, distance effectiveness, and cost-effectiveness. To reap full benefit from this popular and convenient communication medium, follow the basic guidelines regarding the creation and use of e-mail.

E-mail Composition

Although perceived as informal documents, e-mail messages are business records. Therefore, follow effective communication guidelines: write clear, concise sentences; break the message into logical paragraphs; and double-space between paragraphs. Spell check e-mail messages carefully, and verify punctuation and content accuracy. Do limit e-mail messages to one idea per message, and preferably limit to one screen. Include a subject line that clearly defines the e-mail message.

E-mail Practices

Although many people are using e-mail, some individuals do not use it as their preferred method of communication and may check it infrequently. To accomplish tasks more effectively, be aware of individuals' preferred channels of communication and use those channels. Consider an e-mail message the property of the sender, and forward only with permission. Some senders include a note in the signature line that reminds recipients not to forward e-mail without seeking permission.

Side heading

Margins: Use the preset default top, side, and bottom margins.

Font size: Use 12-point size for readability of the report body.

Spacing: DS educational reports and SS business reports.

Single-spaced report—Begin paragraph at left margin; DS between paragraphs.

Double-spaced report—Indent paragraphs 0.5".

Main heading:
- Key main heading in ALL CAPS.
- Position at about 2.1". (Tap ENTER three times if report is set as DS; tap ENTER six times if report is set as SS.)
- Apply 14 point, bold.
- Center-align.
- Tap ENTER twice after heading if report is SS.

Side heading:
- Key at left margin in bold.
- Capitalize the first letter of main word.
- DS above and below side headings if the report is SS.

Enumerated items:
- Align bulleted or numbered items with the beginning of a paragraph.
- SS each item and DS between items. If items are only one line, DS the list.

Page numbers:
- First page is not numbered.
- Second and succeeding pages are numbered in the upper-right corner in the header position (0.5").

Leftbound Report

WARMUP
38a
Key each line twice.

alphabet	1	Melva Bragg required exactly a dozen jackets for the winter trip.
figures	2	The 1903 copy of my book had 5 parts, 48 chapters, and 672 pages.
direct reach	3	Olga, the French goalie, defended well against the frazzled team.
easy	4	Rodney and a neighbor may go to the dock with us to work for Ken.

| 1 | 2 | 3 | 4 | 5 | 6 | 7 | 8 | 9 | 10 | 11 | 12 | 13 |

COMMUNICATION
38b

1. In groups of two, develop a list of the top ten mistakes student writers make in word choice (*to* vs. *too* vs. *two*).

2. Open the data file *word choice*; save as *38b*. At the keyboard, key your top ten list as directed in the file's directions. When finished, delete the directions at the top of the page.

3. Save your changes and print.

   Optional: Post your group's top ten list on the bulletin board or on the class Web page.

4. Open the data file *authors' top 10* and print. You may use a dictionary, reference manual, or online source (e.g., http://www.dictionary.com). Circle the correct word choice and submit to your instructor.

NEW FUNCTIONS
38c

help keywords

change page margins

Margins

Margins are the distance between the edge of the paper and the print. The default settings are 1.25" side margins and 1" top and bottom margins. Default margins stay in effect until you change them.

To change the margins:

1. Click **File**; then **Page Setup**.

2. From the Margins tab, click the up or down arrows to increase or decrease the default settings.

3. Apply margins to the whole document unless directed otherwise. Click **OK**.

Title Page

An attractive cover or title page is designed to enhance a report and to provide important information. Study the illustration below to learn to format an attractive title page of a report.

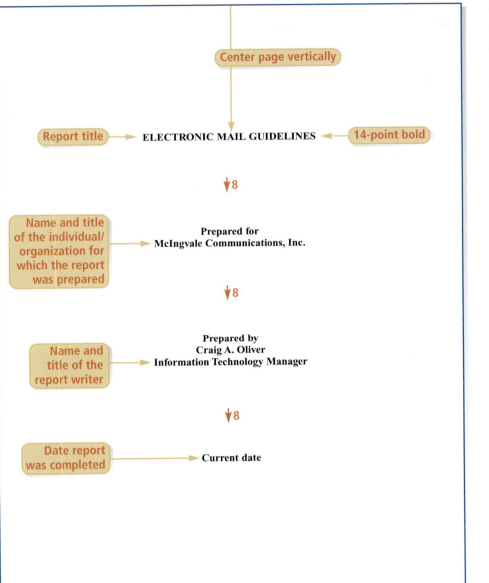

- Apply 14 point, bold.
- Center-align each line.
- Allow near equal space between parts (tap ENTER about eight times.)
- Center the page vertically (**File**, **Page Setup**, **Layout tab**)

APPLICATIONS

[37e-d1]
Unbound Report

1. Key the model report on the next page. Change the line spacing to double. Tap ENTER three times to leave a top margin of about 2.1". Use default side margins.

2. Key the main heading in ALL CAPS. Tap ENTER once. Select the heading; then change the font size to 14-point, bold and center-align the heading. (*Tip:* Tapping ENTER before formatting the main heading prevents the format of the heading from being applied to the body of the report.)

3. After keying and formatting the report, save it as *37e-d1*.

[37e-d4]

Title Page with Borders
Challenge

1. Open *37e-d3*, and save it as *37e-d4*.
2. Add a page border following the directions below.
✳ 3. Expand the space between characters in the report title using the Character Spacing feature. Expanding the space between characters will cause the heading to be more prominent (stand out more).

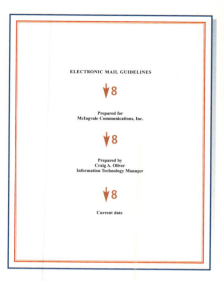

Page Borders

1. The title page, *37e-d4*, should be open.
2. Choose **Format**; then **Borders and Shading**.
3. Click the **Page Borders** tab; then choose a setting, e.g., **Box**. Choose the desired line style, line color, and line width. Click **OK**.
4. Close the document and save your changes.

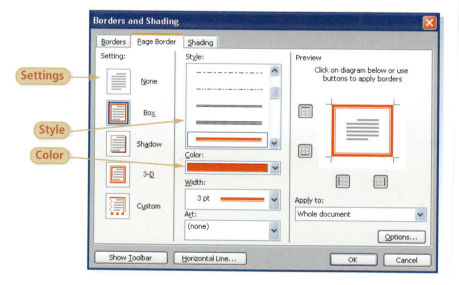

Timely Topics

on casual dress

Many companies have now established casual dress codes. Casual dressing implies that the clothing is appropriate for business yet still commands respect. Examples of casual attire are slacks, khakis, polo shirts, blouses, and other comfortable apparel. Casual dress code does not mean that employees may look sloppy. Tee-shirts, old sneakers, or improperly fitting clothing are not appropriate.

Appropriate dress plays an important role in the impression an employee creates with clients, customers, and even other employees. If you are hoping to climb the corporate ladder, you need to plan your dress carefully and always look professional.

ELECTRONIC MAIL GUIDELINES

Electronic mail, a widely used communication channel, clearly has three major advantages—time effectiveness, distance effectiveness, and cost effectiveness. To reap full benefit from this popular and convenient communication medium, follow the basic guidelines regarding the creation and use of e-mail.

E-mail Composition

Although perceived as informal documents, e-mail messages are business records. Therefore, follow effective communication guidelines: write clear, concise sentences; break the message into logical paragraphs; and double-space between paragraphs. Spell-check e-mail messages carefully, and verify punctuation and content accuracy. Do limit e-mail messages to one idea per message, and preferably limit to one screen. Include a subject line that clearly defines the e-mail message.

E-mail Practices

Although many people are using e-mail, some individuals do not use it as their preferred method of communication and may check it infrequently. To accomplish tasks more effectively, be aware of individuals' preferred channels of communication and use those channels. Consider an e-mail message the property of the sender, and forward only with permission. Some senders include a note in the signature line that reminds recipients not to forward e-mail without seeking permission.

1. Open *brochure* from the data files.
2. Select the entire document, and set the line spacing to double.
3. Position the main heading at about 2.1" by tapping ENTER three times.
4. Change the font of paragraph 1 to Garamond.
5. Apply the format of paragraph 1 to the remaining paragraphs using Format Painter. Do not format the side headings.
6. Bold the first side heading, *Working with Blocks*; change the font to Univers.
7. Apply the side heading format to the second side heading and the main heading.
8. Center the main heading and change to 14 point.
9. Save the document as *37e-d2*.

[37e-d3]
Title Page

1. Prepare a title page for the unbound report completed in *37e-d1*. See the illustration on page 136.
2. Use bold and 14 point for all lines.
✶ 3. Center-align each line using the Click and Type feature.
4. Center the page vertically. Save the document as *37e-d3*.

✶ **DISCOVER**

Click and Type—Switch to Print Layout View. Point to the center of the page to display centered text icon; double-click and key.

ELECTRONIC MAIL GUIDELINES

▼8

Prepared for
McIngvale Communications, Inc.

▼8

Prepared by
Craig A. Oliver
Information Technology Manager

▼8

Current date

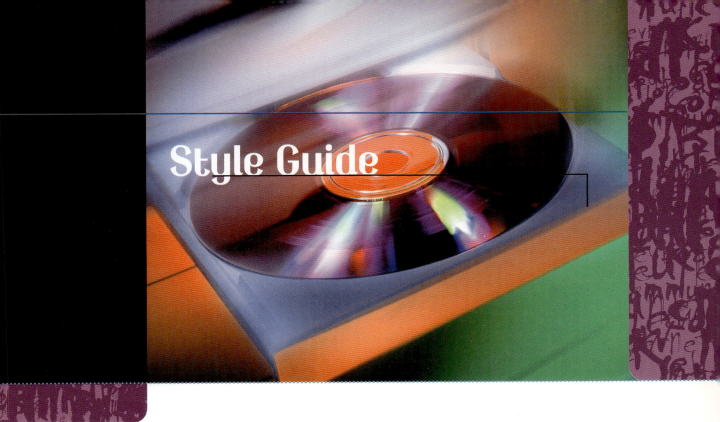

Style Guide

[STYLE GUIDE]

Number Expression

General Guidelines

1. **Use words** for numbers one through *ten* unless the numbers are in a category with related larger numbers that are expressed as figures.
   He bought three acres of land. She took two acres.
   She wrote 12 stories and 2 plays in the last 13 years.

2. **Use words** for approximate numbers or large round numbers that can be expressed as one or two words. Use **numbers** for round numbers in millions or higher with their word modifier.
   We sent out about three hundred invitations.
   She contributed $3 million.

3. **Use words** for numbers that begin a sentence.
   Six players were cut from the ten-member team.

4. **Use figures** for the larger of two adjacent numbers.
   We shipped six 24-ton engines.

Times and Dates

5. **Use words** for numbers that precede o'clock (stated or implied).
   We shall meet from two until five o'clock.

6. **Use figures** for times with *a.m.* or *p.m.* and days when they follow the month.
   Her appointment is for 2:15 p.m. on July 26, 2005.

7. **Use ordinals** for the day when it precedes the month.
   The 10th of October is my anniversary.

Money, Percentages, and Fractions

8. **Use figures** for money amounts and percentages. Spell out *cents* and *percent* except in statistical copy.
   The 16% discount saved me $145. Bill, 95 cents.

9. **Use words** for fractions unless the fractions appear in combination with whole numbers.
   one-half of her lesson   5 1/2   18 3/4

Addresses

10. **Use words** for street names First through Tenth and **figures** or ordinals for streets above Tenth. Use **figures** for house numbers other than **one**. (If street name is a number, separate it from house number with a dash.)
    One Lytle Place   Second Ave.   142—534 St.

Capitalize

1. First word of a sentence and of a direct quotation.
   We were tolerating instead of managing diversity.
   The speaker said, "We must value diversity, not merely recognize it."

2. Names of proper nouns—specific persons, places, or things.
   Common nouns: continent, river, car, street
   Proper nouns: Asia, Mississippi, Buick, State St.

3. Derivatives of proper nouns and geographical names.
   American history   English accent
   German food   Ohio Valley
   Tampa, Florida   Mount Rushmore

4. A personal or professional title when it precedes the name or a title of high distinction without a name.
   Lieutenant Kahn   Mayor Walsh
   Doctor Welby   Mr. Ty Brooks
   Dr. Frank Collins   Ms. Tate
   the President of the United States

5. Days of the week, months of the year, holidays, periods of history, and historic events.
   Monday, June 8   Labor Day   Renaissance

6. Specific parts of the country but not compass points that show direction.
   Midwest   the South   northwest of town

7. Family relationships when used with a person's name.
   Aunt Helen   my dad   Uncle John

8. Noun preceding a figure except for common nouns such as *line, page,* and *sentence.*
   Unit 1   Section 2   page 2   verse 7   line 2

9. First and main words of side headings, titles of books, and works of art. Do not capitalize words of four or fewer letters that are conjunctions, prepositions, or articles.
   Computers in the News   *Raiders of the Lost Ark*

10. Names of organizations and specific departments within the writer's organization.
    Girl Scouts   our Sales Department

Punctuation

Use an Apostrophe

1. To make most singular nouns and indefinite pronouns possessive (add **apostrophe** and **s**).

   computer + 's = computer's   Jess + 's = Jess's
   anyone's   one's   somebody's

2. To make a plural noun that does not end in s possessive (add **apostrophe** and **s**).

   women + 's = women's   men + 's = men's
   deer + 's = deer's   children + 's = children's

3. To make a plural noun that ends in s possessive. Add only the **apostrophe**.

   boys + ' = boys'   managers + ' = managers'

4. To make a compound noun possessive or to show joint possession. Add **apostrophe** and **s** to the last part of the hyphenated noun.

   son-in-law's   Rob and Gen's game

5. To form the plural of numbers and letters, add **apostrophe** and **s**. To show omission of letters or figures, add an **apostrophe** in place of the missing items.

   7's   A's   It's   add'l

Use a Colon

1. To introduce a listing.

   The candidate's strengths were obvious: experience, community involvement, and forthrightness.

2. To introduce an explanatory statement.

   Then I knew we were in trouble: The item had not been scheduled.

Use a Comma

1. After an introductory phrase or dependent clause.

   After much deliberation, the jury reached its decision.
   If you have good skills, you will find a job.

2. After words or phrases in a series.

   Mike is taking Greek, Latin III, and Chemistry II.

3. To set off nonessential or interrupting elements.

   Troy, the new man in MIS, will install the hard drive.
   He cannot get to the job, however, until next Friday.

4. To set off the date from the year and the city from the state.

   John, will you please reserve the center in Billings, Montana, for January 10, 2006?

5. To separate two or more parallel adjectives (adjectives could be separated by *and* instead of a comma).

   The loud, whining guitar could be heard above the rest.

6. Before the conjunction in a compound sentence. The comma may be omitted in a very short sentence.

   You must leave immediately, or you will miss your flight.
   We tested the software and they loved it.

7. Set off appositives and words of direct address.

   Karen, our team leader, represented us at the conference.
   Paul, have you ordered the CD-ROM drive?

Use a Hyphen

1. To show end-of-line word division.

2. In many compound words—check a dictionary if unsure.

   - Two-word adjectives before a noun:
     two-car family

   - Compound numbers between twenty-one and ninety-nine.

   - Fractions and some proper nouns with prefixes/suffixes.
     two-thirds   ex-Governor   all-American

Use Italic or Underline

1. With titles of complete literary works.

   College Keyboarding   *Hunt for Red October*

2. To emphasize special words or phrases.

   What does *professional* mean?

Use a Semicolon

1. To separate independent clauses in a compound sentence when the conjunction is omitted.

   Please review the information; give me a report by Tuesday.

2. To separate independent clauses when they are joined by conjunctive adverbs (*however, nevertheless, consequently*, etc.).

   The traffic was heavy; consequently, I was late.

3. To separate a series of elements that contain commas.

   The new officers are: Fran Pena, president; Harry Wong, treasurer; and Muriel Williams, secretary.

Use a Dash

1. To show an abrupt change of thought.

   Invoice 76A—which is 10 days overdue—is for $670.

2. After a series to indicate a summarizing statement.

   Noisy fuel pump, worn rods, and failing brakes—for all these reasons I'm trading the car.

Use an Exclamation Point

After emphatic interjections or exclamatory sentences.

Terrific!   Hold it!   You bet!   What a great surprise!

[STYLE GUIDE]

[STYLE GUIDE]

Proofreading Procedures

Proofread documents so that they are free of errors. Error-free documents send the message that you are detail-oriented and a person capable of doing business. Apply these procedures after you key a document.

1. Use Spelling and grammar function to check spelling when you have completed the document.
2. Proofread the document on screen to be sure that it makes sense. Check for these types of errors:
   - Words, headings, and/or amounts omitted.
   - Extra words or lines not deleted during the editing stage.
   - Incorrect sequence of numbers in a list.
3. Preview the document on screen using the Print Preview feature. Check the vertical placement, presence of headers or footers, page numbers, and overall appearance.
4. Save the document again and print.
5. Check the printed document by comparing it to the source copy (textbook). Check all figures, names, and addresses against the source copy. Check that the document style has been applied consistently throughout.

Proofreaders' Marks

Mark	Meaning	Mark	Meaning
#	Add horizontal space	/ or lc	Lowercase
‖	Align	⊏	Move left
∼	Bold	⊐	Move right
Cap or ≡	Capitalize	⊓	Move up
	Close up	⊔	Move down
	Delete	¶	Paragraph
∧	Insert	sp	Spell out
	Insert quotation marks	∼ or tr	Transpose
... or stet	Let it stand; ignore correction		Underline or italic

6. If errors exist on the printed copy, revise the document, save, and print.
7. Verify the corrections and placement of the second printed copy.

State Abbreviations

Alabama, AL
Alaska, AK
Arizona, AZ
Arkansas, AR

California, CA
Colorado, CO
Connecticut, CT
Delaware, DE
District of Columbia, DC

Florida, FL
Georgia, GA
Guam, GU
Hawaii, HI

Idaho, ID
Illinois, IL
Indiana, IN
Iowa, IA

Kansas, KS
Kentucky, KY
Louisiana, LA

Maine, ME
Maryland, MD
Massachusetts, MA
Michigan, MI
Minnesota, MN
Mississippi, MS
Missouri, MO
Montana, MT

Nebraska, NE
Nevada, NV
New Hampshire, NH
New Jersey, NJ
New Mexico, NM
New York, NY
North Carolina, NC
North Dakota, ND

Ohio, OH
Oklahoma, OK
Oregon, OR

Pennsylvania, PA
Puerto Rico, PR
Rhode Island, RI

South Carolina, SC
South Dakota, SD
Tennessee, TN
Texas, TX

Utah, UT
Vermont, VT
Virgin Islands, VI
Virginia, VA

Washington, WA
West Virginia, WV
Wisconsin, WI
Wyoming, WY

Addressing Procedures

The envelope feature inserts the delivery address automatically if a letter is displayed. Title case, used in the letter address, is acceptable in the envelope address. An alternative style for envelopes is uppercase with no punctuation.

Business letters are usually mailed in envelopes that have the return address preprinted; return addresses are printed only for personal letters or when letterhead is not available. The default size of *Word* is a size 10 envelope (4 1/8" by 9 1/2"); other sizes are available using the Options feature.

Small envelope. On a No. 6 3/4 envelope, place the address near the center—about 2 inches from the top and left edges. Place a return address in the upper left corner.

Large envelope. On a No. 10 envelope, place the address near the center—about line 14 and .5" left of center. A return address, if not preprinted, should be keyed in the upper left corner (see small envelope).

An address must contain at least three lines; addresses of more than six lines should be avoided. The last line of an address must contain three items of information: (1) the city, (2) the state, and (3) the ZIP Code, preferably a 9-digit code.

Place mailing notations that affect postage (e.g., REGISTERED, CERTIFIED) below the stamp position (line 8); place other special notations (e.g., CONFIDENTIAL, PERSONAL) a DS below the return address.

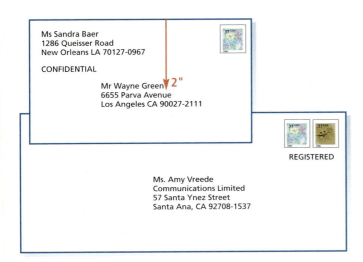

Folding and Inserting Procedures

Large Envelopes (No. 10, 9, 7 3/4)

Step 1	**Step 2**	**Step 3**

Step 1: With document face up, fold slightly less than 1/3 of sheet up toward top.

Step 2: Fold down top of sheet to within 1/2" of bottom fold.

Step 3: Insert document into envelope with last crease toward bottom of envelope.

Small Envelopes (No. 6 3/4, 6 1/4)

Step 1	**Step 2**	**Step 3**

Step 1: With document face up, fold bottom up to 1/2" from top.

Step 2: Fold right third to left.

Step 3: Fold left third to 1/2" from last crease and insert last creased edge first.

Window Envelopes (Full Sheet)

Step 1	**Step 2**	**Step 3**

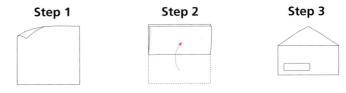

Step 1: With sheet face down, top toward you, fold upper third down.

Step 2: Fold lower third up so address is showing.

Step 3: Insert document into envelope with last crease toward bottom of envelope.

[STYLE GUIDE]

[STYLE GUIDE]

Letter Parts

Letterhead. Company name and address. May include other data.

Date. Date letter is mailed. Usually in month, day, year order. Military style is an option (day/month/year): 17 January 2005).

Letter address. Address of the person who will receive the letter. Include personal title (*Mr., Ms., Dr.*), name, professional title, company, and address.

Salutation. Greeting. Corresponds to the first line of the letter address. Usually includes name and courtesy title; use *Ladies and Gentlemen* if letter is addressed to a company name.

Writer. Name and professional title. Women may include a personal title.

Complimentary close. Farewell, such as *Sincerely.*

Body. Message. SS; DS between paragraphs.

Initials. Identifies person who keyed the document (for example, *tr*). May include identification of writer (*ARB:tr*).

Enclosure. Copy is enclosed with the document. May specify contents.

Copy notation. Indicates that a copy of the letter is being sent to person named.

Letter placement table

Length	Dateline position	Margins
Short: 1–2 ¶s	Center page	Default
Average: 3–4 ¶s	Center page or 2.1"	Default
Long: 4+ ¶s	2.1" (default + 6 hard returns)	Default

Default margins or a minimum of 1".

Block Letter (Open Punctuation)

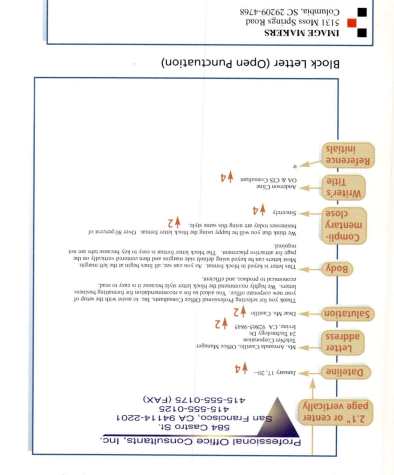

Dateline — January 17, 20--
2.1" or center page vertically

Professional Office Consultants, Inc.
584 Castro St.
San Francisco, CA 94114-2201
415-555-0125
415-555-0175 (FAX)

Letter address
Ms. Amanda Castillo, Office Manager
Telexel Corporation
24 Technology Dr.
Irvine, CA 92865-9845

Salutation — Dear Ms. Castillo

Body
Thank you for selecting Professional Office Consultants, Inc. to assist with the setup of your new corporate office. You asked us for a recommendation for formatting business letters. We highly recommend the block letter style because it is easy to read.

This letter is keyed in block format. As you can see, all lines begin at the left margin. Most letters can be keyed using default side margins and then centered vertically on the page for attractive placement. The block letter format is easy to key because tabs are not required.

We think that you will be happy using the block letter format. Over 80 percent of businesses today are using this same style.

Complimentary close — Sincerely

Writer's title
Anderson Cline
OA & CIS Consultant

Reference initials — tr

Envelope

IMAGE MAKERS
5131 Moss Springs Road
Columbia, SC 29209-4768

Ms. Mary Bernard, President
Bernard Image Consultants
4927 Stuart Avenue
Baton Rouge, LA 70808-3519

Modified Block Letter (Mixed Punctuation)

IMAGE MAKERS
5131 Moss Springs Road
Columbia, SC 29209-4768
(803) 555-0127

October 27, 20--

2.1" or center vertically

Ms. Mary Bernard, President
Bernard Image Consultants
4927 Stuart Ave.
Baton Rouge, LA 70808-3519

Dear Ms. Bernard:

The format of this letter is called modified block. Modified block format differs from block format in that the date, complimentary close, and the signature lines are positioned at the center point.

Paragraphs may be blocked, as this letter illustrates, or they may be indented from the left margin. We suggest you block paragraphs when you use modified block style so that an additional tab setting is not needed. However, some people who use modified block format prefer indented paragraphs.

Although modified block format is very popular, we recommend that you use it only for those customers who request this letter style. Otherwise, we urge you to use block format, which is more efficient, as your standard style.

Both formats are illustrated in the enclosed *Image Makers Format Guide*. Please note that the block format is labeled "computer compatible."

Sincerely,

Patrick R. Ray
Communication Consultant

tr

Enclosure — Enclosure

Copy notation — c Scot Carl, Account Manager

Personal Business Letter

2.1"

Janna M. Howard
587 Birch Circle
Clinton, MS 39056-0587
(601) 555-0177

Current date

> The return address may be keyed immediately above the date, or you may create a personal letterhead as shown here.

Mrs. Linda Chandler
Financial News
32 North Critz Street
Hot Springs, AR 71913-0032

Dear Mrs. Chandler

My college degree in office systems technology and my graphics design job experience in the United States and Taiwan qualify me to function well as a junior graphic designer for your newspaper.

As a result of my comprehensive four-year program, I am skilled in the most up-to-date office suite packages as well as the latest version of desktop publishing and graphics programs. In addition, I am very skilled at locating needed resources on the information highway. In fact, this skill played a very important role in the design award that I received last month.

My technical and communication skills were applied as I worked as the assistant editor and producer of the *Cother Alumni News*. I understand well the importance of meeting deadlines and also in producing a quality product that will increase newspaper sales.

After you have reviewed the enclosed resume, I would look forward to discussing my qualifications and career opportunities with you at *Financial News*.

Sincerely

Janna M. Howard

Enclosure

Résumé

JANNA M. HOWARD

Temporary Address (May 30, 2000)	Permanent Address
587 Birch Circle	328 Fondren Street
Clinton, MS 39056-0587	Orlando, FL 32801-0328
(601) 555-0177	(407) 555-0184

CAREER OBJECTIVE — To obtain a graphic design position with an opportunity to advance to a management position.

EDUCATION — *B.S. Office Systems Technology*, Cother University, Mobile, Alabama. May 2005. Grade-point average: 3.8/4.0. Serve as president of Graphic Designers' Society.

SPECIAL SKILLS

Environments:	*Microsoft Windows®* and *Macintosh®*
Application software:	*Microsoft Office Professional®/ Windows XP®, PageMaker®, CorelDraw®, Harvard Graphics®*
Internet:	*Netscape®, Internet Explorer®*
Keyboarding skill:	70 words per minute
Foreign language:	Chinese
Travel:	Taiwan (two summers working as graphic design intern)

EXPERIENCE — *Cother University Alumni Office*, Mobile, Alabama. Assistant editor and producer of the *Cother Alumni News*, 2004 to present.
- Work 25 hours per week.
- Design layout and production of six editions.
- Meet every publishing deadline.
- Received the "Cother Design Award."

Cother Library, Mobile, Alabama. Student Assistant in Audiovisual Library, 2003-2004.
- Worked 20 hours per week.
- Created *Audiovisual Catalog* on computerized database.
- Processed orders via computer.
- Prepared monthly and yearly reports using database.
- Edited and proofed various publications.

REFERENCES — Request portfolio from Cother University Placement Office.

Standard Memo

Tab (1" from left margin)   **2.1"**

TO:	Executive Committee ↓2
FROM:	Colleen Marshall
DATE:	November 8, 20--
SUBJECT:	Site Selection ↓2

Please be prepared to make a final decision on the site for next year's Leadership Training Conference. Our staff reviewed the students' suggestions and have added a few of their own. The following information may be helpful as you make your decision:

1. New York and San Francisco have been eliminated from consideration because of cost factors. ↓2

2. New Orleans is still open for consideration even though we met there three years ago. New Orleans has tremendous appeal to students.

3. Charleston, San Antonio, and Tampa were suggested by students as very desirable locations for the conference.

Site selection will be the first item of business at our meeting next Wednesday. I'm attaching various hotel brochures for each site. ↓2

xx ↓2

Attachments

Standard Memo with Distribution List

Tab (1" from left margin)   **2.1"**

TO:	Team Leaders ↓2
FROM:	Form Paragraph Task Force
DATE:	Current
SUBJECT:	Initial Meetings with Task Force ↓2

The task force assigned the responsibility for developing form paragraphs to use in key departments of our company plans to work in your department beginning two weeks from today. Please assign two representatives from your department to coordinate the work with us. ↓2

The procedure that the Executive Committee asked us to follow is to collect samples of typical correspondence, meet with departmental representatives to collect additional information, and then to prepare a draft of the form paragraphs for review. After we receive your feedback on the draft copy, we will schedule a meeting to finalize the paragraphs.

Matthew Redfern has been assigned as the task force coordinator for your department. Please direct all communications about the project to him. ↓2

xx ↓2

Distribution List:
    Nestor Garcia, Claims
    Roberta Layman, Underwriting
    Rosa Romero, Agency Services
    Diana Wang, Business Services

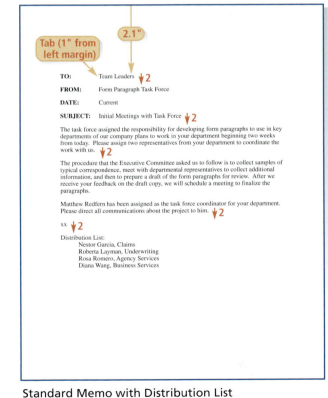

[STYLE GUIDE]

[STYLE GUIDE]

Standard Unbound Report

Margins: Position the main heading about 2.1" (tap ENTER 3 times in DS mode or 6 times in SS mode). Default side and bottom margins.

Spacing: *Educational reports:* DS, paragraphs indented .5". *Business reports:* SS, paragraphs blocked with a DS between.

Page numbers: Second and subsequent pages are numbered at top right of the page. DS follows the page number.

Main headings: Bold, centered, ALL CAPS, 14 pt. or use Heading 1 or Title style, initial cap only.

Side headings: Bold; main words capitalized; DS above and below.

Paragraph headings: Bold; capitalize first word, followed by a period.

NOTE: Styles may also be used for headings.

Report Documentation

Internal citations: Provides source of information within report. Includes the author's surname, publication date, and page number (Bruce, 2005, 129).

Footnotes: References cited are indicated by a superscript number (. . . story.[1]) and a corresponding footnote at the bottom of the same page.

Bibliography or references: Lists all references, whether quoted or not, in alphabetical order by authors' names.

First Page of Unbound Report

Set DS; tap ENTER 3 times

TRENDS FOR BUSINESS DRESS
DS

Casual dress in the workplace has become widely accepted. According to a national study conducted by Schoenholtz & Associates in 2005, a majority of the companies surveyed allowed employees to dress casually one day a week, usually Fridays (Tarr, 2005, p. 23). The trend continued to climb as shown by the 1997 survey by Schoenholtz & Associates. Fifty-eight percent of office workers surveyed were allowed to dress casually for work every day, and 92 percent of the offices allowed employees to dress casually occasionally (Surphin, 2005, p. 10).

Decline in Trend

The trend to dress casually that started in the early 1990s may be shifting, states Susan Monaghan (2005, p. 34).

Although a large number of companies are allowing casual attire every day or only on Fridays, a current survey revealed a decline of 10 percent in 2004 when compared to the same survey conducted in 2003. Some experts predict the new trend for business dress codes will be a dress up day every week.

What accounts for this decline in companies permitting casual dress? Several reasons may include:

1. Confusion of what business casual is with employees slipping into dressing too casually (work jeans, faded tee-shirts, old sneakers, and improperly fitting clothing).
2. Casual dress does not portray the adopted corporate image of the company.
3. Employees are realizing that promotion decisions are affected by a professional appearance.

Second Page of Unbound Report

2

Guidelines for Business Dress

Companies are employing image consultants to teach employees what is appropriate business casual and to plan the best business attire to project the corporate image. Erica Gilreath (2005), the author of *Casual Dress*, a guidebook on business casual, provides excellent advice on how to dress casually and still command the power needed for business success. She presents the following advice to professionals:

- Do not wear any clothing that is designed for recreational or sports activities, e.g. cargo pants or pants with elastic waist.
- Invest the time in pressing khakis and shirts or pay the price for professional dry cleaning. Wrinkled clothing does not enhance one's credibility.
- Do not wear sneakers.
- Be sure clothing fits properly. Avoid baggy clothes or clothes that are too tight.

In summary, energetic employees working to climb the corporate ladder will need to plan their dress carefully. If business casual is appropriate, it's best to consult the experts on business casual to ensure a professional image.

References Page

3

REFERENCES
DS

Gilreath, Erica. "Dressing Casually with Power." < http://www.dresscasual.com> (23 March 2005).

Monaghan, Susan. "Business Dress Codes May Be Shifting." *Business Executive*, April 2005, pp 34-35.

Surphin, Rachel. "Your Business Wardrobe Decisions are Important Decisions." *Business Management Journal*, January 2005, pp. 10-12.

Tarr, Kelsey. "Companies Support Business Casual Dress." *Management Success*, June 2005, pp. 23-25.

(Labels: 0.5", 2.1", 14 pt.)

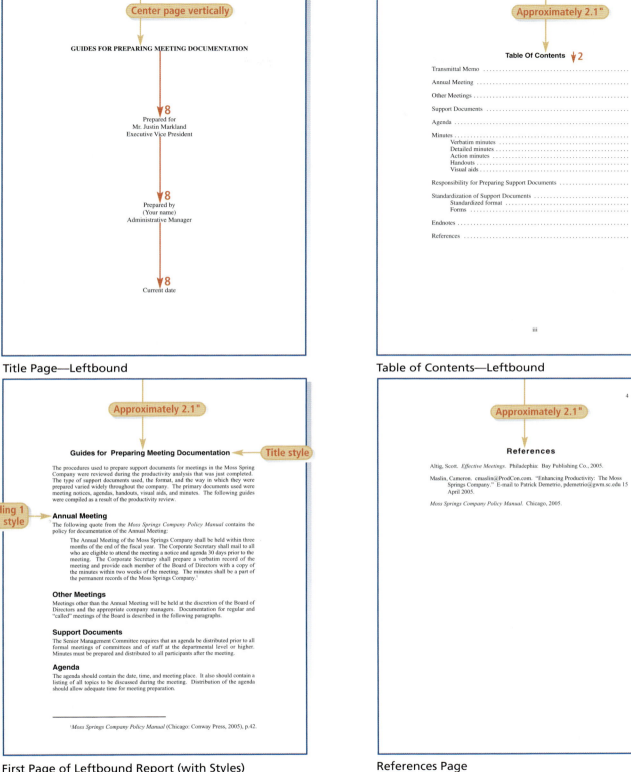

Title Page—Leftbound

Center page vertically

GUIDES FOR PREPARING MEETING DOCUMENTATION

↓8
Prepared for
Mr. Justin Markland
Executive Vice President

↓8
Prepared by
(Your name)
Administrative Manager

↓8
Current date

Table of Contents—Leftbound

Approximately 2.1"

Table Of Contents ↓2

iii

First Page of Leftbound Report (with Styles)

Approximately 2.1"

Guides for Preparing Meeting Documentation ← Title style

The procedures used to prepare support documents for meetings in the Moss Spring Company were reviewed during the productivity analysis that was just completed. The type of support documents used, the format, and the way in which they were prepared varied widely throughout the company. The primary documents used were meeting notices, agendas, handouts, visual aids, and minutes. The following guides were compiled as a result of the productivity review.

Heading 1 style →

Annual Meeting

The following quote from the *Moss Springs Company Policy Manual* contains the policy for documentation of the Annual Meeting:

The Annual Meeting of the Moss Springs Company shall be held within three months of the end of the fiscal year. The Corporate Secretary shall mail to all who are eligible to attend the meeting a notice and agenda 30 days prior to the meeting. The Corporate Secretary shall prepare a verbatim record of the meeting and provide each member of the Board of Directors with a copy of the minutes within two weeks of the meeting. The minutes shall be a part of the permanent records of the Moss Springs Company.[1]

Other Meetings

Meetings other than the Annual Meeting will be held at the discretion of the Board of Directors and the appropriate company managers. Documentation for regular and "called" meetings of the Board is described in the following paragraphs.

Support Documents

The Senior Management Committee requires that an agenda be distributed prior to all formal meetings of committees and of staff at the departmental level or higher. Minutes must be prepared and distributed to all participants after the meeting.

Agenda

The agenda should contain the date, time, and meeting place. It also should contain a listing of all topics to be discussed during the meeting. Distribution of the agenda should allow adequate time for meeting preparation.

[1]*Moss Springs Company Policy Manual* (Chicago: Conway Press, 2005), p.42.

References Page

4

Approximately 2.1"

References

Altig, Scott. *Effective Meetings*. Philadelphia: Bay Publishing Co., 2005.

Maslin, Cameron. cmaslin@ProdCon.com. "Enhancing Productivity: The Moss Springs Company." E-mail to Patrick Demetrio, pdemetrio@gwm.sc.edu 15 April 2005.

Moss Springs Company Policy Manual. Chicago, 2005.

[STYLE GUIDE]

[STYLE GUIDE]

Electronic Mail

Electronic mail (or **e-mail**) requires an e-mail program, an e-mail address, and access to the Internet.

Address e-mail carefully. Key and check the address of the recipient and always supply a subject line.

Format the body of an e-mail SS; DS between paragraphs. Do not indent paragraphs. Limit the use of bold, italics, and uppercase. For business use, avoid abbreviations and emoticons (e.g., :- for wink or BTW for by the way).

E-Mail Etiquette

1. Create a meaningful subject line that is tailored to the specific content. Limit e-mail to one topic.
2. Get to the point quickly; the most important message should appear in the first paragraph. Keep paragraphs focused and short. Use bullets when possible.
3. Capitalize only to highlight proper nouns—do not use all caps for emphasis.
4. Keep paragraphs focused and short. Use bullets when possible.
5. Be clear on the response (if any) you are expecting from the reader.
6. Include your full name and contact information so that a recipient may follow up by telephone or fax if desired. If possible, create a signature that automatically includes this information.
7. Avoid lengthy e-mail messages. Use file attachments when you need to send detailed information.
8. Check spelling and grammar before sending an e-mail. Read your message carefully before sending.
9. When creating your message or reading a message from others, assume the good intentions of the sender.
10. If communication seems tense or unclear, consider talking to the receiver in person or by telephone.
11. Do not forward a chain letter/message.
12. Use company e-mail for company business correspondence only. Companies do have the right to monitor business e-mail accounts.
13. Respond to e-mails you receive within 24 hours if possible.

Landscape Plan - Message

File Edit View Insert Format Tools Table Window Help

Type a question for help

Normal | Times New Roman | 12 | B I U | HTML

To... Les.Grenzeback@sterlingtech.edu

Cc... wdikins@krider.com

Subject: Landscape Plan

Attach... Landscape Plan.doc (24 KB) | Attachment Options...

The landscape plan for your new building has been completed, and a reduced version is attached. Three full-size copies will be delivered to your office tomorrow morning. If you need additional copies, please e-mail me today.

Table Format Guides

1. Key the main heading on approximately line 2.1", or center the table vertically on the page.

2. **Headings:** Center, bold, and key the main heading in all caps. Key the secondary heading a DS below the main heading in bold and centered; capitalize main words. Center and bold all column headings.

3. Adjust column widths attractively, and center the table horizontally.

4. Select the table, change the row height to .3", and then center the text vertically in the cells.

5. Align text within cells at the left. Align numbers at the right. Align decimal numbers of varying lengths at the decimal point.

6. When a table appears within a document, DS before and after the table.

Table Design

COOK OFFICE PRODUCTS

20-- Sales

Sales Agent	Territory	Amount of Sale
Stephanie Acosta	Northwest	$1,157,829
George Cunningham	Central	$4,245,073
Angel Izadi	Southwest	$6,301,625
Joseph Viceroy, Jr.	Midwest	$99,016
Lauren Zimmerman	East	$82,479

Subject/Verb Agreement

Use a singular verb:

1. With a **singular subject**. (The singular forms of *to be* include: am, is, was. Common errors with *to be* are: you was, we was, they was.)

   She monitors employee morale.
   You are a very energetic worker.
   A split keyboard is in great demand.

2. With most **indefinite pronouns**: *another, anybody, anything, everything, each, either, neither, one, everyone, anyone, nobody*.

   Each of the candidates has raised a considerable amount of money.
   Everyone is eager to read the author's newest novel.
   Neither of the boys is able to attend.

3. With singular subjects joined by *or/nor, either/or, neither/nor*.

   Neither your grammar nor punctuation is correct.
   Either Jody or Jan has your favorite CD.
   John or Connie has volunteered to chaperone the field trip.

4. With a **collective noun** (*family, choir, herd, faculty, jury, committee*) that acts as one unit.

   The jury has reached a decision.
   The council is in an emergency session.
   But:
   The faculty have their assignments. (Each has his/her own assignments.)

5. With words or phrases that express **periods of time**, **weights**, **measurements**, or **amounts of money**.

   Fifteen dollars is what he earned.
   Two-thirds of the money has been submitted to the treasurer.
   One hundred pounds is too much.

Use a plural verb:

6. With a **plural subject**.

   The students sell computer supplies for their annual fund-raiser.
   They are among the top-ranked teams in the nation.

7. With **compound (two or more) subjects** joined by *and*.

   Headaches and backaches are common worker complaints.
   Hard work and determination were two qualities listed by the references.

8. With *some, all, most, none, several, few, both, many*, and *any* when they refer to more than one of the items.

   All of my friends have seen the movie.
   Some of the teams have won two or more games.

[STYLE GUIDE]

FUNCTION SUMMARY

Function	Menu Command	Keyboard Shortcut	Toolbar Button
Alignment: Left, Center, Right, Justify	Format, Paragraph, Indents and Spacing tab		▤ ▤ ▤ ▤
AutoCorrect	Tools, AutoCorrect Options		
AutoText: Create	Select Text, Insert, AutoText, New, OK		
Bold	Format, Font, Font tab	CTRL + B	B
Borders: Page	Format, Borders and Shading, Page Border tab		
Borders: Paragraph	Format, Borders and Shading, Borders tab		▣ ▦
Browse Object			●
Bullets	Format, Bullets and Numbering		≣
Center Page	File, Page Setup, Layout tab		
Change Case	Format, Change Case		
Character Effects	Format, Font, Font tab		
Chart	Insert, Picture, Chart		
Clear Formatting	Select text; click down arrow on Style button; select Clear Formatting		
Clip Art and Images	Insert, Picture, Clip Art		▣
Close Document	File, Close		×
Columns—New	Insert, Break, Column break		
Columns—Create	Format, Columns		▤
Columns—Balance	Insert, Break, Continuous section break		
Comment	Insert, Comment		▣
Compare and Merge	Tools, Compare and Merge Documents		
Convert Document to Different Format	File, Save As; click Save as type down arrow, select format; Save		
Copy	Edit, Copy	SHIFT + F2	▣
Cut	Edit, Cut	CTRL + X	✂
Date and Time	Insert, Date and Time, select format		
Diagram	Insert, Diagram		▣
Document Map	View, Document Map		
Document Properties	File, Properties		
Drawing Tools	View, Toolbars, Drawing		▣
E-mail: Send Document	File, Send To, Mail Recipient		
E-mail: Send Document as Attachment	File, Send To, Mail Recipient (as Attachment)		
E-mail: Send Document for Review	File, Send To, Mail Recipient (for Review)		
Envelopes	Tools, Letters and Mailings, Envelopes and Labels, Envelopes tab		▣
Exit	File, Exit		☒
Find	Edit, Find	CTRL + F	▣
Font	Format, Font		Times New Roman ▾

Function	Menu Command	Keyboard Shortcut	Toolbar Button
Font: Color	Format, Font, select color		
Font: Size	Format, Font, select size		
Font: Style	Format, Font, select style		
Footnote	Insert, Reference, Footnote		
Format Painter			
Go To	Edit, Go To	CTRL + G	
Graphic: Move	Select graphic; click Text Wrapping button; choose a wrapping option; point to graphic; and drag to desired position.		
Graphic: Size	Select graphic; drag resize handle. Double-click graphic; Format Picture dialog box, choose Size tab; enter dimensions.		
Graphic: Wrap Text	Select graphic, Format, Format Picture; select wrapping style.		
Hanging Indent	Format, Paragraph, Indents and Spacing tab	CTRL + T	
Header and Footer	View, Header and Footer		
Help	Help, Microsoft Word Help	F1	
Highlight			
Hyperlink	Insert, Hyperlink; click Existing File or Web page; select file or key Web address; OK.	CTRL + K	
Indent	Format, Paragraph, Indents and Spacing tab		Increase Indent / Decrease Indent
Insert File	Insert, File, select desired file, Insert		
Italic	Format, Font		
Keep with next	Format, Paragraph, Line and Page Breaks tab		
Line Spacing	Format, Paragraph, Indents and Spacing tab		
Margins	File, Page Setup, Margins tab		
New Document	File, New	CTRL + N	
Numbering	Format, Bullets and Numbering		
Open Document	File, Open	CTRL + O	
Outline: Numbered	Format, Bullets and Numbering, Outline Numbered tab		
Page Break	Insert, Break, Page Break	CTRL + ENTER	
Page Numbers	Insert, Page Numbers		
Paste	Edit, Paste	CTRL + V	
Paste Special	Edit, Paste Special		
Print	File, Print	CTRL + P	
Print Preview	File, Print Preview	CTRL + F2	
Redo	Edit, Redo	CTRL + Y	

[FUNCTION SUMMARY]

[FUNCTION SUMMARY]

Function	Menu Command	Keyboard Shortcut	Toolbar Button
Replace	Edit, Replace	CTRL + H	
Research Tool	Tools, Research		🔖
Save As/Save	File, Save As or File, Save	F12/CTRL + S	💾
Save as Web Page	File, Save as Web Page, Save		
Section Breaks	Insert, Break; select break type; OK		
Shading	Format, Borders and Shading, Shading tab		🎨▾
Show/Hide			¶
Show/Hide White Space			
Space after Paragraph	Format, Paragraph, Indents and Spacing tab		
Special Characters	Insert, Symbol, Special Characters tab		
Spelling and Grammar	Tools, Spelling and Grammar	F7	✓
Style: Apply	Click down arrow on Style button and make selection		Normal ▾
Symbols	Insert, Symbol, Symbols tab		
Table: Convert Table to Text	Table, Convert, Table to Text		
Table: Convert Text to Table	Table, Convert, Text to Table		
Tables: Adjust Column Width	Table, Table Properties, Column tab		
Tables: AutoFormat	Table, Table AutoFormat		📋
Tables: AutoSum			Σ
Tables: Change Borders and Lines	Format, Borders and Shading, Borders tab		⊞▾
Tables: Change Row Height	Table, Table Properties, Row		
Tables: Create	Insert, Table		⊞
Tables: Delete Rows or Columns	Click in the row or column to be deleted, Table, Delete, Rows or Columns		
Tables: Insert Rows or Column	Position insertion point, Table, Insert, Rows Above or Row Below or Columns to the Left or Columns to the Right		
Tabs: Set	Horizontal Ruler; set Tab Alignment, click Ruler; Format, Tabs		
Template	File, New, On my computer; select tab and select template		
Text Effects	Format, Font, Text Effects tab		
Thesaurus	Tools, Language, Thesaurus	SHIFT + F7	
Track Changes	Tools, Track Changes	CTRL + Shift + E	📝
Underline	Format, Font		U
Undo	Edit, Undo	CTRL + Z	↩
Widow/Orphan	Format, Paragraph, Line and Page Breaks tab		
Wizards	File, New, On my computer; select tab and select wizard		
WordArt	Insert, Picture, WordArt		🅰

Standard Coding Number	Certification Skill Sets	Content Pages	Drill and Page	Application Number and Page
WW03S-1	**Creating Content**			
WW03S-1-1	**Insert and edit text, symbols and special characters**			
	Inserting text, symbols, hidden text and special characters	83 88 147	Drill 3–4, p. 84; Drill 4, p. 89; 30c, p. 97; Drill 4, p. 147	28c-d1, p. 91; 39d-d1, p. 151; 53c-d1, p. 229; 56e-d1, p. 247; Document 5, p. 271
	Deleting, cutting, copying, pasting text and using the clipboard	88 205–207	Drill 4, p. 89; Drill 1–4, p. 205	28c-d1, p. 91; 49d-d1, p. 208; Document 5, p. 271
	Checking spelling and grammar	87	Drill 1, p. 87; Drill 5, p. 91; 30c, p. 97	Documents 1–12, pp. 270–274
	Checking language usage (e.g., Thesaurus)	214	Drill 2, p. 215	52d-d1, p. 222
WW03S-1-2	**Insert frequently used and pre-defined text**			
	Creating text for repeated use (e.g., *AutoText*)	92–93	Drill 1, p. 93	Document 1, p. 270; Document 5, p. 271
	Inserting pre-defined text (e.g., *AutoText* and *AutoCorrect*)	87 92–93	Drill 1, p. 87	28c-d2, p. 91; Documents 1, 5, 6–8, p. 270; Module 9
	Inserting date and time fields	88	Drill 2, p. 88; 30c, p. 97	28c-d2, p. 91; Documents 1–2, p. 270; Documents 6–7, p. 273
WW03S-1-3	**Navigate to specific content**			
	Finding and replacing text	213–214	Drill 1, p. 214	51d-d1, p. 218; 55c-d1, p. 238; Document 1, p. 240; Document 2, p. 270
	Moving to selected content (e.g., *Select Browse Object*, *Document Map*)	81 234–235	Drill 1, p. 82; Drills 5–6, p. 235	54c-d2, p. 236; Documents 6-7, p. 273
WW03S-1-4	**Insert, position and size graphics**			
	Inserting, positioning and sizing graphics, text boxes and shapes	227 242–245	Drill 7, p. 228; Drill 1, p. 244; Drill 2, p. 245; Drill 3, p. 246; Drill 2, p. 256	53c-d1, p. 229; 56e-d1; d2; d3, p. 247; 58c-d1; d2; d3, p. 257; 60c-d2; d3, p. 266; Document 1, p. 268; Document 11, p. 274
WW03S-1-5	**Create and modify diagrams and charts**			
	Creating and modifying charts and diagrams	249–252	Drill 1, p. 250; Drill 2, p. 251; Drills 3–6, p. 252	57e-d1; d2; d3, p. 253; 60c-d1, p. 266; Document 1, p. 268
WW03S-1-6	**Locate, select and insert supporting information**			
	Locating supporting information in local reference materials or on the Internet using the Research tool	220	Drill 2, p. 221	52d-d1, p. 222
	Using the Research tool to select and insert supporting text-based information	220	Drill 2, p. 221	52d-d1, p. 222
WW03S-2	**Organizing Content**			
WW03S-2-1	**Insert and modify tables**			
	Inserting new tables	176	Drill 1, p. 177; Drill 2, p. 178	44d-d1; d2; d3, p. 180; 54c-d1, p. 236; Document 4, p. 271

[MICROSOFT OFFICE SPECIALIST CERTIFICATION]

MICROSOFT OFFICE SPECIALIST CERTIFICATION

Standard Coding Number	Certification Skill Sets	Content Pages	Drill and Page	Application Number and Page
	Converting text to tables	192	Drill 1, p. 192	47c-d1; d3; d6, p. 194; 48c-d4, p. 198
	Applying pre-defined formats to tables (e.g., AutoFormats)	183	Drill 3, p. 184	45c-d3, p. 185; 45c-d4, p. 185; 48c-d2, p. 197
	Modifying table borders and shading	183 188	Drill 2, p. 183; Drill 3, p. 188	45c-d1; d2, p. 184; 46d-d1, p. 190; 48c-d1; d3, p. 197; 54c-d2, p. 236; Document 4, p. 271
	Revising tables (insert and delete rows and columns, modify cell formats)	179 187–189	Drill 3, p. 180; Drill 1, p. 187; Drill 2, p. 188; Drill 4, p. 189	46d-d2, p. 190; 48c-d1; d3, p. 197; Document 2, p. 199; 52d-d1; d2, p. 222; 54c-d1, p. 236; Document 4, p. 271
WW03S-2-2	**Create bulleted lists, numbered lists and outlines**			
	Customizing and applying bullets and numbering	141 232 264	Drills 2–3, p. 142; Drill 2, p. 233	38e-d1, p. 144; 39d-d1, p. 151; 41c-d1; d3, p. 162; 59d-d3, p. 264; 60c-d4, p. 267; Module 9, Documents 5, 10
	Creating outlines	231–232	Drill 1, p. 231	
WW03S-2-3	**Insert and modify hyperlinks**	189	Drill 4, p. 189	46d-d3; d4, p. 190; 48c-d4, p. 198; Module 9, Document 1
WW03S-3	**Formatting Content**			
WW03S-3-1	**Format text**			
	Finding and modifying font typeface, style, color and size	82 214	Drill 1, p. 82; Drill 1, p. 214	27b-d1, p. 85; 39d-d2, p. 151; 58c-d1, p. 257; 60c-d2; d3, p. 266; Module 9, Documents 3, 5
	Applying styles to and clearing styles from text, tables, and lists	183 223 226 232	Drill 3, p. 184; Drills 1–2, p. 224; Drill 4, p. 226; Drills 1, 2–3, p. 232	45c-d4, p. 185; 55c-d2, p. 238; 60c-d2, p. 266; Document 10, p. 273
	Applying highlights to text	228	Drill 8, p. 228	54c-d1, p. 236
	Applying text effects	82 219	Drill 2, p. 83; Drill 1, p. 220; Drill 5, p. 235	27b-d1, p. 85
	Modifying character spacing	139		37e-d4, p. 139; 38e-d2, p. 144; 39d-d2, p. 151; 43c-d3, p. 172
WW03S-3-2	**Format paragraphs**			
	Applying borders and shading to paragraphs	227	Drill 6, p. 227	53c-d1, p. 229; Document 1, p. 240; 56e-d1, p. 247; 60c-d3, p. 267
	Indenting, spacing and aligning paragraphs	84–85 152–154 226	Drills 4–5, p. 84; 30c, p. 97; Drills 1–2, p. 153; Drills 3–5, p. 154; Drill 5, p. 226	27b-d1; d2, p. 85; Document 2, p. 103; 38e-d1, p. 144; 40e-d1; d2; d3, p. 157; 41c-d1, p. 162; 43c-d1; d2, p. 171; Module 9, Document 1, 3

Standard Coding Number	Certification Skill Sets	Content Pages	Drill and Page	Application Number and Page
	Setting, removing and modifying tab stops	98–99 114 182	Drill 1, p. 98; Drills 2–3, p. 99; 33c, p. 114; Drill 1, p. 122; Drill 1, p. 182	30e-d1; d3, p. 100; 31c-d1; d3, p. 102; 33e-d1; d2, p. 117; 35f-d1, p. 126; 36c-d2, p. 129; Document 3, p. 130; 45c-d1–d4, p. 184; 47c-d2, p. 194; Document 1, p. 199; 54c-d2, p. 236
WW03S-3-3	**Apply and format columns**			
	Applying and formatting columns	255–256	Drill 1, p. 256; Drill 3, p. 257	58c-d1–d3, p. 257; 60c-d2; d3, p. 266; Module 9, Documents 12
WW03S-3-4	**Insert and modify content in headers and footers**			
	Insert and modify headers and footers	145 155 233–234	Drill 1, p. 145; Drill 2, p. 146; Drill 6, p. 155; Drill 4, p. 234	39d-d1, p. 151; 40e-d1, p. 157; 41c-d1, p. 162; 42e-d3, p. 169; 43c-d1, p. 171; Document 1, p. 173; 51d-d1, p. 218; 54c-d2, p. 236; Document 5, p. 271
	Insert and format page numbers	145 150	Drill 1, p. 145; Drill 2, p. 146; Drill 3, p. 147	39d-d1, p. 151
WW03S-3-5	**Modify document layout and page setup**			
	Inserting and deleting breaks	146	Drill 3, p. 147	39d-d1, p. 151; 40e-d1, p. 157; 40e-d2, p. 158; 41c-d1, p. 162; 43c-d2, p. 172; Document 12, p. 274
	Modifying page margins, page orientation	140	Drill 1, p. 141	38e-d1–d3, p. 144; 39d-d1–d3, p. 151; 40e-d3, p. 158; 41c-d1; d3, p. 162; 43c-d1–d3, p. 171; 55e-d2, p. 248; 58c-d1, p. 257; Document 11, p. 274
WW03S-4	**Collaborating**			
WW03S-4-1	**Circulate documents for review**			
	Sending documents for review via e-mail	123–125	Drill 3, p. 123; Drill 6, p. 125	35f-d4; d5; d8; d9, p. 126
	Sending documents in an e-mail or as an e-mail attachment	94 123–125	Drills 3–4, p. 123; Drill 5, p. 124; Drill 6, p. 125	29e-d1; d3, p. 95; 35f-d4; d5; d8; d9, p. 126; Document 9, p. 273
WW03S-4-2	**Compare and merge document versions**			
	Comparing and merging documents	221	Drill 3, p. 221	52d-d1, p. 222
WW03S-4-3	**Insert, view and edit comments**			
	Inserting, viewing and editing comments	215	Drills 3–6, p. 215; Drill 7, p. 217	51d-d2, p. 218; 51d-d3, p. 218;
WW03S-4-4	**Track, accept and reject proposed changes**			
	Locating successive changes in a document	216–217	Drill 7, p. 217	51d-d1; d2; d4, p. 218; 52d-d1, p. 222
	Tracking, accepting and rejecting changes	216–217	Drill 7, p. 217	51d-d1; d2; d4, p. 218; 52d-d1, p. 222; Document 5, p. 271

[MICROSOFT OFFICE SPECIALIST CERTIFICATION]

[MICROSOFT OFFICE SPECIALIST CERTIFICATION]

Standard Coding Number	Certification Skill Sets	Content Pages	Drill and Page	Application Number and Page
WWO35-5	**Formatting and Managing Documents**			
WWO35-5-1	**Create new documents using templates**			
	Creating new document types using templates	209-211	Drills 1-2, p. 210; Drill 3, p. 211	50c-d1, p. 212; 57d-d2, p. 254; Module 9, Documents 1-2, 7
WWO35-5-2	**Review and modify document properties**			
	Reviewing and modifying the document summary	225	Drill 3, p. 225	Document 5, p. 271
	Reviewing word, paragraph and character counts (e.g., *Word Count*)	225	Drill 3, p. 225	Document 5, p. 271
WWO35-5-3	**Organize documents using file folders**			
	Creating and using folders for document storage	76	Drill 4, p. 77; Drill 1, p. 110, 134, 205, 244; Drill 2, p. 178, 194	p. 269
	Renaming folders	76	Drill 4, p. 77	p. 269
WWO35-5-4	**Save documents in appropriate formats for different uses**			
	Converting documents to different formats for transportability (e.g., .rtf, .txt)	193	Drill 2, p. 194	47c-d7, p. 195; Document 2, p. 199
	Saving documents as Web pages	193	Drill 2, p. 194	47c-d7, p. 195; Document 11, p. 274
WWO35-5-5	**Print documents, envelopes and labels**			
	Printing documents, envelopes, and labels	78, 119, 121	Drill 5, p. 78; Drill 2, p. 119; Drill 3, p. 119	34d-d1-d5, d7, p. 120; 35f-d1, d3, p. 126; 36c-d2, p. 129; Documents 1-3, p. 130; 49d-d1, p. 208; Documents 1-12, pp. 270-274
WWO35-5-6	**Preview documents and Web pages**			
	Previewing a document for printing	77	Drill 5, p. 78; Drill 1, p. 122	Documents 1-12, pp. 270-274
	Previewing a Web page for publication	193	Drill 2, p. 194	Document 11, p. 274
WWO35-5-7	**Change and organize document views and windows**			
	Revealing formatting and hidden text	83	Drill 3, p. 84	Document 10, p. 273
	Viewing reading layout, normal, outline, full screen, zoom views	138, 166	Drill 1, p. 166	42e-d1, p. 169
	Showing/hiding white space in a document	167	Drill 2, p. 167	42e-d1, p. 169
	Splitting windows and arrange panes	168	Drill 3, p. 169	42e-d2, p. 169

[**INDEX**]

[INDEX]

[INDEX]